The Foreign Policy of France from 1914 to 1945

FOREIGN POLICIES OF THE GREAT POWERS
Edited by C. J. Lowe

The Reluctant Imperialists   C. J. Lowe

Vol. I British Foreign Policy 1878–1902
Vol. II The Documents

The Mirage of Power   C. J. Lowe and M. L. Dockrill

Vol. I British Foreign Policy 1902–14
Vol. II British Foreign Policy 1914–22
Vol. III The Documents

From Sadowa to Sarajevo: The Foreign Policy
of Austria-Hungary, 1866–1914   F. R. Bridge

Italian Foreign Policy 1870–1940   C. J. Lowe and F. Marzari

The
Foreign Policy
of France from
1914 to 1945

J. Néré

*Professeur, Faculté des Lettres et
Sciences Humaines de Brest*

Routledge & Kegan Paul
London and Boston

This translation by Translance
first published in 1975
by Routledge & Kegan Paul Ltd
Broadway House, 68–74 Carter Lane,
London EC4V 5EL and
9 Park Street,
Boston, Mass. 02108, USA
Set in Monotype Garamond
and printed in Great Britain by
Western Printing Services Ltd, Bristol

ISBN 0 7100 7968 0
Library of Congress Catalog Card No. 74–83376

Contents

Preface   *page* ix

1   French Diplomacy in the War of 1914–18   1
    Introduction   1
    Winning the War   3
    Peace Feelers and War Aims   6
    The Armistice   9

2   The Peace Settlement   11
    A Pyrrhic Victory   11
    The Quest for Security   12
    Alsace-Lorraine and the Saar   16
    The Principle of Reparations   18
    Central and Eastern Europe   21
    The League of Nations   23
    Conclusion   24

3   From Versailles to the Ruhr   26
    The Disappearance of the Anglo-American Guarantee   26
    The Efforts to Recover the Anglo-American Guarantee   28
    The Difficulties of Carrying Out the Treaty of Versailles   31
    The 'Eastern Alliances'   38
    Retreat in the Middle East   45

4   The Occupation of the Ruhr, and the Dawes Plan   47
    The Preliminaries   47
    The Entry into the Ruhr and the 'Passive Resistance'   52
    Poincaré Faced with the German Chaos   55
    The Dawes Plan   56
    Central Europe during the Ruhr Crisis   60

Contents

5 The Early Days of the Cartel des Gauches   63
The Implementation of the Dawes Plan   64
In Quest of Security   66

6 The Briand Era   69
The Locarno Treaties and Germany's Entry into the
    League of Nations   71
Thoiry and the Young Plan   76
The Briand-Kellogg Pact   85
The Proposal for European Unity   87
The Early Evacuation of the Rhineland, and the Renewal of
    the German Threat   89
Conclusion   91

7 The Problem of National Defence after the Evacuation
of the Rhineland   93

8 The World Economic Crisis and its Repercussions on
the Foreign Policy of France   100
The End of Reparations: the Hoover Moratorium and the
    Lausanne Conference   102
The Economic Conference at Stresa (September 1932)   107
The End of the Interallied Debts, and the London
    Conference   109

9 The Disarmament Conference and the Rearming of
Germany   117
The Tardieu Plan and Germany's First Sortie   119
The Herriot-Paul-Boncour 'Constructive Plan'   120
Disintegration of the French 'Constructive Plan'   124
The French Plan of the Two Periods and the Resignation of
    Germany from the League of Nations   126
The Note of 17 April 1934   128
German Rearmament and French Disarmament   130

10 The Franco-Italian *Rapprochement* and the Attempt to
Consolidate Central Europe   132
The Franco-Italian Affair   132
Central and Eastern Europe at the Beginning of 1933   134

Contents

The de Jouvenel Mission and the Four-Power Pact   137

The Proposal for an Association of the Peoples of
   Central Europe   141

The Austrian Crises of 1934 and Italian Policy   149

The Rome Agreements (January 1935)   151

The 'Stresa Front'   152

11   The Franco-Soviet Treaty of Mutual Assistance   155

The Non-Aggression Pact of November 1932   156

The Turning-Point of 1933   160

Barthou's Venture   165

The Policy of Laval and the Conclusion of the Mutual
   Assistance Pact   169

12   The Abyssinia Conflict and the Remilitarization of
the Rhineland   173

The Origins of the Abyssinia Conflict   173

The Sanctions   175

A New Attempt at Conciliation: the Laval-Hoare Plan   180

Remilitarization of the Rhineland   184

The Last Attempt at a Rapprochement with Italy   192

13   The Foreign Policy of the Popular Front   195

General Reflections   195

Franco-British Relations and the Negotiation for a 'New
   Locarno'   196

The Tripartite Monetary Agreement and its Political
   Significance   200

The Belgian Defection   202

Franco-German Relations: the Schacht Mission   205

Franco-Soviet Relations   208

Break-Up of the Eastern Alliances   211

The War in Spain: Non-Intervention and Attempt at
   Mediation   214

14   Munich   221

The Calm before the Storm   221

The Annexation of Austria   221

The Preliminaries of the Czech Affair   222

vii

Contents

Britain Appears on the Scene   225
The September Crisis   226
The Consequences of Munich   230

15   The Beginning of the War   233
     The Italian Claims   233
     The Prague Coup   234
     The Policy of Guarantees   235
     Negotiations with the USSR   236
     The Last Hesitations and the Declaration of War   239
     The 'Phoney War'   242

16   Woe to the Vanquished   246
     Military Disaster and Political Disaster   246
     The Impotence of the Vichy Regime   248
     The Impotence of Free France   251

     Conclusion   260

     Appendix: Documents   262
     Introduction   262
     List of Documents   262
     Documents   265

     Select Bibliography   354

     Index   358

Preface

Writing a book on the foreign policy of France from 1914 to 1945 may appear, if not an impossible undertaking, at any rate premature. Indeed, there is an almost complete absence of earlier works which could serve as guides: this is true not only of works of a general nature but most frequently in the case of special studies of even the most important points. What is perhaps more serious, however, is that the papers which are most vital for the purpose of these studies, the archives of the French Ministry of Foreign Affairs, were destroyed or scattered during the disaster of 1940. Some years ago a commission of historians undertook the gigantic task of reconstructing and publishing them but they believed that they could only do this starting from the summer of 1932, and the volumes which have appeared up to now cover only the years 1932–3 and 1936–7. Nevertheless, as the major problems and their possible solutions have varied little over this period, this published material already affords the historian a valuable foundation, and we owe deep gratitude to those who devoted themselves to this thankless task, and without whom the present work could not even have been attempted.

In these circumstances, however, a complete study of French foreign policy could hardly be contemplated. We have limited ourselves to attempting a general understanding of this policy reduced to its most outstanding features. Even within these limits it is still a hazardous attempt: it is not easy for either a foreigner or a Frenchman of the 1960s to recall the state of mind of Frenchmen from 1920 to 1930. We are bound to present highly personal ideas which will doubtless often surprise more than one reader. We take full responsibility for this, of course. However, we cannot end these few words without expressing special gratitude to M. Pierre Renouvin who has trained generations of historians in the disciplines of the history of international relations.

Preface

Chapter 1

French Diplomacy in the War of 1914–18

Introduction

There is a story about the old French geographer A. Demangeon who, when he had to give a course on the British Isles, began by declaring: 'Gentlemen, England is an island; now you know as much about it as I do.' This will serve as an apology for stating first of all that one can understand nothing of the foreign policy of France unless one bears in mind always that France does not have the good fortune of being an island. She is attached to a continent of which she cannot avoid being an integral part. Her capital and her most vigorous provinces are without natural defences of any note and they are within striking distance of an invader advancing into the great plains of northern Europe. It is true that these open spaces which present no obstacles can be crossed in either direction; and the French armies have more than once invaded the Netherlands and the German states, under Louis XIV, Louis XV and Napoleon. In 1914, however, these events were already long past, and France had neither the strength nor the wish to expand into Europe. What had dominated her for several decades was fear – fear of Germany. In 1870 France had a sharp revelation of a superior military power, which conquered her, and which took Alsace-Lorraine from her, disregarding the wish of the population. France never wholly resigned herself to this loss, but she soon had to abandon the illusion that she could recapture Alsace-Lorraine by force, for, since 1871 the population of Germany had continued to increase while that of France remained static, and although the French economy had not remained in the state of stagnation too often claimed, the growth of the German economy had been more extensive and more rapid than hers. French diplomacy sought to counterbalance this German power, which the French had never ceased to believe to be malevolent and hostile. For a long time the only possible counterweight seemed to be Russia, and the conclusion of the Franco-Russian Alliance did in fact give to many French people several years of seeming tranquillity. After 1905, however, the German peril appeared in a new form, for Germany had launched its *Weltpolitik*, or world policy. No doubt this policy was no longer directed exclusively against France, as in the time of Bismarck. Its aim was rather to overthrow the English position; but France, which Wilhelm II and his chancellor Bülow at times contemplated integrating into their system, would have to submit, in their opinion, to the continental hegemony of Germany, which meant in fact that she must lose her independence. The year 1905 symbolized this new threat, for in that year Germany demanded, and obtained, the resignation of the French Minister of Foreign Affairs, Théophile Delcassé.

The threat was from then on, however, no longer perceptible only to diplomats and politicians; it made itself felt every day to much wider strata of the population, for it had spread from the military and political level to the economic level.

It is difficult to imagine today the effect which the modern and dynamic characteristics of the German economy that now seem to us so normal, produced about 1910 on Frenchmen accustomed to more traditional concepts and practices. At this time we find that many socially very conservative French authors analysed Germany as bent on export, and on the conquest of opportunities by its production system; these analyses are reminiscent of the post-Marxist theorists of 'imperialism, the last stage of capitalism'. The French point of view at this time was in fact different: it was not because of her advanced economic development that Germany had become imperialistic; it was imperialistic by nature and economic expansion was for it only one of the means of conquering the world. For example, the very important work published in 1915 by one of the pioneers of economic history in France, Henri Hauser, should be read again. In his *Méthodes allemandes d'expansion économique* (Paris, 1915), he tells us (p.60):

> German industry must appear . . . as a bloc of forces. . . . The economic struggle is a war like other wars. . . . Everything must be organized with a view to the goal to be achieved, which is rational exploitation of the planet. In the field of commerce, as in that of strategy and politics, this methodical organization will achieve the sovereign formula: *Deutschland über Alles.* [or (p. 135)] German

dumping is not a process of economic action, it is a warlike measure in the midst of peace and under the deceitful appearance of peace.

Here we have the basic argument: contrary to practices in other countries, in Germany it is the state which presides over economic expansion (pp.254–5):

> By this concentration of all its energies, by this unity of direction, the economic Germany has become a power which is at least as formidable as the military Germany, and of the same order: a power of domination and conquest.

Winning the War

France did not enter the war in 1914 because of subtle clauses of some secret treaty, or by virtue of special links with threatened Serbia; she did this because her leaders did not think they could take the risk of losing the Russian alliance by too feebly supporting or too harshly restraining Russia in a venture to which the latter was utterly committed. Also, the mass of the population followed because they felt that a war against Germany was inevitable sooner or later, and that there was no use in prolonging the agony of suspense indefinitely. This fatalism explains the comparative passivity of French diplomacy in the international crisis which ended in war: not that they wished for a military confrontation with a formidable enemy, who, there was no doubt, was stronger than they were, but that France, in her continental position, did not consider that she was free to choose.

Once committed to the war, France felt that she was fighting for her independence and perhaps for her very existence. During the first years of the conflict, one single idea took possession of her: to win the war. French diplomacy was then concerned only with reinforcing the cohesion between the allies and achieving new alliances. By the agreement of 5 September 1914, concluded on the eve of the victory of the Marne:

> The British, French and Russian governments undertake not to conclude a separate peace during the present war; the three governments agree that, if there are grounds for discussing peace terms, none of the allied powers can stipulate peace conditions without previous agreement with both the other allies.

This agreement gave each of the three countries a precious feeling of security, but on the other hand it obviously confined their freedom of political action within narrow limits, especially for peace overtures. The quest for new allies is the substance of *Entente* diplomacy, not specially of French diplomacy. One point, however, must be stressed: since the end of 1914 the German army had dug itself into a continuous network of trenches, opposite the French front, which the French troops were unable to penetrate in spite of enormous sacrifices. To achieve victory, and in the meantime to reassure her Russian ally, against whom the majority of the Austrian and German forces were turning, France herself felt the need for new allies: her aim was not only the increase of forces which these allies would bring, but also the possibility of opening new theatres of operations in which, she believed, the military decision would be easier to achieve. Hence France would, generally speaking, be inclined to make greater sacrifices to the countries whose support she wished to enlist and to consider long-term interests or difficulties which would become apparent after victory as less important.[1]

First of all she contemplated Italy, the only great European country which had not entered the war in August 1914. Italy was the ally of Germany and Austria-Hungary, but as far as the latter was concerned, she had territorial claims to assert: provinces, whose population was partly Italian, in the Alpine valley of Alto Adige and in the Istrian peninsula around Trieste. The *Entente* would have no difficulty in promising these enemy lands to the Italians. However, Italy had other ambitions, especially on the eastern shore of the Adriatic, formerly the possession of the Venetian Republic, but at that time inhabited mostly by Slavs related to the Serbs. Here she encountered the resistance of Russia, who regarded herself as the protector of the Slav world. It was owing to France that she obtained satisfaction for the most part. Italy entered the war on 20 May 1915, a great diplomatic success. However, the military result was limited: access to Austria from the Italian side was blocked by the Alpine range.

North of the Balkans, however, the Danube plain presented a wide path without obstacles to Budapest and Vienna; that would be the means of striking at the rear of Austria-Hungary which

[1] In this her attitude differed from that of Britain, for example. Cf. A. Pingaud, *Histoire diplomatique de la France pendant la Grande Guerre*, Vol. I, pp.11–12.

was the weak point of the enemy alliance. Even apart from this brilliant prospect, the immediate need arose of coming to the rescue of little Serbia, who was being threatened by the great Austria-Hungary, and who could not be aided directly because she had no access to the sea. The diplomacy of the *Entente* believed that it had found a great field of action there: in 1912–13, Serbia, Bulgaria and Greece, allied under the aegis of Russia and supplied with French equipment, achieved a brilliant success against Turkey. It was this same Turkey which entered the war on the side of the Central Powers on 19 October 1914. Would it not be possible to re-form the 1912 alliance against Turkey and extend it in such a way that it would also act against Austria-Hungary? There was a great obstacle to this hope: in 1913 Bulgaria, actuated by Austria-Hungary, had turned against her recent allies. Moreover, she had been conquered and had lost many of the advantages she had acquired; and she dreamed of revenge. So we see the diplomats of the *Entente* making attractive promises to Bulgaria, foreseeing even restoration of territory at the expense of Serbia. This proved a waste of time: in September 1915 Bulgaria, in her turn, joined the war on the side of the Central Powers. This failure was so strongly resented that it may have been responsible for the final resignation of Delcassé, the great French Minister of Foreign Affairs.

The diplomacy of the *Entente* was not much happier as far as Greece was concerned. A problem of internal politics was encountered here: the minister Eleutherios Venizelos, who was willing to honour the alliance of his country with Serbia, and who was a supporter of the *Entente*, came up against King Constantine who was supposed to favour Germany. The situation was complicated by the fact that an Allied army under French command had gained a foothold in the Greek port of Salonika at the very moment when Bulgaria was attacking Serbia, and Greece stood aside. In order to safeguard the rear of this expeditionary corps, France would gradually be led to involve her allies in measures which respected Greek neutrality less and less. The army of Salonika, moreover, would remain powerless for all practical purposes until September 1918.

The prospects seemed more favourable as far as the last remaining Balkan State, Rumania, was concerned. She had territorial claims to assert against Hungary, and the influence of French culture there was considerable. Rumania in fact entered the war on the Allied side in August 1916, but perhaps through over-caution, she had allowed the favourable moment to pass and was soon militarily crushed.

Japan, the ally of Great Britain, had declared war on Germany on 23 August 1914. In fact it was up to her solely to immobilize the German positions in China (in the Shantung peninsula) and in the Pacific. Nevertheless, throughout the war, French opinion and even certain leaders beguiled themselves with illusory hopes that the Japanese armies, which had proved their worth against the Russians in 1905, would be induced to intervene in Europe. Neither the reservations of Great Britain and Russia, nor the unequivocal refusals of the Japanese government, could dispel this idea. The result was that France was undecided about opposing Japanese ambitions in China about which Great Britain and the United States, on the other hand, were very concerned.

Hence, during the first years of the war, French diplomacy was preoccupied with immediate problems which need only be recalled briefly, for they have little to do with the permanent factors of French foreign policy.

Peace Feelers and War Aims

Various neutral countries, however, and one of the enemy powers, Austria-Hungary, almost from the beginning of the war tried constantly to find the basis of a possible return to peace,[2] either by diplomatic probings or by talks between unofficial intermediaries. It must be acknowledged that French diplomacy paid little attention to these attempts, since she saw them chiefly as possible traps. Since these peace feelers required great secrecy, the belligerent who became a party to them could always be afraid of seeming to negotiate behind his allies' backs, and hence being disloyal to them, and it is known how much the cohesion of the *Entente* was essential for France. Moreover, the adversary could at any moment reveal these talks and thus give the impression that France was losing confidence in victory, for one of the great pre-occupations of French governments throughout the war was the fear of seeing the country's 'morale' waver. Finally, negotiations

[2] In this connection see F. Charles-Roux, *La Paix des Empires centraux*, and G. Pedroncini, *Les Négociations secrètes pendant la Grande Guerre*.

with Austria-Hungary, even if surrounded by guarantees, could not take France very far: it was from Germany that the dangerous demands could come, and it was from Germany that France herself had demands to make. Hence, without examining all these attempts in detail, we will confine ourselves to examining the most important of them: that of Prince Sixtus of Bourbon-Parma.

Sixtus of Bourbon-Parma was the brother-in-law of the Emperor Karl of Austria-Hungary who had succeeded to the throne in November 1916; he was, moreover, an officer in the Belgian army. He was therefore the ideal intermediary, because of his rank and his connections in both camps. From March to May 1917 he plied backwards and forwards between the Emperor Karl and the president of the French Republic, Raymond Poincaré. The Emperor Karl appeared very generous as far as Germany's affairs were concerned: complete restoration of Belgian independence and the return of Alsace-Lorraine to France which were the two things which the German government of the time, as we know from other sources, absolutely refused to contemplate. On the other hand the Emperor Karl was silent about the Italian claims with regard to Austria. Finally, contrary to what Prince Sixtus gave to understand, Austria-Hungary did not contemplate making a separate peace; furthermore it is doubtful whether she would be able to do so, even if she wished, because being already very weakened, she depended greatly on Germany. Italy, moreover, as soon as she was informed, insisted on the promises made to her by the *Entente*, and the talks soon came to an end. Even this attempt, in spite of the quality of its participants, was not without danger; for in order to dispel Germany's mistrust, which these peace feelers had aroused, the Austrian Minister of Foreign Affairs allowed himself to say in public at the beginning of 1918 that France had petitioned for peace. This elicited a blunt denial from Clemenceau who was then President of the Council.

There was, however, one case of steps taken by a neutral country, which must be treated separately because it has its own characteristics. This was the proposal for mediation made by the United States and developed by Colonel House, who was in the confidence of President Wilson, in the first months of 1916. According to an unofficial agreement signed by House and the British Foreign Secretary, Sir Edward Grey, on 22 February, an international conference could be called at the request of the

Entente; if the Germans refused, 'the United States would probably join in the war against Germany'. One cannot help looking back and thinking of the evils which could have been avoided and the number of human lives which could have been saved, if this initiative had been successful. However, the fact is that the French did not encourage the British, who were themselves hesitant to follow it up, and one may wonder why. In the first place no basis for the future negotiations had been given, and perhaps they did not dare submit in practice the claims which they considered vital, to the arbitration of the United States. But was the decisive trump-card, which United States intervention would have represented for the *Entente*, worth running a number of diplomatic risks for? At this point the disillusioned wisdom of diplomats, as expressed by the following anecdote, must be remembered: When a pretty girl says 'no' she means 'perhaps', and when she says 'perhaps' she means 'yes'. When a diplomat says 'yes' he means 'perhaps', and when he says 'perhaps' he means 'no'.

No doubt President Wilson's 'probably' appeared in French eyes as too improbable a foundation to be relied upon, thereby committing the country's policies to completely new paths.

The United States met with more success when they asked the belligerents at the end of this same year, 1916, to disclose their war aims. Until that time France had taken hardly any interest in this, since the anxiety about victory obliterated everything else. French censorship had tried to avoid discussions of this subject in the press, for fear that excessive claims would give a false impression to the neutral countries and cause the enemy to harden: this was the very result that had been achieved by certain claims expressed by Germany. On the other hand, faced with the American demands, it was Germany who stood aside and not France.

If the document presented by France in the name of the Allies[3] is compared with the Fourteen Points which were made public a year later by President Wilson, one cannot fail to see great similarities on the whole. The French text did not, however, mention the League of Nations, the freedom of the seas, or the publication of peace treaties. It did not state anything definite regarding Poland in order not to contradict the tsar, who was still – for a little while longer – on the Russian throne, and whose fidelity to

[3] See Document 1.

8

the alliance had to be strengthened. Harder words were used regarding Turkey. However, the French and American formulae came back to the same theme, whether the question was that of Belgium or Alsace-Lorraine. One difference catches the eye: where Wilson limits himself to saying, 'the possibility of an autonomous development for the peoples of Austria-Hungary', the French note calls for 'freedom of the Italians, Slavs, Rumanians and Czechs from foreign domination'. France evidently had to take into consideration the point of view of her allies, and the Czechs had already made sure of influential partisans in Paris: Thomas Masaryk, who inspired the Czech independence movement, visited Briand in February 1916; but most of all his influence was extended by that of several great French teachers, such as the historians Ernest Denis and Louis Eisenmann, specialists in Slav questions, and supported by a high official in foreign affairs, Philippe Berthelot.[4]

However, an essential point was left vague in the French official note: that of the guarantee of security. This was at least as important to a France which was invaded and whose very life was threatened, as the restoration of Alsace-Lorraine, which the French could not omit to claim once they were engaged in the war against Germany. But, with regard to this guarantee against a German invasion, other texts written at the same time[5] enable us to see that the French government had already formed a fairly clear idea of this: the question was to detach the left bank of the Rhine from Germany and to make it neutral. The idea which inspired this demand was not political but strategical, bearing in mind the means available for fighting: the course of the Rhine, which is wide and has high banks in many places, was the last large obstacle on which a defensive stand could be made against an offensive from the east.

From the beginning of 1917 several of the guiding lines of French foreign policy were already appearing; we will have to discuss them again at length during the course of this study.

The Armistice

When the German High Command, becoming aware of the attrition of its army and foreseeing that the influx of American

[4] See Document 4.   [5] See Documents 2, 3.

forces would guarantee the Allies an increasing superiority, decided that it was necessary to request an armistice, it was to President Wilson that the request was sent, on 4 October 1918; and it was President Wilson alone who gave the first replies. The Allies protested: they objected to being kept in the background and feared that the conditions indicated in the first place by Wilson would enable Germany to resume the war after having restored its strength. However, the French government was more reticent in its protestations than was the British government: it was bent on dealing tactfully with American susceptibilities, while the press censorship endeavoured not to let the French public suspect any possible disagreements between France and the United States.[6] At this time one of the dominant preoccupations of the Clemenceau government made its appearance.

Wilson, however, lost no time in giving his military chiefs the task of determining the conditions which would effectively put the Germans out of action. It was at this point that the French marshals Foch and Pétain added the occupation of the left bank of the Rhine and certain 'bridgeheads' on the right bank to the evacuation of the countries invaded and the delivery of war equipment. These stipulations were not made exclusively for military considerations; they show political ulterior motives, the wish to take out a mortgage on the conclusion of peace. 'It is obvious', wrote Foch, 'that only the advantages established by the armistice will remain acquired; only those sacrifices regarding territory agreed upon by the enemy when it is concluded will be final.'[7] The innate anxiety for security had already set the French government on this path nearly two years previously.

As a matter of fact, however, the entire armistice was based on political concepts: it was requested by the Germans and granted by President Wilson, on the basis of the Fourteen Points. These, some of which had already been overtaken by events, were the subject of an implementation discussion between the Allies and Colonel House, who was representing Wilson. Britain in particular repudiated the principle of 'the freedom of the seas'. France, however, confined herself to defining the right to reparations. All the territorial disagreements were then sent to the peace conference.[8]

[6] See P. Renouvin, *L'Armistice de Rethondes*, especially pp.131, 133.
[7] Ibid., p.198.   [8] Ibid., pp.214–18.

Chapter 2

The Peace Settlement

A Pyrrhic Victory

We have seen the victorious Allies impose on Germany an
armistice which made it incapable of resuming the struggle. Stark
reality, however, hardly conformed with these brilliant appearances. In order to win this war France had made a prodigious
effort, which literally exhausted her and bled her white: out of a
population of barely forty million inhabitants, she had lost more
than a million and a half men, to which more than 700,000 disabled
have really to be added. This does not include the ravages caused
by the fact that the war was fought basically on her territory; we
will return to this later. The distribution of the losses made the
overall picture worse. In France, which was a country with a
stagnant population, it was a large proportion of the young
people, already few enough, who were lost, especially the future
leaders of the nation: the most recent graduations from the *Grandes
Ecoles* were often reduced by two-thirds. Moreover, the only large
industrial area of France before 1914 – that of the Nord-Pas de
Calais – was completely devastated. If this can be imagined, add
also the moral damage caused to the entire population by more
than four years of suffering and anguish. It is not to be wondered
at that the dominant preoccupation of French opinion was to be
absolutely certain that such ordeals would never again be
experienced.

This threat, however, was not removed. Even after the territorial losses resulting from the peace treaty, Germany still had a
population of more than sixty millions; its losses, in absolute
figures, were hardly greater than those of France which meant that
relatively they were considerably lower. Added to this, the
German population was far younger than that of France. Without
too great a distortion of the facts it could be said that for the
French and the Germans in 1919, the ratio of men of an age to
bear arms was 1 to 2. Moreover, in the case of heavy industrial

potential, even after reconstruction of the devastated French areas the ratio was 1 to 4. For in the 1914–18 war equipment played a dominant part.

The situation was perhaps even more serious: France could not have thought of confronting Germany in 1914 without the Russian alliance. Russia, whose political and administrative weakness and economic backwardness had no doubt been underestimated, seemed at least to offer an almost inexhaustible reservoir of brave and long-suffering soldiers. In 1919, however, no support could be expected from a Russia in the throes of a revolution; moreover, from now onwards she seemed to be a source of dangers which, although not clearly defined, could nevertheless prove formidable.

It is not at all paradoxical to say that from that time the main concern of French diplomacy was to guarantee the safety of a vulnerable and greatly threatened conqueror.

The Quest for Security

The simplest and most basic means of protecting oneself against Germany would be to eliminate it. Not that anyone contemplated genocide at this period. However, there were many Frenchmen who advocated breaking, or at least loosening, the German unity which Bismarck had imposed by force in 1866 and 1871, and returning to the political situation which had followed the Westphalia treaties of 1648.[1] The French government firmly dismissed this argument without hesitation, both from respect for the principle that people have a right to self-determination, and from realism: German unity was now too well established, too deeply rooted, for there to be any hope of ending it.

Various other solutions were contemplated or proposed and some of them were partly put into practice, to lead finally, by a series of compromises, to a hybrid system.

(a) Disarmament

A first solution, which Britain and the United States seemed at times prepared to consider, was to impose total disarmament on Germany. However, this would have morally obliged the Allies,

[1] See in particular a good account of this argument by the historian and politician G. Hanotaux, *Le Traité de Versailles*.

France in particular, to guarantee the integrity of German territory, and this was asking too much of French opinion. Moreover, was it feasible? This was the question asked by the French, especially Marshal Foch. It was impossible to overcome the fact that, owing to the war itself, Germany had had at her disposal for many years millions of experienced men in reserve. Depriving these soldiers of personal and light arms was an unrealistic demand: it would have meant searching every house. The reply to this would be that modern wars are won by heavy armaments, which are much more difficult to conceal. Again, this argument was not without a reply: armaments quickly become outdated, and it was above all the manufacture of new armaments which must be prevented; this presupposed that the activity of a large number of factories could be closely inspected. It would therefore be necessary to set up a system of permanent inspection which in the course of time would not be compatible with German sovereignty.[2]

It was finally decided to reduce the German army to the minimum which would be necessary to guarantee internal order: 100,000 men. On this point two systems came into conflict: whether to recruit these men by short-term or long-term engagements. The first system could not fail to end in a rapid reconstitution of large trained reserves: on this subject the French still remembered the example of Prussia, whom Napoleon I had tried in vain to disarm after having defeated her at Jena in 1806, and who had very quickly regained a large number of troops owing to very short-term service. However, an army formed by long-term engagements would be dedicated to becoming an army of trained officers, whose soldiers would be transformed at the appropriate time into non-commissioned officers ready to train a large number of conscripts quickly. Finally, an army recruited on a twelve-year engagement basis was decided upon.

It must be added that the result of the disarmament of Germany was to subject Germany's neighbours to a strong moral pressure to oblige them sooner or later to disarm likewise; an inequality of *right* between the conqueror and the conquered could not be maintained indefinitely. However, when once all the countries disarmed, the problem would not be solved: the threat would come from the country which would rearm with the greatest

[2] See the argument in G. Castellan, *Le Réarmement clandestin de l'Allemagne, 1930–1935*, and the book by General Nollet, quoted on p.31.

determination and speed, having available the greatest human and industrial potential to achieve this; this would again be Germany. The solution was therefore invalid.

(b) *Detachment of the left bank of the Rhine*

As we have already stated, the origin of this demand was basically strategic: it was only on the Rhine that an offensive from the east could be stopped without too great risks and excessive sacrifices, by a France which was considerably weakened by the war. However, although this argument was irrefutable from a military point of view, to what political reality would it lead? The argument of the French government on this point appeared from 1917: Aristide Briand, the President of the Council at the beginning of 1917, and Clemenceau, who would negotiate on behalf of France in 1919, had the same ideas. The two men were subsequently to come to a violent confrontation regarding the application and the consequences of the Treaty of Versailles; this, however, should not blind us to the profound similarity of their views. The problem was not to annex the left bank of the Rhine to France, but to form one or several independent states there. This would be an answer to all the reproaches which could be made to the Allies for violating their own principles.

It had to be recognized, however, that this solution gave rise to serious objections. In order for military requirements to be fully satisfied, it would be necessary for the line of defence of the Rhine to be held permanently by the French army and her allies; the need to guarantee the safety of the rear area and lines of communication would hence not be compatible with true independence of the Rhineland states. If the military occupation were not permanent, however – on this point the French argument was somewhat uncertain[3] – what would prevent the Rhineland states, once they were really free, from rejoining Germany? The French proposal relied partly on the feelings of the Rhineland population whom the treaties of 1815 had arbitrarily attached to Prussia (and, to a smaller extent, to Bavaria). There was no doubt that the Rhineland people were very different from the Prussians, and did not much like them; many of them would no doubt be pleased to

[3] For the disagreements between Clemenceau and Foch in this connection and the inconsistencies of Foch himself, see Renouvin, *L'Armistice de Rethondes*, pp.305-8.

see an autonomy which would enable them to participate in the same way as Prussia and outside it, in a German state.[4] A whole movement developed in this direction during the course of 1919. It did appear, however, that, except in moments of sharp crisis, only a small minority contemplated an independent, separate existence from Germany.

It would appear that Britain – who, unlike Russia, had not been informed of French wishes in 1917 – strongly refused to take this course, and that the United States had made the same refusal to the French demand. However, the security problem still remained.

(c) *The Anglo-American guarantee offer and the final decisions*
In view of this deadlock President Wilson made his famous offer, on 14 March 1919: to give France an American guarantee against any unprovoked aggression by Germany. Lloyd George also added that this American guarantee would be accompanied by a British one. The offer was made in exchange for France's renunciation of taking from Germany the left bank of the Rhine. Clemenceau scarcely hesitated in accepting – for which he was long reproached in France. Nevertheless he insisted on a temporary military occupation of the left bank of the Rhine by France and her allies, and in the end he obtained it: in principle it would be for fifteen years, with partial withdrawal after every five years. This occupation was supposed to guarantee that the treaty was carried out. But what did it amount to? If one considers the military clauses – the disarmament of Germany – this came back to saying that the occupation would come to an end at the moment when Germany had recovered its strength, and would date in advance the moment when the danger would reappear. If one considers the financial clauses – the reparations, which will be discussed at length later – there was no connection between the duration of the occupation and that of the reparations; this was, moreover, not fixed by the treaty, but everything pointed to its being much longer.[5] In fact the temporary occupation of the left bank of the Rhine, complemented, it is true, by a permanent demilitarization of this region, could only result in guaranteeing

[4] One must not forget that the Germany of 1914, like that of 1919, was a federal state.

[5] Certain American experts suggested introducing into the treaty a time limit of thirty to thirty-five years for payment of reparations.

France a breathing-space in which to tend her wounds and build up her strength.

It must be stressed that during the negotiations Clemenceau finally staked everything on the Anglo-American Alliance, on which the future of the country henceforth depended. This political choice encountered the declared opposition of Marshal Foch, supreme commander of the French armies who feared that, should the line on the Rhine be abandoned, Anglo-American aid would arrive too late. It came up against the reluctance of many military men and politicians, especially the President of the Republic, Raymond Poincaré.[6] However, he kept firmly to the chosen path and did not hesitate to strike at General Mangin, the commander of one of the occupying armies, who seemed to be adopting an attitude too favourable to the Rhineland autonomists.

Alsace-Lorraine and the Saar

France's right to recover Alsace and Lorraine was one of the least discussed points of the peace treaty. Hence we will say only one word on this subject: the return of these two populous and economically active provinces represented a profound aspiration in which justice and sentiment were intermingled, but it did not make any fundamental change in the ratio between the French and German forces. The two million or so people of Alsace-Lorraine more or less represented a kind of numerical equivalent to the French losses in the war. The French claim was based solely on reasons of principle and right, and not on ulterior motives of political balance.

An even more controversial question, however, was grafted on to the Lorraine question: that of the Saar. There France made two requests which were very different and, to tell the truth, even incompatible with one another.

In the north there is no natural fixed boundary between Lorraine or Alsace and the German *Länder*. Before 1815 the border regions of Landau, Saarbrücken and Saarlouis were part of French

---

[6] It must not be forgotten that in France at this period the president of the Republic was not responsible; and he had only a function of representation and not the power to decide general policy. This power belonged to the president of the Council.

territory. They had been removed in the treaties of 1815 as a military precaution against a counterattack from France. Since the beginning of 1917 Briand had formulated what was to become the official French claim: a return to the frontier as it was before 1815. However, in spite of there being certain Francophile elements, especially around Saarlouis, the Saar population had not, during a century of German rule, shown anything comparable to the continuous and unanimous protest of the people of Alsace-Lorraine after 1871. It was clumsy at the very least, on the part of French diplomacy, to bring two such separate issues together.

Above all, the second French claim was of a totally different origin. During the war the Germans had occupied the larger part of the Nord-Pas de Calais basin, the only important coal-mining area which France had at the time. There they had carried out systematic destruction which amounted to a loss of production of 20 million tons over several years, the very years in which France had a particularly imperative and immediate need of this coal for her reconstruction. Now in the Saar there was a coal basin which represented a production of 13½ million tons in 1913. It was therefore natural that France without waiting for hypothetical and risky reparations should wish to guarantee for herself for a certain time, with full ownership, the production of this basin, which implied that during this time the German administration in the mining area should be suspended.

However, the boundaries of the mining and industrial Saar basin did not in any way coincide with those of the districts which had belonged to France before 1815: the industrial basin stretched much farther north. It was economically and humanly hardly possible to introduce political and administrative differences in the middle of the basin. This explained the vigorous opposition of President Wilson to any French annexation in the region which would have cut the basin in half. Finally, after ups and downs which it is not essential to recall, the following compromise was made: France received the ownership of the mines, and the industrial Saar basin was detached from Germany for fifteen years and administered by the League of Nations, after which a plebiscite would decide its fate. The results of this plebiscite, like that which took place after the Second World War as a result of similar claims, proved the German character of the Saar territory.

The Principle of Reparations

There had been no lack of people in France who dreamed that the military solidarity of the Allies could spread and become transformed into a solidarity which would restore Europe. An interallied conference held in Paris in June 1916 expressed the following wish:

> Proclaiming their solidarity for the restoration of the countries which were the victims of destruction, plundering and forced requisitions, the Allies decide jointly to seek ways of restoring to these countries preferentially, or to help them to restore, their raw materials, their industrial and agricultural machinery, their livestock, their merchant fleet.

During the negotiations of 1919 several projects saw daylight which, extending this modest wish, contemplated a general settlement of war costs by a joint effort of the conquerors and the conquered.[7] It was, however, difficult for the French government officially to propose a system of this nature, which would have inevitably eased the burden of their country and on the other hand overburdened their American friends. For example, meeting the war costs by world taxes based on population and wealth was contemplated: this would have reduced the French effort from 30 per cent to 11 per cent of the total, but would have increased that of the United States by 29 per cent, that is, 250,000 millions of francs. Only an initiative from the United States would have enabled the conference to move along this path. Perhaps President Wilson personally would have been open to these considerations of world interest; but public opinion in his country was not ready and he could not think of supplying an argument of this kind to the opposition which he was already encountering there. It was necessary to wait for the Second World War, before a wider and more generous outlook and a more accurate recognition of the new needs resulted in the Marshall Plan.

The fact remains that France had suffered by far the most among the great belligerents: before the war that part of her territory which was invaded and devastated by the German armies produced 94 per cent of the wool products, 90 per cent of the linen yarn, 90 per cent of the iron ore, 80 per cent of the steel, 60 per

[7] See the analysis of one of these projects, 'General Administration of Nations' by Bouilloux-Laffont in A. Tardieu, *La Paix*, p.377.

cent of the cotton fabric and 55 per cent of the coal of the whole of France. Moreover, a large part of the destruction which had been suffered was the result not of military operations but of a deliberate wish to destroy the French economy and to eliminate competitors to German industries after the war. This was particularly clearly shown in a memoir of the German General Staff, dated February 1916, entitled *Industry in Occupied France*.[8] There could be no question of allowing the German economy the benefit of this calculated destruction, any more than of allowing the German navigation companies to profit from the submarine offensive carried out against the British fleet contrary to the laws of war.

In fact, the custom at that time was even that the conqueror would exact an indemnity from the conquered which would cover his war expenditure. Germany had not omitted to do this with regard to France in 1871, and had been prepared to do it again if she had won.[9] The principle of refunding the costs of the war was abandoned in the face of the objections of the American delegate Foster Dulles, which in fact were not only inspired by the Wilsonian idealism, but were also based on realistic considerations: the total repayment of war damages and costs would have been a sum exceeding 1,000 milliard francs, the payment of which no one considered possible. On the other hand, the repayment of damages, the principle of which, moreover, appeared in a general form in President Wilson's Fourteen Points, and which had been defined in the armistice, could not be contested. This included – notably at the request of belligerents such as the British Dominions which had not suffered material damages – not only damages to property, but damages to persons, in other words, war pensions.

However, fixing the total of these damages presented a considerable problem. Not only did it take a long time to draw up the census, but the evaluation of each damage presented considerable elements of doubt: should one adopt the nominal value in 1914, or the replacement value, taking into account the already considerable increase in prices?[10]

---

[8] See extracts from this report in Tardieu, op. cit., pp.309–13.

[9] The German experts contemplated a figure of 300,000 million francs.

[10] It is for this very reason that we have kept here the figures given in francs by the authors of the period. On the basis of the gold-equivalent of 1913, 1 dollar = 5 francs, 1 mark = 1.25 francs. The franc of 1919, which

Faced with the impossibility of achieving a well-established total in good time, many experts suggested fixing a lump sum for the reparations. France refused as a matter of principle: she believed that she should maintain her right to total reparation for damages. She also refused for factual reasons: a final figure could not be fixed without considering Germany's capacity for payment – and clause 232 of the Treaty of Versailles, moreover, recognized to some extent the necessity for taking this capacity into account. However, an estimate based on the situation of the politically and economically disorganized Germany of 1919 could not fail seriously to underestimate the future potential of the German economy, whose rise had been so swift between 1900 and 1914. There was a fear that too low a forfeit might be fixed and published. To give an idea of the extent of the disagreement which took place, the first approximation of the repayable damages was estimated at 350 thousand million francs. This assumed that there was a much greater sum to be paid, owing to the fact that Germany would not be able to pay for several decades, and that it was desirable to take the interest into account. These interests were justified, moreover, since, for example, France had to rebuild all her devastated areas immediately, without expecting annual payments from Germany, and for this she would have to borrow at the market rate. Germany, on the other hand, at the time of the discussion which preceded the signing of the treaty, offered to pay a lump sum of 100 thousand million francs, without interest, payable in fifty or sixty years.

In the light of what happened afterwards, however, it was regrettable that the solution of paying a lump sum did not prevail. It was a serious matter to compel Germany to pledge itself without its knowing exactly what it was undertaking. The fixing of the total sum to be paid and the terms and conditions of payment were handed over to a Reparations Commission whose task, it was seen from that moment, would not be easy.

The work of the negotiations proved open to criticism on another point. The right to reparations was established in the treaty by clause 231:

---

had been detached from the gold standard, was no longer the franc of 1914; but those writing at the time were far from realizing this, and any calculation of actual equivalence would be very risky.

The allied and associated governments declare, and Germany recognizes, that Germany and its allies are responsible, because they caused them, for all the losses and all the damages suffered by the allied and associated governments and their nationals, as a result of the war which was forced upon them by the aggression of Germany and her allies.

The wording of this clause, which was granted as a compensation to the Allies for not having their costs of the war repaid,[11] was particularly unfortunate, for its last phrase seemed to make the right to reparations depend on Germany's being responsible for starting the war. Now the question of the origins of the war of 1914 is highly complex and could not fail to be disputed at great length by historians. The Germans, too, made use of these discussions in order constantly to question the French right to reparations, the basis of which was quite different.

Central and Eastern Europe

The war aims of the French in 1917 foresaw the breaking up of the Austro-Hungarian Empire, while Wilson's Fourteen Points contemplated only the autonomy of the various nationalities of this empire. The situation was the opposite with regard to Poland: the broad lines of her reconstitution were established by Wilson's Fourteen Points, while France had refrained from making any demands from consideration to the tsar. However, it cannot be said that the territorial upheaval introduced in these regions by the peace treaties – and which was subsequently one of their most criticized aspects – owed much to the deliberate policy of one or the other of the victorious states. The latter confined themselves for the most part to recording the accomplished facts: the collapse of the Austro-Hungarian Empire before the armistice, and the occupation of territories, especially by the rebellious Czechs and Poles.

It would have been difficult, moreover, for the Allies to enforce the application of indisputable principles, for the principle of nationalities, which was generally acknowledged by all, came up against insurmountable difficulties on the subject of territory. In many places the different nationalities were intermingled more or less inextricably, one of the most usual combinations being that

[11] Cf. P. Birdsall, *Versailles Twenty Years After*, pp.253–5.

the large towns showed ethnic majorities which were different from those of the surrounding countryside. Nor was it possible, in order to take the often questionable ethnic considerations into account, to separate regions which were economically too closely bound together. The new states must be viable and consequently they must rely as much as possible on geographically well-defined limits – mountains or rivers – and they must also correspond with historical regions which would provide ready-made administrative frameworks.

We will not examine these different rulings here in detail. We will confine ourselves to noting that in general one does not notice a well-asserted French policy resulting in solutions very different from those advocated by the experts of the different countries.[12] This was especially true of Czechoslovakia: nobody then advocated attaching to Germany the Germans of Sudetenland who had, moreover, never formed part of it, and Austria, who claimed them, was not supported by any of the 'Great Allies' on this point.

The most serious confrontation took place over Poland; but this brought Lloyd George, who for some reason regarded the Poles with particular disfavour, into conflict with all the other delegations. One of Wilson's Fourteen Points guaranteed to the reconstituted Poland an access to the sea: the most obvious was the famous 'Corridor', a narrow band of territory between Pomerania and East Prussia, the majority of whose population were Slavs related to the Poles; however, the only port in the region, Danzig, at the mouth of the Vistula, was unquestionably German. The experts none the less advocated assigning the entire region to Poland. In the face of the protestations of Lloyd George, a series of compromises was decided upon: a status of free city for Danzig (this was to be a source of perpetually renewed conflicts), plebiscites in East Prussia, and also – as a result of German representations – in Upper Silesia. The problem of the eastern frontiers of Poland was not settled at the peace conference, neither was that of the duchy of Cieszyn, which was disputed between Poland and Czechoslovakia. We will meet them again, at the very moment when the problem of French policy in central and eastern Europe begins to assume paramount importance.

In 1919, however, it was premature to represent France as the champion and protector of the new states. The Anglo-French

[12] See in particular P. S. Wandycz, *France and her Eastern Allies, 1919–1925*.

conflict which arose at the Peace Conference at the end of March 1919 could create this impression, especially Clemenceau's reply to the Lloyd George memorandum of 26 March.[13] In fact, however, the reason was the apparent discrepancy between two attitudes with regard to Germany which is found again and again throughout this narrative: the attitude of the British who believed that Germany could be morally disarmed by concessions, and the attitude which was that of many Frenchmen, especially at the beginning, who believed that any concession would be regarded by the Germans as a weakness, and would only aggravate the danger.

From the time of the Peace Conference, however, French policy asserted itself on one point regarding the problems of central Europe, even at the risk of contradicting the principles of President Wilson. This was the problem of Austria. Reduced to the German-speaking provinces of the Alps and the Danube and deprived of the Habsburg empire, Austria appeared to be a 'head without a body', and many people wondered whether this small new state was economically viable.[14] The majority of Austrians at the time seemed to wish to be attached to Germany. However, in spite of the right of the people to self-determination, France was opposed to this solution: she could not permit a Germany which, when enlarged by Austria, would be stronger than in 1914. If she failed to obtain from Britain and the USA the proclamation of an 'inalienable' independence of Austria, she would insist, by clause 80 of the treaty, that the attachment of Austria to Germany be subject to the approval of the League of Nations. From that time onwards France would submit Austria to a supervision which would also imply protection, and in particular she would not spare financial assistance. Here again it was the concern for security which inspired French policy and compelled her to avoid any increase in German power.

The League of Nations

It must not be concluded from certain sceptical outbursts on the part of Clemenceau – and he was lavish with them on many

[13] See Document 4.

[14] It is curious to find that, within the same territorial limits, the Austria reconstituted in 1945 never encountered insoluble economic problems; it is doubtful whether the discovery of the oilfield at Zistersdorf would be sufficient to explain this difference.

subjects – that the French in 1919 were as a whole indifferent to the proposals for a League of Nations. In fact many of them, even outside socialist circles, had great hopes of the future of the League of Nations; many writings on this subject by the nationalist historian G. Hanotaux, or by Poincaré's assistant R. Pinon, would no doubt surprise many people today. In fact the French delegates responsible for this problem – Bourgeois and Larnaude – rather incurred the reproach that they took the League of Nations too seriously, and that they wished straight away to make it a collective security system for which opinion in the different countries was far from ready. Their proposal foresaw in particular the formation of an international army, equipped with a general staff, also international, with extensive powers. This proposal was immediately put aside by the British and American delegations, and the text finally adopted made the League of Nations into an interesting debating society which was quite incapable of guaranteeing in itself the disarmed security which was its official objective. Only a few very general provisions could form a point of departure for the endeavour to build up a collective security which was to develop a few years later – unfortunately without a decisive result.[15]

Conclusion

The 1919 treaties were hotly debated in the twenty years which followed.[16] The Second World War, however, was able to correct many of the opinions voiced at that time. Their grave injustice could hardly be maintained any longer by anyone who had known the Europe of Hitler.[17] Was the Treaty of Versailles too hard to be borne by Germany? But what German living after 1945 could not regret the state of things established in 1919?

Two points, however, must be remembered. The first is that the revision clause written into the League of Nations Pact (clause 19) directly imparted a sort of vulnerability to the 1919 treaties and condemned Europe to a troubled future. A second point, on

[15] See Birdsall, op. cit., pp.116–47.

[16] It is essential, in order to obtain an idea of these discussions, to reread the Keynes pamphlets and the reply of E. Mantoux, *La Paix calomniée.*

[17] While severely criticizing other aspects of the treaty, Birdsall writes that it was 'the nearest situation to an ethnographic map of Europe which has ever been drawn up'.

which the French negotiators, Clemenceau in particular, insisted from the beginning, was that the application of the treaties and the preservation of the state of things which they established – ultimately the preservation of peace – depended on a close and permanent understanding between France, Britain and the USA. As it was, the Peace Treaty was not welcomed with unmixed satisfaction in France: to many it seemed incomplete, unfinished, and left many misgivings for the future.[18]

[18] A large number of testimonies, notably that of Paul Cambon.

Chapter 3

From Versailles to the Ruhr

The Disappearance of the Anglo-American Guarantee

On 19 March 1920 the United States Senate failed to ratify the Treaty of Versailles with a constitutional majority. This vote was to have considerable consequences for the whole history of the interwar period. In the first place, the absence of the United States from the League of Nations was going to deprive the latter of a considerable part of its effectiveness. What was perhaps even more serious, however, from the French point of view, was that the guarantee treaty offered to France by President Wilson fell at the same blow, and that the end of the American guarantee also brought about the end of the British guarantee which was an integral part of it. In other words France, who at the time of the peace negotiations had sacrificed the real guarantee, which the separation of the left bank of the Rhine would have constituted, to the double political guarantee, then found herself deprived of anything which could have ensured her security.[1] Naturally Clemenceau, who was the person mainly responsible for the negotiation, was vehemently reproached for this disaster; his adversaries were amazed that he had not provided for an eventuality of which there were many indications, in particular the Republican victory in the American elections of October 1918. André Tardieu, who had been Clemenceau's chief assistant from the time of the peace conference, did his best to reply to these critics, in an article in *L'Illustration* of 20–7 March 1920;[2] he resumed more or less the same argument textually, a year later, in his book *La Paix*.[3] According to him Clemenceau had provided for the risk of non-ratification of the British and American guarantee treaties, by having added to article 429 of the Treaty, which dealt with the temporary occupation of the left bank of the

[1] Cf. especially Briand's speech of 25 February 1926, see Document 15.
[2] See Document 5.   [3] Pp.234–6.

Rhine and provided for its evacuation at the end of fifteen years, the following paragraph:

> If at this time the guarantees against an unprovoked aggression on the part of Germany were not considered adequate by the Allied and associated governments, the evacuation of the occupying troops could be delayed to the extent considered necessary to obtain the aforesaid guarantees.

Hence, Tardieu argued, failing the Anglo-American guarantee, France had only to prolong the occupation of the left bank of the Rhine.

How could one believe, however, that it would be politically and morally possible, in the face of international opinion, to subject Germany to the consequences of a British and American shirking of obligations for which it was in no way responsible? How could one contemplate forcing the Rhineland population to live in a situation which was abnormal and temporary, but which was prolonged indefinitely? In fact, this provision of the Treaty would only have meaning if it constituted a juridical expedient to return thereby to the political detachment of the left bank of the Rhine. In this case, 1920 was the suitable time for preparing for this solution. At the time, however, there was no trace of attempts of any kind by France or her representatives in the Rhineland to support autonomist movements there; these movements were manifested in 1919, and would appear again in 1923, but there was nothing to be found between these two dates.

How can this French passivity be explained? Can we believe that the French were so absorbed in more immediate preoccupations such as reconstruction and reparations that they suddenly forgot the concern for security which had haunted them until then?

The explanation is perhaps a different one; in order to have a real understanding of the problem we must try to put ourselves in the state of mind of the French at that time. They had been so completely absorbed by the war that they had retained a wartime attitude of mind. Germany was still the enemy – which also explains why the French, with a few exceptions, did not attach prime importance to the Rhineland movements. The British and the Americans, however, were by the same token still allies, fundamentally united by a similarity of views and by defence of the same cause. The separations and disagreements which arose could be caused only by transient misunderstandings, or by the intrigues of some 'villains': Lloyd George or Keynes, for instance.

There were, moreover, many reasons for believing that the British and the French were in fact still allies. They sat together at the Supreme Interallied Council, at the Conference of Ambassadors, at the Reparations Commission, at the Commission for Control of German Disarmament, at the Interallied Commission of Occupied Areas, etc. Naturally the task of these bodies was to control the carrying out of the peace treaties, and in certain cases to settle the problems which these treaties had left unresolved. In general, however, the French did not imagine that the Allies who had fought together and who remained united while solving the problems resulting from the end of the war, should not remain so in the future when facing up to the major problem, which was still the same: the problem of Germany. If Arnold Wolfers is to be believed, French confidence in British support was not wholly an illusion, for British diplomacy considered France as the guardian of the British frontier on the Rhine (but the French did not realize that this support, which was to come into effect only as a last resort, could involve a permanently paralysing control of French diplomacy by Britain).[4]

In any case it must be stressed that Clemenceau's choice – to link French security with the Anglo-American alliance – was never seriously questioned by his successors. Clemenceau, Briand and Poincaré came into conflict in violent political struggles in which they often sought arguments in the field of foreign policy. However, these struggles must not blind us to the basic continuity of French diplomacy.

The Efforts to Recover the Anglo-American Guarantee

It is well understood that some responsible statesmen could not entirely share the popular belief that the British and American alliance was still alive – even if they humoured this belief. Thus they tried forthwith, as they were to do later on, to retie the broken threads and once more to make the alliance a reality.

The estrangement of the United States appeared most clearly and had the most visible effects. Again, no doubt, the extent of the

[4] Cf. A. Wolfers, *Britain and France between Two Wars*, especially pp.229ff.

reaction which aroused American opinion against Europe was not fully realized in France. In any case the magnitude of the obstacles did not discourage certain French politicians, especially Briand who became President of the Council again from January 1921 to January 1922. Briand seized the opportunity of the Washington Conference which met in the autumn of 1921, to discuss naval disarmament and the problems of the Pacific. The concern of the professional diplomats of the Quai d'Orsay[5] was to avoid the question of land armaments being raised in this connection. Briand went in person to Washington, and then left before even the purpose of the debate had been broached. This behaviour did not fail to cause surprise, but his reasons become clear when one studies the texts closely.[6] The problem for Briand was to launch an appeal to American opinion in a general and disguised form, and to let it be understood that France was ready to disarm if she could have the benefit of a new international guarantee which would be liable to discourage any new German aggression. This appeal then passed more or less unnoticed.

The year after, it was Clemenceau's turn to undertake a journey to America. He no longer held any political responsibilities, but his moral prestige was considerable and he believed he could once again put it to the service of his country. In a speech delivered at the Metropolitan Opera on 22 November 1922 he suggested a mutual guarantee of the Rhine frontier which was, all things considered, a foreshadowing of Locarno, but a Locarno whose effectiveness would have been far greater because the United States would have been the guarantors.[7]

This was indeed a case of isolated attempts with no future; their main interest is that they reflected a trend. An official and continuous negotiation from 1919 to 1923, on the other hand, took place with Britain.[8] The most important period in this negotiation was from December 1921 to January 1922, when Lloyd George and Briand met in Cannes to prepare the Genoa Conference. This conference was one of Lloyd George's preoccupations: a joint

---

[5] The Ministry of Foreign Affairs in Paris, so called from the location of its headquarters.

[6] See Document 8. [7] See Document 11.

[8] See the Quai d'Orsay publication: *Documents relatifs aux négociations concernant les garanties de sécurité contre une agression de l'Allemagne* (*10 janvier 1919–7 decembre 1923*).

launching of a great effort for the economic rebuilding of Europe. In order to guarantee the success of his initiative, Lloyd George, broadly speaking, appeared to take the French point of view into consideration, and even provided his interlocutor with a proposal for a pact which would again give the French a British guarantee.

Are we then to believe that by forcing Briand to resign in January 1922, his political opponents wrecked a negotiation which had almost achieved its object and which would have again guaranteed the security of France? In France itself the supporters of Briand and the political opponents of his successor Poincaré did not fail to maintain this. If we examine it more closely we find that the negotiation was not so far advanced and Briand's reply to the British proposal[9] shows that there were serious differences between the French and British points of view. Briand requested in the first place that France and Britain should unite their policies on all the problems. In addition he wished for a bilateral treaty: a unilateral guarantee granted to France by Britain would put the former in a position of inferiority. British support would have to be effective not only in the case of a direct attack on French territory, but in the case of a violation of the treaties for German disarmament or demilitarization of the Rhineland region. Finally political agreement must be accompanied by an understanding between the General Staffs.

The negotiation was continued by Poincaré, and it failed on the very objections which Briand had already raised. If Briand had remained in power, would he have withdrawn from his first claims? Would he have succeeded in obtaining new concessions from his British partner? Naturally, the historian cannot provide an answer to these questions. It must also be realized that, with the passage of time, the state of mind of the two peoples differed more and more; in Britain the tendency was to believe that French fears regarding Germany were unfounded, and that it was sufficient to appease them with a few soothing words which did not constitute a real undertaking.[10] Most of all, the impression which was becoming more and more widespread in France was that the British were prepared to make verbal and hypothetical concessions in the field of security in exchange for immediate and

[9] See Document 10.
[10] See, for example, A. J. P. Taylor, *English History 1914–15*, London, 1965.

very real concessions on the part of the French in the field of reparations.

The Difficulties of Carrying Out the Treaty of Versailles

Although the problems of safety and alliances were not neglected during these years it is still true that attention in France was occupied mostly by immediate problems – the constant difficulties encountered by the application of the peace treaties.

(a) Disarmament of Germany[11]

The stipulations of the Treaty were precise on this point. The difficulties and the delays of putting them into practice are all the more worthy of attention.

The Treaty allowed a period, which in any circumstances did not exceed six months, for its military clauses to be applied. The interallied commission in charge of supervising this application, however, remained in office for seven years. The mere comparison of these two figures gives a first idea of the difficulties and the resistance encountered by disarmament.

It must be acknowledged, moreover, that demobilization – in practice putting into unemployment – of hundreds of thousands of men who had no other tradition or future than that of bearing arms, presented formidable problems to the German Republican government, which was still new and lacking in confidence. The Kapp putsch (March 1920) showed the seriousness of this problem. The German Republic, however, when finally victorious over this military *coup d'état*, did not react by taking advantage of their victory in order finally to break the militarism associated with the old order. On the contrary, Germany officially requested the Allies for a revision of the peace conditions in this respect, in particular the establishing of a regular army of 200,000 men; the reason which it gave for this was the communist threat which had reappeared as a result of the troubles following the coup. The Allies refused and at the Spa Conference (July 1920) they insisted that the German army should be reduced to 150,000 men on 1 October 1920 and to 100,000 men on 1 January 1921.

[11] A complete account of this question has been made by General Nollet, who was president of the Commission for Control of German Disarmament. The summary which follows is basically inspired by this account.

During the period that followed, the German government abandoned the idea of obtaining officially a revision of the military peace conditions, and tried various ways of changing them. Finally, this attempt became so obvious that the French and the British – in spite of the tendency of the latter to minimize the problem – came to an agreement at the London Conference (May 1921) to send Germany what was virtually an ultimatum, aimed in particular at the deliveries of equipment and the existence of paramilitary associations, with a threat of extending the occupation. This emphatic and co-ordinated intervention of the Allies, as in previous cases, was at first effective, but the effect gradually diminished. From April 1922 the German Wirth-Rathenau ministry – which was, however, as we shall see, the champion of the 'policy of execution' – resumed on a large scale the methods of obstruction which had been previously prepared, and tried to put an end to the control system officially.

This stubborn resistance was, of course, made easier by the nature of things. Modern warfare is to a very great extent a warfare of equipment. It was naturally impossible to draw up a complete report of war equipment actually in existence at the time of the armistice – no doubt the German military authorities did not possess one. Because of this the control of the destructions carried out did not entirely solve the problem. Large hidden stores of equipment were in fact discovered, for example, hundreds of 105mm howitzer barrels in the bricked-up cellars of a factory in Saxony. It is superfluous to add that a serious control of personal light arms was out of the question.

The destruction of old equipment, moreover, meant nothing; it was necessary to be able to carry out an effective control of manufactures which could be used for war. Here obstacles of a technical or economic order were insurmountable in certain cases. With regard to the chemical industry, for example, how was it possible to forbid the manufacture of products which could end equally well as either fertilizers or explosives? Moreover it was impossible to reduce certain sectors of heavy industry to ruin, and their workers to unemployment, and the Control Commission itself consented to certain departures when faced with the force of economic argument.

Thus the main effort of France was against German effectives under arms or militarily instructed. We have already seen the delay with which the regular army was reduced to the level established by the Treaty. Again, this reduction was compensated for by the authorization granted in June 1920 to increase the police force from 60,000 to 150,000 men; this increase was all the more noteworthy in that the army allowed by the Treaty was in principle justified by the necessities of maintaining internal order, and that the new police had considerable armaments at their disposal, including artillery and armoured vehicles.

This, however, was not all. The Germany of the years following 1918 was the favourite country for commandos and paramilitary associations of all kinds. It would be tedious to give details of these, which would of necessity be incomplete. However, they involved hundreds of thousands of men who could be regarded as irregular soldiers.

When the German resistance to the application of the disarmament clauses is considered in retrospect, there is no doubt that it can be seen as a rearguard action, the instinctive reflex of a profoundly military society which has not resigned itself to a radical change. The French at this time, however, were tempted to conclude from the opposition which they encountered that the Germans wished to prepare a future revenge. These ever-recurring difficulties gave rise to a mistrust, irritation and permanent tension, which could not fail to have their effect in other fields. The history of German disarmament and that of reparations are for the most part parallel.

(b) *The reparations*

The problem of the reparations weighed very heavily on the first years after the war; no doubt it contributed more than anything to weakening Franco-British ties and aggravating Franco-German animosity. There are some who have even maintained that French demands in this matter, by preventing the consolidation of the Weimar Republic, greatly contributed to the development of the desire for revenge in Germany and to the final victory of Hitler. If one compares this heavy political liability with the paltriness of the reparations when actually collected, it is natural to wonder, after the event, whether the game was worth the candle.

The first matter to be explained is, then, the relentlessness with which the French claimed their due. The first reason for this was the feeling of justice, all the stronger in France at this time because the country had suffered so much. It is impossible for a Frenchman, even today, not to consider that the principle of reparations was perfectly just.

However, there is another reason, which we cannot entirely understand unless we disregard what we have learnt since. The common illusion in the aftermath of war was that Europe, completely ruined, would take many years, perhaps generations, to recover. The greatest error of Keynes in his *The Economic Consequences of the Peace* (London, 1920) was to consider the future of the German economy in far too gloomy a light. Now Germany was a country which the war had left intact. The French undoubtedly had a much greater excuse for having the same pessimism with regard to their own country, whose most active regions were mere ruins. They thought that the reparations were absolutely indispensable in order to rebuild their devastated provinces. A few figures will make this conviction easier to understand: in 1922 at the time when the main reconstruction expenses were already committed, France's national debt came to a total of about 250,000 million francs. In spite of a drastic revenue effort, the budget receipts hardly exceeded a tenth of this sum, and the deficit was increasing from year to year. It is not surprising that in France it was believed to be impossible to solve this problem without a massive German contribution. In fact it was impossible: in 1926–8, the franc was reduced to one-fifth of its former value, which was equivalent to reducing arbitrarily the internal public debt by four-fifths; in other words, the majority of French investors, who by tradition invested their money in the public funds which were reputed to be the safest, lost four-fifths of the savings which they had accumulated through severe privations. Such a solution could not even have been imagined in 1919–20.

The history of the reparations is highly complex, not only because of its technical difficulties but because of the major political implications which the various sides believed they could find there: hence the Germans, and soon many of the British, claimed that they could see in the French demands a desire to ruin Germany, while many Frenchmen feared that Germany – who had already rid itself of its internal debt by inflation, as we shall see later – would rapidly be assured of economic hegemony over Europe if it also escaped the burden of reparations. The hope of economic reconstruction or political reconciliation of Europe also inevitably came up against this problem. Hence the activity of the Reparations Commission, bound by the rules of the Treaty, was doubled and then supplanted by the efforts of the governments in order to establish among themselves the payment of the forfeits which it had not been possible to achieve at the Peace Conference. These efforts resulted in a number of interallied, and then international, conferences, which were the favourite instrument of the personal diplomacy of Lloyd George.

The task of the Reparations Commission at this time consisted basically of ensuring and supervising the evaluation of damages. This posed very complex technical problems, since the replacement value of the goods destroyed was particularly difficult to determine during a period of instability of currency and prices. A final estimate of 70,000 million gold marks was made for France's damages, and an estimate of 150,000 million for those of all the Allies combined. However, under the pressure of the English expert Sir John Bradbury this total was finally reduced to 132,000 millions; this figure was adopted officially on 27 April 1921. The reproach has often been made that these evaluations were greatly exaggerated; the exhaustive study by E. Weill-Raynal showed that they certainly were not.[12]

However, as early as March 1920, the Allied governments accepted the idea of the forfeit, by the London declaration, if Germany took the initiative of proposing it. But Germany was in no hurry to take advantage of the opportunity: quite the contrary. So much so that the conference of San Remo (April 1920), seeing that Germany had not fulfilled its undertakings either for disarmament or for the reparations, informed it that the Allies were 'resolved to take any measure, which could be . . . the occupation of a new part of German territory, the result of which would be to guarantee that the Treaty was carried out'.

The next stage was the Spa Conference (July 1920), where for the first time the representatives of the Allies and of Germany came face to face. The encounter was quite uncordial, and the attitude of the German representatives aroused sharp reactions, even on the part of the British government. Germany did not suggest any figure for monetary payments, but finally offered to

---

[12] See E. Weill-Raynal, *La Politique française des réparations* (Paris, 1946). This statement is all the more valuable in that Weill-Raynal, who was a socialist, judged Poincaré's policy harshly.

rebuild the devastated regions by an international syndicate and the delivery of German payments in kind destined for these regions. We shall have occasion to come back to this last point. With regard to the first point – which consisted in fact of making the Germans themselves rebuild what they had destroyed – the French government was perhaps mistaken in not driving the German representatives into a corner and finding out whether their offer was sincere and genuine. However, they came up against a psychological impossibility: the population of the devastated regions would not have accepted seeing the return of bands of those whom they had known as invaders in uniform, even when dressed as workmen, and no doubt they would have had no confidence in the result of their work. The only practical result of the Spa Conference was to determine between the creditors the distribution of the reparations to be collected: France was to receive 52 per cent instead of 55 per cent as hoped.

Complicated and confused discussions were carried out to establish the sum. To this point, which in itself was already a revision of the Treaty of Versailles, the Germans tried to graft yet another: the allocation of the whole of Upper Silesia to Germany, by renouncing the plebiscite stipulated by the Treaty. In January 1921 the power in France fell to Aristide Briand, who was to pass into history as a master of conciliation. This, however, did not lead to the end of the Franco-German confrontations: on the contrary. In short, German intransigence was such that the Franco-British agreement was restored: in 1921 by mutual agreement the French and the British occupied three towns of the industrial area of the Ruhr – Duisburg, Ruhrort and Düsseldorf.

Tension mounted as the doubly significant date of 1 May 1921 drew nearer: on this date the Reparations Commission was to announce the final evaluation of the damages, also Germany was to have paid in fact an account of 20,000 million gold marks, the only figure quoted in the Treaty of Versailles (clause 235). Now only a very small part of this payment had been made, which permitted the Allied governments, that is, Briand and Lloyd George, to deliver an ultimatum to Germany: it must declare its willingness to fulfil its obligations with regard to reparations and disarmament before 12 May, otherwise the Allies would occupy the Ruhr.

The German obligations regarding reparations were henceforth defined by the Statute of Payments of 5 May 1921. The theoretical total corresponded to the figure of 132,000 million established by the Reparations Commission as the minimum total of damages. The terms and conditions of payment, however, considerably lightened the weight of this debt. One part only – that is, 50,000 million gold marks – was represented by bonds A and B, issued in 1921, and this issue was to start immediately. The rest, that is, the greater part, corresponded with bond C which would be issued only when Germany's capacity for payment justified it. Thus France had made very considerable concessions, both in the principles and in the figures.

The Allies' ultimatum, however, had its effect – for a time. The German ministry resigned and its successor (the chief personalities of which would be Wirth and Walther Rathenau) declared their intention of carrying out a 'policy of execution' of the treaty.

Other problems then arose: even if Germany carried out the payments in marks as stipulated, it was not marks that its creditors needed, but values which were legal tender in their own countries or which were universally negotiable. Germany's resources, however, in gold, currency, or foreign currency (even if part of the latter were hidden) would be manifestly insufficient. If the reparations were to be paid in cash, it would then be necessary for Germany to gain large amounts of foreign currencies, in particular by developing its exports far more than its imports. It would then have to compete very keenly with other great industrial exporters, especially Britain; this was one of the reasons why the British fairly soon displayed a tendency to come closer to the German point of view in this matter.[13]

The difficulty of cash payments explained why there was a move towards another form of payments – 'reparations in kind', that is, payments in the form of products. This method was the subject of the Franco-German Agreements of Wiesbaden, 6–7 October 1921: these agreements provided direct arrangements between groups of French victims of the disaster and an organization regrouping the German producers. In fact reparations in kind were also against the interests of industrial exporting countries, because the regions devastated by war would of necessity prefer to receive the products which they needed from Germany without paying for them, than to buy similar products, often at high cost, for example

[13] In this connection see in particular A. Fabre-Luce, *La Crise des alliances*.

from Britain. Hence the consent of the Allies to the Wiesbaden Agreements was not obtained until 11 March 1922, which was too late, as we shall see.

Even apart from this obstacle, payments in kind were not the panacea which some people wished to believe, for agreement between Germany the producer and France the consumer was often very difficult to achieve. The Germans intended, as far as possible, to keep their raw materials – especially coal – and to part only with finished products, in order to stimulate industrial activity; French interests were precisely the opposite. The prices with which the products would be accounted in order to appear on the reparations budget would give rise to interminable discussions, often impossible to settle, since in France as in Germany (although not to the same extent) the currency was unstable and the internal prices varied rapidly, as world prices themselves were subject to sudden changes.[14] In fact there was no way of avoiding the financial and monetary problems.

The 'Eastern Alliances'

While the application of the peace treaty west of Germany, in spite of the clarity of the territorial and political solutions, gave rise to ever-renewed difficulties, the uncertainty and fluidity of the situation continued to grow worse as one went farther east.

The unknown quantities were most formidable in Poland. The reconstitution of the Polish state, which had been divided up in the eighteenth century, had indeed been decided upon by the Allies and carried out there and then. The Polish frontiers, however, were established only in the west, subject to several plebiscites. Nothing had been decided regarding the eastern frontiers, for these were of direct interest to Russia, who had not been represented at the peace conference. There, every kind of uncertainty was present to the highest degree. In this great, partly swampy, plain there were no natural frontiers. Nor could historical frontiers be put forward, since the sizes of the different states had varied considerably over the centuries. It was equally illusory to look for precise ethnographic limits. Poles, Lithuanians, White Russians, Ruthenians and Ukrainians were inextricably mixed: even the Jews formed substantial national minorities. The

[14] See J. Néré, *La Crise de 1929*, p.14.

same uncertainty prevailed in peoples' minds at the time regarding the immediate political future of Russia: the West hardly believed in the stability of the Bolshevik regime, and France in particular, influenced by her alliance with tsarist Russia, set her hopes on counter-revolutionary attempts, especially that of Wrangel which she recognized officially in August 1920. Among the Poles themselves, profound differences appeared between those who had formerly been subject to German, Austrian and Russian rule. The French were predisposed to transfer their traditional sentimental penchant for Poland to those Poles who had fought above all against the Germans while dealing tactfully with the Russians; these Poles, however, were soon dominated by Jósef Piłsudski who, on the contrary, had fought mostly against the Russians, even to the extent of fighting on the side of the Austrians at the beginning of the war. The misunderstanding and mistrust between Piłsudski's Poland and France were never completely dispelled.

Piłsudski's dream was to establish between Germany and Russia a vast federal state including Poland, Lithuania and the Ukraine. France, on the other hand, like the other Allies, contemplated giving Poland, in the east, the frontiers of the former Grand Duchy of Warsaw, which had remained autonomous until 1863. She was all the more inclined to do this because the counter-revolutionaries whom she supported in Russia were nationalists devoted to the territorial integrity of the former empire of the tsars.

In 1919 the Ukraine was in practice separate from the Bolsheviks of Moscow and Petrograd. In the spring of 1920 Piłsudski tried to gain a foothold there. The Bolsheviks reacted to this and during the summer Poland was seriously threatened by the Red Army. At the Spa Conference the Allies decided to send to Poland a Franco-British mission whose somewhat vague objective seems to have been to carry out a kind of mediation between the Russians and the Poles, and to achieve a peace which would preserve an independent Poland – in accordance with the decisions of the Treaty – but one which was reduced to the territories populated exclusively by Poles. However, once there, the purpose of the mission changed, notably because of the intransigence of Russia. Led by General Weygand, who had been the assistant of Marshal Foch, the French element of the mission – without, however, breaking

39

with the British element – became an adviser to the Polish troops, who lost no time in gaining a decisive victory over the Russians at the approaches to Warsaw (August 1920).[15] The Polish-Russian frontier was then established, quite far to the east, by the Treaty of Riga (March 1921).

Since January 1921, however, an alliance had been concluded between France and Poland. It had been arranged at the insistence of Piłsudski in the face of the unwillingness of several statesmen, and also of Foch and Weygand, who considered that Poland was insufficiently consolidated internally, and who also feared that she might involve France in dangerous adventures in the east. However, whether they liked it or not, France and Poland were bound together by the necessity of facing up to Germany. The problem of Upper Silesia was to dominate the year 1921. This important industrial region contained Germany's greatest coal reserves before 1914. It was vital to Poland, because if deprived of it she would be a purely agricultural country and quite powerless against her neighbours. Germany therefore attached great importance to it, as we have seen, to the extent of adopting a conciliatory attitude as far as negotiations for reparations were concerned. For France the annexation of Upper Silesia meant a considerable increase in German industrial potential, which was already much greater than her own. For Britain, Upper Silesia was necessary for re-establishing the German economy, which from this time became a basic preoccupation for her.

The plebiscite of 20 March 1921 gave 717,122 votes to Germany and 483,154 votes to Poland. However, the Germans who dominated the economy had many ways of putting pressure on their Polish wage-earners; and 200,000 Germans who had long ago ceased to live in Upper Silesia had been brought there in special trains to vote. Germans and Poles were intermixed throughout the region. The Poles rebelled in the face of the Anglo-German proposal to assign the whole of Upper Silesia to Germany; a real war with the German commandos ensued. This new warlike manifestation was accompanied by a sharp diplomatic conflict between Britain and France, in spite of the fact that the latter country was led by Briand, the man who had promoted

[15] This was subsequently an additional subject for dispute between the French and the Poles, whether it was Weygand or Piłsudski who was the true victor in the battle of Warsaw. We will return to this later.

conciliation and understanding with Britain. Finally, the problem was submitted to the League of Nations, who on 20 October decided to divide the industrial area.

The situation among the states which succeeded Austria-Hungary seemed much clearer: apart from the duchy of Cieszyn, which we will discuss later, and a few other exceptions which would not have important consequences, the frontiers were established definitively by the peace treaties. Here too, however, there was an important factor of instability: this was Hungary. The most dominant nationality of the former Habsburg Empire, she was the least favoured by the treaties, in that she had the largest number of national minorities outside her frontiers and the least number of foreign minorities within her frontiers. Even during the 1919 negotiations, the communist regime of Béla Kun, who established himself in power in Hungary for a few months, represented nationalist resentments just as much as revolutionary aspirations and it ended in an armed conflict between Hungarian and Rumanian troops. After the fall of Béla Kun in July 1919, Hungary adopted a monarchical constitution, and it was on this that the ex-Emperor Karl based his hopes of restoration: Austria in fact was turning away from her old dynasty to dream of union with Germany.

French policy with regard to this problem is not very easy to define, and doubtless it had not been clearly established from the beginning. The aim was obviously to achieve a politically stable and economically viable situation in the Danube region. The breaking up, or 'Balkanization', of this region had been greatly criticized since 1919: there were already visions of these new states, which were too small, suffocating behind the customs walls which they were themselves building. Now, according to the example of the German *Zollverein*, a customs union without a political federation could hardly be imagined. It seems that the French Ministry of Foreign Affairs, and especially its general secretary Maurice Paléologue, had indulged in this dream at the beginning of 1920. Hungarian sources even claimed that France had given Hungary to expect territorial improvements, on condition, of course, that these were achieved peacefully and with the agreement of the adjoining countries. In any case the great Allied powers, France included, were officially hostile to the restoration of the Habsburgs, which would have seemed to threaten the independence or the newly acquired increase in power of the new states. This is what the interallied communiqué of 2 February 1920 maintained.

The advent of the war between Russia and Poland further complicated the problem. In fact the Czech trade unions refused to allow the passage of arms and supplies destined for Poland. The Hungarians, on the other hand, in accordance with historical precedents, offered their armed support to Poland. This, however, would have implied the entry of Hungarian troops into Slovakia, which, some hoped and some feared, would mean Hungary's annexing at least part of Slovakia and thus keeping a common frontier with Poland: in this way she would no longer have been completely surrounded by hostile countries. These countries, however, reacted promptly and vigorously: on 14 August 1920 Czechoslovakia and Yugoslavia promised each other armed assistance should Hungary make an unprovoked attack.

The year 1921 was marked by two attempts to restore Karl von Habsburg in Hungary, one in March and the other in October. The treaties of 23 April 1921 between Rumania and Czechoslovakia, and of 7 June 1921 between Rumania and Yugoslavia, were the response to this threat. It was the combination of these three bilateral treaties – Czechoslovakia-Yugoslavia, Czechoslovakia-Rumania, Rumania-Yugoslavia – which made up what was known as the Little *Entente*. About the same time France gave up her attempts at an understanding with Hungary. In connection with this, Paléologue was replaced at the Quai d'Orsay by Philippe Berthelot who supported the Czechs. Perhaps the French leaders also perceived that the best way to consolidate the Europe of the Danube was not to fuel the quarrels between the states which succeeded the Austro-Hungarian Empire.

Nevertheless the Little *Entente* appeared at first as a manifestation of independence towards the 'Great Allies', especially France. Certain French publicists, the nationalist Jacques Bainville, for example, did not welcome its formation with enthusiasm. It was only later, from 1924 to 1926, that France associated herself – still by separate treaties – with the three countries of the Little *Entente*.

This mere comparison of dates already shows how debatable are certain current ideas on the relationships between France and the small countries of central and eastern Europe. These countries have been described as 'clients' or 'satellites' of France: we have already seen, and we shall have the opportunity of seeing again, that they scarcely hesitated to affirm their independence. It has been claimed that France wished to squeeze Germany in a 'Slav corset': at the time when Franco-German tension was at its highest, the 'corset' was not made. There are some who have even suggested that France had sought in these eastern alliances a substitute for the failing Anglo-American guarantee: we cannot see that this search was very keen even at the very time when this guarantee disappeared, and when the forming of new ties with Britain seemed very problematical.

Nevertheless many people in France, even among responsible men in politics and diplomacy, believed that they had found in these new countries the elements of a new 'reverse alliance' – still necessary in the face of German power, but which could no longer be guaranteed by Russia since the Bolshevik revolution. It was, however, a strange illusion.

In the first place, there was no comparison between Russia with her vast territory and resources and her population of nearly 200 million inhabitants, and these states of such modest dimensions: Poland had a population of about 30 millions, Rumania 16 millions, Czechoslovakia 14 millions and Yugoslavia 12 millions. Moreover, these populations were not homogeneous. Both Poland and Rumania contained important foreign minorities; Yugoslavia was the result of a union between neighbouring, but often rival, peoples – the Serbs, the Croats and the Slovenians. The worst situation was that of Czechoslovakia, which was a largely artificial structure uniting two very distinct peoples, the Czechs and the Slovaks, and including, moreover, three million Germans.

External perils were added to these internal weaknesses: Poland, who could consider herself as one of the countries of medium importance, was held as in a vice between two equally hostile giants, Germany and Russia. Rumania was in conflict with Russia over Bessarabia. Yugoslavia had come up against Italy on the subject of the Istrian peninsula and the Dalmatian coast.

France's four future allies were not, moreover, and never would be, allies among themselves. No doubt Poland and Rumania had an agreement, but this was limited to the event of a threat from Russia. There was, no doubt, a Little *Entente* between Czechoslovakia, Yugoslavia and Rumania; but the latter was directed exclusively against Hungary, and in no circumstances could it be extended to serve as a support to Czechoslovakia against a possible German threat. On the contrary, Czechoslovakia, almost up to her last moment, disbelieved the possibility of danger from Germany, and gave her attention almost exclusively to Hungarian affairs.

The most serious situation, however, was that Germany's two neighbours, Poland and Czechoslovakia, regarded one another with an instinctive and deep-rooted hostility. A circumstantial reason for this hostility can be found: the Cieszyn Affair. The duchy of Cieszyn formed part of historical Bohemia. It included the only coal-mining area available to Czechoslovakia, and at the same time provided a railway network which was indispensable to communications between Bohemia and Slovakia; the majority of its population was, however, Polish. The problem, which the peace treaties left unsolved, was settled a little later by a partition which the Poles considered was to their disadvantage. Nevertheless, this territory was not of vital importance to Poland. In fact, there was between the Poles and Czechs, who speak very similar languages, a real incompatibility of temperament. Their temperaments could be compared with those of Don Quixote (Polish) and Sancho Panza (Czech) but without the faithful affection which united the two Spanish heroes. In 1919 Poland was still an aristocratic, rural, Catholic society, whose members were often impulsive and liable to dream; the Czechs belonged to an industrial country and appeared to be rationalist and matter-of-fact bourgeois. Outwardly the Czechs set their hopes on Russia, where they hoped to see a democratic evolution, whereas in the eyes of the Poles nothing good could come from Russia. The natural affinities of the Poles were with the Hungarians, whom the Czechs watched and particularly feared. The efforts of French diplomacy led to several attempts at an understanding between Poland and Czechoslovakia, but these did not achieve any results. The representatives of France would lead a miserable life unless they adopted, purely and simply, the prejudices of the country in which they were living.

To sum up, Poland and the Little *Entente* would be less of a support to France against Germany than a burden which complicated her relations with Russia and Italy. Why, in that case, did France undertake and persist in a policy of eastern alliances which, moreover, removed her further from Britain, who always had reservations with regard to undertakings in central and eastern Europe?

There are two replies to this question. First of all one must imagine a sort of 'theory of dominoes': consolidation of Europe could be achieved only by strict observance of the treaties, and any revision of one point must by degrees unleash a whole series of claims resulting in chaos, and providing Germany with the best pretexts for calling its own obligations in question.

The second reason is that these small countries, in themselves powerless, could, if they came under the influence and domination of their near neighbour Germany, provide it with a formidable addition of resources. The German ambition of *Mittel Europa* was well known in France, and its most moderate expression, as given by Friedrich Naumann in a book which caused considerable repercussions, had been translated into French during the war. French policy in these regions was therefore defensive, and could be described as negative.

Retreat in the Middle East

During the war the Allies had visualized a complete break-up of the Turkish Empire; no doubt it is necessary to view in this, beyond the effect of the mental attitudes of war, the consequence of the rivalries of the great powers around the Straits, of the famous 'Eastern Question' which had been one of the main preoccupations of European diplomacy in the nineteenth century. France had a special interest in these regions, owing to a very ancient tradition of protecting the Christians of the Levant. However, in her concern for the balance of power, France was obliged to claim as her sphere of influence a much greater part than the area of Syria and Cilicia in which Christians were numerous. As early as December 1918, France retroceded the richest territory of her area to Britain: the part which included the oil of Mosul.

The Treaty of Sèvres (10 August 1920) was immediately called in question by the Turkish nationalist revolt led by Mustapha Kemal. France did not persist and by the agreement of 20 October 1921 she renounced her occupation of Cilicia. The question of the Straits, which had to be demilitarized and neutralized under international protection, still remained. Faced with the advance of Mustapha Kemal, the French and the British adopted different attitudes: the French abandoned the position of Chanak (September 1922), which controlled the Dardanelles from the Asian side. There followed a period of sharp tension with Britain, who wanted a firmer attitude towards the Turks. However, it would be a great exaggeration to see this as a serious conflict between French and British policies. The British involvement in the Straits and in the conflict which then took place between Greece and Turkey is above all the result of the personal policy of Lloyd George: the latter did not obtain full support on this point either from the Dominions or even from a section of his majority, and this was indeed one of the causes of his downfall. Moreover, the Chanak affair was not the sign of a wish on the part of France to play a systematic trick on Britain, with whom she had a disagreement on the subject of reparations. It was rather the result of a general policy of prudence, even weariness, a policy which was hardly in accordance with the image of a militarist and dominant France, so widespread at the time in the foreign press.

Chapter 4

The Occupation of the Ruhr, and the Dawes Plan

We now come to one of the most discussed and most criticized acts of French foreign policy between the two world wars. It is a point which remains on the whole not well known because the principal actor in the drama, Raymond Poincaré, did not continue his Memoirs up to this period, and the complete archives on the subject have not yet been published. We can, therefore, only try to understand what happened, as it appears from the outside, and partly by reasoning; this kind of understanding will hardly be made easier by the numerous polemical hypotheses which very quickly came to obscure the facts.

The Preliminaries

(a) Requests for a moratorium: German inflation

On 14 December 1921, the German government asked the Reparations Commission to grant it a postponement of the payments due on the following 15 January and 15 February, at the same time making provision for a request for an even longer payment period. Thus no sooner had a plan for a statute for reparations, already falling far short of original hopes, been put on its feet after two years of discussions and clashes, than everything seemed again open to question.

There was violent reaction in France. At that very moment Lloyd George was preparing an important international conference for the reconstruction of the European economy, especially for resuming relations with Russia, now under Soviet rule. Briand expected to graft on to these British proposals his own plans, which were directed towards political security, by demanding not only the reaffirmation of the British guarantee to France, but also, in a form as yet undefined, guarantees for the new states of central and eastern Europe. A large number of French political figures was convinced that Briand was prepared to pay for these, doubtless uncertain, guarantees with new, very concrete and very serious concessions in the matter of reparations. Conscious of too strong an opposition to his policy, Briand resigned and was replaced by Poincaré who was regarded as the champion of intransigence.

Germany, however, obtained a partial delay in March 1922, on condition that it applied a plan for financial reforms, the purpose of which was to put it in a position to resume the payments. On 12 July the German government requested a further postponement. In August Poincaré replied, at the interallied conference in London: no moratorium without pledges of production. It was in the face of this demand, formulated by the president of the Republic, that Briand had preferred to resign. By pledges Poincaré understood the direct management of German national forests and the mines of the Ruhr, by the Reparations Commission, in order at least to guarantee the stipulated deliveries of wood and coal. He did not obtain satisfaction. In practice, Germany found itself granted a moratorium of several months.

These requests for a moratorium were based on the situation of the German currency. The mark, like the currencies of the main belligerent countries (with the exception of the United States), had been detached from gold in 1914. The gold mark, which was worth 17 paper marks in December 1920, was worth 46 in December 1921, 65 in March 1922, 90 in June, 349 in September and 1,778 in December. It was the classic phenomenon of collapse of the currency due to galloping inflation. However, it took by surprise the people of the time, accustomed to the stable currencies of Europe before 1914, and hit them hard. Also, the most fantastic explanations for this were given, some of which are directly related to the subject of this work. In Germany and in certain British circles, the reparations were blamed for causing the collapse of the mark. In France, people were inclined to the view that the Germans deliberately ruined their currency in order not to pay the reparations.

A scientific explanation of the phenomenon has naturally to be much more complex.[1] First of all it is out of the question that the payment of reparations, still very small, could have set in motion a phenomenon of such magnitude. What occurred was a general crisis, not restricted to Germany, which was connected with the

[1] We have attempted this elsewhere; cf. J. Néré, *La Crise de 1929*, pp.22–30.

aftermath of the war and the political and administrative weakness of certain governments such as that of the German Republic. It must, however, be added that the great economic crisis of 1921, which had resulted in a brutal fall in prices and massive unemployment, had spared Germany and had given rise in certain German economic circles to the idea that inflation and currency depreciation were all in all profitable to their business, acting as a sort of exportation bonus. Finally, the Germans, even the most experienced, did not for a long time understand the real mechanism of the problem, or the extent of the damage which it caused.[2]

(b) *The question of interallied debts*
At about the same time a new, or at least a forgotten, element came to complicate and aggravate the situation in the eyes of the French. This was the problem of war debts contracted by the European Allies among themselves and to the United States. In 1919 the American delegation was opposed to proposals to divide all the war costs between the Allies. Then the affair seemed to become dormant. On 9 February 1922, however, the American Congress created the World War Foreign Debt Commission, whose responsibility was to recover war debts. Now all the debtors had always considered that their payment was bound up with that of reparations. Hence, in May 1922, the French government made known that it could pay nothing until matters became clearer in the problem of the payment of reparations by Germany.

However, on 1 August 1922, the British government published the Balfour Declaration, in which it declared itself ready to cancel all its credits with regard to its Allies and Germany on condition that the United States for their part were prepared to abandon their war credits; this condition, coming at this time, made the British generosity quite unrealistic. The British government, moreover, undertook never to receive either from Germany or from the Allies more than would be necessary to pay the American government. The Balfour Declaration had a hostile reception in France because in practice it amounted to breaking the solidarity of the debtors and indirectly obliged France to contemplate paying war debts without being guaranteed the payment of the reparations.

[2] On this subject we have at our disposal the evidence of Lord d'Abernon, the British Ambassador to Berlin and very much a Germanophile.

The state of mind of French people at that time must be understood: they began to fear that, with one moratorium after another, Germany would never pay the reparations. At the same time they thought that they would be obliged to pay their debts to the United States: the latter in fact had an excellent means of putting on pressure, by refusing to agree to any new loan to the recalcitrant debtors. The French sense of justice was deeply offended: they could not accept that, having paid so much in blood and devastation, they must pay in money too, while Germany, the cause of all their suffering, would pay nothing. Moreover, this new demand made their financial prospects particularly gloomy.

(c) *French finances*

The restoration of the economy and the costs of reconstructing the devastated areas meant that the French budget was constantly in deficit during these years. However, the successive governments made a vigorous effort to recover: from 1919 to 1921 the actual receipts increased from 13 to 23 thousand million francs, while expenses were reduced from 40 to 33 thousand million. In 1922, however, the trend was reversed: 35 thousand million in receipts, 45 thousand million in expenses.[3] Also, the franc which had recovered in 1921 began to slide again: the dollar increased from 10·81 francs in April 1922 to 14·62 francs in November.[4] Would France, sinking under burdens which were too heavy for her, suffer an inflation and currency depreciation similar to those which were rife in Germany? Hence came the inspiration to mount a supreme effort to escape the threat of this fate.

(d) *Poincaré*

Raymond Poincaré, President of the Council since January 1922, had to pay special attention to these problems, for he was one of the rare French statesmen who really understood financial problems.

In any case the personality of Poincaré must be remembered here, even if it is not considered the decisive factor of the Ruhr affair. As is well known, Poincaré was a native of Lorraine, the

---

[3] The figures are those of A. Sauvy, *Histoire économique de la France entre les deux guerres*, Vol. I, Paris, 1959, p.367.

[4] The figures are those of Sauvy, op. cit., Vol. I, p.445.

country which for many centuries had been the great French border country against Germanism, and he had the ardent patriotism of the Lorraine people. However, he also had in common with many of the natives of Lorraine, caution and level-headedness. A scrupulous and meticulous jurist, a very hard worker, he seemed to lack imagination and intuition. This was more or less what his old enemy Clemenceau meant when he was reputed to have made this sally: 'Poincaré knows everything but he understands nothing.'

When the Treaty of Versailles was drawn up, Poincaré, who was then President of the Republic, was considered to support the view of Foch, who wished to detach the left bank of the Rhine from the rest of Germany, against Clemenceau, who had abandoned this approach in favour of the Anglo-American guarantee. He did not, however, try to force his own point of view: he withdrew when faced with the risk of a political crisis in France. When Poincaré gave up the presidency of the Republic, he accepted the presidency of the Reparations Commission; by choosing such a post after the highest honour, he showed clearly that in his opinion the reparations problem was of prime importance.

When Poincaré decided on the occupation of the Ruhr, he was accused in Germany, in Britain and even in France (by the extreme Left opposition) of having a motive other than the one he declared; he was accused of the ulterior motive of breaking Germany by striking at the heart of its economy and profiting by its downfall, in order to achieve detachment of the left bank of the Rhine which had been refused at the time of the negotiations of the Treaty of Versailles.

This view, although it has no documentary foundation, is still very widespread today. For the time being we will confine ourselves to pointing out that, in questioning a man like Poincaré, this view comes up against a certain psychological improbability.

(e) *Doubts regarding the 'German industrial party' and the*
   assumption of power by Chancellor Cuno

It is not sufficient, however, to argue in general terms. If we refer to contemporary documents, especially those of the direct assistants of Poincaré such as Jacques Seydoux or René Pinon, we find that there is in France a particular animosity towards the

'German industrial party'. We must understand by this term something far greater than the little 'populist' party of Stresemann, who nevertheless was fairly representative of it. For it was said that the industrial magnates had either directly or indirectly dominated all the succeeding German governments since 1919. They also took over from the military and land-owning classes as champions of German nationalism (they were even accused, I do not know on what basis, of being the cause of the 1914 war). On the other hand they profited beyond doubt from the inflation and the fall of the mark which ruined so many of their compatriots: the collapse of the exchange stimulated their exporting industries; they produced at low prices by paying their workers in devalued marks; and they themselves lost nothing since they converted their possessions into real values (factories, equipment) or appreciated foreign currencies. From this to the accusation that they had deliberately caused the collapse of the currency, in order not to pay the reparations, to eliminate any debt, and thus to provide an irresistible competition to their foreign rivals – there is only one step, often taken.

Would it not be possible, by occupying the Ruhr basin, the heart of their power, to break these modern feudalists, and thus fortify oneself against a renewed offensive by the Germans in the near future? This was a tempting but vague idea. There is nothing to prove that Poincaré tried to make it into a practical proposition. He could, however, have been subconsciously influenced by the state of mind of those around him.

At the end of this year, 1922, however, a government presided over by Chancellor Cuno came to power in Germany. Cuno was the first minister to be openly supported by the nationalists; the first who, as it were, officially represented the industrial party, which until then had seemed to act by indirect pressure, and behind the scenes. The march of events seemed then to press inexorably towards a trial of strength.

The Entry into the Ruhr and the 'Passive Resistance'

(a) The discussions of January 1923

On 14 November 1922 Germany claimed a complete moratorium of three or four years, with the exception of deliveries in kind intended for the reconstruction of the devastated regions. However, this restriction was an illusion, for Germany was even late in its deliveries of wood and coal. This was indeed the problem of the reparations – or of the end of the reparations – which was presented in all its magnitude. The interallied conference in Paris (2–4 January 1923) was once more going to look for solutions.

At this conference, Poincaré presented a complete plan. The interallied debts would be paid by remittance of category C bonds,[5] representing the credit from reparations. German finances would be reorganized under the control of a Guarantees Committee set up in Berlin. Finally, a hold over local pledges, in the Rhineland and in the Ruhr, would guarantee the deliveries in kind.

The British government, presided over by Bonar Law, opposed this programme with a very complicated plan of which we shall mention only the main provisions here. Going one step further than the Balfour Declaration, the British government renounced all Britain's credits with regard to her former allies, on condition that the latter accepted the clauses provided for the German debt: postponement for two years, then progressive resumption of payments in cash, whose total would not exceed that of the interests of the debt, which would thus become perpetual; there was no question of taking securities.

The Bonar Law plan which was, moreover, greatly criticized by the Italian and Belgian delegates, was categorically rejected by Poincaré: France would lose any real guarantee of being even partially paid by Germany, while her debt to the United States would still stand in full.

(b) *The entry into the Ruhr*

When the Reparations Commission had duly ascertained the German omissions in the deliveries of wood and coal on 11 January 1923, the French and Belgian governments sent an 'Interallied Mission of Control of Factories and Mines' (MICUM) into the Ruhr. This mission consisted of a group of engineers, protected by troops, designed to guarantee the fulfilment of the pledges of production. In fact, the operation very quickly resulted in an extension of the military occupation of this region of the right bank of the Rhine.

The legality of this occupation has been hotly debated. The text of the Treaty of Versailles on which it is based is as follows:

[5] See above, p.37.

The measures which the allied and associated Powers will have the right to take, in the case of voluntary omission by Germany, and which the German government undertakes not to regard as acts of hostility, can include acts of economic and financial prohibition and reprisals, and in general, other such methods as the respective governments may consider necessary in the circumstances.

The occupation of territories beyond the Rhine did not then appear among the sanctions explicitly provided for. Was it, however, excluded? Legally, it seems that the Allied governments were left with very great latitude. In fact Britain had taken part in the occupation of Düsseldorf, Duisburg and Ruhrort; on several occasions she had accepted the idea of occupation of the Ruhr, at the same time seeking ways of delaying putting it into practice. In January 1923 Britain broke away from the operation, but she lacked a juridical basis for opposing it. Her objections developed basically on political and economic levels.

(c) The 'passive resistance'

Germany's reaction was clearly much more drastic. On 13 January the German government suspended all payments in kind to France and Belgium. It forbade railway officials and employees[6] to obey the orders of the occupying authorities. The strike spread quickly to the private sector.

Such was the 'passive resistance'. The idea – like that of the occupation of the Ruhr – had been discussed for a long time. The German nationalists saw it as a means of questioning the Treaty of Versailles as a whole. It is, however, difficult to imagine how they visualized making this weapon effective.

In fact passive resistance, although it was an inconvenience to France, was not of a nature to break her will or to paralyse her action. With technicians sent from France she succeeded in restarting the essential public services. The entire occupied region was enclosed in a customs cordon. Germany, moreover, was the first victim of the passive resistance. Its economy, cut off from the Ruhr, was partially paralysed; the compensations which had to be paid to those who had been ordered not to work completed the ruin of German finances and currency.

It certainly seems that the Germans had calculated that international opinion would be shaken by this crisis and that Britain

[6] The German railways had already been state-owned for a long time.

and the United States would force France to yield. Britain, however, was no more disposed on this occasion than on any other to become deeply involved in Europe. She tried to intervene by diplomatic and possibly financial pressures. However, contrary to an often-recurring illusion, 'international finance' did not, by its own power, have the means of making a country of the size of France yield, and its possibilities even of determining the course of currencies were limited: the dollar, which was worth 14·98 francs in January 1923, was increased in September only to 17·69 francs; the slide of the franc was hence no greater during the Ruhr crisis than in the previous year.

(d) The end of the 'passive resistance'

As could be foreseen, German resistance was exhausted far more quickly: it became impossible to finance it, since the mark had practically lost all value. On 12 August 1923 Chancellor Cuno resigned and was replaced by Gustav Stresemann. On 26 September Stresemann officially abandoned passive resistance. Soon agreements were made between the MICUM and the various industries of the occupied regions: productive use of the pledges seized could begin. Poincaré had thus won the match.

Poincaré Faced with the German Chaos

However, the success itself of French policy was going to present it with problems whose magnitude and whose very nature were unexpected. The passive resistance had united Germany into a bloc which was more or less unanimous against the occupying country. When the policy had been abandoned, Germany seemed on the point of breaking up in the financial and moral confusion which followed this capitulation. During the whole of the last quarter of 1923, chaos seemed to have become a permanent feature. While troubles and attempts at nationalist armed coups occurred in various places, especially in Bavaria, the extreme Left seized power in Thuringia and Saxony. The central government reacted to this by declaring a state of emergency, that is, by practically handing over legal authority to the army. During this time, in the occupied territories of the left bank of the Rhine, a sudden rebirth of autonomists or separatists, who had scarcely been heard of since 1919, was witnessed.

Faced with this situation, Poincaré remained uncertain. He was reproached in various quarters for this attitude. According to certain French nationalists, Poincaré at that time let slip the opportunity of achieving a final triumph by making Germany form part of a French system: certain large German industrialists in particular seemed ready to negotiate very extended agreements of association with France. It is certain that Poincaré resolutely restrained attempts of this nature, but it may be wondered whether these attempts corresponded with very definite future views.

Criticism has been expressed more often in a different direction. Poincaré, forgetting his objective of reparations – or perhaps never having put it forward except as a pretext – was supposed to have deliberately tried to destroy German unity. However, it has never been possible to support this assertion with proofs. The very diversity of the Rhineland movements and the lack of co-ordination in their actions are indications that they were not 'remotely controlled' by the French authorities. Above all, we have the evidence of one of their inspirers, Dorten: he complained that he had encountered only scorn on the part of Poincaré, except for a very short time, towards November 1923. The only measure contemplated by the French government was the formation of a Rhineland issuing bank, which would have established a special currency distinct from German currency. This project greatly alarmed Stresemann, who did everything possible to out-manœuvre him. However, from the beginning of 1924 the French authorities abandoned the Rhineland movements to their fate, which was often tragic.

The solution for which Poincaré finally settled will give us the key to his attitude even better than do his refusals and apparent hesitations.

The Dawes Plan

(a) *The committees of experts*

The proposal to submit the solution of the reparations problem to a committee of international experts had been proposed many times, and it was known that the United States approved of this. Poincaré had refused it, before the occupation of the Ruhr and again at the height of the crisis. However, on 30 November 1923, he accepted it. Naturally it was wondered why Poincaré had suddenly retreated when he was victorious, or why he had under-taken so serious an action, then finally accepted what he had begun by refusing.

But, if we examine it more closely, was it still the same pro-posal? In fact the basic purpose of the committees of experts first considered, was to determine Germany's capacity for payment, a study which could hardly fail to end in a reduction of Germany's debt and a postponement of payments; this result became more and more certain, the more serious grew the financial crisis in Germany. However, what France accepted on 30 November was the formation not of one committee but of two different com-mittees of experts. One of them would in fact study Germany's capacity for payment; but it was specifically stated that it must take into account capital exported from Germany and find means for its return. The other committee – formed, moreover, at the request of the French representative Louis Barthou – was to study the methods to be taken to balance the budget and to stabilize Germany's currency.

Now this was the main point: it had become obvious to every-one that Germany would not be able to pay any reparations until its finances had been put in order and its currency re-established. To threaten it with having this task carried out by an international commission which would inevitably infringe its sovereignty, would oblige it indirectly to make of its own accord the necessary effort, from which it had shrunk until that time. The threat of a Rhineland issuing bank, which would give separatism a strong support, would have the same effect. The result was not long in coming: Stresemann and Schacht hastened to create a new currency whose stability would henceforth be fiercely defended. This was the price of German unity and recovery. It was even maintained that in this respect the occupation of the Ruhr had been profitable to Germany, by obliging it to make the abso-lutely necessary recovery.[7]

(b) *The Dawes Plan*

What were the main characteristics of the plan which was finally worked out by the experts, and accepted by the interested govern-ments in April 1924?

[7] This opinion was expressed in particular by the great German historian Erich Eyck, in *Geschichte der Weimarer Republik* (Erlenbach, 1956–7).

The Occupation of the Ruhr, and the Dawes Plan

Unlike the missions originally set up by the different committees, this plan was concerned entirely with a new settlement of the problem of reparations. This settlement, according to the total of the first annuities provided for, implicitly entailed a further reduction of the total debt. Obviously this meant new concessions by France.

What France obtained in return, however, was decisive. The German payments were henceforth guaranteed by pledges, established by the experts, recognized by all creditors and accepted by Germany: mortgages on the German railways and industry, deductions from various German taxes. There would be established in Berlin an international commission responsible for the supervision of German currency, a railways commissioner, a commissioner for revenue from the Reich, and a general agent for reparations, the American Parker Gilbert, upon whom fell from then on the responsibility for solving the problem of transfers. By this compromise France exchanged her freedom of action with regard to Germany and her illusions regarding the magnitude of what she could expect to receive, for the certainty of being paid to a certain extent.

(c) *The policy of Poincaré*

We can now attempt an appraisal of the judgments which were passed on the Ruhr operation. These judgments are on the whole severe, although not without contradictions. Poincaré is generally reproached with having displayed excessive intransigence for too long, only to make a badly disguised climb-down in the end. Moreover, what made the criticism more serious – but at the same time more difficult to accept completely – was that this final defeat had followed immediately on an indisputable tactical success. Having launched a solitary attempt, in the face of the declared opposition of Britain and the disapproval of America, to bend Germany, who had risen in unity against the French, he would have made it capitulate, resisting all the international pressures while he was in the midst of the fight; however, no sooner had he conquered than he yielded and abandoned all the possible fruits of victory. There was something incomprehensible about this.

Perhaps, however, the problem was badly put, in attributing to Poincaré far more ambitious intentions than he in fact had. Was the problem one of redoing the work which, in the eyes of French nationalists, had been badly done at Versailles, and of breaking the political unity of Germany? In spite of the reproaches of some of his supporters, Poincaré had not really tried to do this. Was the problem one of putting an end to concession in the matter of reparations, of demanding the full payment of the theoretical debt which had been determined in 1921? In this case we could indeed speak of a retreat on the part of Poincaré, for the Dawes Plan undoubtedly implied a new reduction of the German debt. However, if Poincaré simply thought that he was about to see a total disappearance of the reparations, that it was necessary to break this chain of concessions followed by new claims, and to obtain real payments for France in a definite manner, even if they were reduced to a minimum, then he had achieved his purpose.

Does this mean that it was not possible to discern any signs of hesitation or uncertainty in the behaviour of Poincaré? One cannot go as far as that, for one cannot ignore the support given, even for a short time, to the Rhineland movements, which had formerly been so despised and subsequently so lightly sacrificed. In that autumn of 1923, Poincaré found himself in an embarrassing situation: it had been uncertain for several weeks what would become of Germany as a unity. Had Poincaré then thought of taking advantage of the situation in order to achieve political objectives which had been for a long time dormant? It seems rather that he feared the establishment of a military dictatorship in Germany, under the pretext of restoring order, one which would hasten to destroy the Treaty of Versailles.[8] The Rhineland operation would then have been an immediate defensive reaction, which would no longer be justified once the Weimar Republic had been maintained and consolidated.

The fact remains that Poincaré, no doubt basically from lack of imagination, set in motion in Germany a crisis out of proportion to the limited objectives he finally achieved. Must we think that if it had not been for the occupation of the Ruhr, hatred of France and the desire for revenge would not have gained ascendancy over democratic and moderate forces in Germany? This is a question which had been hotly debated and which history evidently cannot solve.

[8] See R. Pinon, *La Bataille de la Ruhr*, p.337.

Central Europe during the Ruhr Crisis

The increasing opposition of the French and British points of view placed the countries of the Little *Entente* in extreme difficulty. In fact they put their hopes for the consolidation of the peace treaties on the support of the two great western powers for whose concord they wished above all else, and they were careful to make it known that there was no question of their taking France's part against Britain.[9] The attitude of Poland, too, did not basically differ on this occasion.[10] Eduard Beneš, who was more or less constantly in charge of Czech foreign policy, was particularly alarmed about the occupation of the Ruhr at a time when this policy seemed to be meeting with success: at the time of the great crisis of the autumn of 1923, far from rejoicing at the possibility of the disintegration of Germany, he feared a restoration of the monarchy in Bavaria which could have had repercussions in Hungary.[11] Moreover, during the year of the Ruhr problem, the Czechs and the Poles were mostly occupied with quarrelling between themselves; since the Cieszyn Affair had been settled for the time being, the little village of Javorina, in the Tatra mountains, provided them with a subject for dispute.

Nevertheless, the Franco-Czech Alliance was concluded in January 1924. It seems that, on the part of the Czechs, this was done as a last resort: the ideal was the League of Nations in which all states, large and small, were equal in principle. The League of Nations had not, however, appeared particularly effective during these troubled years; in the Corfu incident in particular, it had not been able to protect Greece from Italian reprisals.[12] The Czechs were therefore obliged to accept a powerful protector. The Franco-Czech Alliance, however, applied only in the case of a restoration of the Habsburgs or the Hohenzollerns, or in the case of an *Anschluss*. It was not directed against Germany as such, and had nothing to do with an 'Eastern barrier'.[13]

The period from 1920 to 1924 had seen France and Britain drawing progressively further and further apart – to the extent of open opposition in 1923 – even though since the negotiation of

[9] R. Machray, *The Little Entente*, London, 1929, pp.228–32.
[10] P. Wandycz, *France and her Eastern Allies*, p.272.
[11] Ibid., pp.275, 281.   [12] Ibid., p.295.   [13] Ibid., pp.300–2.

the Treaty of Versailles, the whole of French policy had been founded on the understanding between former allies. In explaining this paradox one is obviously tempted to criticize the actions of statesmen – those of France, or those of her neighbour – or to blame misunderstandings, and particularly the hidden motives which each mistakenly attributed to the other. However, the reason goes deeper than this. France and Britain misunderstood each other because the two countries were fundamentally different. One reasoned in space, the other in time.

Britain was a world power which had to face immediate pre-occupations everywhere at the same time. Her anxieties were India, China, the Dominions and the United States, and the dis-organization of the European economy. She had to find equally immediate solutions; she could not indulge herself by looking to future possibilities which might involve the entire planet: there were too many unknown quantities. Now, for the present, solutions by conciliation or concession were the most economical. Moreover, since one is always inclined to believe what is most advantageous, she naturally assumed that there would be no war in Europe in the foreseeable future.

France might well possess the second colonial empire in the world at this time; but for all that she did not, and could not, have a world view of problems. With the exception of Indo-China, far away at the other side of the world, all her important colonies were in Africa, away from the main world currents; even Dakar, in spite of its position, did not in any way play a part comparable with that of Singapore or Hong Kong. The colonies tended to take part in French provincial life, but a study of French foreign policy during this period can more or less completely ignore them.

On the other hand France, in the grip of fixed geographical positions in Europe, was inevitably obsessed with historical precedents. Neglecting, perhaps unduly, difficulties which she knew were temporary – especially economic difficulties – she was haunted by the conviction that Germany would recover its power, and the fear that at the same time the old Germanic demons would recover all their strength. One cannot understand French reactions during these years unless one constantly bears in mind this agonizing vision of a future fraught with danger.

From then onwards, until 1939, French policy was constantly faced with a problem which was almost insoluble: to obtain, since there was no alternative, co-operation between France and Britain, whose diplomatic efforts were based on entirely different foundations. However, French statesmen, even with a common goal, hesitated between two methods: either to adapt themselves as completely as possible to British points of view and feelings, or to endeavour to 'wake up' the British by making them understand dramatically the serious nature of French anxieties.

Chapter 5

The Early Days of the Cartel des Gauches

In the elections of May 1924, the majority in the French Chamber was reversed: after the 'Chambre bleu horizon', elected under the aegis of Clemenceau and the 'National Bloc', the 'Cartel des Gauches' had now come to power. Did this mean, as was so often said, that the policy of Poincaré and the occupation of the Ruhr were repudiated by the French electorate? It should be noted in this connection that the elections of 1924 simply showed a return to the French political situation as it had been recorded in all the elections since 1902 – the radicals and socialists had an indisputable, although not a sweeping, majority which varied little; the 1919 elections were an exception. Poincaré, however, had kept away from the election campaign, wishing to show thereby that his foreign policy was that of the nation and not of one party. If we examine the ministerial declaration of the new government, presided over by Edouard Herriot, we see that far less time was occupied with criticism of the methods of the previous government, that is, the 'policy of isolation and force', than with the affirmation of a political constant: defence of the rights of France and of her security.[1]

However, 1924 marked the beginning of a fundamental change in atmosphere. After four and a half years of war followed by four years of tension both with Germany and with former allies, the morally exhausted French people needed to believe in peace, to believe that the settlement of the exasperating problem of reparations, which seemed to be in sight, would naturally lead to the settlement of all international problems. This optimism was

[1] See Document 12. We must remember that in the French parliamentary system, when a new cabinet presents itself before the Chambers, it publishes a 'Declaration' which consists of a general statement of its policy, and which can be compared with the 'Speech from the Throne' in Britain or the 'Message on the State of the Union' in the United States.

nevertheless very far from being as sure and as free from mental reservations as the insular optimism: the French still felt in their heart of hearts that they were threatened, and trusted the triumph of a pacifist democracy in Germany only with trepidation. On one point, however, the French Left of 1924 allowed themselves to cherish an illusion: this was that the triumph of the Labour Party in Britain at the same time would naturally enable harmony and the necessary sharing of views to be re-established between the two countries. They were quickly to realize that the difference in point of view between the two nations was far more fundamental than any difference in internal policy and that the Labour Party was in many respects the most insular of all the British parties.

The Implementation of the Dawes Plan

The acceptance in principle, on the part of the different governments, of the conclusions of the committees of experts, was far from guaranteeing the final solution of the problem. Not only did the ratification of the Dawes Plan appear at a dangerous time in Germany, when the elections of May 1924 showed a noticeable rise of nationalism, but a large number of technical questions, whose details we cannot examine, still had to be settled. There were other questions which had political implications: since the desired result of Poincaré's measures of coercion could be considered as achieved, was it not necessary to determine under what conditions these measures themselves, the economic isolation of the occupied German territories, and the military occupation of the Ruhr, would be ended? This was the main object of the Franco-British discussions at the interview at Chequers (21–2 June 1924), at the Franco-British Conference in Paris (8–9 July 1924), and finally, at the London Conference (16 July–16 August 1924) to which Germany was admitted. The French idea was to associate the withdrawal from the Ruhr with the most extensive application of the Dawes Plan. Curiously, however, Herriot tried at first to avoid completely the discussion of this problem – naturally without success. It seems that he himself was deceived by the campaign led against Poincaré in the face of international opinion, a campaign which had found echoes in the French opposition. Poincaré, we must remember, was accused of having initiated the Ruhr expedition, not with a financial aim, but with a political one, in order to destroy Germany. However, was not the occupation of the Ruhr connected, in the mind of Herriot, with the problem of French security, about which he did not intend to compromise? Now one of the great reproaches directed against Briand in 1922 had been precisely that he had connected the two separate problems of security and reparations, which meant that France had had to make dangerous concessions on one point or another. Thus, just as he was yielding over the withdrawal from the Ruhr, Herriot asked the military authorities, Marshal Foch, and his representative, General Desticker, whether this evacuation would in any way compromise the safety of France. Desticker replied that, on the contrary, the French troops would be much safer, should trouble arise, if certain of their elements had not ventured as a spearhead into the Ruhr.[2] Finally, France announced on 16 August 1924 that the Ruhr would be evacuated within a maximum period of one year.

However, in exchange for this goodwill gesture, Herriot obtained from Britain a decision which was to have far-reaching consequences, as we shall see later. The British troops occupied the Cologne area on the left bank of the Rhine, which was vital for railway connections between France and the Ruhr. This area was to be evacuated in January 1925 if Germany had fulfilled all the obligations of the Treaty by this date. It could be agreed that the implementation of the Dawes Plan was equivalent to fulfilling the financial obligations. There remained the military obligations. During the period of 'passive resistance', the functioning of the commission for inspection of German disarmament had been made a practical impossibility. In the autumn of 1924, France carried out a general inspection, which revealed numerous German shortcomings. As a result of this the Cologne area was not evacuated on the appointed date. A first result of this was that France was not obliged by indirect pressure to evacuate the Ruhr before the date which she herself had fixed.

A further criticism regarding the negotiation was directed against Herriot, in particular by Weill-Raynal:[3] this criticism was that he had not made the evacuation of the Ruhr subject to the settling of the question of interallied debts. It must be remembered that the British premier Bonar Law had proposed a complete plan

[2] See E. Weill-Raynal, *Les Réparations allemandes et la France*, Vol. III, p.80.
[3] See especially Weill-Raynal, op. cit., pp.39–45.

for settlement of the reparations in January 1923; one of its features was the unconditional renunciation by Britain of her war credits from France. The Labour leader Ramsay MacDonald had made a declaration to the same effect when he was in opposition. Now when Herriot put forward this question at the Chequers interview, the British authorities replied that their former offer could not be maintained, following a 'new development'. It is very doubtful whether Herriot could have made Britain go back on this refusal, which was never explained, but which nevertheless is perfectly explicable: Poincaré had finally obtained far more in the matter of reparations by the Dawes Plan than Britain had visualized in 1923; as a result Britain's own sacrifice appeared useless from that time onward. This was an indirect confirmation of the effectiveness of the occupation of the Ruhr.

In Quest of Security

Edouard Herriot proved conciliatory over financial questions, about which he in fact understood very little. He was, however, haunted by the concern for security:

> My country has a dagger pointed at her breast, a centimetre from the heart. United efforts, sacrifices, war deaths, all will have been in vain, if Germany can again resort to violence. . . . I would rather say straight away that I would prefer that France was not paid, if this meant renouncing her security. . . . I am speaking to you from the bottom of my heart, and I assure you that I cannot renounce the safety of France, which would not be in a condition to endure another war.

These words were intended to persuade MacDonald to resume negotiations on the Franco-British mutual guarantee pact, which had been interrupted in 1922. MacDonald, who belonged to the Labour wing which had shown itself unfavourable towards British intervention in the war of 1914, categorically refused; he was thus less accommodating even than Lloyd George.[4]

However, at about the same time a new possibility appeared: that of replacing a limited guarantee by effectively establishing collective security. We have seen that the opportunity had been

[4] Weill-Raynal, op. cit., p. 46, from G. Suarez, *Une Nuit chez Cromwell* (Paris, 1930).

missed at the time of the drawing up of the Treaty of Versailles. But since then, work had been done at the League of Nations. In order to achieve the general disarmament which was one of the great Wilsonian objectives, it had been recognized that a pre-condition was to establish a security system. But what system? On this point two proposals came into conflict: a French one, providing geographically limited, bilateral and multilateral pacts; and a British one, which accepted only a general treaty of mutual guarantee. The 'Resolution XIV' which was adopted at the 1922 session offered a compromise between the two concepts, by providing

> a defensive agreement, open to all countries, which pledges the parties to give effective and immediate assistance according to a previously established plan, should one of them be attacked, provided that the obligation to come to the aid of an attacked country is limited in principle to countries situated in the same part of the world. However, in cases in which one country runs a particular risk of being attacked, special measures must be taken for her defence in carrying out the aforesaid plan.

The Herriot government purely and simply rallied to the British proposal which had been taken up by the Labour Party. It remained to establish the means by which universal assistance could be effectively applied. The great difficulty was to determine who was the aggressor, and hence to establish a definition of aggression. The solution found was compulsory arbitration. The aggressor would be the one who refused to have recourse to arbitration or would not accept the conclusions and would then have recourse to force. Edouard Herriot then presented the famous trilogy, of which the successive conditions were as follows: arbitration, security, disarmament. The Council would decide upon application of sanctions against the aggressor by a majority of two-thirds: the paralysing rule of unanimity would be removed.

The Geneva Protocol thus formed, and enjoying the support of both France and Britain, was adopted unanimously by the League of Nations Assembly. France ratified it immediately. There was a moral element in this universalism which appealed to the French Left: it was no longer a question of coalitions whose aim was to defend particular interests, but of a union of all countries to make justice prevail and to guarantee peace.

Britain, however, did not ratify the agreement, for in November 1924 the Conservatives had taken over from the Labour party. We must understand this British refusal. For countries with limited interests the difference between a universal and a regional pact was a moral, rather than a practical, one: if an aggressor appeared in a part of the world where they had neither interests nor significant resources, their condemnation, whatever their theoretical obligations might be, would be of symbolic value only and would not pledge them to very much. Britain, on the other hand, whose presence was felt all over the world, would run the risk of being actually involved in any conflict resulting from the application of sanctions against an aggressor.

There remained the fact that France, having played in succession the card of practical possibilities and that of idealism, had been the loser on both tables. The government of the Cartel des Gauches could only reap the benefits of Poincaré's policy, which it had professed to reject; for the rest, especially on the fundamental question of security, its first balance-sheet was heavily in the red.

Chapter 6

The Briand Era

On 17 April 1925 Aristide Briand became Minister of Foreign Affairs. He remained in this office, in several cabinets of different shades of political outlook, until 8 January 1932, shortly before his death. This exceptionally long ministerial life was not, as sometimes happens, contrivance on the part of a person so unobtrusive as to cause offence to no one. On the contrary, Briand stamped French foreign policy with such an imprint that veritable myths have been created about him. To his supporters he was an apostle, a man of peace and universal reconciliation, and Briand himself was not above cultivating this image. To his opponents he was a dupe, the dupe of Germany and especially of Stresemann, who by his simple-mindedness and imprudence had seriously compromised French security. Apostle or dupe, is it not fundamentally the same picture viewed through different spectacles? What was the truth about Briand and his policy?

It is not possible to answer this question with certainty because he was the most secretive of men; comparison with his famous opponent Stresemann will clearly demonstrate this aspect of his character. On the death of Stresemann, his Papers were published: in these Stresemann himself expressed his worries, his aims and his methods most clearly. The French writer Georges Suarez had access to the personal papers of Briand, about which he wrote an extensive work; but in them we find nothing from Briand himself, apart from his speeches and public declarations. His papers consist of letters and notes which had been sent to him. Briand rarely made confidences.

In 1925 Briand already had a long political career behind him. This began with the extreme Left, as often happens in France. In 1905 Briand left the socialist party and rose very quickly to power. This rise was to be favoured by a sort of miracle. In 1905 the disguised religious war between the Catholic Church and the laity, which had been raging since the beginning of the Third Republic, if not before, reached its most acute stage: the separation of the Church from the State, which broke the ancient ties at one blow. Aristide Briand was the chairman of the committee for the Law of Separation in the Chamber, and he succeeded in transforming this weapon of war into an instrument of mutual tolerance. Did he acquire from this his confidence in his power to solve any conflict, no matter what its nature?

Briand was then President of the Council several times, especially during a large part of the First World War. He held this office again in 1922. He did not at that time prove particularly weak with regard to Germany; on the contrary, it was he who decided to occupy Düsseldorf, Duisburg and Ruhrort in March 1921 and who delivered the ultimatum of May 1921 to the German government, but from that time, as we have seen, he tried to regain the British and American guarantees.

In 1924, although Briand had again moved towards the Left, he remained independent of the Cartel and did not belong to the first Herriot cabinet. However, at the time of the debate on the ratification of the London Agreement of August 1924, he revealed some of the guiding thoughts of his foreign policy:

> Isolation means danger. Isolation is the setting in motion of acts which one cannot avoid. Isolation is recourse to force, followed by other measures. It is what happened when anger and impatience were the dominant emotions, when faced with the bad faith of Germany. The situation grew worse and worse and it was necessary to escape from it at a given time. What I find best in the London Agreements, what makes me vote for them with eagerness, is this:
>
> > Let us put aside the questions of quibbling over millions of gold marks which will or will not be repaid. What does that signify when the problem is perhaps to avoid spilling the blood of hundreds of thousands of men yet again?

If we ignore the indifference to the matter of reparations – which was easy to assume once their settlement had been obtained – what do we find in these phrases? That France, who needs peace, cannot achieve it in a durable form without agreement with her former allies. However, had Clemenceau, Briand's old opponent, said or thought anything different in 1919?

One element remains which results from the contrast in the temperaments of Briand and Clemenceau. This is what could be called the method, or rather the art, of Briand. We find a sample of this in the article in which he gave his first impressions as delegate to the League of Nations.[1] Already we see his gift for toning down too sharp distinctions, for creating the half-light conducive to harmony. Above all we must imagine this born parliamentarian in the great international parliament of the League of Nations, delivering from the platform the ritualistic words which everyone expects and which offend no one, and then 'lobbying', drawing to one side into a window-recess those whom he must persuade, insinuating his ideas, and adapting himself to the character and interests of each one of them. Flexibility and adroitness, guided by profound knowledge of men, these, even more than the gift for oratory enhanced by a stirring voice, were Briand's main weapons. We will now study him through his actions, without ever forgetting that very often the part played by his personal initiative will be limited by the existing situation and the action of his opponents.

The Locarno Treaties and Germany's Entry into the League of Nations

The immediate cause of the Locarno negotiations was the refusal of the Allies to proceed with evacuation of the Cologne area in January 1925. This refusal caused strong reactions in Germany: the German Minister of Foreign Affairs, Gustav Stresemann, set himself as a primary task the achievement of the evacuation of the Rhineland, both to restore to Germany its freedom of action, and because, it seems, he had taken the threat of Rhineland separatism very seriously. However, surely the simplest way to end the occupation of the Cologne area was actually to fulfil the obligations of the Treaty regarding German disarmament, since it was the non-observance of these obligations which had motivated the keeping of allied troops in Cologne. Stresemann does not appear to have contemplated this solution: seeking the support of the nationalists in his internal policy he could hardly dissolve their paramilitary organization, the *Stahlhelm*, the main target of French recriminations, any more than he could paralyse the efforts of von Seeckt to re-establish the Supreme Headquarters, when he had actually left it to him to restore the order and authority of the central power at the time of the disturbances of 1923.

[1] See Document 13.

Rather than do this, Stresemann set out on a new and daring path: to offer to France a guarantee agreement, an undertaking not to compromise by force her frontiers of 1919. The Germans had frequently been advised to take this step by their British friends, especially the ambassador to Berlin, Lord d'Abernon. This advice on the part of the British, who did not believe in the German desire for revenge, was quite natural. However, it was less natural for nationalists such as Stresemann to take it. What decided Stresemann, according to his declarations, was the concern to put an end to the occupation of the Rhineland, to avoid its being replaced by international control, and also to avoid the conclusion of a Franco-British assistance agreement. Stresemann must have been very badly informed on the latter point if he considered this possible after the failures of 1924. It seems rather that he wished to make his offer the starting point of a vast negotiation which was to have ended in a more or less extensive revision of the Treaty of Versailles.

Be that as it may, when Briand again became Minister of Foreign Affairs, he was in the presence of the German proposal for a Rhine pact, which was addressed both to Britain and to France and already contemplated the accession of Italy. This proposal did not at first arouse enthusiasm either in Britain or in France. The General Secretary of Foreign Affairs, Philippe Berthelot, even advised against a purely Franco-British agreement, because this limited France's freedom of action with regard to German disarmament, just as the Dawes Plan already limited it in the matter of reparations.[2]

Nevertheless, Briand decided to follow up the German proposal. He did this apparently because it now seemed to him the only way to renew the ties between France and Britain. Britain, who did not wish to guarantee France on her own in the future, could not morally refuse to preside over a Franco-German reconciliation which she had pressed for for so long, nor could it fail to please her to resume her role of arbiter of Europe. The possibility that she too would appear as an arbiter was sufficient to make Italy's agreement certain.

However, the mutual guarantee of the Franco-German frontier

---

[2] See Document 14. This view is all the more remarkable in that Berthelot had been dismissed from favour by Poincaré. For the enmity between Poincaré and Berthelot, see the novel by Jean Giraudoux, *Bella* (Paris, 1926).

by France, Germany, Britain and Italy was only the starting point, more or less undisputed, of the negotiations. There were much bigger plans on all sides. First of all, Briand obtained without much difficulty an extension of the guarantee of the Belgian frontier. Stresemann set forth at one fell swoop the programme of German claims, which were concerned not only with the Rhineland problems, but with the question of responsibility for the war, the eastern frontiers of Germany, the restitution of German colonies, etc.: in short, a considerable revision of the Treaty of Versailles. It seems that Briand did not commit himself one way or the other on this programme, confining himself to obtaining a postponement of the majority of the questions.[3] Thus the main point which would enable us to determine what Briand's policy was exactly remains vague: was he prepared to revise the Treaty, or did he think on the other hand that an atmosphere of appeasement would gradually remove any demand for revision?

At that time, however, the most arduous negotiations revolved round Germany's eastern frontiers. It refused to guarantee them – in fact it demanded the revision of the German-Polish frontier – and confined itself to offering arbitration agreements to Poland and Czechoslovakia. Britain on the other hand continued to refuse any guarantee to the states of central and eastern Europe. Now France, henceforth the ally of both Poland and Czechoslovakia, was faced with a formidable problem: if Germany attacked Poland (at that time Czechoslovakia was hardly thought of) and if France came to the aid of Poland by attacking Germany, would she not become guilty of a violation of the Locarno Treaty, and would she not then risk having Britain and Italy intervene against her? The final result was an ambiguous solution which Briand and Stresemann interpreted differently: Franco-Polish and Franco-Czech treaties were added to the series of Locarno Agreements (16 October 1925); the other countries had official knowledge of these, but did not in any way participate in them. The relentlessness of Briand in pressing the French obligations to help Poland and Czechoslovakia at the very moment when he was proceeding towards an agreement with Germany is, however, significant on two counts: it showed in the first place that the Slavonic alliances were not created by France with a view to hostility against Germany, but with a view to consolidation of a basic order in

[3] G. Suarez, *Briand, sa vie, son œuvre*, Vol. VI, pp.117–18.

Europe; it also showed that Briand probably saw the preservation of treaties rather than their revision as a basis for establishing a lasting peace.

If we wish to pass judgment on the Locarno Agreements today, we must obviously view with considerable detachment the vehement outbursts which greeted their publication. Germany renounced the restitution of Alsace-Lorraine, and even re-militarization of the Rhineland, no longer under coercion, but of its own free will; this appeared to be a considerable concession, but Stresemann explained constantly that in his opinion Germany was not in a condition to wage war against France in the fore-seeable future. France renounced acting alone against Germany – except in the case of her eastern allies – but this was exactly what Briand, who was aware of the disproportion of the actual forces of the two countries, wished most of all to avoid. Britain and Italy acquired, or thought they acquired, considerable diplomatic prestige as arbiters of Europe, or at least, of the main European question: doubtless they were undertaking to guarantee the Franco-German and Germano-Belgian frontiers and the de-militarization of the Rhineland, but the execution of this guaran-tee, subject to the procedures of the League of Nations, afforded by that very fact a wide margin of interpretation. The Locarno Treaty was above all a beginning, and very different consequences were expected from it: for the Germans, a revision of the peace treaties, for many Frenchmen, their consolidation. Thus it was an eminently diplomatic piece of work, which consisted of postpon-ing the problems and relying on time to solve them.

One of the conditions – or necessary consequences – of the Locarno negotiations was the entry of Germany into the League of Nations. This had been regarded by many Germans and British as bound to occur a very short time after the signing of the peace treaty and as a logical consequence of it. At this time France had reservations; she considered that Germany must first of all prove its good intentions and good conduct for a certain number of years. The difficulties raised by the question of German dis-armament and that of reparations quite naturally delayed the admission of Germany.

Briand adopted a different attitude: considering the reparations problem as solved, and ceasing to consider the total disarmament of Germany as a preliminary condition, he himself wished to see

Germany as a member of the League of Nations, reckoning that it would be subject, like the other members, to obligations, whose very definition had been under discussion for several years. It seemed therefore that since the main powers were now in agreement, the question would be settled very quickly; in fact it involved yet another year of bargaining and conflict.

The first difficulty arose from Germany's demand to obtain a permanent seat in the Council of the League of Nations. This demand may seem natural, but what was less so was its claim to forbid the creation of new permanent seats at the same time for the benefit of other powers. For example this placed Poland, who had numerous differences with Germany which were liable to be debated at the League of Nations, at a disadvantage. It would also thwart other ambitions such as those of Spain and Brazil. Finally Germany obtained satisfaction, but Brazil left the League of Nations.

While the debate about permanent seats in the Council occupied the front of the stage, another question, which was in fact far more serious, also required delicate negotiations. This was the question of the new obligations which Germany would assume and, more precisely, that of clause 16 of the League of Nations Pact,[4] which stated the principle of assistance to a country which was the victim of aggression, and sanctions against the aggressor. Now Stresemann declared that Germany should not be compelled to observe this clause, since it was in a special situation; it was disarmed by the Treaty of Versailles, while the other countries were not. If it then carried out the obligations of help and sanctions as stated in clause 16, it would be the appointed defenceless victim of the aggressor state.

The argument appeared to be largely theoretical, since in that case, the other states of the League of Nations would be obliged to come to Germany's rescue. It was, however, accepted; and in order to understand the importance of this concession, it must be borne in mind that Stresemann in fact was thinking of a very real situation. In his opinion – which was not that of his successors – Germany was not in a condition to face an armed conflict with France, nor could it think of attacking Poland, whom France would immediately assist. However, Germany was in league with Russia, as a result of the Rapallo Agreement of 1922, which

[4] See Document 35.

Stresemann confirmed and in fact extended in 1926. If, then, Russia attacked Poland, and France, invoking clause 16, intervened on behalf of the latter, Germany would not offer her any assistance, and would even refuse the passage of troops coming to the aid of Poland. The latter would be doomed to a defeat from which Germany would not fail to profit.[5] This explains why Poland soon registered deep disapproval with regard to the Locarno policies and their outcome.

Thoiry and the Young Plan

The Dawes Plan, which was operating normally, was, however, only a temporary arrangement, although the limit of its duration had not been fixed in advance. Nevertheless, it was seen that attempts to achieve a definite settlement of the reparations problem were quickly renewed in various quarters.

(a) The Thoiry interview (17 September 1926)

A few days after the official admission of Germany to the League of Nations, Briand, accompanied by his assistant Hesnard, who was to act as interpreter, met Stresemann privately at an inn near Geneva. We have two reports of this interview, one from Stresemann himself, and the other from Hesnard, obviously inspired by Briand, and the two accounts differ very greatly.[6] Many questions were broached; once again the German paramilitary associations were discussed, with no more result than on previous occasions. However, one of the problems dealt with was relatively new: that of commercialization of the German reparations debt. It is known that this debt was represented theoretically by series of bonds. However, they had never been offered to the public. Now this 'mobilization' of the bonds would have given Germany's creditors, especially France, great advantages. Firstly, if this had been carried out on a large enough scale, it would have supplied in one fell swoop more liquid money than the annuities stipulated; it would then have spread the French credit for example into a large number of hands, in practice, those of international

---

[5] See in particular Stresemann's Papers on this subject (French translation, Paris, 1932–3, Vol. II, p.50).

[6] This difficulty seems to have been overlooked by Weill-Raynal, who slavishly follows Stresemann's account.

financiers, notably Americans: in this way a permanent cause of direct Franco-German confrontation would be removed, and this would be a valuable advantage both for those who wished for a Franco-German *rapprochement* and those who simply wished that France would not be isolated in the face of German ill-will and British and American disapproval.

However, if the German debt became commercial, it would be subject at the same time to strict repayment obligations. Now the German political debt profited from two possibilities of mitigation. In the first place, by virtue of the Treaty of Versailles (clause 234), Germany could always seek for a reduction or a moratorium, and request an examination into its capacity for payment. Secondly, according to the clauses of the Dawes Plan, it was obliged to pay only in national currency, since conversions into foreign currencies would devolve on the general reparations agent and would be authorized only in so far as they did not compromise the German exchange rate. Obviously international capitalists would not agree to buy the reparations bonds unless Germany would agree to renounce these two protective clauses.

If Germany made this sacrifice, however, what would it get in return? According to Stresemann this was a matter of early withdrawal from the Rhineland and the relinquishing of French claims in the Saar. The account of Hesnard, which was certainly supervised by Briand, gave no precise information of this nature. However, it seems unlikely that Stresemann would consider conceding very important advantages to France without being obliged to do so and without making very high demands in return, which would be precisely what was closest to his heart.

Nevertheless, if we accept Stresemann's account on this point, the policy of Briand is extremely questionable. He would in fact have contemplated giving up an essential guarantee of French security at a time when the indispensable substitute – fortification of the frontiers – had not been undertaken, nor was it financially possible. In order to understand Briand's action, we must bear in mind the French situation at that time. France had experienced a serious currency crisis since the spring of 1925, and in July 1926 the franc seemed on the point of collapse like the mark three years previously. It was then that an appeal was made to Poincaré, who was to save the situation brilliantly. Poincaré did not hesitate to retain Briand as Minister of Foreign Affairs; and Briand did not fail to use this as a justification for declaring that his foreign policy, ratified by all the important responsible parties, was the only possible one.

In September 1926, however, the fate of the franc was still in the balance, and Briand did not perhaps have absolute confidence in the ability of Poincaré to save the situation. He knew that a committee of financial experts, which he himself had had appointed, had come to the conclusion that a large loan from abroad was necessary to stabilize the franc. The only possible large subscribers, in Britain and the United States, would perhaps not be available, since the question of interallied debts had not been finally settled. It is possible that Briand then thought that the mobilization of the German reparations bonds was the only possible solution and that it answered the immediate need.

Poincaré, however, contrary to all expectations, succeeded in saving and stabilizing the franc without any foreign aid, and the Thoiry interview was not followed up. In connection with this failure, the French and German approaches were again very different. Once more we will adopt that of Stresemann, which appears the more logical: Briand abandoned negotiations which had ceased to serve any purpose when the franc no longer gave cause for alarm. We will add personally that Briand hastened to cover his tracks to eradicate the proof of what was, according to us, notable rashness.

(b) *Settlement of interallied debts*

France was the last country to make agreements for payment of her debts to her allies, or, to use a more technical term, to consolidate debts which were floating until that time. There were several reasons for this delay. First, France could not contemplate providing for settlement of her debts before the Dawes Plan had been put into force, which would guarantee the beginning of the payment of German reparations. Soon after this a financial and currency crisis resulting in a rapid fall of the franc was to pose, together with the question of the right, the question of the material possibility, of payment. The problem was further complicated by a change of attitude by Britain: in a debate in the House of Commons on 10 December 1927, the Chancellor of the Exchequer claimed that any payment made by the European debtors to America should be accompanied simultaneously and *pari passu* by a proportional payment effected on behalf of Britain. This position was very much a reversal not only, as was obvious, of the Bonar Law propositions of January 1923, but even of the Balfour note of 1922.

Above all, the negotiations which took place in 1925 and at the beginning of 1926 came up against a fundamental obstacle. France requested a safeguard clause which would provide for a revision of the payments if 'for a reason independent of the wish or power of France, one of the constituent elements of the nation's assets was substantially reduced'. The United States stubbornly refused this clause, which would have established an indirect but real link between the interallied debts and the reparations. France was consequently in a much worse position than Germany, who was protected by a capacity-of-payment clause which was included in the Treaty of Versailles. Similarly, France obtained nothing equivalent to the transfer clause, protecting German currency, which had been introduced by the Dawes Plan. These two clauses were of special interest to France in her financial position at that time.

Finally, the French government signed agreements with the United States on 29 April 1926 and with Britain on 12 July 1926. It was practically obliged to do so at a time when its experts did not believe that it was possible to stabilize the franc without having recourse to foreign credit, that is, in practice, British and American credit. It was known that the United States and Britain would not grant these credits without a previous settlement of the problem of debts. Nevertheless, these agreements shocked French opinion so much that it did not seem possible to submit them to parliamentary ratification immediately, and from 1926 to 1929 they were carried out in the form of provisional arrangements.

As a result of these agreements and the Dawes Plan, France's position with regard to debts and reparations appeared as shown in Table 6.1 on page 80.

It would appear that the payments France was to receive from Germany greatly exceeded what she would have to pay to Britain and the United States. However, this did not represent the true situation. First, the excess in favour of France would be much diminished after the first years, that is, at a time when the German payments appeared uncertain. Moreover, a considerable part of the German payments, which were reckoned in marks, were in

Table 6.1

Years of the Dawes Plan (31 Aug.–31 Aug.)	Annual instalments due to the USA	Annual instalments due to Britain	France's part of the German annual instalments
	(millions of gold marks)		
1926	126	126	591
1927	126	82	748
1928	136	123	888
1929	136	164	1293
1930	147	204	1356
1931	168	255	1356
1932	210	255	1356
1933	252	255	1356
1934	315	255	1356
1935	336	255	1306
1936	378	255	1281
1937	420	255	1269
1938	441	255	1264
1939	462	255	1264
1940	483	255	1264
1941	504	255	1264
1942–57 annually	525	255	1264
1958–86 annually	525	286	1264
1987	494	286	1264
1988		286	1264

fact carried out at the time by payment in kind. Finally, the German payments were to be made in marks, and were converted into foreign currencies only to the extent that this conversion could not harm the German currency. The sums owed by France – shown in marks in Table 6.1 to make comparison simpler – were to be paid entirely in dollars and in pounds sterling. It was therefore very likely that after a few years France would have to pay out more dollars and pounds sterling than she could hope to obtain from Germany.[7]

[7] On this point see the exhaustive discussion by E. Weill-Raynal, *Les Réparations allemandes et la France*, Vol. III, pp.385–9.

(c) *The causes of the revision of the Dawes Plan*

The Dawes Plan was by its nature a provisional arrangement. It organized the payment of annual instalments whose number had not yet been established. In principle the total German debt remained the one which was determined in 1921. In fact the Dawes annual instalments could cover only the interest on this debt, which would thus become perpetual. This was a questionable situation, which could not continue indefinitely. Of course the Germans, while carrying out the Dawes Plan, never ceased to demand its revision, reduction of the annual instalments, and a final settlement which would let them know at last the total that they would have to pay.

The general agent of reparations, the American Parker Gilbert, also wished for a speedy revision of the Dawes Plan for obviously different reasons. The responsibility for the transfer, that is, the conversion of the marks paid by Germany into foreign currencies, devolved entirely on Parker Gilbert. Because of this there was the risk that Germany would consider itself free from any constraint in this respect and would set off again on the path of financial rashness. At the end of 1927 Parker Gilbert found that he was obliged to send a warning to Germany about its budgetary extravagances. Another, often published, reason could be added to this: Parker Gilbert could not be unaware that if the Dawes Plan were carried out easily, this would be owing to the plentiful short-term credits which the Americans were granting to the Germans in various forms. If for any reason these credits were slowed down, a currency crisis, involving a crisis in the execution of the Dawes Plan, would almost inevitably ensue. Would it not be better to carry out in a 'cold' state a revision which, if imposed under 'hot' conditions, could again present a risk of seriously disturbing international relations?

The real problem was that of France's attitude. We shall in fact see not only Briand, but his President of the Council, Poincaré, hasten to fall in with the suggestions of Parker Gilbert. How could Poincaré, who was formerly so intransigent on the subject of reparations, now so willingly be a party to negotiations which could not fail to involve France in new concessions and considerable sacrifices?

Many answers to this question have been put forward. Two of

these were based on the declarations of Poincaré himself. First, the problem was one of establishing a more precise relationship between the reparations and the interallied debts within the framework of a new Plan. To this certain commentators have added that Poincaré, who was in great embarrassment over obtaining ratification by parliament of the agreements regarding the debts, was counting on obtaining this ratification more easily within the framework of a general agreement which included debts and reparations. This reason, however, does not seem very conclusive: why should the adoption of several proposals, all involving sacrifices, be made easier by their being presented all at once?

A second reason, invoked by Poincaré and his colleagues, was the procuring at last of the commercialization of the German debt which had already been considered at Thoiry. However, we shall see that this commercialization, which was in fact the result of the Young Plan, would give only very meagre results. We must then look beyond the official justifications for the probable ulterior motives.

Firstly, Poincaré may well have had the same idea as Parker Gilbert: it was better to carry out a revision which was inevitable in any case, 'cold' rather than 'hot', and not to wait for a crisis which could well mean the end of the reparations.[8] If Germany, lacking foreign credits, again pleaded the impossibility of paying, the situation would be back to what it was in 1922, but without its any longer being possible to have recourse to actions such as the occupation of the Ruhr; and the result of all the efforts made since then would be destroyed. Thus, by consenting to the establishment of the Young Plan, Poincaré would have tried to avoid what in fact happened in 1931-2.

There is, however, another reason. We have shown that the intransigence of Poincaré in 1923 was explained also by the difficulties of the French financial situation. But in 1928 the reconstruction of the devastated regions had been almost completed. The franc was stabilized, in fact from the end of 1926 and by law in 1928, at a fifth of its pre-war value; the sacrifice of the French investors was therefore achieved. Strictly speaking, France no longer needed the German reparations unless it was to pay her

[8] For the expectation of this crisis, which some people counted upon, see Weill-Raynal, op. cit., Vol. III, pp.401, 416, 524.

war debts. Under these conditions, Poincaré, as well as Briand, was prepared to make a general settlement of the questions still in the balance; this, it was hoped, would enable the peace to be strengthened.

(d) *The Young Plan*

The alteration of the Dawes Plan was officially recommended by Parker Gilbert in December 1927. The negotiations were announced by the different powers in September 1928, and in December of the same year a new committee of experts was called together. The Young Committee submitted its report in June 1929. The whole of August 1929 was taken up with the first intergovernmental conference at The Hague with a view to implementing the conclusions of the experts. A second conference was held at The Hague in January 1930. The Young Plan was finally put into operation in May 1930. The simple enumeration of dates gives some idea of how laborious this negotiation undertaken 'in cold blood' could be.

In fact, serious diplomatic crises again brought France into conflict, first with Germany and subsequently with Britain, as had become the custom over the question of reparations. On the German side the main difficulty came from the financial expert, Dr Schacht, who tried to take advantage of the final settlement of the reparations to raise the question, not only about the allocation of colonies to Germany, but also about the recovery of Polish provinces which it had held before 1914. The most disturbing feature of these claims was that they were a symptom, for at this time it was not Dr Schacht who was directing Germany's policy. The clash with Britain was much more serious at the time, for it brought the French representatives into conflict with Philip Snowden, Chancellor of the Exchequer; he wished both to reduce the German responsibilities and to increase Britain's part, as the experts had foreseen it. After very keen discussions, he obtained largely what he wanted, and France pushed very far her desire for conciliation.

The final result, the Young Plan, appeared to be a definitive settlement of the reparations problem, and because of this, it openly represented a reversal of the Treaty of Versailles. Germany was from then onward relieved of the system of guarantees and pledges of the Dawes Plan and was under a moral obligation only to carry out the new plan; on the other hand it renounced the benefit of the transfer and safeguard clauses.

Henceforth it was the debts of the Allies to the United States which formed the largest part of the German debt, as it was now defined. According to the French expert Jacques Seydoux, the Young Plan was 'like a small house flanked and dominated by an enormous tower, this tower being the total debt to the United States'.

Two series of annual payments were provided for: thirty-seven 'non-deferrable' or 'unconditional' instalments of 660 million gold marks each[9] were to represent the reparations as such. In addition, a 'deferrable' part of the first thirty-seven instalments, and the whole of twenty-two subsequent instalments, made a total which was approximately equivalent to the debts of the Allies to the United States, the settlement of which was spread over the same number of years. The total payments to be made by Germany were reduced to about 40,000 million gold marks, and the future prospects of the new plan promised France only slightly more than half the sums spent on reconstruction of the devastated areas; less than 7,000 million gold marks were involved, as against 13,000 million marks for the payment of France's debts to her allies. This was the extent of the sacrifices freely agreed to by France, without considering any pressure of economic necessity.

From then on the interallied debts became the great problem. As soon as the report had been presented by the committee of experts, the agreements for the settlement of these debts were submitted to the French Parliament. The Chamber of Deputies resigned itself to ratifying the Washington Agreement (20 July 1929) by 300 votes to 292, after adopting a resolution which declared:

> That the charges imposed on the country by the agreements must be covered exclusively by the sums which Germany must pay France in addition to those intended for reparations.

The Senate voted for similar arrangements, but of course they had no juridical value as far as the United States was concerned. From this time onward everything depended on the effective operation of the Young Plan. In spite of all the sacrifices which it

---

[9] It must be remembered that a Dawes Plan typical annual instalment amounted to 2,500 million gold marks.

implied, this plan was ratified by the Chamber on 29 March 1930, by a very large majority: 527 votes to 38 with 21 abstentions.

There is a final point to be mentioned. The Young Plan at last made possible the mobilization and commercialization of the German debt. In fact the first Young Plan loan was launched in June 1930.[10] However, this totalled only about 300 million dollars, that is, 1,268 million marks. This sum was comparable in size to one Young Plan annual instalment; the French contributions represented 28 per cent of this total, about as much as those of the United States (29 per cent), and much more than those of Great Britain (16 per cent). It will be seen from these results that commercialization of the German debt was far from being the panacea which was hoped for at one time.

The Briand-Kellogg Pact

Up to now we have seen Briand engaged in long-standing problems and even in solutions which were in the process of development. We shall now begin to study his most personal initiatives.

Since 1921 the movements to 'outlaw war' had developed seriously in the United States,[11] where there were both supporters and opponents of the League of Nations. Briand was kept informed of these efforts and was even in contact with certain of their promoters who otherwise had very different leanings: Levinson for one side; Nicholas Murray Butler and Shotwell for the other side. Hence he reiterated their phrases in the message which he sent to the American people on 6 April 1927, for the tenth anniversary of the entry of the United States into the war.

> France would be ready to subscribe publicly with the United States, to any mutual undertaking which would 'outlaw' war according to the American expression, for the two countries. Renunciation of war as an instrument of national policy is a concept already well known to the signatories of the League of Nations Pact and the Locarno Agreements. Any undertaking signed in the same spirit by the United States with another nation such as France would make a

[10] There is a fundamental difference between this Young Plan loan and the Dawes Plan loan of 1924; the basic aim of the latter was to enable the mark to become stabilized and it was not directly connected with the German reparations debt.

[11] See J. B. Duroselle, *De Wilson à Roosevelt*, Paris, 1960, pp.194–201.

great contribution in the eyes of the world to widening and strengthening the foundation on which an international peace policy is built.

Of course, as has often been stressed, this proposal could hardly have any practical consequences. There was no foreseeable possibility of a war between France and the United States. However – and here we have a very characteristic example of Briand's method – the idea was to create a moral link between the French and American peoples, to change the atmosphere of distrust, even of hostility, which reigned in the United States towards France, whom they accused of 'militarism'.

In fact, in view of the favourable welcome with which Briand's suggestion was received by the American people, it was changed into an official proposal on 20 June and submitted to the United States ambassador in Paris. The reaction of the American administration, however, was at first much more reserved. Finally, the Secretary of State, Frank Billings Kellogg, replied on 28 December:

> It seems to me that, instead of being content with a bilateral declaration of the kind suggested by M Briand, the two governments could make a much more spectacular contribution to world peace by uniting their efforts to obtain the agreement of all the main world powers to a declaration whereby these powers renounced war as an instrument of national policy.

The original proposal was thus completely transformed and could from then on be concluded only at the cost of a long and difficult negotiation. In fact, in a general text, France could only accept the illegality of wars of aggression. This was not only a problem of maintaining the right to legitimate defence, which no one disputed. It was also necessary to preserve the possibilities of mutual assistance as written in the League of Nations Pact and the Locarno Agreements, as well as France's individual alliances – which were all, moreover, of a purely defensive nature.[12] However, Briand's formula included a serious difficulty: the definition of 'aggressor' and 'aggression'. The United States refused to allow herself to become involved in the discussion of formulae which the League of Nations was beginning to develop in this connection. To eliminate any objection, Kellogg declared on 28 April 1928:

[12] See Document 42.

In the event of the signatories of the treaties of Locarno and the neutrality treaties agreeing to the American proposal, every violation of these treaties or agreements would thus constitute an infringement of the multipartite treaty. . . . The violation of a multipartite treaty against war by one of the parties would automatically free the other parties with regard to the State which has violated the treaty.

Finally, the Pact was signed in Paris on 27 August 1928. About fifty nations agreed to it, of which many had reservations; one of the few who did not have any was Japan, who was to be the first to violate the agreement.

Much ironical comment has been made on the unrealistic nature of the Briand-Kellogg Pact. There are some who have estimated that its consequences were more damaging than useful, notably its interference with the functioning of mutual assistance. Others were naturally disappointed that the persistent effort made by Briand since 1921 to recover the contact with the United States had finally failed.

These criticisms and disappointments seem excessive, and it is not even certain that the final formula of the 'open to all' treaty was more disadvantageous to France than the original proposal of a bilateral agreement, for the United States were from this time onward party to a treaty which put them in contact – without binding them – with the main countries of Europe; if one of them had recourse to war, the United States were affected and could, if the general atmosphere permitted it, enter into talks with the other countries, especially the victims of the act of aggression. An American administration which believed it possible and desirable to intervene in world affairs now had a juridical basis on which to do so.[13]

The Proposal for European Unity

We now come to the Briand initiative which seems the most difficult to understand. About 1930 the idea of a 'United States of Europe' was the very pattern of academic utopias, which none of those responsible for the policy of a large country would dream of taking seriously. As for the vision that Europe, failing to unite,

[13] See in particular the *Documents Diplomatiques Français* (DDF), 1st series, Vol. I, pp.163–7, 10 August 1932 (comment on an electoral speech by Stimson about the Briand-Kellogg Pact).

would one day be crushed between Russia and the USA: some of those in his confidence attributed it to Briand, but it went back to Napoleon I, and it was not yet possible, at the time of which we are speaking, to appreciate its prophetic nature.

However this may be, Briand launched his idea, in a speech delivered at the tenth assembly of the League of Nations, on 5 September 1929, in the following terms:

> I believe that there should be some kind of federal link between peoples who are grouped together geographically, like the peoples of Europe. These peoples should be able to come into contact at any time, to discuss their common interests, and to make joint resolutions. In a word, they should establish between them a tie of solidarity which will enable them, at the desired moment, to face up to serious circumstances, should these arise. . . .
>
> Obviously the association will function most of all in the economic field: this is the most immediate necessity. I believe that in this field we can succeed. I am also sure, however, that from the political or social point of view, the federal link could be beneficial, without interfering with the sovereignty of any of the nations which might form part of an association of this kind.

We note immediately the vagueness, and possibly the ambiguity, of such a proposition. The mere possibility of discussing common interests, even of making common resolutions, does not necessarily imply the existence of a federal link; and many specialists in constitutional law would dispute whether this federal link could 'not interfere with the sovereignty of any of the nations'. This presentation can be explained by the concern not to startle the participants and also – which seems to reveal much of Briand's method – by the desire to leave all doors open, in order to be able to adapt and manipulate the initial proposal according to the reactions of the participants.

Another comment can be made straight away: although the world crisis had not yet exploded at that time, Briand was, in the beginning, relying on the economic preoccupations of his listeners, but his main concern was to achieve a political organization. He had already revealed this train of thought during his negotiations with Lloyd George at the time of the conference at Cannes, in December 1921 and January 1922.

As a result of his speech, Briand was asked by twenty-seven states to prepare a memorandum which was submitted to them on

17 May 1930.[14] This memorandum contained more specific proposals: the formation of European institutions (whose powers, it is true, were not strictly defined), a system of arbitration, security and international guarantees for the whole of Europe (to which Briand perhaps attached most importance), and finally the establishment of a common market.

This was still nothing more than a rough sketch. Nevertheless the memorandum obliged each of the interested countries to reveal their ulterior motives. Britain made a very cautious response, as she seemed to wish to consider only an economic co-operation, and showed that her ties with the Commonwealth were stronger than those with Europe. Germany counted on vast and vague claims. Contradictory trends were revealed in the replies of the other states. Finally, the proposal was abandoned for practical purposes, at least on the political level. This was Briand's most marked failure.

What, however, had he wished to do; and what, in his mind, would this initiative have achieved? Was it, as has been claimed, a withdrawal position of a statesman disappointed in his attempts to re-establish the ties with Britain and the United States, a statesman who would then have attempted a 'continental' policy to oppose 'maritime' powers? We believe the opposite: the possibility, which was expressly provided for in the memorandum, of inviting 'a power outside Europe which does or does not form part of the League of Nations', could properly be applied only to the USA. Briand might also have thought that offering Britain the possibility of joining Europe without clearly offering any new guarantees, would provide her with the best means of overcoming her insular reflexes.

However, the failure was all the more serious for that. Briand had done his utmost to release European policy from apparently insoluble problems, by placing it in a new atmosphere and by directing it towards new horizons. It is useless to say that the attempt was premature, but the fact that it could not be achieved was an ill omen.

The Early Evacuation of the Rhineland, and the Renewal of the German Threat

The occupation of the left bank of the Rhine was to be ended in

[14] See Document 16.

1935 if it were accepted that the Treaty of Versailles had actually been put into effect on the appointed date, in 1920. That is to say, it was possible to find reasons for extending it beyond this limit. However, the last French troops left the Rhineland on 30 June 1930. In this way the first fundamental objective of Stresemann's policy had been achieved.

However, this premature evacuation was part of Briand's policy and to some extent it was the inevitable price. Briand had indeed endeavoured not to connect it with any particular agreement, to make it appear, not as the result of a deal, but as a goodwill gesture on the part of France. In fact he was not entirely successful here, and the evacuation was connected more or less directly with the adoption of the Young Plan. Above all, however, the military occupation of German territory could not be reconciled for long with the striving for general appeasement which was the hallmark of Briand's policy.

But it is a mistake to reproach Briand for having compromised the security of France by this act. Merely to gain an extra breathing-space of a few years was no longer of great importance. The essential thing was that France had recovered sufficiently, especially on the financial level, to replace one security system, which was unavoidably precarious, by another, which it was hoped would be more lasting.[15]

However, far from sanctioning the appeasement, the evacuation of the Rhineland was on the contrary followed by a renewed outbreak of manifestations in Germany. In the evacuated territories these were first of all not only highly spectacular *Stahlhelm* demonstrations, but an official visit of the President of the Republic, Marshal Hindenburg, during which he questioned the demilitarization of the Rhineland which Germany had nevertheless freely confirmed by the Locarno Agreements. Then in the German elections of September 1930, Hitler's party achieved a sudden electoral boost and become one of the main factors of German policy, since it now had more than a hundred seats in the Reichstag.

Under the Hitlerite pressure, the German government – which no longer included Stresemann, who had died in the autumn of 1929 – was to make use of a more and more aggressive diplomacy. Its most striking gesture was the proposal for an Austro-German

[15] See Chapter 7.

customs union, announced in March 1931. Now, according to all precedents, this customs union foreshadowed a political union, and this directly contravened the peace treaties.

This time, France, including Briand and his warmest supporters, reacted energetically. At her request, the Council of the League of Nations submitted the proposal to the International Court of Justice at The Hague. Britain supported the French position on this occasion. Even before the official decision of the Court at The Hague, Austria and Germany abandoned their proposal. Nevertheless, Briand would hardly survive this affair.

Conclusion

We can now attempt to answer the questions raised by Briand's policy.

One point appears certain: it seems impossible to us that Briand was the dupe of Stresemann. As his entire career shows, Briand was too subtle and experienced a politician to be deceived by anyone, no matter whom. Moreover, Stresemann was not trying to deceive; not only his nationalist past, even his physical appearance would have made it difficult for him, and he had always made his intentions very clear. The publication of Stresemann's Papers in 1932 had the effect of a bombshell on one section of French opinion. However, Briand could not have been ignorant of the substance of these papers. It is hardly more likely that Briand – like part of the French Left – had banked on the triumph of a 'good' democratic and peaceful Germany. He was too well aware of the difficulties of the Weimar Republic. His game was certainly deeper and more subtle.

One of the elements of this game is, however, clear and indisputable: since 1921 Briand, who was very much aware of the threat which weighed upon French security, looked for means to counteract it by strengthening the closest possible ties with Britain and the United States, in the forms permitted by circumstances, and right to the end this effort was unrelenting.

Should the analysis end here? Were not the famous speeches by which Briand made such an impression on French and international pacifist opinion only a stage production designed to guarantee his popularity in his own country and to prepare the moral understanding between France and the Anglo-Saxon countries which was indispensable to a political understanding? This would be an excessive simplification of the actions of a complex personality. It can hardly be doubted that Briand sincerely tried to create a European atmosphere which would be unfavourable to a renewal of claims and conflicts, and which by this very fact would enable a gradual consolidation of the Europe of the Treaties to take place; finally, it is extremely doubtful, contrary to what some of his followers later maintained, that he contemplated a territorial revision which could not have failed to bring about more troubles and bloodshed. The ambiguity which he maintained on this point was in some way part of his method; it was the price to be paid for his ability to conjure away the conflicts which could not be resolved.

Finally, it can perhaps be maintained that if Briand deceived anyone, it was himself; he probably overestimated the effects of his skill as a conciliator. His chief failure, doubtless, was not that he had not transformed the mentality of Germany after 1919 by waving a magic wand, but that he had confirmed the false sense of security of the British partner whom he should have made aware of danger.

Chapter 7

The Problem of National Defence after the Evacuation of the Rhineland

By evacuating the Rhineland, the French army lost the line of defence of the Rhine which Foch – and many other generals – had declared indispensable; she also lost the advantage of having the Ruhr, the heart of the German economy, within the range of her heavy artillery. All the foundations of national defence were thus overturned. This is why the French government was careful to make this gesture only after France, having recovered her finances, had been able to begin construction on what was to be a substitute for the Rhine defences: the Maginot Line.

The 'Maginot Line complex' has since aroused a great deal of misunderstanding, criticism and mockery; it has, moreover, weighed so heavily on French diplomacy, that it is necessary to make a careful analysis of its origins and the reasons for it.

The first and most valid reasons depended on the actual condition of France. She was, as we have seen, very inferior to her probable opponent Germany, in human and economic resources. The possibility of confronting Germany without an initial advantage to compensate for this inferiority must therefore be excluded from the calculations of those responsible for her destiny. From this arose the need, which we shall discuss at length later, to preserve the legal superiority over Germany which had been created by the Treaty of Versailles: unilateral limitation of German armaments.

It was necessary to go further than this, however: in the First World War a country of static population had been bled white. Even another victory, if it were achieved at the same price as that of 1918, would be the end of France. The reactions of the French differed in this respect from those of their Polish allies, for example. The Poles took courage from the thought that they multiplied more rapidly than the Germans and that consequently they would have the advantage in the long run. It is not at all surprising, or particularly meritorious, that in these conditions the French should be profoundly pacifist. However, the French military men whose professional obligation was to foresee the possibility of a war in spite of everything, had to solve this problem first and foremost: if war nevertheless broke out, how could it be conducted in a way which would spare as many lives as possible?

To find the solution, the technicians – and public opinion perhaps even more so – were guided by the lessons, real or imagined, of the First World War. The military doctrine of 1914 which was based on the superiority of the offensive had been held responsible for the enormity of French losses. As an extreme reaction against equally extreme statements, it was now accepted without question that the defensive was less costly. A thorough, and to some extent a statistical, analysis of some of the great battles of the war could have awakened some doubts, but it was not done at this stage.

Another idea became grafted on to this one, and although it was quite separate, nevertheless it was often confused with the previous one: the idea that the defensive is from the military point of view superior to the offensive. In fact this led people to believe that the use of modern methods made a war of movement impossible, and imposed a war of positions.[1] This was precisely the doctrine of Marshal Pétain, but it must not be thought that it was confined to one man and his followers. When Foch achieved victory in 1918 he did so by the methods of the war of attrition, and did not attempt to restore a war of movement. Those who were successively responsible for national defence after 1930 – Maxime Weygand, who was a disciple of Foch, and then Maurice Gamelin, who was a disciple of Joffre – did not fundamentally alter Pétain's teaching.

However, it was not only on the military level that the defensive seemed superior; it seemed to have imposed itself on both the political and the moral levels. By confusing a war of aggression with offensive tactics once war had been declared, the tendency was to believe that the defensive alone was worthy of a peace-loving people. The following text which escaped as evidence from the pen of a writer who set himself the task of analysing critically a

[1] See on this subject the very characteristic development by the author Jean de Pierrefeu between his war memoirs, *G.Q.G. secteur 1* (Paris, 1920), and his curious later reflections, *Plutarque a menti* (Paris, 1923).

mass of memories and testimonies on the First World War is very revealing in this respect:[2]

> . . . If the defensive wins the day, if it wins the approbation of the heads of all countries as it directly won that of the actual combatants, it will begin by guaranteeing complete security against aggression and it will gradually bring about the elimination of war by the conviction that any offensive is doomed to failure. In August 1914 the German offensive was doomed to a grand failure. This failure did not take place because the offensive came up, not against a defensive, but against another offensive more desperate, more illogical and more blind than itself. The less blind offensive drove back the more blind offensive and the world lost a unique opportunity of demonstrating the ineffectiveness of a war of aggression, of demonstrating the impenetrable defence which a less populated, even less well armed country could offer, but whose soldiers resisted bullets with a parapet, artillery with a trench, onslaughts of men with barbedwire entanglements. . . . If Vauban had written: 'One man well entrenched is worth six who are not', the work containing this phrase should not have remained unpublished, for if a man of his knowledge had been able to establish this ratio of one to six, what could not one say today when all the progress achieved in the manufacture of arms gives to the defensive everything that it takes away from the offensive?

The task which fell to the military authorities was therefore quite naturally to prepare in advance this 'impenetrable defence'. This was why the evacuation of the Rhineland was accompanied by the beginning of work on the site of a continuous fortified line, which covered the entire length of the Franco-German frontier and was called the Maginot Line. It was a mistake when its effectiveness was later questioned: during the campaign of 1940 it was not crossed but taken from behind, which is a quite different matter. Nevertheless, one may wonder what was the real objective in the mind of the General Staff: did they wish to set up a line of defence which was absolute, immutable and destined to show in advance the futility of any Franco-German war? Or was it merely to permit economy of manpower which was indispensable to an army suffering from a shortage of men? We are obliged to ask the question because the Maginot Line had two gaps: one, which was of secondary importance, was in Lorraine; but the other was

---

[2] Jean Norton Cru, *Témoins* (Paris, 1929), p.445, n.1. See also pp.174–5, 310, 432, 481 (in which the effectiveness of assault tanks is challenged).

fundamental; since the line stopped at Longwy, it left the entire Franco-Belgian frontier open.

The gap along the Lorraine frontier is explained by the fact that when the first Maginot Line, which was to be completed in 1934, was designed, the French General Staff still hoped that when 1935 came, the Saar would remain under the control of the League of Nations, or on failing this, France could recover the French-speaking districts and thus base her defences on the course of the river Saar.[3]

The absence of a continuous fortified line along the Franco-Belgian frontier was infinitely more serious, for both the historical precedent of 1914 and permanent geographical considerations indicated that if an invasion one day took place, it would in all probability take place there, all the more so because the very existence of the Maginot Line would prevent its being attempted elsewhere. A whole complex of reasons, diplomatic, strategic and technical, were put forward to explain this omission which was only too obvious.

Belgium, whose status of neutrality guaranteed by France, Britain and Prussia had not protected her from invasion in 1914, had concluded a defensive alliance with France in 1920. It would then hardly seem in accordance with the spirit of this alliance to separate Belgium from France by a fortified line. Why then did they not build this fortified line along the German-Belgian frontier and share the costs? In fact, an attempt in this direction was made by the French statesman André Tardieu, but without result. Besides, surely, if one thought about it, the surest way of protecting Belgium from invasion was to make such an invasion pointless by preventing it from entering French territory in any circumstances? Why should German forces be launched into Belgium if, no sooner had they crossed the country than they came up against a permanent, impregnable, fortified line?

Diplomatic reasons, however, were reinforced by technical considerations: the building of a continuous fortified line, which would be of little use in the wooded hills of the Ardennes, which, it was thought, would be an adequate natural barrier, became impossible at the boundary of Nord, the French département. This area, in fact, together with the adjacent Belgian regions, formed a more or less continuous industrial and urbanized zone.

[3] *Documents Diplomatiques Français* (DDF), 1st series, Vol. IV, pp.644–5.

Now the Maginot Line was basically a system of gun emplacements, and therefore it needed open ground in which guns could be fired without obstruction: obviously it was out of the question, in peacetime, to flatten entire districts of houses and factories for military purposes. It was not possible, either, to consider building the line of French resistance behind a vital industrial region; it was necessary to establish it in front, in Belgian territory, and as far forward as possible, to include the important centres of Brussels, Antwerp and Liège.

Here lay the uncertainty of the true objective of the Maginot Line. According to certain responsible French military men, General Weygand in particular, the existence of the Maginot Line did not imply a purely defensive strategy; its aim was to economize on manpower in order to make it possible to form a large manœuvring formation whose very purpose was to operate in Belgium.

Examination of the French plans of operation, however, showed the limits of this concept, which had appeared so attractive since it enabled technical and diplomatic obstacles to be avoided. In fact, it was not a question of taking the offensive into Germany, nor even of accepting a 'battle of encounter' between two armies, both on the move. What was expected was that in the event of a threat of German aggression, the Belgians would appeal to the French for help soon enough for the latter to have time to improvise a line of defence behind the Meuse and the Albert Canal (the latter connected Antwerp with Liège and thus the Scheldt with the Meuse). This hope was based on two illusions. One was a military illusion, which we have already discussed: that is, that the tactical superiority of defensive strategy over the offensive was indisputable, and that when two modern armies met, it was always possible to freeze them within a few days into a war of positions. There was also a diplomatic illusion: that Belgium would always behave as a faithful ally; now, we shall see that all the efforts of the latter country were directed towards a gradual return to her state of neutrality, or at least towards not becoming too deeply involved with French policy.[4] The risk was then, however, that Belgium would call for France's help at the last moment, too late to entrench the defence at the only serious obstacle on the

[4] See for example on this subject DDF, 1st series, Vol. I, pp.650–1 (3 November 1932) and 1st series, Vol. II, pp.788–9 (20 March 1933).

Belgian plain: the watercourse of the Meuse and the Albert Canal. Hence the entire security of France rested finally on the arrangements of a neighbouring state which was too weak to defend itself.

Up to now we have discussed only the checking of a possible invasion. This operation alone, however, could not guarantee victory. On what factors did the French General Staff base their hope for a final favourable decision?

France, who was too inferior to Germany in war potential, could hope for victory only with the help of her allies, that is, Britain and the USA. Here again, the precedent of the First World War influenced all minds: it was thought that the greater resources of the Anglo-Saxon world would finally be decisive. However, it was also known from experience that this help was slow in coming. Hence the defensive strategy of the French General Staff was designed not only to save manpower; it was also a policy of delay. At the same time the Locarno Treaty regained its full value. One of the reproaches made in certain circles regarding the Treaty was that, by its nature of mutual guarantee, it made preliminary military discussions designed to provide for certain eventualities very difficult in practice. But what did this matter? The long war of positions which would be maintained in the first place would give Britain time to re-arm and to concert her action with that of France. Meanwhile, Britain had no need for any preliminary joint plans to wear down German resistance by a maritime blockade; it was reckoned, owing to the League of Nations system, that this maritime blockade would be completed by a blockade of the aggressor by land, without which it would be rendered ineffective. One of the most widespread illusions at the time – not only in France – was the belief in the omnipotence of economic weapons. As for the USA, it was reckoned that their industrial power would finally give the Allies a superiority of equipment which would guarantee victory. The question as to how these armaments would be paid for apparently remained obscure.

This concept of national defence explains why French diplomacy, the further we advance into this period, did everything possible to establish the closest possible ties with Britain, and to try to renew them with the USA: there was no other alternative.

On the other hand, was not a purely defensive strategy incompatible with the alliances which had actually been concluded with

Poland and Czechoslovakia? It would be sufficient for Germany to remain on the defensive with regard to France, to crush these little countries without reprieve. This argument has often been defended and the experience of 1938 as well as that of 1939 confirmed the correctness of it. However, the military men in charge in France did not reason this way. Confident in the omnipotence of the defensive they advised their allies that they too should entrench themselves in fortified lines, and there await events. The Czechs meekly also built a 'Maginot Line' which, moreover, could be based on effective natural barriers. The Poles, however, who were less discerning, raised the objection that the nature of their country did not lend itself to these methods. The French military men, in no way convinced, attributed these objections to the peculiar temperament of the Poles, or even to their inexperience in modern warfare. The reactions of General Weygand were typical in this respect: when he was sent to Poland in 1920 at the time of the advance of the Russian armies, he gave the Poles advice which they did not take, and he did not succeed in transforming a war of rapid movements into a war of positions in the Western style.[5]

Thus the French policy of national defence was based at the same time on indisputable national necessity and on obsolete military concepts. However, these were so closely linked together that no new ideas could succeed in separating them. France, being too weak, could not adopt a doctrine of offensive. It did not follow from this that her enemy could not obtain decisive results from this doctrine.

[5] See Weygand's Memoirs, Vol. II. *Mirages et réalité*, Paris, 1957.

Chapter 8

The World Economic Crisis and its Repercussions on the Foreign Policy of France

The economic crisis which broke out in the USA in the autumn of 1929 and which soon spread throughout the world, caused such a deep shock that it could not fail to have considerable influence on international relations. We will not attempt to define this influence in general terms here,[1] and will confine ourselves to a more detailed investigation of the points which most directly affected French diplomacy.

France was affected later than many other countries by the crisis, and, apparently at least, less deeply. It was only towards the end of 1931 that she felt the world depression directly. This delay, however, was traditional in the history of French economy and several reasons can be found for it: the economy of France was balanced as a whole, without a clear predominance of either agriculture or industry; foreign trade at this time played only a very limited part; most of all, a very large sector, in agriculture and even in industry, was composed of family enterprises which applied for credit in a very small way, if at all, and could thus quite easily live for a time on their reserves. Finally, owing to her demographic weakness, France was a country of immigration; in times of economic slowing down, foreigners were naturally the first to be dismissed; the result was that the scourge of unemployment seemed to rage less fiercely in France than in other industrial countries.

Of course, analysis must not end here. It is necessary also to consider the situation of the countries which played the largest part in what could be called France's external situation. Germany and Britain were both very seriously shaken in 1931. The result

[1] We have attempted to do this elsewhere; cf. our article in *The Great Depression Revisited* (The Hague, 1972).

was that Britain's foreign policy was both weakened in its available means and dominated more than ever by economic interest; this likewise reduced the support which France could expect from her traditional partner. As for Germany, it was plunged into internal convulsions which only made it more alarming to its neighbours.

As for Eastern and Danubian Europe, whose political equilibrium was so delicate in any case, this part of the world was made up of countries which lived mostly on the export of their agricultural products. Agricultural prices were those most affected by the crisis; in four years they were lowered by more than 50 per cent.[2] It can be imagined how these countries could be weakened and threatened by this, until they became completely dependent on whoever could offer them a remedy for their difficulties. Now France, who was herself an agricultural country, did not complement economically the countries which she protected politically. Germany, an industrial country and a great importer of agricultural products, had in this respect an enormous potential advantage.

In addition to these economic factors connected in some way with geography, it is necessary to consider financial factors which were in fact historical. The period which followed the First World War had seen a fundamental upheaval of European currencies, many of which had been either annihilated or very much reduced in value by inflation. All those countries who understood the mechanism in time, and who were able to 'export' their capital, did so, that is, they converted it from a currency in process of rapid depreciation into other currencies which were considered more stable.[3] France, like the others, had suffered from this exportation of capital at the time of the devaluation of the franc. The 1929 crisis caused a renewal of this migration of 'floating' capital, but this time it was in France that the others took refuge: France, whose economy the crisis seemed to have spared and who was fiercely to defend the stability of the franc which she had just re-established.

To say that floating capital came to take refuge in France is a metaphorical way of making it understood that foreigners bought francs at the Bank of France, and gave her in return gold or,

[2] See J. Néré, *La Crise de 1929*, especially p.83.
[3] See Néré, op. cit., Chapters 1, 2.

rather, foreign currencies which prudence advised her to convert into gold. In this way the gold holding of the Bank of France increased. At one time France thus 'held' 25 per cent of the gold stock of the world, as against 55 per cent in the USA.[4]

This apparent wealth – for the gold deposited in this way at the Bank of France, in exchange for paper francs, which could always be presented for repayment, did not belong either to the Bank or, usually, even to French people – aroused a great deal of jealousy and animosity against France on the part of the countries who suffered the worst from the crisis. Theories were seen to blossom forth, according to which the crisis was due to an unequal distribution of gold in the world, and therefore France was held to be in some way responsible. Another image, which was equally absurd, was superimposed on the image of a militarist France: that of a plutocratic France profiting from the misfortunes of others. Objective analysis of economic mechanisms never prevails against passionate reactions aroused by the state of the purse.

Thus even in the years which only slightly affected the French economy, the world economic crisis considerably weakened France's position with regard to other countries.

The End of Reparations: the Hoover Moratorium and the Lausanne Conference

The world economic crisis assumed a dramatic character in Central Europe from May 1931, when the largest bank in Austria, the *Kredit Anstalt* belonging to the Rothschild group, went bankrupt. Immediately the financial foundation of the German economy itself was threatened, not only because of very close business relations between the two countries but above all from the fact that Germany, like Austria, depended largely on short-term foreign credits, and that panic, which knew no frontiers, would risk involving a massive cancellation of these credits. In June 1931 Germany appealed to international co-operation, contemplating a loan and at the same time questioning the payment of reparations. President Hoover, although at first unwilling, put forward on 20 June his proposal to postpone all payments of intergovernmental debts for a year; this included both the reparations and the interallied debts.

[4] E. Weill-Raynal, *Les Réparations allemandes et la France*, Vol. III, p.652.

Naturally, this proposal could be carried out only with the agreement of Germany's European creditors. France, without denying the necessity for immediate help, understood that an emergency measure should not call in question a permanent right. For this reason she replied with a counter-proposal[5] on 24 June: Germany would naturally be exempt from the deferrable part of the Young Plan annual payments; on the other hand it would pay the non-deferrable part, but

> ... The French Government declared itself ready ... to place at the disposal of the Bank of International Payments a sum equivalent to its part for one year of the non-deferrable annual payment, ... the liquid assets thus paid to the Bank ... could immediately be used to improve credit in Germany, as well as in the countries of Central Europe and especially those where the suspension of the implementation of the Young Plan for a year could cause a financial or economic disturbance.

After several discussions whose purpose was to solve points of detail, the USA and France came to an agreement on 6 July. The other European creditors had agreed on their part: the payment of intergovernmental debts was in effect suspended from 1 July 1931 to 30 June 1932. Fifteen days had passed since President Hoover had put forward his proposal.

France has nevertheless been accused of having deprived the Hoover Moratorium of its effectiveness by her procrastination. This was a curious exaggeration of the psychological aspect of the financial panic which shattered Europe at the time: there was nothing imaginary about its causes; on the contrary, they were only too real. This was so true that the Hoover Moratorium, which was limited to one year, immediately proved inadequate. Negotiations were undertaken without delay with a view to granting the issue of a large international loan to Germany. Before she agreed to this, France naturally requested economic pledges and political guarantees: German customs would be allocated to the service of the loan, of which the Bank of International Payments would become the 'trustee'. Germany would stop making claims for revision of the Treaty of Versailles for ten years – the period of payment of the new loan; it would disband

[5] See extensive excerpts from this reply in Weill-Raynal, op. cit., pp.620–1.

the *Stahlhelm* and would recognize its eastern frontiers.[6] Germany, however, refused to give any political guarantee.

A committee of experts was then formed to study the question of credits necessary to Germany. It adopted the name of its American president, Albert Wiggin. In its report, published on 18 August, it estimated that the success of the indispensable international loan was subject to two conditions, or the elimination of two risks:[7]

> The first is the political risk: until important causes of internal political difficulties in Germany have been eliminated, the continuous and peaceful economic progress of this country cannot be guaranteed; this is the first and basic condition in order for Germany to deserve credits. The second condition refers to Germany's external undertakings: as long as these private and public undertakings imply either continuous snowballing of Germany's external debt, or a disproportion between German imports and exports of such magnitude that it could threaten the economic prosperity of other countries, it is unlikely that the future lender can consider the situation to be stable or secure.

Hence two facts had to be acknowledged: on the one hand, the launching of a large international loan was linked with general policy, which confirmed the French idea; on the other hand, the operation of the Young Plan was again back in the melting-pot.

The President of the Council, Pierre Laval, made his way to the USA to examine with President Hoover the problem of war debts and reparations as a whole. However, the two men achieved only a very general agreement, on 25 October 1931, which in fact did not pledge them to anything:[8]

> As far as intergovernmental obligations are concerned, we recognize that before the Hoover year of suspension has expired, an arrangement to cover the period of economic depression may be necessary; our two Governments make all reservations for the terms and conditions of this arrangement.

[6] The source of this information is J. Wheeler-Bennet, *The Nemesis of Power* (London, 1954); we do not have the publication of the *Documents Diplomatiques Français* for this period, which would enable us to make a cross-check.

[7] Extensive extracts from this report are in Weill-Raynal, op. cit., pp.648–9.

[8] Ibid., p.652.

While Pierre Laval confirmed verbally that France would not pay her war debts if she did not receive any reparations, the American Congress proclaimed its hostility to any cancellation or reduction of governmental debts.

Meanwhile, on 19 November, the German government requested a meeting of the special consultative committee provided by the Young Plan. This committee presented its report on 23 December, boldly stating the problem in its entire breadth:[9]

> The Committee would not feel that it had accomplished the whole of the task entrusted to it, or justified the confidence placed in it, if it did not draw the attention of the Governments to the unprecedented seriousness of the present crisis, whose magnitude indisputably exceeds the 'relatively short depression' contemplated in the Young Plan and in view of which the 'safeguard measures' which it contains were provided. The Young Plan, whose annual payments increased, presupposed a constant development of world trade, not only in volume, but also in value; it was thought that in this way the burden of the annual payments would become less and less for Germany. Nothing of the kind had occurred. Since the Young Plan was put into force, the volume of world commerce has declined; at the same time the exceptional lowering of gold prices has greatly increased the actual weight of the German annual payments, as with all payments drawn up in gold.
>
> In these conditions, the financial difficulties of Germany, which are to a great extent the source of the increasing paralysis of credit throughout the world, make a concerted action necessary, which only the Governments can undertake. . . .
>
> In this connection, the following considerations appear to us to be particularly important. In the first place, any transfer from one country to another, made on so large a scale that it destroys the balance of accounts, can only accentuate the present chaos. Secondly, it is advisable not to lose sight of the fact that any alleviation in favour of a debtor country, which is incapable of bearing the burden of certain payments would run the risk of transferring this burden to a creditor country, which, being itself a debtor, would be unable to support it. An adjustment of all intergovernmental debts [reparations and other war debts] to the present troubled situation of the world – an adjustment which should be made without delay, if we wish to avoid further disasters – is the only lasting measure which is capable of restoring the confidence which is the very foundation of economic stability and true peace.

[9] Ibid., pp.662–3.

It was thus clearly recognized that the Young Plan was from now on unworkable; but at the same time, and for the same reason, revision of interallied debts was obligatory by the same economic arguments.

Meanwhile, the intergovernmental conference whose purpose was to draw practical conclusions from the report of the experts, was adjourned to await the results of the French elections of May 1932. These were a triumph for the Left and brought Edouard Herriot back into power. In his ministerial declaration the new President of the Council upheld the rights of France. However, together with this affirmation of principle he gave indications of his willingness for a complete negotiation, political as well as economic.

However, the Lausanne Conference (16 June to 9 July 1932) could be concerned officially only with the question of reparations. After complicated and sometimes dramatic negotiations, it achieved the following result: the total German debt determined by the Young Plan was abandoned in favour of a final payment of 3,000 million marks, and whose payment – which, moreover, never took place – must take place only after a moratorium, the duration of which was not fixed. World economic reconstruction, which appeared among the objectives of the Lausanne Conference, was committed to the care of a future conference.

Hence France capitulated all along the line. Was this because of the weakness of Edouard Herriot? There was undoubtedly an element of weariness and resignation to the inevitable, of which glimpses could be seen in the articles in the *Dépêche de Toulouse* which was one of the strongest supports of the new government.[10] However, at the same time it was hoped that in time, if not immediately, France would receive compensations with regard to general policy and interallied debts.

A further proof that general policy had in fact never been absent from the discussion can be seen in the proposals made to France by Franz von Papen, the new German chancellor, on 28 June: a consultative agreement and military discussions between France and Germany, in exchange for recognition of Germany's equal rights over the question of armaments, abandonment of the gold standard by France and a redistribution of gold reserves through-

[10] See Document 17.

out the world.[11] These conditions were obviously unacceptable to France, who would have had to make positive concessions in exchange for vague promises. Nevertheless, these separate Franco-German talks alarmed Britain so much, it seems,[12] that she hastened to conclude a 'confidence agreement' with France which consisted of an undertaking by both countries to consult with each other on all the important questions of the moment. Herriot was enthusiastic in his acceptance of this agreement, in which he saw a considerable strengthening of ties with Britain which was the chief aim of French diplomacy. Moreover, it was officially understood that the ratification and enforcement of the Lausanne Agreements were subject to a satisfactory settlement of the question of interallied debts.

In fact, however, the Lausanne Agreement marked the end of the reparations. How did this happen? In France the temptation has often been to trace the source and main responsibility for this to the Hoover Moratorium, which had created a precedent for suspension of the reparations; and it was maintained that by his moratorium Hoover had undertaken a sort of moral engagement regarding the interallied debts. This argument does not appear entirely convincing: the Lausanne Agreement was concluded not so much because of the precedent but because the financial situation which had occasioned the Hoover Moratorium demanded new measures; if the reparations had not been abandoned in practice, they would, in any case, never have been paid. However, the same financial and economic arguments which were valid against continuation of payment of reparations, were from then onward equally valid against the payment of interallied war debts.

The Economic Conference at Stresa (September 1932)[13]

The purpose of this conference was to come to the aid of those Central and Eastern European countries which were particularly affected by the economic crisis. France had already attempted to include this aid in the negotiations which had resulted in the Hoover Moratorium; it had been discussed again at the Lausanne

[11] Weill-Raynal, op. cit., pp. 690–1.

[12] This is the argument of W. E. Scott, *Alliance against Hitler*, p.49.

[13] Documentation for this episode can be found in the *Documents Diplomatiques Français* (DDF), 1st series, Vol. I, pp.327–30, 382–6.

Conference. Moreover, the work had been prepared by the economic commission which had been set up within the framework of Briand's project for European union.

Two measures were proposed by both France and the conference of the agricultural states of Central and Eastern Europe which had met shortly before in Warsaw: stabilization of cereals by means of preferential agreements guaranteeing turnover of all exportable surplus; and the establishment of a monetary fund whose purpose would be to take up the frozen agricultural bonds of the issuing and private banks. In this respect France was in agreement not only with her traditional friends – which was obviously not a coincidence – but also with former enemies such as Hungary and Bulgaria.

On the other hand, France came into direct conflict with Britain. The latter had been a great importer of agricultural products from Central and Eastern Europe. However, she had just granted a customs preference to the rival products of her Dominions, by the Ottawa Agreements. She was therefore asked to reverse a policy which she considered to be one of the foundations of the restoration of her economy. Preferential agreements in favour of agricultural Europe would likewise have meant a discrimination against the USA.

As far as Italy and Germany were concerned, they tended to dismiss any general preferential agreement, from which France could derive moral benefit, in favour of bilateral agreements whose purpose was to enable them to strengthen their own positions in Central Europe.

A conciliation position was found, which formed an agreement between France, Italy and Germany: the interested large countries would help the medium-sized Central European states either in the form of a financial contribution or in the form of an equivalent customs preference; this latter form would be particularly suitable for Italy and Germany, while the financial contribution would be adopted by both France, who was not a great importer of agricultural produce, and Britain, who did not wish to put her overseas suppliers at a disadvantage.

Nevertheless, altercation between France and Britain was not avoided: it arose in connection with financial aid. Britain maintained that the contributions to this fund should not originate from budgetary allocations but from advances from central banks.

It is probable that there was more to this opposition than a technical subtlety: Britain, in fact, did not wish to become too deeply involved in a policy of economic reconstruction in Central Europe, the purpose of which was at the same time to consolidate French influence there.

What is interesting about this episode is that it shows how the economic preoccupations revived by the crisis began to complicate or even cast doubt upon the political alignments which existed previously. The connection between the economic problems of Central Europe and the problems of general policy were to be even more in evidence a little later.

The End of the Interallied Debts, and the London Conference

(a) *The non-payment of 15 December 1932*

The question of interallied debts was put forward implicitly and explicitly in the Lausanne Agreements. France had always proclaimed the existence of a direct connection between these debts and the reparations; there could be no question of paying the one without receiving the other. As far as Britain was concerned, the overall arrangements which she had proposed on several occasions in fact linked them both together: this was especially so in the case of the Bonar Law Plan.[14] Also, the documents signed at the end of the Lausanne Conference made the provision that ratification and implementation of the reparations agreement should be subject to a new settlement of the question of debts.

This is why, as the date on which an instalment on the interallied debts, 15 December 1932, approached, France asked the United States for a new examination of the question, and a moratorium while this examination was taking place.[15] The USA, however, had always explicitly refused to recognize any legal connection between the war debts and the reparations, and the negotiation was undertaken in difficult conditions. In the first place, France had little to offer in the domain of the compensations which were referred to vaguely on the part of the Americans: commercial concessions and disarmament.

The main preoccupation of French diplomacy at this time,

[14] See Chapter 4.

[15] DDF, 1st series, Vol. I, pp.683–5. Official memorandum from France to the United States, 10 November 1932.

however, seems to have been above all to maintain unity of action with Britain in this domain. In fact, if the USA emphatically asserted their right, they would not be opposed with the same intransigence of principle to the examination of each debtor's capacity of payment. In this respect France and Britain were not in the same situation. An acute financial crisis had obliged Britain to detach the pound sterling from gold, and a large currency transfer could still compromise its fragile position. As far as France was concerned, the payment of interallied debts which had fallen due would weigh upon her budget, which already showed a deficit. On the other hand, the franc was stable and the currency reserves were plentiful enough to meet the transfer: this, it was understood, was on condition that a financial panic would not involve a withdrawal of foreign capital invested in France; but the French government had scruples about calling this possibility to mind.

In the Franco-British talks on this subject which were held on 8 December 1932[16] in view of the American refusal, the British government, at first hesitant, chose payment; the main reason for this seems to be that British financiers finally feared the repercussions which a non-payment could have on British commercial credit. France, however, would then have a justification for denouncing the Lausanne Agreement and regarding the Young Plan as still in force. In order to avoid this possibility, which it dreaded, the British government threatened that if France did this, Britain would in her turn claim the payment of France's debt to her. Hence the solidarity which had apparently been established at Lausanne did not withstand the first difficulty.

Herriot, 'sickened'[17] by the attitude of the countries he had regarded as France's chief friends, nevertheless resigned himself to asking the French Chamber for the authorization to pay the sum due; this was refused by 402 votes to 196, which resulted in his resignation. When the next sum was due to be paid, France was imitated by the other debtor countries. This was, in practice, the end of the interallied debts.

The legitimacy of the attitude then adopted by France could hardly be disputed, from the French point of view. The general economic argument regarding the inopportuneness of large inter-

[16] Report in DDF, 1st series, Vol. II, pp.190–200.
[17] This word is used in the text of the report.

national financial transfers without commercial counterbalance at this time of crisis was also perfectly valid. It must also be recognized, however, that non-payment could not have happened at a worse time. First of all, the American political situation – the interregnum between the election and the entry of Franklin D. Roosevelt into office – made it impossible to undertake a negotiation in good time. Then the USA were approaching the most critical point of their financial crisis and could not fail to take very badly the refusal of France, whom they believed rich, to make a payment of which they were all but in need.

(b) *The London Conference*
The non-payment of 15 December 1932 produced a violent anti-French reaction in American public opinion.[18] On the diplomatic level, however, there was no open split. In his first interview with the French ambassador, President Roosevelt declared that he was ready to negotiate.[19] But this negotiation was never actually undertaken, since the Americans suggested that a payment, in some form or other, of the deferred due payment would be a necessary prelude to the opening of discussions; and the French government did not believe that they could bring their parliament to reverse their decision without giving them the assurance of a re-examination of the whole problem of debts.

This problem, moreover, appeared to have much better chances of solution within the far greater framework of reconstruction of the world economy. This task, to which the Lausanne Conference, occupied with immediate concerns, could not devote itself, was to be the subject of a new international conference which was intended to take place in London during 1933.

Without tackling the whole of the economic problems as they were presented at the London Conference,[20] we will limit ourselves to noting that the approach to this general discussion seemed to have infinite possibilities. In fact, France was basically in agreement with Britain over the question of interallied debts; moreover, she believed that she was in agreement with the USA in thinking that a general stabilization of currencies was an indispensable condition for resumption of business, and on this point the two countries came into conflict with Britain. This was a good

[18] DDF, 1st series, Vol. II, pp.317–18, 347–8.   [19] Ibid., pp. 414–17.
[20] See J. Néré, *La Crise de 1929*, Chapter 7.

opportunity for France – whose attitude in both cases was in accordance with that of the experts – to pursue a policy of conciliation between the USA and Britain, and by means of economic bias to achieve the political understanding among the three great liberal powers which was essential for world peace.[21]

These brilliant prospects faded rapidly. At the time of the Franco-British discussions of 17 March 1933,[22] the French minister asked his partners what measures should be taken in the event of depreciation of the dollar; he did not receive any definite reply.

However, matters were rapidly to take a completely new turn. Roosevelt, who preferred personal interviews to large spectacular conferences, wished to prepare for the future conference by separate talks, first of all with qualified representatives from France and Britain. He invited Edouard Herriot as the representative of France.[23] The position finally adopted by Herriot on the question of debts predisposed American opinion in his favour, and this would permit free speaking. The French government, of which Herriot was no longer a part, hastened to entrust him with a special mission to Roosevelt.[24]

Herriot was still on the vessel sailing towards the USA when the American authorities confronted him with the idea of a customs truce for the duration of the economic conference.[25] The French cabinet, faced with an emergency, was caught completely unawares. It declared that it was ready to accept a customs truce, but not without reservations.[26] However, its main concern was the possibility of depreciation of the dollar, which would overthrow all its ideas; the cabinet was (and would be for several years, whatever its political shade) in fact very much attached to the classical economic concept, according to which the crisis would end only with the return in confidence which was itself conditioned by the restoration of monetary stability. Then the USA, which had been regarded as a firm support in maintaining sound doctrine, seemed to be effecting a violent reversal.

This was not the end of France's surprises at a time when the USA, spurred on by the crisis in its acutest phase, was on the point

[21] DDF, 1st series, Vol. II, pp.665–9 (20 February 1933).
[22] DDF, 1st series, Vol. III, pp.1–4.   [23] Ibid., pp. 148–9 (5 April 1933).
[24] DDF, p.220 (13 April).   [25] Ibid., pp.244–5 (19–20 April).
[26] Ibid., pp.276–8, 288 (21 and 22 April).

of undertaking new experiments, without having any preliminary ideas clearly established.[27] On 24 April Herriot described his first impressions of America: the problem was first and foremost to obtain with France's support an increase in prices, perhaps after a preliminary stabilization of Anglo-American exchange,[28] by the formation of a common fund. Obviously Herriot and his experts were clinging to this hypothesis. However, the French government became alarmed in the face of American haste.

> It is extremely difficult to establish a customs truce in a system of almost general monetary instability. . . .

and laid down as the main condition:[29]

> actual stability of the main currencies which are at present devalued, in such a way that the present rates are maintained and in order to avoid economic disturbances which would oblige us to apply new exchange surcharges.

In fact, when the depreciation of the currency of one country brought about at least a temporary advantage, which could be considerable, for exports from that country, a practice had been established in the great monetary crisis of 1920–3, for the countries threatened to compensate this advantage by a temporary exchange surcharge; this had been applied in particular by Britain when dealing with Germany.

Meanwhile the Americans were becoming impatient and Herriot made it known:[30]

> We venture to insist on a reply concerning fundamental principles by tomorrow morning at the latest. . . . To be more precise, the plan for a common fund is approximately as follows. The fund would be made up by the three partners, for totals which will be determined, and the contributions will be made in their respective currencies. The purpose would be to maintain the stability of these currencies, for the franc, at its present value, for the pound and the dollar, at rates which will be determined. According to the trends, the fund would sell or buy the currency whose stability had been achieved.

This proposal was still not very precise, for in the minds of the Americans at this time it meant both lowering the dollar and raising the pound sterling,[31] and it was most unlikely that the

[27] See Néré, op. cit., Chapter 8.   [28] DDF, 1st series, Vol. III, pp.300–1.
[29] Ibid., pp.331–2 (27 April).   [30] Ibid., pp.332–3 (27 April).
[31] Ibid., p.328 (26 April).

British would agree to such an action. In any case, not only did the French government not hasten to reply as far as the common monetary fund was concerned, but it emphasized its reservations concerning the proposal of a customs truce in view of the devaluation of the dollar.[32] This earned the government very lively representations from its ambassador in London, de Fleuriau – a very rare occurrence in the annals of diplomacy:[33]

> To apply an exchange surcharge to imports from the United States in the present state of affairs, immediately after M Herriot's mission and a few weeks before the economic conference, would be an act whose consequences would be very dangerous for our country. . . . This would be like throwing out a challenge to the American government, whose attitude to us is certainly better than formerly, and to the world conference on which the solution of the war debts and the confirmation of the Lausanne Agreements depend.

In any case, American disappointment was very keen.[34] Had France let slip the opportunity for co-operation with the USA, which, starting from the monetary and economic fields, might not only have promoted an agreement on the question of debts, but perhaps have arrived finally at a political co-operation which would have been vital to France? Roosevelt, in any case, in his first contact with Herriot, had made approaches in this direction, especially with regard to disarmament:[35]

> The President, who is in favour of the British plan, admitted to us certain of its inadequacies; in particular he realizes that temporary control must be replaced by a permanent and mobile control.
> He declares that he is disposed to sign the disarmament convention, except for the section concerning security, for which he would not obtain the consent of the Senate. As far as security is concerned, however, he says that, within the limit of his own powers, he is ready to make a declaration according to which:
> (1) He would send an observer to the conference entrusted with the definition of the aggressor;
> (2) He would reserve the right to approve the decision relating to the aggressor;
> (3) In this case, he would renounce the rights of neutrality, that is, any protection of American citizens having dealings with the aggressor.

[32] Ibid., p.388 (1 May).
[33] Ibid., p.389 (2 May).
[34] Ibid., pp.465–6 (10 May).
[35] Ibid., p.314 (25 April).

Indeed, it was still a long way from the political guarantees which France needed, as we shall see. However, since it was a question of countries which, like Britain and the USA, were reluctant to bind themselves in advance by definite undertakings, the habit of co-operation and solidarity could finally prove decisive.

We are allowed to dream. However, the apprehension and the instinctive recoil of those responsible for French policy at a time when they were about to join themselves economically with a country in the throes of finding its way, can also be understood. This was not only the fear of the leap into the unknown. From that time onward it was obvious to discerning minds that the preoccupation of the Americans with raising world prices first of all would incite them not only to devalue the dollar, but to wish to devalue the franc and all the currencies still attached to the gold standard.[36] This would necessarily involve an increase in prices expressed in all the national currencies. Now the French had recently undergone a depreciation of the franc by four-fifths, and it was psychologically impossible for them to accept lightheartedly a new fall. Three years later they would be forced to it by necessity.

Be that as it may, after the failure of the preliminary meetings in Washington, the fate of the London Conference was sealed in advance. It foundered on the problem of the connection between a monetary and a customs truce, and ended with the formation of the 'gold block' which for several years was to widen the gulf between France and the Anglo-Saxon countries. We believe that there was above all a close link between the return of the USA to political isolationism, which was to assert itself more and more, especially from 1934 onwards, and the recognition of the need which Roosevelt had in mind for developing an actual national self-sufficiency which did not correspond with the original intentions of many Americans.[37] The very violence of the message which Roosevelt addressed to the London Conference, which in effect resulted in the breaking up of the latter, could only be explained by the disappointment of a great hope.[38] In any case,

[36] See in particular DDF, 1st series, Vol. III, p.472 (12 May 1933).
[37] See DDF, 1st series, Vol. IV, pp.287–90.
[38] See Néré, op. cit., pp.135–7, which we do not view in the same light today.

France's withdrawal before the prospects opened by the American proposals was explained by the fear of monetary risks and not by the defence of narrow commercial interests, for the exchange surcharge, which caused the split, was not in the end applied to American products.[39] However, there is obviously a difference between renouncing a right and temporarily abstaining from exercising it.

The balance-sheet of the effects of the economic crisis on France's foreign policy was thus heavily in the red: she would no longer receive any reparations, and the question of debts, as well as the disagreement in currency matters, from then onward separated her fundamentally from her essential allies, Britain and the USA. The stability of the new European states, which was another of the great aims of her diplomacy, was undermined more than ever from within as well as from without. Other repercussions were also to make themselves felt in the most unexpected quarters.

[39] DDF, 1st series, Vol. IV, pp.136–8, 182, and Document 22.

Chapter 9

The Disarmament Conference
and the Rearming of Germany

On 2 February 1932 the Disarmament Conference met in Geneva, under the presidency of the British delegate, Arthur Henderson. To a certain extent, this meeting was the more or less inevitable ending of a very long procedure. General disarmament had been stipulated theoretically by the Treaty of Versailles. A 'preparatory commission' had sat in Geneva from May 1926 to January 1931, and although it did not achieve very concrete results, it became morally difficult to put off the plenary conference indefinitely. This conference was far greater than the League of Nations itself, since it included the USA and USSR.

The Disarmament Conference acquired special importance from the international climate in which it opened. The year 1931 had been a troubled one, the euphoria surrounding the Briand-Stresemann dialogue was fading, and general disarmament appeared as a means of returning to that happy era.

The threats of political conflicts, as yet vague, impressed public opinion all the more, in that they were accompanied by an economic crisis which was becoming more and more serious. Everyone tended, in a more or less confused way, to establish a connection between the two phenomena. Above all it was believed at this time that political anxieties were largely responsible for the economic depression. Everyone relied upon disarmament to disperse all the clouds. It is interesting to note that this idea, which was raised in particular in politically advanced circles,was associated with the most traditional economic concepts. In fact, to see the economic crisis as a result of political unease is equivalent to saying that it was above all a 'crisis of confidence'; and that it was more important to reassure economic agents than to take positive measures implying an active intervention by the state in a domain which until then had been reserved for private initiative.

To be more precise, many classical economists paid most attention in the crisis to the fact that expenditure, especially public expenditure, exceeded receipts, and as a basic remedy they recommended deflation, that is, reduction of expenditure to the level of receipts. Now what more convenient method could be found to reduce public expenditure than that of disarmament?

The political aspect of the problem, however, must be examined more closely. The belief that it was the presence of powerful armaments which created the risk of political conflicts, rather than the opposite, was very widespread at the time in Britain and the USA, and also in part of the French Left, especially among the socialists who during this period were kept away from power by a rule which they had themselves established. On the contrary, those responsible for French policy who knew that France, perhaps the most completely armed country of continental Europe, was also a profoundly peaceful country, considered that this was mistaking the effect for the cause. According to them, if security and political stability were finally established, disarmament would follow quite naturally. On the other hand, to disarm France before these conditions were achieved would be to aggravate the dangers instead of reducing them. The French leaders then found themselves in the grip of an insoluble dilemma: to maintain the legal margin of superiority of French armaments – which as we have seen, was necessary to compensate for the superiority of the German potential – was to risk alienating her more and more from the support of the Anglo-Saxons who were equally indispensable, in the long run, to French security.

At this very time, the German threat was growing greater. We now have a tendency to consider that the accession of Hitler in Germany, on 30 January 1933, marked the beginning of a new era, the beginning of the road to war. Perhaps we are right, but at the time it was not so regarded. Many people, especially in Britain, believed for a long time that an understanding with Hitler was perfectly possible. Conversely, in the most threatened countries such as France and Poland, it was considered that the threat of German nationalism had assumed a particularly virulent form even before the advent of Hitler, from 1931 or 1932. G. Castellan in his thesis, *Le Réarmement clandestin de l'Allemagne*, dates the official German rearmament on a large scale from the 'Plan for Reorganization of the Army' officially announced on 26 July 1932

by von Schleicher, the Minister of the *Reichswehr*.[1] The work of
the Disarmament Conference was often to give the impression of
being subjected to a race: the problem was to achieve a disarmament agreement soon enough to prevent, or at least to limit,
German rearmament.

We have available a devastating documentation of the Disarmament Conference describing very involved discussions in
which questions of procedure prevailed over the fundamental
questions. We would need to devote a whole book to the study of
this event in its entirety. We will limit ourselves here to recording
the main stages, concerning both the development of French
attitudes and the course of German action.

The Tardieu Plan and Germany's First Sortie

As soon as it had met, the Disarmament Conference was presented
with the detailed plan of the French minister André Tardieu, who
took up the ideas already maintained by France at the time of the
development of the League of Nations Pact.[2] Starting from the
principle that actual disarmament at a given instant does not
prevent rapid rearmament of nations who have sufficient potential
at their disposal, and that effective repression of aggression was the
very condition of security and therefore of peace, Tardieu proposed basically the formation of an international force, under the
aegis of the League of Nations, to which all the states would submit their offensive weapons. Of course, putting this force into
operation required a definition of the aggressor and of aggression,
relying notably on compulsory arbitration. It was necessary to
revive the Geneva Protocol.

This plan naturally encountered opposition from the states
which were not members of the League of Nations, like the USA
and the USSR, since it was based on the conferring of decisive
powers to the League of Nations. However, it also presupposed
such a change of accepted ideas on the sovereignty of states and
their relationship with their armed forces that even those who
theoretically proclaimed their support of the concept of collective
security recoiled from it.

[1] G. Castellan, *Le Réarmement clandestin de l' Allemagne, 1930–1935,* especially
p.77.
[2] See W. E. Scott, *Alliance against Hitler*, p.39, and R. Binion, *Defeated
Leaders*, pp.312–13, on the Tardieu plan. Cf. our Chapter 2.

On 22 June President Hoover of the USA replied with a proposal, whose execution was much easier to imagine, but which went nowhere near the root of the problem: it was the elimination of certain weapons, and the reduction of others by a third or a quarter. Even this apparently simple proposal raised considerable problems regarding its execution.[3]

The extent of the disagreement thus revealed between the peaceful powers was obviously a high trump-card for the nationalist leaders of Germany. They could thus make use of a weapon which proved very effective: they left the conference. In order to save it, and to achieve at no matter what cost a disarmament agreement regarded as an end in itself – an agreement which would obviously be of little value if Germany were not a signatory – many countries, especially Britain and the USA, put pressure on France to induce her to make concessions. In these circumstances, Germany's breaking-off gesture, which was made on 16 September 1932, had one precise object: to obtain the proclamation that it might profit from equality of rights over the question of armaments, before any negotiation was made. The dilemma was thus clearly stated: either general disarmament, or rearmament of Germany. In France it was already widely thought that Germany would prefer the second condition.[4] However, the pressure on France in favour of disarmament was reinforced with a new argument, more definite and less disputable than the others, which influenced in particular, besides Italy, the eastern allies of France: it was necessary to disarm, above all to prevent Germany from rearming.

Since they could not thus withdraw into an attitude of intransigence, those responsible for French policy again had to show great imaginative powers.

The Herriot-Paul-Boncour 'Constructive Plan'

Our documents enable us from now on to follow closely the origin of the new French plan. The dominating idea of the government was to prevent large-scale rearmament of Germany, of which there were ever-increasing premonitory symptoms. To achieve this, however, it was necessary to obtain the support of

[3] DDF, 1st series, Vol. I, pp.66–8, 153–7. See Document 24.
[4] See for example DDF, 1st series, Vol. I, pp.439–43.

Britain and the USA and the approval of international opinion.[5] Hence the necessity to impress them with daring proposals calculated to dispel the impression that France always acted as a brake.

The French proposal was complex.[6] It offered the conference the choice between two solutions: the 'maximum plan' and the 'minimum plan'.

The 'maximum plan' consisted of 'replacing permanent national forces with organically international forces', each state keeping only a militia at its disposal. In the opinion of its authors this plan offered several advantages: since the international force became the basic one, it enabled Germany to be given an equal right to national forces, that is, the militia. Moreover, since the plan for German rearmament seemed to be 'to incorporate the advantages of a professional army prepared for a rapid offensive with those of a conscripted army of the militia type who would supply a large number of trained reserves', the problem was to remove from Germany this professional army prepared for an offensive, since in any case it would have at its disposal a militia in the form of paramilitary associations. It was, moreover, possible to see in this militia formula a reflection of French pacifist tendencies which went back to the 'New Army' of Jean Jaurès: the idea that short-term militia, whose members remained citizens rather than soldiers, were suitable only for defensive operations and consequently would make their state unsuitable for a war of aggression.

If the other countries rejected the maximum plan, France would then be in a good diplomatic position to fall back upon the 'minimum plan', which would revive that of Tardieu: the permanent national forces would be maintained, but part of them would be kept constantly available so that they would be immediately at the disposal of the League of Nations Council, with a view to preventing or suppressing an act of aggression; heavy bomber aircraft would be at the disposal of the League of Nations and civil aviation – which could easily be transformed into bomber aviation – would be made international.

The maximum plan came up against very strong objections from responsible military men, especially General Weygand. He was particularly hostile to the militia system which, he said,

[5] Ibid., pp.476–91 (18 October 1932).
[6] The fullest statement of this proposal appears in a report from the War Ministry of 14 October 1932, DDF, 1st series, Vol. I, pp.439–43.

would end by leaving the Maginot Line undefended and vulnerable to a sudden attack.[7] However, as the responsible politicians pointed out to him, this plan was not limited to its military aspect: since it included considerable actual disarmament on the part of France, it put her in the position of exacting, in return, new guarantees of security. These, which had been worked out in detail by the French service of the League of Nations, were themselves complex, in order to take into account the positions of the main interested states.[8]

> Past experience – especially the failure of the 1924 protocol – proves that in the organization of peace, that is, the enforcement of security on the political and juridical level, it is impossible to make significant progress as long as we try to achieve solutions of a universal order. Any attempt of this kind, in fact, encounters a double obstacle: on the one hand the great aversion of the American government to making long-term undertakings which would automatically involve her in complications in Europe, and on the other hand the necessity for the British government not to offer any guarantees whose fulfilment would run the risk of her coming into conflict with the United States.

Hence two pacts were provided: basically, there was a general one known as a 'consultative pact', of which the USA would form a part and which, therefore, nothing would prevent the British Empire from signing. The general agreement to limit armaments would be associated with the consultative pact. Superimposed on this pact there would correspond, on the disarmament level, a regional European disarmament convention which would contain more definite guarantees. The general consultative pact would obviously be based upon the clauses of the Briand-Kellogg Pact, and would include an obligation to hold joint consultations should an occurrence arise which would disturb the peace, to prohibit the export of weapons to the country which had violated the pact; if necessary, to prohibit all commercial and financial relations with that country; and finally, to refuse to recognize any situation resulting from the violation of international agreements. The European regional agreement would 'establish the right to assistance in a case in which a European territory within the jurisdiction of one of the signatory powers were attacked by

[7] DDF, 1st series, Vol. I, pp.476–91, 543–53, 614–30.
[8] Ibid., pp.499–503 (19 October 1932).

foreign forces or invaded by them'. The granting of the assistance would be decided by the Council of the League of Nations, by simple verification of the fact of the attack or invasion; accordingly the League of Nations Council would appoint a verification commission in each country. It was not reckoned that Britain would take part in this regional agreement, any more than she would be required to give up her regular army to adopt the militia system.

When once the French proposals had been officially presented,[9] they immediately came up against a preliminary difficulty: of necessity they would require long discussions and, as the American delegate for example pointed out, it was important in the first place to bring Germany quickly back into the conference.[10] There was a grave risk of Germany's trying to isolate the principle of equal rights from the French plan as a whole, thus eliminating the essential counterbalancing clauses.[11] In one of the Franco-British discussions in which Herriot recognized the great political benefit of the Lausanne Conference, although they revealed above all the opposition of their points of view, Ramsay MacDonald insisted that it was necessary to come to an agreement on the conditions by which equality of rights could be recognized. To this Herriot replied that in order to discuss equality of rights, it was necessary to know what Germany understood by this.[12] He became involved by the same token in unofficial talks not only with Britain and the USA but with Germany and also Italy – talks in which France, deprived of the support of her allies on the Continent,[13] was always at a disadvantage. MacDonald, who was anxious to speed up matters, declared that nothing would be achieved if a comprehensive discussion of equality of rights was contemplated first; to this Paul-Boncour replied that Germany wished to take as a point of departure what could only be a point of arrival. Finally, agreement was reached on the following formula:[14]

(1) The governments of the United Kingdom, France and Italy have declared that one of the principles which must serve as a guide to the

[9] The complete text, which is too long to be reproduced in our Documents, appears in DDF, 1st series, Vol. I, pp.710–18 (14 November 1932).

[10] Ibid., Vol. II, pp.6–9, 27–8.   [11] Ibid., pp.116–20.

[12] Ibid., pp.120–6 (3 December 1932).

[13] Reports of these conversations, especially DDF, 1st series, Vol. II, pp.148–56, 160–72, 216–25.   [14] Ibid., p.240 (11 December 1932).

Disarmament Conference must be to grant to Germany, as well as to the other powers disarmed by the Treaty, equality of rights in a system which would comprise security for all nations, and that this principle must be expressed in the agreement which will contain the conclusions of the disarmament conference.

This declaration implies that the reciprocal limitations of armaments of all countries must be written into the proposed disarmament agreement. It is clearly understood that the terms and conditions of application of such an equality of rights remain to be discussed at the conference.

(2) On the basis of this declaration, Germany has declared that it is prepared to resume its place at the Disarmament Conference.

Disintegration of the French 'Constructive Plan'

When Germany had resumed its place at the Conference, discussion of the French plan could begin. This proved disappointing. Misunderstandings accumulated, especially on the subject of security guarantees, the essential counterbalance to the French concessions on the question of armaments. Germany, with the support of Italy, was opposed to the very principle. Moreover, to make this opposition more effective and more threatening it let it be understood that, if the question of security were insisted on, it for its part would openly put the question of revision of the peace treaties, seeing that security guarantees would be acceptable only if they applied to a European statute accepted by all interested parties.[15] This threat was sufficient to prevent Poland, for example, from supporting the French plan without reservations.

However, it was above all Britain's attitude which paralysed any effort to build up security. France had been careful to limit requests with regard to Britain and did not require her to adhere to the European pact but only not to prevent its functioning, and for this reason to accept a precise definition of the obligations arising from clause 16 of the League of Nations Pact. Even this was refused. The attitude of Britain resulted in – or served as a justification for – the abstention of the Scandinavian countries and the Netherlands, and the hesitation of Belgium.[16] How could one continue to speak of collective security under these conditions?

Germany, on the other hand, also refused to accept the transformation of the national armies into militia, thus indicating its

[15] Ibid., pp.336–8 (29 December 1932).   [16] Ibid., pp.37–8, 635–7.

wish to keep the regular army granted by the Treaty of Versailles while developing paramilitary associations in addition. This refusal, moreover, was to give it a considerable tactical advantage on the diplomatic level.

For the time being the refusals of Germany and Italy were obstructing the conference, and this prompted Britain to ask France for further concessions. As Paul-Boncour, who was nevertheless a convinced champion of international institutions, observed with bitterness:[17]

> If a country has only to obstruct treaties and blackmail other powers, so that from fear of what this country will do another which keeps its promises is asked to make sacrifices, an intolerable situation will be created.

This, however, is what MacDonald was going to do with his plan of 16 March 1933. For the first time he presented exact figures: 200,000 men for each of the French, German, Italian and Polish armies. There was no longer any question of security guarantees, but the MacDonald Plan took up certain parts of the French plan which had won wide approval in the general discussion:[18] the obligation to take into account premilitary or paramilitary training, when calculating manpower; the need to subordinate total abolition of military aviation to the establishment of an effective inspection system; and finally, standardization of the types of continental European army. Thus that point of the French plan which seemed the most dangerous and which had been most criticized by those responsible for French security, was to be presented as a major concession to France, in exchange for which new counter-claims were going to be made.

The MacDonald Plan was adopted as a basis for discussion, as it seemed to be the only way of saving the conference. It received in particular the approval of the American delegation, but the latter made an important step in France's direction by advocating reinforcement of the disarmament inspection clauses, while the very idea of inspection was repugnant to British opinion.[19] This was the fleeting moment when Roosevelt, who was preparing for the international economic conference in London, contemplated

[17] Ibid., pp.804–8 (13 March 1933).
[18] See a very optimistic summary of this discussion as a whole, DDF, 1st series, Vol. III, pp.238–42.　　　[19] Ibid., pp.393–400.

Anglo-Franco-American co-operation in the main international fields.[20] However, with the failure of Roosevelt's proposals, this American advance soon lost all its impetus. The basic question was to know what would be done if the inspection revealed any failure to observe the disarmament agreement; if Germany rearmed, for example. In this case Britain and the USA agreed only to consultations with the other signatories of the convention; they did not agree that France could consider herself as immediately freed from her disarmament obligations. The USA also refused to determine in advance the attitude they would adopt should such failure be ascertained.[21] Under these conditions inspection, even strict inspection – and doubts could be entertained on this point, from the example of the Nollet mission[22] – could in no way constitute a security guarantee which would be a substitute for the proposed mutual assistance. Nothing of the French plan remained.

The French Plan of the Two Periods and the Resignation of Germany from the League of Nations

The French government then had recourse to a new plan which was proposed in June 1933.[23] This plan officially recorded the great retreat of France, who no longer made the accomplishment of concrete disarmament measures dependent on the establishment of a security system. It was true that the new plan insisted on inspection measures and stipulated 'arrangements whose aim was to draw inferences from any violation of guarantees offered'. But what arrangements did France have in mind? According to Daladier, the Minister of War, these were of several kinds: first, in the case of violation of the agreement, the other signatories could resume their freedom of action and rearm. However, this would be insufficient, for the time lost would be difficult to regain; and so it would be necessary to contemplate breaking off all economic and diplomatic relations with the aggressor state.[24] Thus one would be within the scope of sanctions according to

[20] See Chapter 8.
[21] DDF, 1st series, Vol. III, pp.676–91 (18 June).
[22] See Chapter 3.
[23] DDF, 1st series, Vol. III, pp.897–9; see also Document 24.
[24] DDF, 1st series, Vol. IV, pp.457–65.

article 16 of the Treaty of Versailles which were far less effective than mutual assistance; but it had proved impossible to organize this assistance in Europe without the effective co-operation of Britain.

However, the great innovation of the proposal was the establishment of a four-year trial period, during which the states whom the peace treaties left in free possession of their armaments would accept limitations of these, without yet being restricted to actual disarmament. The idea of this trial period had developed during the conference discussions: everyone accepted that disarmament could be carried out only in stages. Besides, some time was needed, both to install the inspection organizations and to transform regular armies such as the *Reichswehr* into short-service armies. Nevertheless, urged by Britain and the USA to specify what disarmament measures she would accept at the end of the trial period, France risked finding herself at that time in a particularly dangerous situation. Was the French government then reduced to a Micawberish policy, hoping that something would turn up to get her out of her difficulties?

The documents give us, however, some indication of the thoughts of the French leaders. In the first place, information about German rearmament was increasing, and France repeatedly drew the attention of her partners, especially Britain, to this fact.[25] She hoped perhaps that in a few years the world would have become more clearly aware of the danger of Hitler, and that this would change the general conditions of international politics.

To be more precise, France could set her hopes on the diplomatic manœuvres which she was carrying on parallel with the Disarmament Conference and which were beginning to bear fruit. Hence the USSR proposed a text which was largely in accordance with French views for the definition of aggression.[26] Such a definition was necessary as a preliminary to sanctions or mutual assistance. Thus Italy, too, who at the beginning of the conference was still taking Germany's part, now undertook to conciliate between the German and French views.[27] France, who could not confront Germany with her own forces alone, had to

[25] Ibid., especially pp.14–19, 118–28, 150–1, 295–8, 350–3, 373–6, 711–12.
[26] See Chapter 16.
[27] See DDF, 1st series, Vol. IV, especially pp.196–7, 270–1, 302–8, 359–62, 412–15, 417–20, 435–8. Cf. our Chapter 10.

do or accept many things in order to be sure of the maximum possible support.

In fact, in that autumn of 1933, her position again seemed favourable. She obtained the agreement of Britain, the USA and Italy to the principle of the trial period. As far as inspection was concerned, the USA were in favour and Italy too; and Britain had not formally opposed it. Finally, France, Britain and the USA seemed to be in agreement over avoiding any rearmament of Germany (at least beyond that contained in the MacDonald Plan).

It was because of this very opposition to rearmament that Hitler left the Disarmament Conference on 14 October 1933 and immediately afterwards withdrew Germany from the League of Nations. In this way he began his series of outbursts of temper which proved so profitable; it must be pointed out, however, that in this matter his nationalist predecessors had already shown him the way in 1932.

Now that Germany had left, what was to become of the Disarmament Conference? It finally decided to continue its work, even avoiding long adjournment, partly at the insistence of France. What were her reasons for this? The first problem was not to give Germany an excuse for rearming openly, by alleging that the other powers had failed in their moral obligation to disarm:[28] it was also a question of avoiding becoming involved in discussion about disarmament in new talks between five countries, which was always to France's disadvantage;[29] finally, France now hoped to maintain the diplomatic and moral unity which she had managed to achieve around her.[30] These hopes were dashed for the most part, however: the Conference sat until April 1935, but there is nothing to be gained from following its work further.

The Note of 17 April 1934

Even before Germany had dramatically left the Disarmament Conference and the League of Nations, it had several times made approaches with a view to direct Franco-German talks. The spirit of such talks could be glimpsed from the confidential remarks of the German minister Funk to the French ambassador's deputy:[31] Germany was absolutely determined to rearm, for the acknow-

---

[28] DDF, 1st series, Vol. IV, pp.468–70.   [29] Ibid., pp.522–6.
[30] Ibid., pp.655–8.   [31] Ibid., pp.557–60.

ledged reason that military training was necessary for the education of young people and for the whole of the German people;
since it assumed that France for her part had no wish to disarm,
there was in its opinion, in the principle of equal rights, some
common ground between the two countries. It declared that it
was ready to offer France, without any further definition, political
guarantees which obviously did not guarantee anything.

However, France for a time allowed herself to become involved
in bilateral discussions at which Germany put forward its new
demands:[32] an army of up to 300,000 men, with the same weapons
as the other nations, especially the allocation of fighter aircraft, for
these could not be obtained by simple conversion of civil aircraft.
The French army in its turn would be reduced to 300,000 men all
inclusive: until then it had been accepted that equality applied
only to the home army, the French colonial troops being in
addition to these.

On 17 April 1934 the French government cut short any new
concession by a note declaring that it 'solemnly refused to legalize
German rearmament, that this made negotiations useless and that
France would from then on guarantee her security by her own
methods'.

This note has been hotly debated. According to André
François-Poncet, who was then the French ambassador to Berlin,
the French cabinet was itself divided with regard to it, and the
Minister of Foreign Affairs, Louis Barthou, was in favour of
carrying on negotiations.[33] Without questioning the statement
of François-Poncet, the origin and the reasons for this refusal can
be understood. France, as we have seen, had been gradually led
to make very important concessions for the very purpose of preventing the German rearmament which she was now asked to
accept officially and hence, in a way, to legalize. Why should she
have agreed to bilateral agreements, when all her efforts had
always been devoted to making problems international in order
not to remain face to face with her too powerful neighbour?
Could it really be hoped that German rearmament could be
controlled and limited by a new treaty? Such a hope seemed
somewhat naïve at this juncture. A hardening of the French

[32] On this point we follow the account of J. B. Duroselle, *Histoire diplomatique de 1919 à nos jours*, pp.175–8.

[33] See A. François-Poncet, *Souvenirs d'une ambassade à Berlin*, pp.175–9.

attitude had been perceptible since the autumn of 1932, in ministers of the Left such as Daladier and Paul-Boncour, well before the reversal of the majority following the events of February 1934.[34] That is to say, to those responsible for French policy this hardening seemed to be a necessity. Doubtless it was not always understood by Anglo-Saxon opinion. However, by trying to conciliate the latter by constant concessions, she had strengthened their impression that the danger so often invoked by the French was in fact largely imaginary. This illusion was one of the main causes of the final catastrophe.

German Rearmament and French Disarmament

Because the Disarmament Conference did not result in the signing of an agreement, after three years of debates and many negotiations behind the scenes, it must not be concluded that it had no practical results. On the contrary, it had some very important consequences.

Firstly, and paradoxically, it enabled German rearmament to be effected without opposition or emphatic reactions on the part of the other signatories of the Treaty of Versailles. This rearmament was achieved, partly in secret and partly openly, and therefore in stages; however, every time France considered taking action, objections were made that by doing this she would risk destroying the Disarmament Conference, and that the problem was no longer one of seeing that the Treaty of Versailles, already rendered out of date by the very fact of the conference's having been called, was respected, but one of signing the future agreement.

At the same time, however, France actually disarmed. This was partly the result of the budgetary deflation policy by which all French governments between 1932 and 1936 strove in vain to solve the economic crisis. Diplomatic considerations, too, worked in the same direction: it was necessary to gain support at the Conference by making goodwill pledges; and then, what was the use of building the modern equipment which technicians declared indispensable if it must soon be destroyed in the carrying out of the future agreement? The French plan of July 1932 expressly stipulated the stoppage of certain manufactures from the beginning of the trial period. The French General Staff protested

[34] See J. Néré, *La Troisième République, 1914–1940*, pp.141–4.

more shrilly.[35] The time had come to ask the most serious question: had the government, which defined the missions of the army, given sufficient thought to putting it into a condition in which it could carry them out?[36]

[35] See for example DDF, 1st series, Vol. II, pp.20–1, 266–8, 597–600.
[36] Ibid., pp.457–9; see also Document 26.

Chapter 10

The Franco-Italian *Rapprochement* and the Attempt to Consolidate Central Europe

The Franco-Italian Affair

Every stage of the Disarmament Conference was marked by a weakening of France's position in Europe; and the rise of Hitler in Germany only increased France's anxieties. Accordingly, successive French governments tried to restore the situation and to set up new diplomatic alliances. The first idea to present itself was that of achieving an understanding with Italy.

Since the unification of Italy, which was due to a great extent to France's support, Franco-Italian relations had known more moments of tension than phases of friendliness. An attempt to explain why this was so would involve us in an analysis of the psychology of peoples which would be for the most part outside the scope of this work. Nevertheless, during the First World War the two nations had fought side by side. Italy, however, had been deeply disappointed in the peace treaties which had not given her the advantages she had expected: the promises which Britain and France had made during the war, especially on the subject of the Dalmatian coast, had not been recognized by President Wilson and consequently they had not been honoured. Curiously, though, it was not against the USA or Britain but against France, that Italy harboured resentment.

It should not be forgotten that there was also a certain number of private disagreements between Italy and France which were always liable to become acrimonious.

The first of these concerned the respective navies of France and Italy. Italy demanded naval equality, chiefly for prestige reasons, but also because her geographical configuration made her very vulnerable to an attack from the sea. The Washington Conference of 1922 had sanctioned this equality for battleships. France, however, did not accept it for light craft: cruisers, torpedo boats and submarines. She herself in fact had to divide her fleet between the Mediterranean and the oceans, and guarantee lines of communication between the various parts of her empire; this was vital because in the event of a European war she would have to bring back to metropolitan France important contingents of troops stationed in the colonies. Italy did not have such responsibilities.

To this naval rivalry were added the African rivalries. Italy disputed the preponderant part played by France in the international port of Tangier. On the other hand, Tunisia, which was a French protectorate, included a large colony of Italian immigrants, on whom the agreements of 1896 had conferred notable privileges (retention of their nationality, Italian schools) which tended to make them a 'state within a state'. In October 1918 France had not renewed these agreements, which had expired, and the problem remained in abeyance.

Tunisia, like the French Sahara, bordered on Tripolitania which was an Italian possession. France and Britain had promised that if they received the former German colonies they would give considerable colonial compensations to Italy. This promise had hardly been carried out. Italy, under the pretext of enlarging Tripolitania, cherished ambitions as vast as they were vague in the direction of Lake Chad; the realization of these ambitions would have cut the French empire of Africa in two.[1]

In Africa, however, Italy had set her sights on Ethiopia; a first attempt to take possession of that country had resulted in the Adowa disaster in 1896. But Italy had kept the coastal possessions of Eritrea and Italian Somaliland which were of no interest except as a point of departure towards the Ethiopian hinterland. France, for her part, had important economic interests in Ethiopia, and its port of Djibouti, which was the starting-point of the French railway to Addis Ababa, was Ethiopia's only outlet to the sea. In 1906 an Anglo-Franco-Italian agreement had considered a future division of the country into areas of influence. However, after 1919 France had made herself the protector of Ethiopia, which she had caused to be admitted to the League of Nations in 1923, and she had not taken part in a new Anglo-Italian agreement of sharing the zones of influence in 1925.[2]

[1] *Documents Diplomatiques Français* (DDF), 1st series, Vol. II, pp.609–14.
[2] Ibid., pp.404–6.

The Franco-Italian Rapprochement

Since 1928 Franco-Italian discussions had taken place which were to solve these various disputes; an idea appeared at the beginning of 1932 to exchange Italian non-involvement in North Africa for French non-involvement in Ethiopia.[3] The French Ministry of Foreign Affairs contemplated this suggestion without enthusiasm:[4] the policy of division into areas of influence did not seem to it to be in accordance with the principles of the League of Nations.

However, this dispute as a whole acquired special importance owing to the Franco-Italian rivalry in Central Europe.

Central and Eastern Europe at the Beginning of 1933

In studying the Stresa economic conference,[5] we have already seen how deeply agricultural Europe was affected by the crisis. However, the few industrial countries of Danubian Europe had hardly fared better. In March 1933 Czechoslovakia recorded the enormous figure of 878,000 unemployed out of 13 million inhabitants. As for Austria, from the economic point of view, she had the appearance of a chronic invalid. This state of affairs made the already fragile and unsure unit even more vulnerable and caused considerable complications in an already difficult political situation.

Even between France and Poland, although they were united by an acute awareness of their common danger, the alliance was difficult in practice. Understanding and confidence never prevailed uninterruptedly between the French and Piłsudski who had been in fact the leader of the Polish state since 1926. The Poles, who had always had a keen pride, did not readily tolerate the presence of the French military mission which had nevertheless been sent to help them to form their army, and in August 1932 they got rid of it.[6] At the same time, the policy of Briand and the Locarno Agreements created in them a real desertion-complex, and Piłsudski declared outright to the French military attaché: 'We must beware. France is going to abandon us, France is about to betray us. This is what people are thinking and I have to tell you about it.'[7]

In addition to this there were other reasons for anger. After

[3] Ibid., pp.391–5.   [4] Ibid., pp.389ff.   [5] See Chapter 8, pp.107ff.
[6] DDF, 1st series, Vol. I, p.145.   [7] Ibid., pp.590–4.

1919 many Poles came to work in France, especially in the coal basin of the north, but far from being absorbed into the population they formed a separate group, as they had formerly done in Germany, with their schools, their churches and their societies. This offended people in France, a country which extends a welcome to newcomers in proportion to the rate at which they become assimilated. Moreover, Poland had appealed to French capital to a great extent, in order to develop her industries. There resulted what was from then onward to be a classic situation: in the eyes of the Poles, France never sent enough money, but at the same time her capital 'colonized' Poland, exacting exorbitant privileges.[8] The French who had dealings with Poland were often disconcerted by her sensitive nationalism and her over-imaginative liveliness. These feelings often showed through, as for example in the memoirs of the French ambassador to Warsaw, Jules Laroche.[9]

In contrast to this, the French felt much more at home with the reasonable attitude of the Czechs, especially with the apparent pliability and skilfulness of Eduard Beneš who conducted their foreign policy. Since 1930 the Little *Entente* seemed to be acquiring a permanent organization which could only strengthen its stability.[10] The faults in the system were nevertheless numerous. From July 1932 the awakening of a Slovakian independence movement, under the influence of the economic crisis, was apparent.[11] As far as Yugoslavia was concerned, the bitterness of the antagonism between Serbs and Croats had got the upper hand of her parliamentary institutions.

The external threats which weighed upon the stability of the system were even more formidable. Some of these were traditional, one would be tempted to say unalterable. They were in the first place the Hungarian territorial claims which were all the more dangerous in that they were ill-defined and, as it were, unlimited, whether it was merely the recovery of a stretch of Rumanian territory, or the annexation of Slovakia or Croatia, or even a return to the 'Great Hungary' of 1914.[12] The Little *Entente*, however, in spite of the time that had elapsed, still continued to fear the restoration of the Habsburgs above all else; on this point,

[8] Ibid., pp.668–9.   [9] J. Laroche, *La Pologne de Piłsudski (1926–1935)*.
[10] DDF, 1st series, Vol. II, pp.679–82.   [11] Ibid., Vol. I, pp.138–9.
[12] Ibid., Vol. II, pp.89–91.

too, the diplomatic alliances discussed were quite different.[13] But the serious problem was that while some people – in Hungary, and perhaps also in Italy and even in France – saw the restoration of the Habsburgs as an effective means of preventing the *Anschluss*, in the countries of the Little *Entente*, especially Czechoslovakia curiously enough, the cry went up: 'Better the *Anschluss* than the restoration of the Habsburgs'.[14]

Now the most immediate threat hung over Austria. In 1931 the attempt at an Austro-German customs union had set in motion a major diplomatic crisis. From the advent of Hitler in Germany in January 1933 the danger assumed other more insidious forms, owing to the existence in Austria of a Hitlerite party of growing importance: Austrian Nazis who had taken refuge in Bavaria could always attempt a show of force across the frontier; above all, however, if the Nazis who remained in Austria seized power in one way or another, how could the other powers act against this disguised annexation without exposing themselves to the charge that they had been interfering in Austrian internal policy?

One sign of the anxiety caused at this time by this region was the importance which diplomacy, especially that of France, attached to an incident which would appear minor in other circumstances.[15] A consignment of light weapons of Italian origin was discovered in the Austrian factory of Hirtenberg, a contravention of the peace treaties: Austria's official explanation was that these were weapons sent for repair. Many suspicions were voiced, especially that the arms were in fact on their way to Hungary where they were intended for groups of Croatian émigrés who wished to attempt a coup against Yugoslavia. However this may be, France used very forcible means of putting on pressure to have the arms returned to Italy, to the extent of calling in question the launching of an external Austrian loan. The incident illustrates particularly the secret plan, attributed to Italy, of forming under her aegis an Austria-Hungary-Croatia unit – perhaps under Habsburg rule – and of guaranteeing thus her supremacy in the Danube basin, at the same time breaking up Yugoslavia, her Adriatic rival.

---

[13] Ibid., pp.505–11.   [14] Ibid., pp.443–5.

[15] Very copious documentation in DDF, 1st series, Vol. II. See in particular pp.531–2.

The Franco-Italian Rapprochement

The de Jouvenel Mission and the Four-Power Pact

The threat which Italy could thus present to the equilibrium and stability of Central Europe, as well as her tendency to take sides with Germany at the Disarmament Conference, made it particularly important for France to try to gain the goodwill of this possible enemy, who was at the same time one of the guarantors of the Locarno Treaty. Britain, moreover, urged the French leaders towards this attempt at an understanding. The nature of the Fascist regime did not at that time appear a sufficient obstacle. As a matter of fact it was a minister of the Left, Joseph Paul-Boncour, who decided to make the decisive gesture by sending on a mission to Rome, not a professional diplomat, but a politician who likewise belonged to the Left, Henri de Jouvenel.[16]

However, the general instructions given to de Jouvenel[17] showed how difficult his task would be. His mission must have great aims: he was to avoid 'reducing the negotiation as a whole into concessions with regard to details'; he was not to try to 'improve relations between France and Italy for several months, but on the contrary to establish during these months[18] the principles of a lasting agreement which would unite the interests of the two countries for a long time'. But at the same time it was France who seemed to be making the demands on practically all points: she wished to regain complete freedom of action in Tunisia with regard to the Italian nationals; at the same time she could not give very clear indications regarding territorial concessions in Africa, nor could she satisfy Italian ambitions in Syria and the Lebanon since she was guiding these two countries towards independence; she also hoped to eliminate Italian claims with regard to Yugoslavia. In exchange, she hardly considered anything but offering associations of interests, with Italy providing the manpower and France providing the capital. However, the French government was counting above all on the similarity of views which must prevail between France and Italy on the subject of interallied debts and international financial policy (since the two countries were attached to the gold standard). And it was

[16] For de Jouvenel's mission, see R. Binion, *Defeated Leaders*, pp.178–85.

[17] DDF, 1st series, Vol. II, pp.609–14 (10 February 1933).

[18] Since de Jouvenel was a member of Parliament he could be given only a temporary mission lasting six months.

very much in the interest of both Italy and France to maintain the independence of Austria from Germany. On the one hand Italy enclosed within her frontiers of 1919 a German-speaking minority in South Tyrol, or Alto Adige, and it was to be feared that this minority would succumb to the attraction of a 'Greater Germany'. Above all, the attachment of Austria to Germany would have restrained Italy from having any ambition to dominate in the Danube basin. Here, apparently, was the true basis for a possible agreement.

In the first detailed discussion between de Jouvenel and Mussolini,[19] the head of the Italian government declared that as far as he was concerned, the fundamental problem was that of the organization of Europe. Alluding only in vague terms to the revision of the Hungarian frontiers, Mussolini put forward a precise proposal on the other hand with regard to the 'Polish Corridor': this was to give Germany a strip of territory ten to twenty kilometres wide along the Baltic to connect it with East Prussia. In comments addressed to Paul-Boncour,[20] de Jouvenel defined a policy which was to gain more and more adherents: France should not persist in an intransigent attitude which no longer corresponded to the actual strength of France, but on the contrary, by making what could be called 'cold' limited concessions at times, she would avoid having more serious ones forced upon her under the pressure of an immediate danger. To this Paul-Boncour immediately replied by reasserting France's desire to preserve the territorial integrity of her allies.[21] The two trends which first appeared at this point continued to diverge until 1939.

On 18 March Mussolini presented de Jouvenel in good and due form with a proposal for 'agreement and co-operation among the four Western powers'.[22] From the first, this text appeared singularly dangerous; it stressed the revision of the treaties and the equality of Germany's rights with regard to armaments, and it made it clear that the intention was to institute a directorate of four powers (Britain, France, Italy and Germany) who would impose their will on the other European states in case of need. This then was the dominating ambition of Mussolini who saw it

[19] DDF, 1st series, Vol. II, pp.729–32 (3 March 1933).
[20] Ibid., pp.757–61 (8 March 1933).
[21] Ibid., pp.775–6 (10 March 1933).
[22] DDF, 1st series, Vol. III, pp.15–16.

as a supreme ratification of his prestige. However, a system of this kind would be particularly unfavourable to France who, deprived of the support of the small states of Europe, would very often find herself one against three.

Hence, on 24 March France reacted with a counter-proposal,[23] which carefully eliminated all the dangerous aspects of the original proposal. The League of Nations Pact was stressed above all, and the agreement among the four powers was reduced to a simple undertaking to co-operate; the allusion to the revision of the treaties was reduced to a reference to clause 19 of the League of Nations Pact, and there was no mention of Germany's rights in the matter of armaments. Instead there appeared the concern for 'restoration' of European economy.

On 26 March – the very haste was significant – appeared a MacDonald-Mussolini proposal.[24] This insisted on revision of the treaties and concession of equal rights to the countries vanquished in the First World War. The agreement of British and Italian views at this point illustrates in a striking manner how difficult the French diplomatic position was and how little in actual fact she could rely on British support, in spite of all the concessions she had made and in spite of the 'confidence pact' which had been signed at the end of the Lausanne Conference.

A month passed in negotiations about which it is futile to go into details. It is the result which matters, and here the result was clear. A German counter-proposal of 24 April[25] revealed the whole extent of the ground gained by France: Germany took up the French formulae, and, referring to the League of Nations Pact, declared itself 'mindful of the rights of every state which was not covered by them' (which eliminated the idea of a directorate of four); the clause on the revision of the treaties was likewise drawn up in a very cautious manner. On the other hand Germany insisted on equal rights with regard to armaments, although it would undertake to achieve this equality only by stages over an initial period of five years (and not at the end of this first period as stipulated in the last French proposal at the Disarmament Conference). In this conciliating attitude one can see Hitler's concern to reassure international opinion for the time being, but one can also see the methodical mind of the Germans: it was useless to

[23] Ibid., pp.70–1; see also Document 27.   [24] Ibid., p.117.
[25] Ibid., pp.303–4.

reveal their great plans for overthrowing Europe while they did not have the means to carry them out; the reconstitution of the German army must come first.

The final text of the Four-Power Pact,[26] on the other hand, was very vague in its definition of how equality of armaments was to be achieved. Next to the reference to clause 19 of the League of Nations Pact (revision of the treaties) appeared the reference to clause 16 (sanctions against the aggressor) from which Germany had actually tried to exempt itself when it entered the League of Nations, and the reference to clause 10 (the territorial integrity of the various states).

This was apparently an unprecedented diplomatic success for France.[27] It was so complete that one no longer wonders why the Pact was never ratified or put into practice. The question is rather to find out why it was signed. It could be thought that Mussolini considered it as satisfying his prestige, or at any rate his vanity. As for Hitler, no doubt he needed a breathing-space in which to carry out his plans and also to lull his opponent to sleep between two dramatic events; moreover, it would have been ill-advised on his part to refuse Mussolini a satisfaction which in fact did not bind him to anything. Since Italy, France and Germany were for once in agreement, Britain was obviously not going to raise any difficulties.

The negotiation of the Four-Power Pact was given a bad reception by Poland, who threatened on this occasion to resign from the League of Nations[28] and began to display feverish diplomatic activity to counteract it.[29] The French representative displayed annoyance at this, seeing it as primarily a reaction of offended pride and a concern for prestige. However, it might be supposed that the feeling of danger had enabled the Poles to see into the future. If we accept that they were not aware of the Mussolini plan regarding the Danzig Corridor, which was nevertheless spreading through the embassies,[30] they could argue that any consolidation of Central Europe, obviously the aim of the attempt at a Franco-Italian understanding, could only transfer German expansionism towards the East. In this case Poland would be the first victim. Accordingly she herself tried to approach her

[26] Ibid., pp.592–4 (30 May 1933); see also Document 28.
[27] De Jouvenel expressed his satisfaction, DDF, 1st series, Vol. III, pp.666–70.   [28] Ibid., pp.552–3 (22 May).   [29] Ibid., pp.782–5 (28 June).
[30] Ibid., Vol. II, pp.262–3.

two formidable neighbours. She could not hope for more than friendly neutrality from the USSR, who was absorbed in her task of internal reconstruction. The important thing therefore was to divert the German threat. Over this question certain Poles took courage from the thought that Hitler, who was of Austrian, not Prussian, origin, would be more anxious to achieve the *Anschluss* than to restore the territorial unity of Prussia.[31] A cause-and-effect relation may be seen between the Four-Power Pact and the German-Polish pact of non-aggression of 26 January 1934: Poland was able to turn the first German threat from the East to the South.

The reaction of the Little *Entente* to the proposal of the Four-Power Pact had been in the first place as hostile as that of Poland. In its communiqué of 25 March 1933[32] it declared:

> The States of the Little *Entente* cannot recognize that the cause of good relations between various countries is served by agreements whose aim is to dispose of the rights of third parties, whether these agreements oblige their signatories to make concrete decisions, or whether the latter aim only to put pressure on countries other than those who made these agreements. . . .
>
> The States of the Little *Entente* also regret that in the recent negotiations the idea of revisionist policy has been emphasized.

French diplomacy exerted itself to reassure the alarmed Danubian states and could prove to them that she was looking after their interests effectively. In a new communiqué of 30 May[33] the Little *Entente* noted the modifications which had been made to the original texts and concluded, while categorically condemning the revision of the frontiers:

> In these conditions, the States of the Little *Entente*, having received all adequate guarantees that the Four-Power Pact could not affect their interests, hope that the decisions of the Four Powers on the questions concerning them can mutually bring them closer together and strengthen their spirit of co-operation and thus bring about tranquillity in Europe, especially in Central Europe.

The Proposal for an Association of the Peoples of Central Europe

The way now seemed clear for the great Franco-Italian negotiation

[31] Ibid., pp.585–8; see also Laroche, op. cit., p.141.
[32] DDF, 1st series, Vol. III, pp.80–1.   [33] Ibid., pp.594–7.

the aim of which was to consolidate Central Europe. This was
the main reason, if not the only one, which decided France to
be a party to the formation of a Four-Power Pact which was
always calculated to upset her public opinion and that of her
allies, even though its harmful content had been removed.

(a) *The political conditions*

Immediately, however, political preliminaries and conditions,
revealing all the difficulties of the project, appeared on every side.
First a note from the Czech Ministry of Foreign Affairs[34] which
tried in a way to prescribe the very method of the negotiations:
first of all to postpone the final signing of the Four-Power Pact,
then to communicate any proposal made by France and Italy, even
before it had been discussed, to the Central European countries
concerned who would thus have as it were a right to a preliminary
veto. At the same time Czechoslovakia presented all her basic
demands at once: repudiation of the *Anschluss*, for which it would
be necessary to obtain the agreement not only of France and Italy,
but also of Austria, Germany, Poland and Britain, a mutual
guarantee of non-aggression between Hungary and the Little
Entente, with the 'confirmation' by Italy, France and possibly
Britain. It was only after this political armistice that economic
negotiations could be undertaken.

French diplomacy reacted with energy. De Jouvenel, fundamentally blaming Czech thought, wrote on 28 June:[35] 'To undertake a negotiation concerning the Danube countries, repeating
"neither Italy nor Germany" is to go back to checkmate. One
should say "either Italy or Germany".'

However, the French ambassador in Prague, Léon Noël, himself considered the procedure envisaged by Beneš too long and
too complicated, while the danger to Austria was immediate.[36]
Paul-Boncour, the Minister of Foreign Affairs, approved these
reservations:[37]

If we agree that pacification of the Danube countries of Europe in
fact consists of Italy's renouncing certain political aims and especially
any idea of dissociation of the Little *Entente* or disintegration of one

[34] Ibid., pp.770–2 (24 June).
[35] Ibid., pp.778–81; see also Document 30.
[36] DDF, 1st series, Vol. III, pp.802–5 (1 July).
[37] Ibid., pp.892–4 (13 July).

of its members,[38] it is advisable not to make this renunciation impossible by ostensibly desiring Italy to reverse her decision in conditions which would wound her pride.

Generally speaking, the negotiation at this point came up against the personal ideas of Beneš who appeared to be leading the Little *Entente*. Beneš did not believe that Italy was sincere and thought that there was an agreement on general policy between her and Germany.[39] And so he wished to demand from Italy, as a preliminary, a declaration repudiating the *Anschluss*; Mussolini refused to do this because it would wantonly offend Germany and cut off all communications with it before the negotiation with France had yielded any substantial results. Mussolini for his part wished to obtain the same public declaration against the *Anschluss* from the Little *Entente*; but the Little *Entente* evaded this, so giving rise to the suspicion that it was more or less resigned to Hitler's seizure of Austria, whether she regarded it as inevitable in any case, or even that this prospect seemed less formidable than others and that basically the Little *Entente* would adapt itself to it.[40] In general Beneš appears to have greatly overestimated the strength of his position[41] and to have underestimated the German danger. Even the first steps towards Czech rearmament seemed rather absurd: an increase of the manpower of the police force by 500, for example.[42] In relation to France, the contrast between the pride and the excitable imagination of the Poles, and the reasonableness and flexibility of the Czechs, was more apparent than real.

Disregarding the greater or lesser far-sightedness of some or other of these, we must still not underestimate the reality and the extent of the political difficulties. One of the chief difficulties was obviously the revisionism of Hungary, for it led this country into flirtations with Germany.[43] Moreover, in a radio broadcast, the Hungarian minister Goemboes launched a vehement appeal for revision of the treaties, for which he was expecting Mussolini's

---

[38] It is evidently Yugoslavia which is meant here.
[39] DDF, 1st series, Vol. III, pp.892–4 (note referring to a telegram of 2 May 1932).
[40] Ibid., pp.833–6 (5 July).
[41] See for example ibid., pp.860–3 (8 July).
[42] Ibid., pp.488–9 (15 May).
[43] Ibid., pp.787–9 (29 June).

support.[44] At the very least he hoped to obtain for Hungary what had been granted in principle to Germany: equality of rights with regard to armaments.[45] Czechoslovakia would resign herself to the necessity of recognizing this principle, while taking certain precautions.[46] On the other hand, if the question of revision of frontiers were raised in Geneva, Beneš would counter immediately by demanding that arrangements for protecting the minorities be made general.[47] The treaties had in fact imposed on the new states, which they had formed or considerably enlarged, special protective measures for the national minorities which they included; in this there was a concern for fairness with respect to the vanquished countries. But these, especially Germany, were not subjected to the same restrictions and this inequality in its turn could seem unfair. However, an initiative by the Little *Entente* on this subject would have been highly dangerous; it would be the opening of a Pandora's box of all kinds of recriminations and claims. Hence France acted with the greatest firmness in dissuading Czechoslovakia from taking this path.[48] We have here, however, a striking illustration of the fact that the smallest revisionist spark could by degrees set Europe on fire.

Meanwhile the strengthening of the Nazi terrorist campaign forced Austria to take immediate precautions. She asked France to authorize her to form special auxiliary corps in addition to the army and police stipulated by the peace treaty. France agreed to turn a blind eye subject to certain conditions, including the consent of other governments directly concerned.[49] Britain adopted a similar attitude, but subject to Italy's agreement.[50] In contrast, France was opposed to the duration of this auxiliary corps being increased to two years instead of one, which then seemed the length of time for which the Disarmament Conference was likely to run.[51] At the same time she insisted on the confidential nature which she wished to preserve for the affair, while Austria wished to obtain a formal public authorization by the powers con-

[44] Ibid., Vol. IV, pp.140–1 (3 August).
[45] Ibid., pp.186–9 (11 August) and passim.
[46] Ibid., pp.110–11 (31 July), pp.163–4 (6 August).
[47] Ibid., pp. 174–5.
[48] Ibid., pp.68–71; see also Document 29.
[49] DDF, 1st series, Vol. IV, pp.53–5 (22 July).
[50] Ibid., pp.128–9 (1 August).
[51] Ibid., pp.193–4 (14 August).

cerned.[52] Thus a new dilemma was brought to light: the favourable treatment which it was desired to reserve for Austria, in order to put her in a position to resist the Nazi intrigues more successfully, would throw doubt not only on equality between the nations but also on the question of the peace treaties and their possible revision. One can imagine the hesitation of French diplomacy in these conditions.

On the other hand, any Franco-Italian negotiation could not fail to cause alarm very directly from the Yugoslav side. Yugoslavia obviously stipulated as a preliminary to any negotiation, especially of an economic nature, that Italy must renounce any territorial ambition on her part.[53] Mussolini gave the required assurances verbally:[54] it seemed in fact that he no longer reckoned upon the imminent breaking-up of Yugoslavia which he had openly considered the year before. This assurance, however, did not eliminate the risk of indirect conflict. Italy, in fact, in order to be mistress of the outlet to the Adriatic, was trying to get a foothold in Albania, a little country adjoining Yugoslavia which was torn by internal struggles of a tribal nature. Now Yugoslavia strongly opposed any right to military intervention in Albania by Italy.[55] Albanian internal disturbances thus presented a risk of bringing about war between the two countries. But perhaps more serious still, the Nazi threat could force Italy to send troops to Austria, a type of reaction which, basically, would fit in well with French general policy. In this case, however, Italy could establish a link with Hungary which would be liable to set off the Yugoslav defence mechanism;[56] should this happen, Yugoslavia would mobilize.[57] On this side the deadlock was therefore complete.

Such then was the political situation of this vast group of countries which France was trying to harmonize and unite in order to meet Hitler's threats with a united front, should this be necessary.

(b) *Economic projects*

To achieve this united front, French diplomacy endeavoured to turn the discussion to the field of economics: 'It is by first creating a unity of interests between the states of Central Europe that we

[52] Ibid., pp.271–3 (31 August).   [53] Ibid., pp.44–6, 265–6.
[54] Ibid., p.58.   [55] Ibid., pp.216–17.   [56] Ibid., p.541.
[57] Ibid., p.579.

can subsequently hope to see a cooling down over the questions which divide them.'[58]

The calm which it was hoped to achieve from economic agreements consisted implicitly of recognition of the political and territorial *status quo*.[59] However, it was evidently necessary first of all to eliminate from the debates any preconditions or even any visible tendency of a political nature, and to 'neutralize' them somehow.[60] The insistence on the economic factor was obviously a result of the world crisis and the pressing anxieties which it aroused in all countries; the economic recovery of Austria, for example, seemed to be the necessary condition for this country to be able to resist internal and external subversion by the Nazis. However, it might also have been that the political and diplomatic leaders of this period, who were still basically ill-informed about the complexity of the economic problems, believed somewhat confusedly that it was possible to create miraculous solutions in this abstruse field which would enable them to find a way out of inextricable political situations.

The first project, which was, moreover, still very vague, was developed by de Jouvenel:[61] his idea was that of a vast commercial association of the Danube countries which had been discussed incessantly since the break-up of the Austro-Hungarian Empire, and which had been taken up again the previous year by the French statesman André Tardieu. The novelty of this idea, however, was that de Jouvenel considered that Italy, without being a full member of the association, should derive special advantages from it.

The negotiation was actively pursued on this basis after the special mission of de Jouvenel had ended.[62] Mussolini showed real interest in it, and there were visible signs of improvement in Franco-Italian relations. For a time Mussolini even considered joint research by the gold-bloc countries on monetary reorganization in Central and Balkan Europe.[63] However, competent French authorities soon perceived how far this project lacked

---

[58] Ibid., p.269.
[59] Ibid., Vol. III, pp.892–4; Vol. IV, pp.307–8, 363–4.
[60] Ibid., Vol. IV, pp.229–30.
[61] Ibid., Vol. III, pp.778–81; see also Document 30.
[62] On this point R. Binion fails through lack of information.
[63] DDF, 1st series, Vol. IV, pp.24–5, 229–30.

realism: how could stabilization of the Danubian currencies be attempted as long as the chief currencies, the dollar and the pound sterling, were not stable?[64] They therefore quickly fell back on a far more modest plan, which was communicated to Italy in the form of a memorandum on 10 September 1933.[65] Its most notable feature was perhaps that which concerned procedure: the idea was to launch a Franco-Italian initiative, whereby France showed clearly that she did not agree to exert an exclusive influence in the Danube basin nor to counterbalance Italian influence in this region. The aim of this initiative was, firstly, not to allow two rival economic groups to form: Italy-Austria-Hungary on the one side and the Little *Entente* on the other; here the political intention showed through clearly in spite of carefully chosen words. In order to avoid the formation or continuation of opposing blocs, economic organization and co-operation by bilateral agreements was recommended, which seemed somewhat contradictory. The memorandum was more precise on one point, however. The ports of Trieste and Fiume, which were formerly the Austro-Hungarian Empire's only outlets to the sea, had been dormant since their reunion with Italy: it was necessary to revive them. A memorandum by Paul-Boncour, intended for the French ambassadors, also considered the formation of unions of Danubian producers and assessment of export or import quotas.[66]

However, even in the best circumstances, the French memorandum was only an outline to be filled in. Even its basic principles did not appear to be accepted by France's Danube allies without reservations, since at the Sinaia Conference they were continuing to set up another project which had been in preparation for a long time: that of the economic organization of the Little *Entente*.[67] In fact, these discussions, carried out under conditions of extreme discretion, even with regard to France, seemed to yield only very modest results. The problem appeared rather to be a threat, whose precise definition was avoided and which was allowed to hover over Austria and Hungary in order to bring them to repentance. The real effect, on the other hand, was probably to hasten Italy's reply.

[64] Ibid., p.640.
[65] Ibid., pp. 327–9; see also Document 31.
[66] DDF, 1st series, Vol. IV, pp.246–8.
[67] Ibid., pp.500–10.

This came on 30 September in the form of a memorandum[68] which filled in the French outline in a manner which was very favourable to Italian interests. It stipulated that the Danube countries should grant preferential treatment to the non-Danube countries who normally had a negative commercial balance with them: this of course referred to Italy. Furthermore it was necessary to revise the problem of the debts of the Danube countries, which implied that their creditors (primarily France) would have to agree to making sacrifices. Finally, the plan must be prepared during discussions between the signatories of the Four-Power Pact and the 'successor states' of the former Austro-Hungarian Empire: Italy, which was the only country to belong to both groups at the same time, would thus be sure of playing a leading part.

The Italian memorandum was received very unfavourably by the statesmen of the Little *Entente*, more so, however, by the Czechs and the Yugoslavs than by the Rumanians. France herself, however, hardly seemed disposed to make sacrifices and to consent to Italy's gaining the advantages which nevertheless seemed to be in de Jouvenel's line of thinking. Faced with the insistence of the Italian delegate, who demanded an immediate agreement at least on the principles, the French representative, Germain-Martin, merely suggested recording 'the agreement of the two governments on the expediency of the proposed undertaking'.[69]

This was far from what had been expected. It had been shown that the economy did not provide a miraculous solution to political problems. On the contrary, the economic difficulties were only added to these. To ask for exceptional privileges as a matter of urgency for Austrian industry, owing to the seriousness of the imminent threat hanging over the country, was to impose equally exceptional sacrifices on Czech industry at the height of its crisis. Even among countries with similar political interest, like those of the Little *Entente*, attempts at economic agreement did not get very far.[70] The countries which succeeded the Austro-Hungarian Empire were becoming less and less complementary, each one trying to equip herself in the economic sectors in which she was lacking. As for France, she was in the throes of a worsening

[68] Ibid., pp.512–14.
[69] All the documentation on this affair is found in DDF, 1st series, Vol. IV, pp.500–12.   [70] Ibid., pp.44–6.

economic situation; and she did not have the strong resolution nor, perhaps, was it in her power, to pay the necessary price for diplomatic success.

The Austrian Crises of 1934 and Italian Policy

Meanwhile a serious internal crisis was added to the threats from the outside and made the survival of an independent Austria even more hazardous. The Austrian chancellor Dollfuss had, in theory, the choice of two methods of facing the Nazis: either he could gather together all the forces devoted to the political freedom of the country, or he could establish an authoritarian regime which would deprive Hitler's supporters of the facilities provided by a democracy but would also deprive the social democrats of these facilities. During the autumn of 1933 Dollfuss steered more and more definitely towards the second path. He had a new constitution drawn up, which was authoritarian and corporate.[71] At this time the words 'corporate system' immediately suggested Italian fascism. At the same time Dollfuss and his colleagues visualized the formation of a kind of single party, the 'Patriotic Front', into which to entice the socialist troops. Naturally, the social democrats reacted to this, and their relations with the government rapidly deteriorated.[72] The socialists threatened the government with a general strike, to which Dollfuss replied with the threat of martial law. Finally, in February 1934, the socialists were crushed in Vienna in a war in the streets which lasted several days and in which even artillery was used. This new disaster, one year after Hitler had come to power in Germany and several days after the Paris riot of 6 February, was reflected sorrowfully in French democratic opinion.[73]

French diplomacy, which was conducted at that time by governments of the Left, a part of whose majority were socialists, had done everything in its power to avoid this outcome. Since June 1933 France had tried to put pressure on the Austrian government, at a time when she was issuing a loan.[74] In September Paul-Boncour wrote to his representative in Vienna:[75]

[71] Ibid., pp.229, 367–8.   [72] Ibid., pp.561–2.
[73] Is the author permitted to draw upon his personal recollections here?
[74] DDF, 1st series, Vol. III, pp.718–20.
[75] Ibid., Vol. IV, p. 383.

Any dictatorship, or even any policy which sets a large part of the workers' democracy against the Austrian government in its difficult struggle, would make our efforts to support it unworkable, which efforts we could no longer even continue without contradicting ourselves.

The representations increased, but Dollfuss brushed them aside: if he did not accept German interference in Austrian internal policy, how could he accept French interference?

Italy, on the other hand, actively supported and perhaps even demanded the new trend of the Austrian state.[76] Hence fascism, contrary to Mussolini's former declaration, seemed to become an export commodity. Italy was obviously taking advantage of the new international situation, which apparently made her indispensable, to increase her demands in all fields. In this way, however, the ideological factor crossed swords for the first time with French national policy, on the subject of a Franco-Italian *rapprochement*. As it grew in size this new element finally considerably weakened the organization of resistance against Hitler.

At that time, however, the support given by Mussolini to Dollfuss's resistance against the Nazis became only more pronounced. In March 1934 the Rome Protocols were signed: these included an agreement to undertake political consultations and to develop economic relations between Italy, Austria and Hungary.[77] But although these agreements separated Hungary from Germany in particular, they tolled the knell of French efforts to form a vast Danube community cemented by the Franco-Italian agreement. More than ever the Little *Entente* and the Italian system formed two separate and hostile blocs.

However, the Hitler Putsch, so often foretold,[78] was finally launched in Vienna on 25 July 1934. The Nazis temporarily took control of the city, by surprise, and the chancellor Dollfuss was assassinated at the Chancellery. Immediately, however, Mussolini concentrated four divisions at the Italian-Austrian frontier, the Hitlerite blow was averted and power in Vienna was returned to Schuschnigg, who continued the policy of Dollfuss.

Did this event give some meaning to the opinion of Beneš who,

[76] Ibid., p.521.

[77] R. Albrecht-Carrie, *France, Europe and Two World Wars*, p.262.

[78] DDF, 1st series, Vol. III, pp.41–2, 194–5, 833; Vol. IV, pp.53–5, 59, 80–1, 89–90, 106–9, 169, 215, 216, 337–40, 757–60.

in his less guarded moments, declared that it was not necessary to make concessions to Mussolini because his interest obliged him to protect Austria? This opinion was in fact rash, for Mussolini, having proved that he was indispensable, would not fail more than ever to demand the counter-claims to which he considered he had a right.

The Rome Agreements (January 1935)

Meanwhile an incident occurred, the truth of which, still unknown, gave rise to innumerable speculations. On 9 October 1934 King Alexander of Yugoslavia, who had arrived in France on an official visit, was assassinated, together with the French Minister of Foreign Affairs, Louis Barthou, by a Croatian terrorist in Marseilles. The assassin belonged to the secret organization 'Ustasha', which was protected by Mussolini who, moreover, refused to extradite the criminals. However, the theory that Mussolini knew of the attempt in advance and encouraged it cannot be verified, and it is not very likely.[79] The incident had serious consequences, however. Yugoslavia's tendency to lean towards Germany, which had already been demonstrated in the economic field, became more pronounced.[80] Much was said at the time about Yugoslavia's having lost confidence in France and her regime, because of the ineffectualness of the French police, who were incapable of protecting the country's illustrious guests. However, there were more serious consequences than this blow to French prestige, which, after all, was an isolated incident. The Yugoslav government could not fail to be offended at the care taken at that time by French diplomacy with regard to Italy, for the effort which France had made to consolidate Central Europe with Italy's support had ended in a kind of paralysis: France was hindered by the Little *Entente* in her efforts to forestall the *Anschluss*, especially in playing her Italian card; however, on the other hand, she could no longer support Yugoslavia as much as the latter expected, if she attached any importance to an understanding with Italy.

Nevertheless, the new Minister of Foreign Affairs, Pierre Laval, took up Penelope's work again. During a visit to Rome in

[79] J. B. Duroselle, *Histoire diplomatique*, p.186.
[80] See for example DDF, 1st series, Vol. III, pp.183–4.

January 1935 he prepared a 'Danube Pact' with Mussolini, an undertaking by both countries not to interfere in the internal affairs of her neighbours; this was to be signed by Austria, Germany, Czechoslovakia, Yugoslavia, Hungary, Italy – with the possibility of the approval of France, Poland and Rumania. France and Italy also agreed to act together in the event of unilateral rearmament of Germany and in the event of a threat against Austria.[81] However, the main point of the 'Rome Agreements' consisted of the settlement of undecided African problems between the two countries, and this settlement was exceptionally favourable to France: subject to certain very slight territorial rectifications, Italy accepted the renunciation of the privileged status of Italians in Tunisia. Naturally Mussolini, who was then in a strong position, had obtained something far more important which could not be represented in the actual text of the agreements: France's non-intervention in Ethiopia. Was this only a withdrawal from an economic point of view, as Laval asserted later? Or was it a concession to Mussolini of freedom of action in all fields, as he understood it? In all likelihood, nothing specific was stated in this discussion, of which there was no written report.[82]

The 'Stresa Front'

On 16 March 1935 Hitler announced the re-establishment of compulsory military service in Germany: the German army would from then on consist of thirty-six divisions instead of the seven stipulated by the Treaty of Versailles. At the same time the French army consisted of thirty divisions.

It was from this time that the criticisms generally levelled at France's foreign policy changed their direction. Until then it had been accused above all of intransigence, and of lack of generosity and breadth of outlook; as we have seen, the note of 17 April 1934 again incurred charges of this kind. Now other commentators – or sometimes the same ones – were to be astounded that, faced with the new German defiance, France had reacted only with

[81] W. E. Scott, *Alliance against Hitler*, pp.216–17.
[82] On this point we can only return to the discussion of P. Renouvin, *Histoire des relations internationales*, Vol. VIII, part 2, pp.78–80; see also Document 34.

words. We have already had occasion, and will have again, to find explanations for the core of the problem. We will confine ourselves here to pointing out that it was hardly possible for French diplomacy, which was controlled by the public opinion of the time, to make such sudden changes of direction.

In fact, French diplomacy was not directed towards an individual reaction but was striving, as it had always done, towards establishing a collective action. Its basic problem was to bring Britain, on whom she relied by tradition, and Italy, who had been the object of her approaches for only a few years, into a common position. The problem was not a simple one, for Britain, while appearing favourable to the Franco-Italian *rapprochement* in principle, still refused to support it by taking on new undertakings in Central Europe. As for Italy, while being a party to the negotiation with France, she had so far handled Germany carefully and avoided publicly taking up a position against it, except of course over the question of Austria. Italy's concern was probably not to remain in practice the only one to defend Austrian independence; and this, together with the more or less implicit promises of Pierre Laval, made her decide on this occasion to take the plunge. As far as Britain was concerned, it seems that the progress made in public opinion by the ideas of collective security made it difficult for her to abstain completely from now on.

Be that as it may, a conference between France, Britain and Italy which met in Stresa on 11 April 1935 ended on 16 April with an official declaration by the three powers. This declaration indicated the intention to 'oppose, by all suitable means, any unilateral repudiation of treaties which is liable to endanger the peace of Europe'; it confirmed the necessity of maintaining the independence and integrity of Austria. The next day, at the suggestion of the same powers, the League of Nations Council condemned the German attitude and decided to 'define the economic and financial measures which could be applied' in the event of a new initiative of a similar nature. Britain agreed, then, to seem to take the path of sanctions which she had always declined to do until that time.

France had therefore achieved a brilliant diplomatic success, but one which, like all successes of this nature, was of value only in so far as there was a readiness to follow words with deeds. Ironic comments on the unrealistic nature of the Stresa declarations have not been lacking, especially in retrospect. These declarations, however, were followed by Franco-Italian military discussions in June 1935. In these a collaboration of the two countries was considered, in the event of a German attack either on Austria and Italy, or even on France, including the possibility of sending an Italian contingent to the Rhine, or – most important – French units to Central Europe, passing through Italian territory. The future prospects opened in this way could be of considerable importance.[83]

[83] DDF, 2nd series, Vol. II, pp.642–5.

Chapter 11

The Franco-Soviet Treaty of Mutual Assistance

The attempt at Franco-Italian agreement and the Franco-Soviet negotiation appeared to be simultaneous and, for the most part, parallel. They both seemed to arise from the same source: the weakening of the French position, a more and more definite threat presented by Hitler's Germany. Furthermore, as W. E. Scott has stressed, these two diplomatic movements supported, rather than contradicted, one another. In spite of their opposing political ideals, relations between Soviet Russia and fascist Italy were never bad, and for the French government, negotiating at the same time with both of them was a considerable trump-card with regard to public opinion: it showed that French diplomacy was inspired by national interest and not by ideological preferences, and the criticisms from the Left against the *rapprochement* with Italy, and the opposition from the Right to the negotiations with Russia, were made more difficult.[1]

However, this analogy must not be taken too far, because these two diplomatic actions were, from the French point of view, of a quite different nature. The understanding with Italy originated basically from French initiatives to which Mussolini was a party, with a greater or less degree of sincerity or ulterior motive; he had vast ambitions, in the opinion of his protagonists, since his aim was to establish European equilibrium on new foundations. In the Franco-Soviet negotiations, on the other hand, the initiative came from the USSR and France at first received it with many reservations; even those among the French who appeared most in favour of this new diplomatic link tended to attribute to it far less importance than the Soviet protagonists appeared to do.

Do we again find here an indirect ideological opposition? Yes

[1] W. E. Scott, *Alliance against Hitler*, p.125.

and no. The policy of the *cordon sanitaire*, which was used by France in particular against the Bolsheviks, had been abandoned at least since 1922 and had never been resumed; the Soviets, however, continued to be haunted by the fear of 'capitalist encirclement'. The USSR for her part had gradually abandoned – at least for a historical period beyond which diplomats scarcely glanced – her primary concern for universal revolution in favour of 'construction of socialism in one single country'; this development, however, was not clearly discerned in the West. From the purely French point of view, two other factors intervened: in the first place the USSR still seemed a long way away, while Italy was very near; a certain effort of imagination was needed to give the Soviet factor its full value. But above all, since the Rapallo Agreement of 1922, the USSR seemed to the French to be the partner of German 'vengeance' – perhaps far more than she really was. All this explains the distrust, or perhaps the lack of interest, displayed by the French in the face of the Soviet advances.

The Non-Aggression Pact of November 1932

The signing of pacts of non-aggression with her neighbours had been a basic element of Russia's policy since 1922, and even more so since the Briand-Kellogg Agreement of August 1928.[2] In 1930 proposals were made to Poland in this direction and similar ones to France at the same time. However, that year Franco-Soviet relations were rather bad, particularly since they were marked by a customs tariff dispute.

In May 1931, however, France agreed to undertake a double – political and commercial – negotiation with the USSR. How did she come to this decision? We can only put forward theories on this subject. It seems doubtful that the concern to put an end to the tariff war was the predominant factor: Franco-Soviet trade was in any case much reduced, and its development encountered obstacles which, as we shall see, were difficult to overcome. The alarm caused by the events of the spring of 1931, especially the proposal for a customs union between Germany and Austria, could have played a part. However, we may wonder – and it

[2] *Documents Diplomatiques Français* (DDF), 1st series, Vol. II, pp.53–61 (23 November 1932). Historical account of Franco-Soviet relations drawn up by the Quai d'Orsay for the use of the President of the Council.

would be a remarkable historical irony for those who know the events which followed – whether the attitude of Poland was not a determining factor. Poland in fact was the country most directly threatened by the German revisionist agitation whose violence had doubled in 1931, and she could not turn down the opportunity of improving her relations with her other large neighbour. The fact that relations between Poland and France at this time were strained was not an argument against this; in fact, the Polish leaders suspected France of thinking of abandoning them. This suspicion was not justified and France had hardly any reason not to bring her attitude on the subject in line with that of Poland.[3]

However this may be, the fact that these two negotiations were parallel and simultaneous is remarkable. In August 1931 the French and Soviet negotiators came to an agreement on a proposal for a pact. In August 1931 Poland too made known her approval of the French attitude and her wish to adopt a similar one, and in fact a Polish-Soviet pact of non-aggression was initiated on 26 January 1932. France, like Poland, made her final agreement subject to the conclusion of a similar pact between the USSR and Rumania. However, an obstacle arose here: as a result of the events of 1919 Bessarabia, which had formerly been under Russian control, had passed into the hands of Rumania. The USSR had never recognized this transfer of territory. Consequently, the Soviet-Rumanian negotiations came up against the contradictory claims of the Soviets, who wished to mention in the pact the existence of their territorial claims, and of the Rumanians who wanted the pact to give a guarantee of their possession of Bessarabia. First Polish and then French mediators endeavoured on the other hand to find a formula vague enough for nothing to be deduced from it on the subject. How much would a pact of non-aggression based on such an ambiguity really have been worth? Why did the Soviets concern themselves only with these claims with respect to Rumania, when they also had territorial claims with respect to Poland? So many questions could be asked, to which there was not necessarily any answer.

W. E. Scott, the remarkable historian who dealt with the Franco-Soviet negotiations, thought that he could detect a deliberate slowing down on the part of the French, during the

[3] On this point we differ from the interpretation of W. E. Scott, op. cit., p.16.

autumn of 1931 and the spring of 1932. Our documents do not enable us to settle this question, but we can discuss some of the reasons put forward. One of these referred to a Franco-German *rapprochement*[4] during this period. This *rapprochement*, however, does not seem to have been real: the policy of Pierre Laval during this period must not be judged by what it was at a later date.

Another reason was the Japanese question. It is certain that the USSR viewed Japan's advance into China with alarm, especially after the proclamation of the independence of Manchukuo on 1 March 1932. On the other hand, rumours of a Franco-Japanese alliance were spreading at this time, and the international press, especially that of China and the USSR, were happy to echo this.[5] But what exactly was the position?

According to our documents Japan did in fact make overtures to France in July 1932, albeit in the form of indirect probings.[6] The first evidence of the goodwill which Japan hoped for would obviously be the attitude of the French representative at the League of Nations commission in Manchuria. Herriot, the president of the Council, immediately sent a reply to his ambassador in Tokyo: 'Please evade the offer courteously . . . taking care not to leave any trace which could make our attitude towards the League of Nations or the signatories of the Treaty of Washington appear ambiguous.'[7]

A little later the political directorate of the Quai d'Orsay explained, in terms which were quite severe to Japan, why the French government could not recognize Manchukuo.[8] In fact, how could France compromise her relations with Britain and the United States, which she considered fundamental, by Far-Eastern questions which were of secondary importance to her? One thing is certain: French policy with respect to Japan was conducted with great caution, because French possessions in East Asia, especially Indo-China, would hardly be in a position to resist a Japanese attack.[9] However, there is a gulf between this caution and active collusion with Japan.

[4] W. E. Scott, op. cit., p.27.
[5] Ibid., p.43; DDF, 1st series, Vol. I, pp.422–3.
[6] Ibid., pp.7–9. The historical account made by the sub-administration of Asia-Oceania, ibid., Vol. II, pp.444–9, does not mention a previous attempt.
[7] Ibid., Vol. I, p.15 (11 July 1932).
[8] Ibid., pp.302–5 (11 September 1932).
[9] Ibid., Vol. II, pp.444–9.

If the reasons for slowing down the Franco-Soviet discussions before May 1932 were not obvious, apart from the personal position of André Tardieu, the acceleration of these talks after the advent of the Cartel des Gauches on the other hand cannot be denied. It must not be forgotten that the new President of the Council, Edouard Herriot, had already become the apostle of the *rapprochement* after his first visit to the USSR in 1922. Again, however, the attitude of Poland had played an important part. On 25 July 1932, the Polish-Soviet Pact had been signed, its ratification by Poland remaining subject to the conclusion of a Rumanian-Soviet pact. Three days later, a note from the Quai d'Orsay intended for the President of the Council, prepared the final conclusion of the Franco-Soviet Pact.[10] It expressly stated that 'the progress of the negotiations carried out by the States adjoining the USSR is such that . . . the French government will shortly be led to establish her intentions'.

It was proposed in the note to make several modifications to the proposal of August 1931, but these were not of basic importance.

On 1 September Edouard Herriot sent a sharp warning to Rumania through his ambassador in Bucharest:[11] France would delay her signature of the Franco-Soviet Pact only until the conclusion of a Rumano-Soviet pact, and only in so far as Rumania was 'reasonable'

> . . . by renouncing any demand which they could not reasonably hope for the Soviet government to accept, that is, any formula whose aim would be directly or indirectly to sanction the USSR's recognition of the annexation of Bessarabia.

Finally, Poland and France decided to disregard the stubborn resistance of the Rumanians.[12] The Franco-Soviet Pact of non-aggression was officially signed on 29 November 1932.

What did this mean to French diplomacy? A memorandum from the Minister of Foreign Affairs[13] gives us a glimpse. In the first place the treaty removed any grounds for Soviet propaganda against France, especially over the question of disarmament. Secondly, the USSR would from then onward be neutral in a Franco-German conflict, instead of leaning at least indirectly

---

[10] Ibid., Vol. I, pp.118–22.
[11] Ibid., pp.245–7.   [12] W. E. Scott, op. cit., pp.65–6.
[13] DDF, 1st series, Vol. II, pp.53–61.

towards Germany. The revisionist ambitions which threatened Poland in particular would thereby be discouraged. Finally, this pact brought the USSR 'into the atmosphere' of the League of Nations to which she did not belong. On the other hand, however,

> It would be a serious mistake to wish to transform [the treaty] into a 'reversal of alliances'. It marked only a balance of agreements contracted by the USSR; a balance which Russia wished to achieve to avoid giving the impression of being a trump-card in Germany's political game, and to avoid the risks of a German economic protectorate.
>
> Politically, the USSR wished to preserve the freedom to remain neutral between France and Germany, and no more could be asked of her.

One sees that those responsible for French diplomacy attached a largely negative value to the Franco-Soviet Pact of non-aggression, and at the time did not infer from it any very ambitious future prospects.

The Turning-Point of 1933

The coming to power of Hitler in Germany was of special significance to the USSR. Not only had the new master of Germany violently proclaimed his anti-communism, but also in his book *Mein Kampf*, written ten or so years previously, he had flaunted territorial ambitions directed towards the East, which could be fulfilled only at Russia's expense.[14]

Meanwhile, the first Soviet reactions to the new German government were cautious and hesitant. German-Soviet relations cooled considerably only after May 1933, and this was the prelude to a general change in their trend.[15] The secret collaboration between the *Reichswehr* and the Red Army ended during the summer.[16]

Can it be said that the friendly approaches to France by the Soviets progressed at the same rate as the widening of the gap with Germany? Generally speaking, this is no doubt true, but in detail matters were not quite so simple.

Before ending the close relationship which she had maintained

---

[14] W. E. Scott, op. cit., p.79.   [15] Ibid., pp.94–5.   [16] Ibid., p.97.

with Germany for ten years, the USSR had taken a big step towards France in a field which at the time was very important in the eyes of the latter country. Until that time the USSR had always proved hostile to the French positions at the Disarmament Conference. However, on 6 February 1933 the Soviet delegate Maxim Litvinov declared that the concept of security was of immense importance, that the French proposals on this point should be taken very seriously and, to give further weight to this intervention, he proposed a definition of the aggressor which would be essential to the establishment of a system of mutual assistance.[17] As W. E. Scott rightly points out, a political reversal of this nature could not be a reply to the accession of Hitler, which had happened only a few days previously: the Soviet government which was, moreover, known for its caution and the slowness of its reactions, could not have had sufficient time to come to a decision of such importance. How, then, could it be explained? Was it merely a way of showing France that the USSR took the newly signed pact of non-aggression very seriously? The idea was, in fact, a manœuvre of far greater proportions, for in July 1933 the USSR signed 'agreements for the definition of aggression' with all her neighbours – including Rumania, who from that time ceased to be an obstacle – and also with Czechoslovakia and Yugoslavia. Now this definition was extremely detailed and comprehensive.[18] It referred not only to the military measures which are usually considered, but also:

the support given to armed irregulars which, having formed on her territory [the aggressor's] have invaded the territory of another state, or [the] refusal, in spite of the request of the invaded state, to take all the steps in her power on her own territory to deprive the aforesaid irregulars of any assistance.

The text further defined that no act of aggression could be justified by 'the internal situation of a state, for example, its political, economic and social structure; the alleged faults of its administration, troubles resulting from strikes, revolutions, counter-revolutions or civil wars'.

A state threatened by revolutionary subversion could not have spoken otherwise. At the same time the USSR abandoned in practice the idea of revision of the peace treaties which she had

[17] Ibid., pp.107–8.   [18] DDF, 1st series, Vol. IV, pp.114–18.

continued to uphold until that time; this was simply because revision would in fact result in war.[19] In short, in order to achieve her internal transformation peacefully, the USSR had become pacifist and hence conservative: there was room here for an agreement with France, even apart from the German question.[20]

France obviously welcomed with gratitude the new attitude of the USSR to the Disarmament Conference, and supported without reservations the Soviet definition of the aggressor.[21] On the other hand, the signing of the Four-Power Pact, even in its final, and much softened, form, could hardly be regarded as a friendly gesture in the eyes of the USSR who was implicitly excluded from the European agreement. In fact Litvinov informed the French ambassador of his misgivings:[22] not only did he fear the formation of a European directorate turned against the Soviets, he feared that the effect of the operation would be to divert the German revisionist appetites towards the East: his deductions thus linked up with those of Poland. A surprising fact was, however, that far from causing a hardening of the USSR attitude in the face of this new manifestation of 'capitalist encirclement', the Four-Power Pact was not followed by any, even transient, cooling of the Soviet attitude towards France. It merely promoted a closer relationship between Russia and the Little *Entente*, who felt the same misgivings. Furthermore, the Four-Power Pact had an unexpected after-effect which was, however, indicative of the state of mind of both Italy and the USSR at the time: this was the signing of an Italo-Soviet pact of 'friendship, neutrality and non-aggression', on 2 September 1933.[23] Both countries derived a sort of counter-assurance from this, which succeeded in depriving the Four-Power Pact of any threatening ulterior motive.

The USSR immediately marked her intention of completing another stage on the way to a *rapprochement*; she offered France a 'secret verbal agreement' of political co-operation. The very cautious memorandum which was drawn up on this occasion by the political directorate of the Quai d'Orsay, deserves careful

[19] W. E. Scott, op. cit., pp.109–10.

[20] For an explanation of Soviet development even before Hitler's rise to power, see also DDF, 1st series, Vol. III, pp.630–6.

[21] W. E. Scott, op. cit., pp.108–9.

[22] DDF, 1st series, Vol. III, pp.206–7.

[23] Ibid., Vol. III, p.773; Vol. IV, pp.9–10, 354–6.

examination, more especially because the document, although official, was intended for internal use and could therefore be expressed more freely.[24] Those responsible for French diplomacy at this time seemed to consider that the German-Soviet agreement of Rapallo was still fully in force; hence they expressed their fear that a Franco-Russian *rapprochement* could seem to be directed against Britain, 'with whom the *entente* is still the basis of all French policy'. The document is also revealing in what it omits to say: there is no allusion either to the ideological antagonism between the Russian communists and the German Nazis (the good Italo-Soviet relations could explain why this aspect had been neglected), or even to Hitler's coveting of Russian territory.

However, the visits to Russia of Edouard Herriot – from then on removed from power – and subsequently of the Air Minister, Pierre Cot, were to provide the opportunity for the Soviet leaders to make proposals which went much further.[25] From now on the question was one of common defence, and this was even referred to in official discussions.[26] The first reaction of the Minister of Foreign Affairs, Joseph Paul-Boncour, to this approach indicated uneasiness:[27]

> By appearing . . . to consider only Germany, and the pursuit of European agreements which would be likely to coincide with our views, is not the USSR really concerned most of all with Japan and prompted by the ulterior motive of committing us in Asia?

Nevertheless, Franco-Soviet collaboration had from now on enthusiastic advocates, the French ambassador to Moscow, Charles Alphand, and the Air Minister, Pierre Cot (who was then a radical-socialist and only later became a 'fellow traveller' of the communists). There was, however, a striking contrast between the general political views which they outwardly displayed and the practical measures which they considered likely to be accepted by the French government. Charles Alphand was not afraid to write:[28]

> After the failure of the British and American agreements of the Treaty of Versailles and the creation of equilibrium by the protocol

[24] Ibid., Vol. IV, pp.32–3 (19 July); see also Document 32.
[25] W. E. Scott, op. cit., pp.118–20.
[26] DDF, 1st series, Vol. IV, p.345.
[27] Ibid., p.425. On the subject of this fear of being drawn by the USSR into a conflict with Japan which would result in the loss of Indo-China, see also ibid., pp.470–1.   [28] Ibid., pp.427–31 (27 September 1933).

of 1924, in the middle of the difficulties in which the British Empire and the United States are struggling, which make concrete undertakings with regard to European affairs more and more unlikely, this is only a system based on agreement with the USSR and Turkey which, in present circumstances, may guarantee French security.

However, he proposed only a 'technical collaboration' matched with a 'benevolent neutrality'. A little later he explained the reason for this:[29]

> I do not believe that the Soviets agree to bind themselves in a concrete manner with any capitalist state. . . . The question is not one of an alliance, which I do not consider materially possible under the present circumstances. . . .

It was necessary for France merely to keep her place in the economic and technical development of the USSR, so that this place would not be taken by Germany.

Pierre Cot for his part recommended an 'industrial agreement' between France and Russia,[30] even if this was only to prevent France being overtaken by the United States in the training of Russian technical personnel![31]

We will add that the economic agreement itself encountered serious obstacles: the USSR was basically trying to import industrial equipment; she would be prepared to pay for this with agricultural produce, but France, affected by the crisis, tended on the contrary to forbid the import of agricultural produce; the fact that she was more or less self-sufficient with regard to agriculture was thus an actual handicap for France in her relations with Russia, as with the countries of the Danube. The USSR might give many industrial orders on credit, but it was impossible for the French government to guarantee these credits, as long as the USSR refused to repay the numerous French holders of Russian stocks and public or private loan bonds contracted under the tsarist regime. Success was achieved merely in making provisional arrangements of limited scope, based on certain raw materials such as petroleum.[32] And so trade between Russia and Germany remained greater than trade between Russia and France.[33]

[29] Ibid., pp.701–4 (5 November 1933).
[30] Ibid., pp.570–2. [31] Ibid., pp.613–14. [32] Ibid., pp.76–9.
[33] In 1935 exports to Russia still only represented 1·1 per cent of French exports. W. E. Scott, op. cit., p.213.

On the whole, France appeared very reluctant to enter into agreements with the USSR beyond the pact of non-aggression, which had a fundamentally negative scope and permitted some relaxation of the relations which had so far been strained. The massive support which the Chamber of Deputies gave to this pact in May 1933 (554 votes against 1, and 41 abstentions)[34] must not create any illusions. On the contrary, it is unlikely that an act heralding a radically new political trend would have obtained even from the Right such almost unanimous support.

Barthou's Venture

Nevertheless, it was at this very moment that Paul-Boncour, the Minister of Foreign Affairs, would have undertaken a secret negotiation with the Soviets with a view to concluding an alliance.[35] Paul-Boncour's endeavour would have been concerned with the following points: in the first place France did not wish to undertake any obligation which would be liable to involve her in a conflict in the Far East. We know that this was in fact what the Minister and his services feared most, but this fear should be easy to calm, for France could be only a very feeble help to Russia in a struggle against Japan. Then Paul-Boncour, who was an enthusiastic supporter of the League of Nations, tried to bring any agreement with the Soviets within the framework of this organization. It was therefore necessary, as a preliminary condition, that the USSR should ask to be admitted into the League of Nations. This was an important matter, not only on the symbolic level, but also from a practical point of view, for clause 16 of the League of Nations Pact was the only means of co-ordinating Soviet action with that of Poland, Rumania and Czechoslovakia in the event of a war with Germany and, which was even more important, of avoiding the Locarno Agreement's working against France in the event of her coming to the aid of the USSR against Germany.

If accurately reported, this negotiation is of interest in that it already sketches the outline for the future agreement. On the other hand, it was to take place in such secrecy (only the President

---

[34] Ibid., pp.112–15.
[35] Ibid., pp.134–8, 146–9. Here Scott's account is based on retrospective evidence, basically that of Paul-Boncour. It is evidently unlikely that it will ever be verified by diplomatic documents.

of the Council, Chautemps, and two high officials of the Ministry of Foreign Affairs were to be informed of it) that it could not pass through many of the stages on the way to an agreement which of necessity would have to be public, ratified by Parliament and by public opinion.

Be that as it may, whether it was to meet a French demand, or whether it was within the framework of a more general policy, the USSR began to make approaches to the League of Nations in December 1933.[36]

However, it was Louis Barthou who made the decisive gestures. This is all the more important in that it appears paradoxical. Louis Barthou was the Minister of Foreign Affairs in the cabinet of the National Union which had been set up in France after the riot of 6 February 1934. He himself as a statesman was regarded as a conservative, even a nationalist; during a great part of his career he had been associated with Raymond Poincaré. No one, therefore, was more qualified to reassure the political circles of the Centre and the Right to whom a *rapprochement* with Soviet Russia could cause alarm on the ideological level.

At the same time, Barthou had made the Franco-Russian Alliance before 1914; he was therefore familiar with the problems of diplomatic co-operation between countries with different political systems (at that time there was a strong antithesis between tsarist, reactionary Russia and democratic France, which was the only republic among the great European states). On the other hand Barthou was one of the few statesmen of the time to have read *Mein Kampf*, or at least, to have taken it seriously. Finally, the note of 17 April 1934[37] made France face her actual situation, without any possible illusion. The first task was then to make a complete examination of France's diplomatic position and the present or future support of which she could avail herself.

During a visit to Brussels in March 1934, Barthou had been able to ascertain that Belgium above all wished to limit her commitments with France.[38] Then, at the end of April, it was Poland's turn. She still remained just as ill-disposed towards Czechoslovakia, but the great and distressing new feature was that by the German-Polish pact of non-aggression of January 1934, Poland seemed to have made the choice between her two great neighbours. It was no longer Poland who would support the Franco-Soviet *rap-*

---

[36] Ibid., p.147. [37] See Chapter 9. [38] W. E. Scott, op. cit., pp.164–5.

prochement as she had done in 1932; quite the contrary. Czechoslovakia, on the other hand, appeared favourable to the entry of the USSR into the League of Nations, which the Little *Entente*, moreover, was ready to recognize officially.[39] Besides, Barthou knew that the commercial influence of Germany was being exerted more and more on Yugoslavia and Rumania. The balancesheet thus appeared heavily negative. It was becoming a matter of urgency to do something to turn the tide.

It was precisely at the end of April 1934 that Barthou, who had hesitated until then, resumed the Franco-Soviet negotiations. He met Litvinov in Switzerland during May. The basic result of their talks was the institution of a proposal for an 'eastern Locarno'.[40]

The problem was to build up a quite complicated diplomacy, which consisted basically of two connected parts. The first part was a 'treaty of regional assistance' which would be signed by Russia, Germany, Poland, Czechoslovakia and the Baltic States, and whose purpose was to guarantee complete application of clauses 10 and 16 of the League of Nations Pact; a specific example of this application was that in the case of, say, aggression on the part of Germany, Poland would be bound to leave the way open for the movement of Russian troops to combat the aggressor. The form of this treaty, which was reminiscent of that of Locarno, was intended to establish a certain continuity with the diplomatic instruments of the Briand era, and to avoid coming into conflict with international opinion. The inclusion of Germany in the treaty, thus ensuring its mutual character would, it was thought, forestall British prejudices.

France, however, since she was not part of Eastern Europe, was not included in the future regional treaty. Therefore, she had to sign a special agreement with Russia: Russia would undertake the same commitments with regard to France as if she were a signatory of the Locarno Agreements; France would undertake the same commitments with regard to Russia as if she were a signatory of the East European Treaty. This second proposal was obviously of a different nature from the first; it seemed to constitute a step towards a pure and simple Franco-Russian alliance.

Thus it was to the second proposal that Britain objected, when

[39] Ibid., p.166.
[40] Ibid., pp.168–9, 176ff. Scott's account of the 'eastern Locarno' is based upon British, American and German diplomatic documents.

Barthou informed her of his intentions in July 1934. The British government asked for Germany to be included in the Franco-Soviet Pact and not only in the regional pact; thus the principle of mutual and reciprocal agreement of the Locarno Pact would be observed. Barthou yielded, and he had to promise also that if the Eastern pact were signed, negotiations for a disarmament meeting would be resumed and would in fact grant equal rights to Germany.

Britain, now won over, had no apparent difficulty in obtaining Mussolini's agreement to the proposal thus modified.[41] Germany refused as was expected and, perhaps, reckoned upon, but it was clever enough to draw out its reply, instead of giving an immediate and blunt refusal. On the other hand, Barthou had certainly not hoped for and perhaps not even foreseen the other obstacle which now became apparent: the refusal of Poland. Poland's reply of 27 September 1934 refused any obligation to Lithuania; she displayed great aversion to undertaking commitments with regard to Czechoslovakia; and she demanded the participation of Germany (which by now had made known its refusal) and a clause specifying the upholding of the German-Polish Agreement of January 1934. The real reason for the Polish refusal was this: in the event of a German-Russian war she could not consider the entry of Russian troops into Polish territory, for it was in this way that the partitions of Poland had begun in the eighteenth century.[42] There was nothing imaginary about this fear, as subsequent events were to show. However, the fact still remained that the policy of a Franco-Soviet *rapprochement* had for the first time encountered the most serious dilemma, and the immediate result of the Polish refusal was obviously the end of the proposal for an 'eastern Locarno'.

In the end, the only definite result of Louis Barthou's venture was the admission of the USSR to the League of Nations. This took place, not without difficulties,[43] in September 1934. The admission of the USSR encountered the opposition of Switzerland, Belgium and the Netherlands in particular, and also of a certain number of Latin American countries. Soon afterwards Barthou was assassinated at Marseilles, and thus there is no knowing what direction he would subsequently have given to French diplomacy.

[41] Ibid., p.181. [42] Ibid., p.187. [43] Ibid., pp.199–201.

The Franco-Soviet Treaty of Mutual Assistance

The Policy of Laval and the Conclusion of the Mutual Assistance Pact

Louis Barthou had let it be understood on a number of occasions that should his proposal for a multilateral regional agreement fail, he would simply have recourse to a Franco-Soviet agreement. This, however, could be merely a method of exerting diplomatic pressure. Here too was another irony of history: Pierre Laval, who succeeded him in Foreign Affairs and who had to carry out his predecessor's undertaking, insisted for his part on his wish to achieve a Franco-German agreement.

At this stage, however, he was not yet inclined to go to any lengths to obtain it. The settlement of the Saar problem must not be seen as an indication of a policy of appeasement, for France was bound by formal undertakings: according to the Treaty of Versailles, whose application she constantly claimed, the Saar must decide its fate by a plebiscite in January 1935. Laval simply arranged for the plebiscite to be carried out in an orderly way, without any unnecessary diplomatic tension. The Saar voted 90 per cent in favour of returning to Germany. If Hitler said in this connection, 'The French have finally missed the opportunity of a preventive war',[44] he manifested on this occasion a remarkable lack of understanding of the conditions in which French policy could be practised.

Laval, however, showed his personal bent even more by trying to revive the Eastern Pact in spite of the failure already recorded. He tried to satisfy the Polish demands,[45] but Polish intransigence soon put this desperate attempt to an end.

On the other hand Laval and his President of the Council, Pierre Etienne Flandin, were acting in accordance with a constant trend in French diplomacy when they again attempted a joint policy with Britain.[46] In February 1935 the two countries published a joint declaration with a view to a general settlement which would be freely negotiated between Germany and the other powers. The basis of this declaration was the proposal to conclude simultaneously an Eastern pact of mutual assistance, a Danube pact, a disarmament agreement which would guarantee equal rights to Germany (who would at the same time resume her place in the League of Nations) and finally – and here was the great innovation – an air pact of mutual assistance which would be confined to the

[44] Ibid., p.208.   [45] Ibid., p.210.   [46] Ibid., pp.219–22.

countries of Western Europe. Germany, however, showed that it intended to negotiate the air pact and to put aside all the rest.

The official announcement immediately afterwards of the re-establishment of compulsory military service in Germany in March 1935 hastened events. After visiting Berlin and Moscow, the British ministers themselves were converted to the idea of a Franco-Soviet pact,[47] which until that time they had always regarded with distrust. Pierre Laval then decided to sign the agreement (May 1935). Flandin and Edouard Herriot boasted in their Memoirs that they had forced Laval into an act which was distasteful to him. On the other hand, it would have been difficult for him to postpone it any further without putting an end to any policy of *rapprochement* with the Soviets and pushing them towards Germany, which would not be a good method of making the Germans more amenable. At least Laval and his staff – for he was supported in this by his General Secretary, Alexis Léger, who was not later implicated in collaboration with the Germans[48] – strove to remove anything of an automatic nature from the pact, to keep it within the framework of the League of Nations and to make it compatible with the Locarno Agreement.[49] In these conditions the 'immediate' nature of the mutual assistance stipulated in the event of aggression could be argued. At least France obtained one assurance without which she could not have considered signing the pact: an official declaration by the British government that it would not consider the new treaty incompatible with that of Locarno, and that if France came to the assistance of Russia as a victim of unprovoked aggression by Germany, Britain would not be obliged at the same time to come to the assistance of Germany.[50]

Such was the history of the Franco-Soviet Pact, in its broad outlines. To a great extent its conclusion seems to have been the effect of circumstances, the result of Hitler's shows of force rather than the well-ripened fruit of a deliberate trend in French policy. It has been said, not without apparent justification, that Pierre Laval who concluded the pact, saw it as an instrument of diplomatic pressure, the aim of which was to come to an agreement with Germany. However, even putting aside the role and the individual ideas of various people, one may wonder whether the treaty of

[47] Ibid., p.238.   [48] Ibid., p.245.   [49] See Document 33.
[50] W. E. Scott, op. cit., pp.249–50.

mutual assistance was not founded upon a basic misunderstanding.

What the French, who welcomed it most readily, saw above all in the Franco-Soviet *rapprochement* was its negative effect: from that time onward Germany could not make use of Russia's resources. This is what Colonel de Lattre expounded in 1933.[51] This is again what the influential political commentator, René Pinon, wrote on 15 May 1935 after the pact had been signed.[52] France thought also of her eastern allies, especially Poland: from then on the USSR, far from threatening them with an attack from the rear, could support their resistance.[53] Such a concept was still a long way from that of the reverse alliance which had justified the Franco-Russian agreement before 1914. It is curious that it was not often considered that Russia, with no ocean to protect her, might have to endure a direct land battle with Germany. What would happen then? Russia would only have to do what France herself counted on doing: enclose herself behind a line of entrenchments and wait.[54] So it may be understood that even at the moment of signing the pact of mutual assistance, France evaded the military agreement which the Soviets demanded: there was no need for precise agreements between General Staffs to put into operation a 'strategy' created in this way. In April 1936 one of the chief advocates of the Franco-Soviet *rapprochement*, the ambassador to Moscow, Charles Alphand, again wrote:[55]

> The main object of the pact of mutual assistance is to confront German expansionism with such a bloc as we could hope would prevent an attack. It establishes between France and the USSR, owing to their interests in common, joint tactics in peacetime in order to oppose war. . . .
>
> The chief interest of the alliance with Russia is to establish this force on our side and to prevent it from being on the side of our enemies. Moreover, I persist in considering that the chief means of collaboration with the USSR in the case of war would be the support given to our allies in the way of equipment, provisions, raw materials and munitions, to the extent that this would seem necessary to these allies themselves.

What did the USSR, for her part, expect from the French alliance? It is difficult to find this out directly. However, we can suppose that the Russians, unlike the French, were not certain

---

[51] Ibid., p.140. [52] Ibid., p.252. [53] Ibid., pp.197, 245.
[54] Ibid., p.266. [55] DDF, 2nd series, Vol. II, p. 63.

that a future war would be reduced to two immobile fortified fronts facing one another: this did not correspond with their experience of the 1914 war. Similarly, they did not perhaps have the same confidence in the strength of the Polish screen. If in this case they calculated that a German offensive directed against themselves would actually give rise to a French counter-offensive, they were going to be seriously disillusioned.

Chapter 12

The Abyssinia Conflict[1] and the Remilitarization of the Rhineland

In June 1935 France was closer than ever before to establishing the system of European security which had been her aim since 1919, and to which she had for a long time subordinated the abandoning of her privileged military situation. Several months later the entire structure was demolished and France found herself more threatened than ever, and finally set upon the downward path which would end in the disaster of 1940. We are truly at the turning-point of this history, at the point where it is of the greatest importance to understand what in fact happened. However, to explain one of the two great events under consideration, which are chronologically and also logically connected, we are still reduced to hypotheses.

The Origins of the Abyssinia Conflict

We have seen[2] that Italy's interest in East Africa goes back to before 1896. However, it was manifested in different ways in different periods; after the failure of the first military attempt, Italy had tried to reserve a zone of influence for herself by agreement with the two other interested countries, France and Britain. Disappointed in this, she tried at one time the method of a direct *entente* with Ethiopia, with whom she concluded agreements in 1928. From 1932 onwards, however, Italy reverted to a more active policy and the idea of securing French non-intervention appeared. Perhaps the threat of an economic and demographic penetration by the Japanese in Ethiopia in the autumn of 1933 was

---

[1] The terms Ethiopia and Abyssinia are not perhaps strictly synonymous from the geographical point of view; however, we will use either term regardless, as was the practice at the time.

[2] See Chapter 10.

173

to hasten events.[3] Perhaps also the failure of the Franco-Italian agreement for a Danubian union at about the same time succeeded in deciding Mussolini to look for satisfaction elsewhere. Be that as it may, from the end of 1934 the problem was presented in an urgent form.

The opportunity, or the pretext, was supplied on 5 December by the Walwal incident. This encounter between Italian soldiers and Abyssinian warriors was not the first and was followed by many others. This was not at all surprising, for it happened in territory in which the frontier between Abyssinia and Italian Somaliland had not been demarcated; it was, moreover, a desert through which nomads wandered and frequently crossed from one country into the other. However, the importance of this incident lies in the fact that it gave rise to a number of procedures: a procedure of direct conciliation, then of arbitration, between Italy and Ethiopia, but there was also recourse to the League of Nations. While this was taking place, Italy made military preparations which were all the more conspicuous because the troops had to pass through the Suez Canal. At the same time, France and Britain found that they were obliged to begin negotiations with Italy. France complied first, by the Rome Agreements of January 1935 which we have already discussed. The British, on the other hand, seemed at first to be playing a game of hide-and-seek with the Italians. It is probable, however, that talks took place unofficially, since during the month of June the British Foreign Secretary Anthony Eden made a proposal to Italy: Britain would concede to Ethiopia an access to the sea, at the expense of British Somaliland, to facilitate Ethiopian territorial and economic concessions to Italy. Since the offer seemed insufficient to Mussolini, on 31 July the League of Nations instructed the three powers, France, Britain and Italy, to find the basis for a compromise. This was what they did at the tripartite conference on 16–18 August 1935 in Paris; France and Britain agreed to offer Italy a privileged economic position in Ethiopia, and the nomination of Italian technical advisers in the Ethiopian administration, police and army. It can be pointed out that several situations of this nature before 1914 developed sooner or later into the formation of

[3] See C. Rousseau, *Le Conflit italo-éthiopien devant le droit international* (Paris, 1938), pp.33–5, and the fuller discussion in C. J. Lowe and F. Marzari, *Italian Foreign Policy 1870–1940* (London, 1975).

veritable European protectorates. Mussolini, however, was not satisfied with this; he demanded 'controlled disarmament of Ethiopia'. On 4 September Italy put before the League of Nations a memorandum which amounted to an act of accusation against Ethiopia whom she tried to have considered as unworthy of her membership of the League of Nations; in particular Ethiopia was reproached with not observing international regulations on the arms trade, and on slave detention and trade. Again, on 18 September, the League of Nations adopted a plan offering Ethiopia 'international assistance' to carry out reforms, while recognizing that Italy had a 'special interest' in that country.

What must be remembered about this long preliminary period is that both Britain and France seemed prepared to go quite a long way to satisfy Italian ambitions, and that the League of Nations did not seem very concerned, in fact, with preserving the sovereignty of one of its members. The anxiety to preserve peace then appeared at that time to be of paramount importance.

The Sanctions

Nevertheless, Italian troops entered Ethiopia on 3 October 1935. On 18 October the League of Nations established the aggression and voted for sanctions to be applied to Italy, according to clause 16 of the League of Nations Pact,[4] and the sanctions were put into practice by the member states during the month of November. Austria, Hungary and Albania, however, declared that they were against the sanctions and would not apply them. Switzerland made reservations and put forward her neutral status as a reason. Germany and Japan were no longer members of the League of Nations; the United States had never been a member.

These were the bare facts. Nevertheless, they presented many problems, to which only tentative solutions can be offered. In the first place, why did Mussolini have recourse to force while the negotiations, which had been undertaken because of his manœuvres of intimidation and his excellent diplomatic position, could give him the greater part of what he wanted? The reason usually given is that Mussolini wanted, even more than the acquisition of Ethiopia, to guarantee a military glory for Italian fascism, which could be acquired without too many risks. Many Italian texts,

[4] See Document 35.

now made public, give decisive confirmation of this explanation, if everything which was written or said in fascist Italy can still be taken as the truth. At the same time, however, Mussolini declared that he was prepared to face a conflict with the whole of Europe,[5] a boast hardly in keeping with the prudent behaviour of Italy in 1939. This doubt therefore remains: did Mussolini really believe that the League of Nations and the great powers would react?

This leads to a second question. Italian aggression was beyond dispute and the decisions made by the League of Nations were dictated by law. However, this was not a legal matter; the decision to set in motion this or that Genevan procedure is always of a political nature. Until then, many acts such as Japanese action in Manchuria, or the violations of the peace treaties by Germany, had not aroused the same reactions on the part of the League of Nations members, especially Britain. In fact, this was the first time that the sanctions mechanism had been put into operation. Why then did Britain, and with her the majority of the other nations, decide to act this time? The first explanation to come naturally to mind can, it appears, be dismissed. Britain had important interests in this part of Africa, especially in the region of Lake Tana, on which one of the sources of the Nile depends. However, Italy had already recognized these interests, which would have been much more surely guaranteed by a bilateral negotiation such as that of 1925. With regard to the 'imperial route' passing through the Red Sea, in what way was it more threatened if the Italians, while keeping the coastal possessions which they had held for a long time, spread towards the interior? We are then led to another hypothesis: Britain was coming round to the ideas of collective security which France had upheld for a long time, and the two united nations could not fail to carry with them the little states, especially those of Europe, which were already linked to one or the other and for whom an effectively operating system of collective security was after all the best safeguard.

But what do we understand by 'collective security'? The time has now come to attempt to define this concept. We can do this with the help of the British 'Peace Ballot', whose results were made known on 17 June 1935 (see Table 12.1).

[5] See Count Pompeo Aloisi, *Journal, 25 juillet 1932 – 14 juin 1936,* French trans., Paris, 1957, p.294.

Table *12.1*

Question 5: Do you consider that if a nation is bent on attacking another, the other nations should act jointly to force her to stop by:

(a) Economic and non-military measures?

Yes	No	Undecided	Abstained
10,027,608	635,074	27,255	855,107

(b) If necessary, by military measures?

Yes	No	Undecided	Abstained
6,784,368	2,351,981	40,893	2,364,441

In other words, a very large majority of those who replied to the questionnaire were prepared to carry out economic sanctions against the aggressor; but if it meant going as far as war, the majority was reduced considerably. This was food for thought for a government which could, moreover, realize that when their backs were to the wall, a certain number of people who were in principle in favour of sanctions would flinch.

We have mentioned Britain. However, there was a very widespread hope among pacifist peoples at the time that purely economic measures would be sufficient to make the aggressor draw back, and thus avoid a war. In France there was nothing comparable with the 'Peace Ballot'; but there were, nevertheless, indications which suggested similar conclusions. There was the case, for example, of the 'Manifestos' of the intellectuals which as we know formed a method widely used in France to express opinions on burning issues. On the occasion of the war in Ethiopia there were three main manifestos. The first, the *Manifesto of French Intellectuals for the Defence of the West and Peace in Europe*, which appeared on 4 October, was definitely hostile to sanctions against Italy. The *Manifesto for Respect of International Law* was published on 5 October. It considered that it was 'the duty of the French government to join in the efforts of all those governments which fight for peace and respect of international law'; the caution of the terms of this 'sanctionist' manifesto must be remembered. Finally, a *Manifesto for Justice and Peace* of 19 October, while unequivocally condemning Mussolini's venture in Ethiopia, again stressed this reservation regarding practical action:

Another European war would be an irreparable disaster. It is not because we refuse to approve of Monsieur Mussolini that we are prepared to accept such an evil. Not only would a general conflict be a calamity for civilization and for the entire world, it would also be another crime against the peoples who would be involved in this tragedy.

In the case of the Italo-Ethiopian conflict of 1935, what could be expected of purely economic sanctions? One must of course guard against the temptation of being a prophet in retrospect. There was, however, a precedent: that of the 1914–18 war. At that time France and Britain, the rulers of the seas, had organized the blockade against their enemies, Germany and Austria-Hungary. Then, however, it was a question of belligerents who did not shrink at any act of war and in particular did not show any great respect for the rights of neutral countries. Nevertheless, several years had been necessary to make this economic blockade truly effective, and the Central Powers had resisted for four years in spite of the considerable needs created by total war. No doubt the Italian economy, which lacked raw materials, was more vulnerable than that of Germany, but the requirements of the war in Ethiopia were in no way comparable with those of a world war.

In view of this precedent, it cannot be said that the application of sanctions was slow. The enormous complexity of the problems arising must be taken into account. We will take just one example, that of mutual assistance: the sanctions had very different repercussions in the different countries which applied them and, within each country, in the various sectors of activity and different businesses. How could an equitable distribution of the costs and losses expressly stipulated by the pact be ensured?

Other, more serious, criticisms referred to the insufficient extent of the sanctions. Why, it was asked, was the embargo on arms and essential war materials not extended to metallurgical products, to coal and to oil? In fact, Italy could easily obtain from Germany coal, iron and steel which would pass through Austria. The main discussion at the League of Nations was concerned with oil, which is vital to a motorized army. The oil stocks in Italy were estimated at three or four months' consumption in February 1936,[6] that is, five months after the beginning of hostilities and three months before the end. It was also necessary to take into

[6] P. Bartholin, *Les Conséquences économiques des sanctions*, p.119.

account substitute products, with which we have since become acquainted, and the possibilities of transferring oil purchases to countries which would not be bound by a League of Nations decision. Thus, American oil exports to Italy increased from $2,600,000 for the period November 1934 to May 1935 to $6,300,000 for the period November 1935 to May 1936.[7]

In other words, the application of purely economic sanctions required a great deal of time in order to be effective. This method assumed that Ethiopia would be able to put up a long resistance against the invader. Certain contemporary accounts, in fact, give one to believe that a long war was expected. However, this was minimizing the difference between the technological level of the opposing forces and the extent of the Italian preparations, which were a matter of public notoriety.

According to certain commentators, the measures affecting trade in Italian goods would not necessarily make themselves felt before a long period of time had elapsed: 'The aim pursued . . . seems to have been, first and foremost, to strike at the weak point of the fascist economy: its currency shortage'.[8] This, however, was the view of classical economists whose ideas had not been changed by the unorthodox experiments occasioned by the world crisis. In fact, by strict measures of national self-sufficiency and by a rigorous control of foreign trade and of the entire economy, Italy was able to resist even the financial blockade for a long time.

Everything leads us therefore to the conclusion formulated shortly afterwards by an objective analyst who was, however, a supporter of the principle of sanctions: 'In order for sanctions to be effective, a complete embargo of long duration is necessary, and for this a blockade is imperative.'[9]

Certainly a maritime blockade was easy to carry out against Italy, a country enclosed by the Mediterranean: in practice it was sufficient to forbid her trade to pass through the Straits of Gibraltar and the Suez Canal. By this operation, even before Italy was 'brought to her knees', the armies invading Ethiopia would be completely isolated.

However, a blockade was an act of war. It was not without danger even for the British fleet, which had become old-fashioned, and whose superiority of number over the Italian fleet was not

[7] Ibid., p.66.   [8] Ibid., p.16.   [9] Ibid., p.265.

overwhelming. Above all, it involved pacifist peoples in a course of action which they had not in fact contemplated.

A New Attempt at Conciliation: the Laval-Hoare Plan

On 18 October 1935, at the suggestion of Britain and France, the League of Nations decided to impose sanctions on Italy. On 14 December the public heard of the existence of a plan drawn up by those responsible for French and British diplomacy, Pierre Laval and Sir Samuel Hoare, which granted to Italy a very large part of her objectives. The brutal confrontation of these two facts requires an explanation which, again, can only be hypothetical.

Various theories have been put forward. One of them questions the attitude of the French government which, it maintained, was very different from that of the British government – especially as regards the manœuvres of Pierre Laval. He was supposed to have set out to sabotage the policy of sanctions on which Britain was determined. In actual fact, Laval did not act alone: he had the approval of his Council of Ministers, in spite of certain discordant voices. The fact is that France was in a particularly difficult position: she was much more devoted to the task of consolidating Central Europe and therefore to the *entente* with Italy, than was Britain; on the other hand, she had always been the champion of collective security, and in this respect she really could not openly oppose Britain.

But what of Britain herself? Was she so resolute in her position? Her government, too, was divided, but the majority did not seem to have resolved to go very far in the matter of sanctions. It was even possible to say that Laval's policy provided an alibi for British action – or inaction.[10]

Are we then to suppose that the two governments, in order to satisfy their public opinion – or at least the British opinion at the time, as French opinion was very divided – made a show of adopting the policy of sanctions, while basically resolved to seek an understanding with Italy? Everything is possible, of course. However, the French and British governments of the time, no novices, would have displayed a most extraordinary lack of responsibility in deliberately adopting a course which accumulated every possible disadvantage, since it could not fail to arouse

[10] M. Gallo, *L'Affaire d'Ethiopie*, p.181.

Italian resentment and at the same time to end in publicly recording the failure of the security system based on the League of
Nations.

While awaiting other documentary proofs than the retrospective Memoirs of invariably partial statesmen, we may consider a
third theory which would explain by a series of miscalculations
and false steps the incoherence of the policy followed during this
period. Mussolini, relying on precedents, did not perhaps believe
that Britain, enticing France along with her, would really have
recourse to the application of clause 16 of the League of Nations
Pact. Similarly, the British and French governments, like all
governments of the time, were very inexperienced in economic
matters, as we have already had occasion to point out. Perhaps
they did not estimate in advance the difficulties and inevitable
delays of the course of action they were undertaking. Perhaps also
they thought that once the mechanism of sanctions had been set
in motion, Mussolini would be alarmed at the consequences and
would become more amenable, and that an agreement would
become possible which would put an end to hostilities while
respecting, outwardly at least, the fundamental interests of
Ethiopia.

On the contrary, however, Mussolini hardened his attitude,
having been convinced that Britain would not go as far as war.
Then again, when all the specific problems of imposing sanctions
were revealed, it was found that a long preparation would be
necessary. Now it appeared that since mid-November the British
government had known through its ambassador in Addis Ababa,
that Ethiopia could not resist indefinitely;[11] and since it thought
that it had a free hand after the elections of 14 November, it
hastened to back-pedal. After 1 December, according to the
Journal of Aloisi, Robert Vansittart, one of the chief officials of the
Foreign Office, made extensive offers to Italy, which implied
direct possession of a large part of Ethiopia and a share in the
control of the remainder.[12]

Such was the origin of the Laval-Hoare Plan, which was pre-

[11] Ibid., p.201.
[12] Ibid., pp.198–9. It must be noted that Vansittart was not one of those
who later were to advocate 'appeasement'. It is therefore an oversimplification
to identify the partisans of conciliation in Ethiopia with the partisans of
concessions to Hitler.

pared by the two ministers on 7 and 8 December, ratified by the British Cabinet on 9 December, and by that of France on 10 December. This plan went further than the Vansittart proposals, but its principles were the same.

However, this plan could obviously not succeed unless it had the approval of Italy and Ethiopia before it was made public, for opinion in favour of sanctions, in France and in England, still had all the enthusiasm of a new venture and could not understand a volte-face or a retreat, the full reasons for which, moreover, would be difficult to disclose. Simultaneously, Mussolini displayed caution and Ethiopia refused, and journalistic indiscretions revealed the terms of the plan.

Immediately, those in favour of sanctions in both countries flared up and branded the Laval-Hoare Plan as a 'reward for aggression', which of course it was. The British government, as was the custom, yielded to opinion; Sir Samuel Hoare agreed to be the scapegoat and resigned in order to save his colleagues politically. However, while resigning he justified his policy:[13]

> I was shocked at the thought that we could lead Ethiopia to believe that the League of Nations could do more than was in its power, and that, when all was said and done, we would be faced with a terrible disappointment on the day that Ethiopia was completely destroyed as an independent State.

Pierre Laval did not have the same resources as his British colleague; he was President of the Council, and it was not a political custom in France, as it was in Britain, to allow a ministry, which admitted to being deceived over an important point, to remain in power. One can suggest the difference in temperament of the two nations as a reason for this, but also the fact that in France a replacement ministerial combination is always easy to find.

Pierre Laval, then, tried to put up a brave front, and until the end of December he maintained a small majority in the Chamber. However, he was progressively abandoned by the radicals, whom he could not do without, for the Chamber which resulted from the 1932 elections tended towards the Left. On 22 January 1936 he also resigned.

The departure of these two men put an end to their attempt at

---

[13] House of Commons sitting of 19 December 1935 (Hansard).

conciliation, the success of which in any case was not guaranteed. However, we must note that there did not result for all that a sanctions policy any more energetic and daring, an additional proof that this policy had encountered more formidable obstacles than the manœuvres of two politicians. Moreover, the collapse of Ethiopian resistance soon succeeded in solving the problem: in May 1936 Italian troops reached Addis Ababa, and the war as such was ended.

The price of this affair, however, was very high. Fascist Italy, whom it was believed possible to associate with the consolidation of Europe, was thrown towards Hitler's Germany with whom she had had an affinity from the beginning. At the same time, just as the system of collective security appeared to be entering the realm of positive action, it suffered a defeat from which it was not to recover, and the public's confidence in the League of Nations was fundamentally shaken. Even if it were regarded simply as the loss of certain illusions and a return to reality, it can hardly be said that this new consciousness of reality had a tonic effect. On the contrary, the mutual recriminations resulting from this failure poisoned the atmosphere, especially between the French and the British.

Perhaps the most serious consequence, however, concerned the cohesion and force of internal resistance in France. Until then, in spite of press polemics, prompted by the policy of Briand, for example, the French leaders, although they belonged to different parties, had succeeded in coming to an agreement on a common policy, by putting national interest before any ideological preference and in making it acceptable to the country. The Ethiopian war was the first occasion on which the two Frances confronted each other, with an unyielding violence in the field of foreign policy. The supporters of each policy considered that the very security of the country was irreparably compromised by their opponents' policy. For those opposed to sanctions, the alliance with Italy was the very foundation of French security, and there should have been no hesitation in sacrificing the agreement with England for the sake of it: this showed an extraordinary misunderstanding of the facts of the problem of national defence. For the supporters of sanctions, there was no safety for France outside collective security, and the opportunity to put it into practice should not be allowed to pass at any price; as far as the Franco-Italian *rapprochement* was concerned, they denied it any importance. It must be said, however, that both sides argued in complete ignorance, for the people at that time knew very little about the Franco-Italian negotiations: the frustrated plans like that of the Danubian economic union were only known from the very recent publication of the *Documents Diplomatiques Français*. The Rome Agreements themselves were not published at the time, for it would have been difficult for Mussolini to declare that he was entirely satisfied with the official text; but the existence of these secret agreements led to much speculation.

From that time on, French diplomacy, which was in any case in the grip of very formidable problems, was to be paralysed in addition by the violence of the divisions of public opinion.

Remilitarization of the Rhineland

(a) The Preliminaries

That Hitler was resolved sooner or later to rid himself of the Locarno Agreements could hardly be doubted: his programme could not otherwise be carried out. The Ethiopian affair gave him an exceptional opportunity, since the Locarno guarantors, Italy and Britain, were openly in conflict.

Indeed, from the beginning of 1936, French diplomacy could see the warning signs of a denunciation by Germany of the Locarno Treaty. Judging by the campaigns of the German press, the pretext seems at first to have been the military talks between France and Britain. The object of these talks was very limited, and it was connected with the Ethiopian war: Britain asked for France's support in the event of Italy's attacking her fleet in the Mediterranean. Germany, however, was for some time disposed to maintain that separate military talks between two of the signatories violated the spirit of the Treaty.[14] To allay these real or imagined fears, the Quai d'Orsay was prepared to consider parallel Anglo-German military talks in a favourable light.[15]

Finally, however, Hitler preferred to make use of the Franco-Soviet Pact as an argument. The problem of the compatibility of this pact with the Locarno Agreements had been questioned from the beginning, as we have seen, and the French negotiators had

[14] DDF, 2nd series, Vol. I, pp.17, 25, 31–5, 71–6. [15] Ibid., pp.111–12.

taken great precautions to guarantee it. The final text had satisfied Britain and Italy in this respect, but not Germany. However, when the Franco-Soviet Treaty was signed, Hitler had evaded the juridical discussion proposed by France; he had even said that he would continue to apply the Agreement.

It was in connection with the ratification of the Franco-Soviet Treaty by the French Parliament that the German leaders decided to renew the affair. The atmosphere in France had changed greatly since the signing of this treaty; a large proportion of the Right, after having accepted it, had now become hostile to it.[16] This can be explained by concern for the internal policy, the fear that the Franco-Soviet alliance would strengthen a trend favourable to the Popular Front. Another element had been recently revealed: the French General Staff had expressed clear misgivings on the prospect of a ratification. We know this from a note[17] of 27 January 1936 whose origin was not defined but which, according to a cross-check,[18] must have come from General Gamelin himself. This note let it be understood that Germany would seize this opportunity to reoccupy the left bank of the Rhine. It stressed, moreover, with new clarity, that the Franco-Russian Alliance, if complemented by a military agreement, was incompatible with the Franco-Polish Alliance. Finally, it noted the alarm of Belgium, who did not wish to be involved in a war for Russia on the strength of being a signatory of the Locarno Agreements. It was known that the entire French defence system was closely bound up with Belgium.

Were the reasons put forward in this memorandum the only ones which explained this new attitude of the General Staff? Ideological motives also come to mind, but they are unlikely in the case of General Gamelin, who was politically much more flexible than his predecessor Weygand. Was it possible that, during the months which had passed since the signing of the treaty, the French General Staff had become aware that the Franco-Soviet Alliance implied something quite different from a purely material and unilateral aid supplied by Russia to the eastern allies of France? Could it mean that Russia would reckon on a

[16] P. Renouvin, *Histoire des relations internationales*, Vol. VIII, part 2, pp.91–2.

[17] DDF, 2nd series, Vol. I, pp.152–4; see also Document 38.

[18] Ibid., pp.444–6; see also Document 39.

French offensive to extricate her if she were attacked by Germany, and that under these conditions, the Franco-Russian Alliance would force France to change her strategy radically? This strategy, as we have seen, seemed to be dictated by the demographic situation of France. It is by no means impossible that this sudden change on the part of the General Staff influenced the French nationalist press whose editors were often in contact with high-ranking officers and who were thus aware, not of the secrets of national defence, of course, but at least of the state of mind of the French Supreme Command.

Be that as it may, from the beginning of 1936 those responsible for French policy were expecting a remilitarization of the Rhineland and were considering what steps to take should this contingency arise. The Minister of Foreign Affairs several times stressed the need for a preliminary consultation with Britain.[19] Unfortunately, the French ambassador in London did not paint a very encouraging picture of future prospects: London did not think that France could have recourse to force in order to maintain the status of the demilitarized Rhineland area; to the British it seemed unjustifiable.[20] At the same time, however, the new Minister of Foreign Affairs, Pierre Etienne Flandin, questioned those responsible for military matters: what counter-measures could be considered?[21] General Maurin, Minister of War, pretended not to understand. In fact, he replied in a memorandum of 12 February:[22]

A sudden reoccupation of the whole or a large part of the demilitarized zone would of necessity result in certain precautionary measures on our part. *We would not know in fact whether this was a question of a prelude to an attack.*[23]

This dialogue of the deaf continued for a time, and then the Minister of Foreign Affairs lost patience and wrote in a new memorandum of 24 February:[24]

The War Minister is not giving an exact reply to the questions he has been asked. By contemplating precautionary measures which could be adopted immediately, and counter-strokes on the rearmament

---

[19] Ibid., pp.78–9, 174–5.   [20] Ibid., pp.273–6.
[21] Ibid., p.220 (7 February 1936).   [22] Ibid., p.247.   [23] Our italics.
[24] DDF, 2nd series, Vol. I, pp.317–18 (24 February 1936).

level, at distant dates, he in fact sees a reoccupation of the Rhineland area by the Reich as a favourable opportunity to obtain new credits. ... It must be established that the letter from the Minister of War only refers to certain 'guarantee' measures ... whose purpose would be to secure us against a *further* development of German initiative; it contains nothing about the initiatives which France would take to intimidate her enemy or to make the enemy retreat.

A memorandum from the Air Minister, however, confirmed that in the opinion of the military authorities the reoccupation of the Rhineland did not constitute a sudden attack requiring an immediate counter-action.[25]

(b) *The crisis*

On 7 March the expected event took place: Hitler announced to the French ambassador that he denounced the Locarno Treaty and that he was sending 'symbolic detachments' of the German army to the Rhineland. The President of the Council, Albert Sarraut, the Minister of Foreign Affairs, Flandin, the military Ministers and their chiefs of General Staff met immediately. We do not have a record of this meeting and we know only indirectly of what took place there, from the account of a meeting which was held the next day at General Gamelin's home; this meeting was limited to those responsible for military affairs, and its purpose was to reply to the demands made by the government.[26] It was decided to refer the matter immediately to the League of Nations Council.[27] At the same time, however, the dialogue of the deaf had been resumed between the civilians and the military. General Gamelin appeared to have heard the question: 'Are you in a position to hold out?' which would imply a case in which the Germans, not content with occupying the demilitarized zone, would attack France directly. However, at the same meeting Admiral Durand-Viel heard an entirely different question, which was much more probable according to the facts we have: 'Are you in a position to drive the Germans out of the Rhineland?' To this Gamelin replied that if French troops entered the Rhineland, this would be war, and that it would first of all be necessary to carry out general

[25] Ibid., pp.377–8 (2 March).
[26] Ibid., pp.444–6; see also Document 39.
[27] This was made by a telegram from Flandin to the Secretary-General of the League of Nations; ibid., pp.430–1 (8 March 1936).

mobilization and guarantee the support of Britain, Belgium, and also Italy, the other Locarno guarantor. This last condition, at least, could obviously not be applied.

However, the representatives of the powers who had signed the Locarno Agreement, apart from Germany, met in Paris on 10 March. Again, we do not have a record of this meeting. We know of it only indirectly, from a memorandum from Flandin to his diplomatic representatives.[28] From this we know that there were two opposing points of view. Britain considered that her obligation to give assistance would apply only in the event of a direct attack against France, and seemed ready to accept the *fait accompli* in the Rhineland. France and Belgium insisted that it was necessary to respect all the pledges which had been undertaken and to re-establish the former situation in the Rhineland and the respect of international law.

French diplomacy was immediately aware of the repercussions which this new failure of Germany to meet its obligations would have throughout the world, if it were again allowed to pass unchallenged.[29] To be more precise, the small European states had a premonition that France would no longer be able to come to their rescue, and they began to think that they would have to change their policy and turn towards Germany.[30] This was why, in spite of the disappointments he had already experienced, Flandin insisted on setting in hand a positive course of action. Having been disappointed as far as the army was concerned, he asked the navy to study the possibility of taking securities with a view to forcing Germany to negotiate: seizure of the German island of Heligoland in the North Sea, blockade of a German port, seizure of German ships.[31] The navy hastened to prevent these 'demonstrations which are as reckless as they are ineffectual', and which could only be made, moreover, with the support of the British fleet.[32] As for the Army General Staff, they contemplated only an occupation of part of the Saar or Luxembourg for the same purpose.[33] The same conditions always reappeared: no

[28] Ibid., pp.493–4 (11 March 1936); see also Document 40.
[29] Ibid., p.525 (12 March 1936).
[30] Ibid., pp.379–80, 420–1, 548–9, 646–7.
[31] Ibid., pp.501–2 (10 March 1936).
[32] Ibid., pp.502–3 (11 March), pp.522–4 (12 March 1936).
[33] Ibid., pp.504–6 (11 March 1936).

action could be taken without a mandate from the League of Nations; first of all, the whole of the 'covering' forces would have to be established, that is, a partial mobilization would have to be instituted, and if Germany reacted this would have to be followed quickly by general mobilization; in any case there could be no question of immediate operations, for France did not have an expeditionary force available which would be ready at any time to act.[34]

On 14 March, however, the League of Nations Council ascertained that Germany had failed in its international obligations – and did not decide upon any action. On 19 March the Locarno powers proposed to submit the problem of compatibility of the Locarno Agreements and the Franco-Soviet Pact to the International Court of Justice at The Hague, and asked Germany to limit its effectives and its occupation zone in the Rhineland, while awaiting the verdict. On 24 March Hitler refused.

And this was all. Later we shall see the negotiations which were undertaken with a view to replacing the Locarno Treaty, which was rendered null from that moment. The deed was, however, accomplished: Hitler had reoccupied the Rhineland, violating the Treaty of Versailles and the Locarno Treaty, without arousing any reaction from the League of Nations, from the other signatories of the Locarno Agreements, or from France herself.

(c) *An attempt at interpretation*

This lack of reaction was doubtless the fact most fraught with consequences in the period 1919–39. It is generally admitted today that at that moment France let slip the last opportunity of stopping Hitler without starting a general war, without even risking anything except limited military operations from which she had the best chances of emerging the victor. It is therefore of particular importance to try to understand the motive for French passivity.

Many explanations have been put forward. One of these concerns French internal policy. France, it is said, was on the eve of legislative elections – not a very propitious moment for heroic resolutions on the part of those who would soon be rendering an account to the voters. In this connection some even blame the rapid progress achieved by the Popular Front in the country at this time, and even the functioning of democratic institutions

[34] Ibid., pp.696–9.

which made the country incapable of facing a serious crisis. In fact, however, as we have seen, if a desire for action were shown anywhere, it was shown by politicians, and especially by Flandin, the man responsible for diplomacy.

According to another theory, France did not dare to undertake a venture in which she would come up against the British veto. It is certain, and it was known beforehand – for nothing was done on the spur of the moment in these circumstances – that Britain was not in favour of a French intervention which could lead to armed conflict, especially to protect the demilitarized status of the Rhineland, of which her public opinion no longer approved. There are some who even said that this British unwillingness was a revenge for the Ethiopian affair in which France had given little support to Britain. This opinion, however, seems mistaken. In fact, on 2 September 1935, Laval had asked Anthony Eden whether Britain would apply the 'Covenant' as firmly in Europe as she intended to do in East Africa; Eden's reply was cautious.[35] It was certainly not that Britain was less interested in Europe than in Africa. However, she wished to take only limited risks, while an operation against Germany appeared very formidable to everyone.

It is always a temptation for a French historian of this period to put all the responsibilities on Britain. In the present case, this explanation would be inadequate, for it would have overlooked a basic element which was revealed in the documentation. From the beginning of the crisis to the end, the slight inclination to action on the part of politicians came into conflict with the resolute opposition of those responsible for French military affairs. It is their attitude which must be explained.

According to one argument, the French army was not organized for the action which was required of it at that time; it did not have available an intervention force which was ready to go into action immediately and independently of the rest of the troops. The armoured divisions which Paul Reynaud had requested in vain the previous year on the advice of Colonel de Gaulle are considered in retrospect. We think, however, that this explanation is insufficient; we cannot believe that the General Staff would have been incapable of improvising such a force, if it had considered that an intervention was not running too serious risks.

In the opinion of the General Staff all the indications were

[35] A. Eden, *Memoirs*, Vol. I, London, 1960, p.294.

indeed that an advance of French troops into the Rhineland would result in a total and prolonged war against Germany; and it considered that, since the beginning of 1936, Germany had been stronger than France. It is advisable to stop at this assertion, which is surprising to the reader today.

On 10 March 1933, during a discussion with British ministers, the French Minister of War, Edouard Daladier, estimated that the effectives of the German forces, taking into account the formations which had just been completed by Marshal Goering, were much greater than those of the French army.[36] He admitted, however, that France still had a greater amount of equipment available. Of course this pessimism was only accentuated in the years that followed, as Germany rearmed more and more openly. A memorandum of 18 January 1936 from the General Staff[37] took stock of the situation. The date is important, for there was still no question of replying to a request for intervention. At that moment the 'lack of balance' of power in favour of Germany was accentuated by the fact that, because of the Ethiopian conflict, France had to guard her Italian frontier. The conclusion of the memorandum is worthy of consideration:

> The present French programme can only oppose the intensive rearmament of Germany, an artillery powerful both in quality and quantity, and a mass of tanks which is almost 2,000 units for the armoured divisions alone, with an artillery system based on equipment in service during the 1914–18 war, limited armaments and anti-tank defences, especially as far as the fortified areas are concerned, and a total strength of modern tanks which is hardly a third of our needs.

This lack of balance[38] in favour of Germany obviously referred to permanently armed forces. However, since Germany had had no obligatory military service from 1920 to 1935, France must still have had the advantage as far as trained reserves were concerned. This explains Gamelin's demand that general mobilization should take place before any military action. This demand, it could be said, was sufficient to discourage the government.

[36] DDF, 1st series, Vol. II, pp.777–85.

[37] Ibid., 2nd series, Vol. I, pp.116–20; see also Document 36.

[38] There are obviously questions to which we cannot provide an answer at present: why did the French army intelligence service not re-establish the facts about the real situation of the German forces? Or, if it did so, why did no one believe it?

The analysis can be taken much further, however. Throughout the crisis the coolness of the French military authorities contrasted with the alarm of the diplomats. Were the military unaware that they were taking part in disastrous events?

In the first place they considered that just as official German rearmament had been preceded by secret rearmament, so the operation of 7 March only made official the remilitarization of the Rhineland which had already been carried out in secret.[39] From their strictly professional point of view, however, the re-entry of German troops into the Rhineland was not as serious as it appeared. Since, in the event of war, the French army would not in any case go to fight beyond the line of defence which had been provided so long ago, what did it matter that German troops came to occupy a glacis where in any case no offensive was contemplated, and to border the Maginot Line at which, it had long been reckoned, they would be stopped?

In short, France's inaction in March 1936 was the logical consequence of both the pacifism of the French people and also the purely defensive military doctrine which was closely bound up with it.

The Last Attempt at a Rapprochement *with Italy*

One of the consequences of remilitarization of the Rhineland was that Czechoslovakia, who had been over-optimistic for too long, from now on felt as threatened as Austria, and many wondered whether it would be possible for France to come to the aid of her Central European allies once the Germans had fortified their western frontier. In fact, another means of intervention in Central Europe was being considered on the French side: that of passing through Italy.[40] There was therefore an attempt to re-establish the Franco-Italian military *entente* which had been outlined at the time of the Stresa Agreements.

On 2 March 1936 – the German troops had not yet entered the Rhineland but they were not expected to delay long – the French

[39] DDF, 2nd series, Vol. I, pp.696–9.
[40] DDF, 2nd series, Vol. II, pp.139–41, and especially pp.642–5. Memorandum from the General Staff: direct assistance to Czechoslovakia by sending units to Central Europe, and the joining of the armies of the Little *Entente* and those of Italy.

Minister of Foreign Affairs asked the League of Nations to launch a final appeal to Italy and Ethiopia, with a view to opening negotiations. Each could now see more clearly than in December 1935 that Ethiopia would not hold out for long, and that only sanctions which could result in military consequences would be effective.

France failed to establish a rapid procedure for opening these negotiations.[41] However, Mussolini did not at first discourage France's direct approaches. On several occasions the French ambassador in Rome stated that Italy was prepared to restore the Stresa front.[42] On one occasion Mussolini declared to him that in his opinion the Gamelin-Badoglio military agreements were still in force, and that he was still prepared to defend the line of the Danube; as far as Czechoslovakia was concerned, he did not have any obligations towards her other than those of the League of Nations Covenant, but: 'As soon as I am secure in Africa, I will uphold these stipulations, for I will become the most conservative of all.'[43]

His tone soon changed, however. Italy showed her impatience over the delay with which the sanctions were removed, and began to seek an arrangement with Germany over the question of Austria.[44] This development was already perceptible before the Popular Front government came to power and gave him an additional pretext.[45] However, political ideology does not seem to have played any part in this latter attempt at a Franco-Italian *rapprochement* of which the USSR, moreover, did not disapprove. Litvinov in fact declared to the French diplomat, Massigli:[46]

> Ethiopia does not interest me; it is necessary to see whether it is possible to obtain adequate pledges from Italy with regard to her general policy in Europe; if these pledges are sufficiently well defined, it will be worth while to say no more about it.

Was Mussolini's originally conciliatory attitude, however, not merely a pretence, the purpose of which was to be given a free hand as long as the victory in Ethiopia had not been finally achieved? Or was Mussolini the conqueror waiting not only for

---

[41] For the procedures contemplated see DDF, 2nd series, Vol. II, pp.91-2.
[42] Ibid., pp.26-41 *et passim.*
[43] Ibid., pp.148-9 (18 April).
[44] Ibid., pp.401-3, 414-15, 424-8.
[45] Ibid., pp.432-3.
[46] Ibid., pp.313-14 (14 May).

others to 'say no more about it' but for them to pay even more dearly than ever for his co-operation in Europe? Be that as it may, French diplomatic attempts achieved nothing. An Austro-German agreement published on 11 July[47] 'gave the relations' between the two countries 'a normal and friendly character'. Germany would not interfere in the internal affairs of Austria. Austria would behave like a German state without injuring her relations with Italy.

In this way, what had always been the strongest tie between France and Italy had, to all intents, disappeared, for a time at least: the concern for preserving Austrian independence.

[47] Ibid., pp.656–7.

Chapter 13

The Foreign Policy of the Popular Front

General Reflections

As a result of the legislative elections of May 1936, a Popular Front government with socialist leadership was formed on 6 June with Léon Blum as president. It is necessary to point out this fact, since from then onwards – although for only a short time – it would no longer be possible in France to separate foreign from internal policy. Now the socialists who played the main role in the new ministry had never previously participated in the responsibilities of power; they had therefore neither the experience nor the traditions. It is true that the Ministries of National Defence and Foreign Affairs were entrusted to the radicals, whose party had on the contrary nearly always been associated with government. However, Léon Blum was to play the most important part personally, especially in the diplomatic field.

In this connection, the political past of Léon Blum gave rise to certain questions. In opposition he was distinguished by a very marked pacifism; he had been a zealous apostle of disarmament. In addition, he considered that in his actions he was bound by the programme of the Rassemblement Populaire. In the field of foreign policy[1] this programme usually barricaded itself behind harmoniously balanced general formulae which, when all is said and done, caused little inconvenience to a diplomat. However, it declared itself clearly in favour of collective security, since it had been drawn up before the failure of the attempt to impose 'sanctions' on Italy. It contained, moreover, as a legacy of former socialist and communist campaigns against the Treaty of Versailles, a somewhat hazardous formula for the 'adjustment of treaties which are dangerous to the peace of the world', which could be useful as an argument to both Hitler and Mussolini. The

[1] See Document 43.

Popular Front had, however, originally been formed to fight against fascism; was it possible to separate this fight completely from foreign policy?

In these difficult conditions, Blum adopted a very cautious policy. The problem was above all to maintain or to re-establish national unity to face foreign countries. This was obviously one of the conditions of effectiveness, but Blum's ideas went much further; he feared, as he said later, that France would one day find herself faced with a civil war further complicated by an external war.[2] He therefore endeavoured to conduct a policy which could not give a handle to any violent opposition. While launching the great rearmament effort long advocated by military specialists, which had been made possible by the abandonment of the dogma of budgetary equilibrium, he endeavoured first and foremost to make his diplomacy appear both very pacifist and free from any ideological inspiration,[3] so that it would be the diplomacy of the whole nation and not of one party. At the same time he worked so closely along the traditional lines of French foreign policy that the first negotiation we have to relate, which was begun before the advent of the Popular Front, continued without interruption or noticeable deviation after Léon Blum had taken office.

Franco-British Relations and the Negotiation for a 'New Locarno'

The denunciation of the Locarno Treaty, even independently of its immediate consequence – the reoccupation of the Rhineland – had presented France with a formidable problem, for the Locarno Agreements were the only tie which Britain acknowledged having with France. Would the British government take advantage of Hitler's gesture to regain complete freedom with regard to Europe? Or, on the other hand, would France obtain at this juncture a guarantee of Franco-British mutual assistance, which was her constant endeavour? In February 1936 a memorandum from the Army General Staff presented the problem with surprising exactitude:[4]

> By the German gesture Britain is freed from her Locarno obligations which imposed on her a very inconvenient impartiality, and pre-

---

[2] It should not be forgotten that the electoral victory of the Popular Front was in no way a landslide victory: 5,400,000 votes as against 4,200,000 to its opponents.   [3] See Document 44.   [4] DDF, 2nd series, Vol. I, pp.299–300.

vented her from concluding any military agreement with us. Without hindrance she can now with France face their common enemy on the Rhine, the common frontier, by concluding a mutual assistance treaty extended by a military agreement. Hence the Anglo-Franco-Belgian bloc may be finally welded together and its massive strength may be a compensation for the loss of the Rhineland no man's land.

However, if we do not strike while the iron is hot, it is to be feared that the British, on reflection, will declare that they will be satisfied with a 'new Locarno', which is already being discussed in British newspapers, and which would merely be the Rhineland pact, from which the clauses concerning the demilitarized zone would have disappeared. In this way the drawbacks of Locarno would be retained, without any compensation for the loss of advantages which it involves.

On 19 March, while proposing to submit the Franco-German disagreement over the interpretation of the Locarno Agreements to the Court at The Hague, France, Britain and Belgium were mutually guaranteeing their territories in the event of German aggression; but this was purely a measure of conservation which was valid until the conclusion of the negotiation to be undertaken with Germany, of which they did not prejudge the issue.

It is true that shortly afterwards France obtained another advantage which she had long wished for in vain:[5] the beginning of Franco-British military talks. These, however, held in London on 15 and 16 April, proved singularly deceptive: they dealt solely with the question of logistic problems which the embarkation of two British divisions for France, fifteen days after the start of hostilities, would present; the British representatives had been formally ordered to refuse to take part in any discussions on the use of these forces, that is, on plans of operations.[6] Moreover, if Britain seemed in principle to take the course of rearmament, even before the reoccupation of the Rhineland, this rearmament appeared to be basically 'insular' and was concerned primarily with aviation, the navy and measures for defending the country. Thus it was only indirectly connected with French concerns.[7]

Nevertheless, in spite of the intransigence of Hitler, who refused in particular any limitation or control of his armaments in the

[5] Setting aside the discussions which have already been mentioned about the possibility of an Italian attack against the British fleet in the Mediterranean.   [6] DDF, 2nd series, Vol. II, pp.155–64.   [7] Ibid., Vol. I, pp.268–72.

Rhineland, Britain continued to show a preference for negotiations which would include Germany. The reasons for this appeared particularly clearly in the confidences imparted to the French ambassador in Berlin by a British diplomat. On the one hand, British opinion was not yet convinced of the aggressive nature of Hitler's Germany, and there was the risk that little support would be given to the government for automatic assistance to France, unless Hitler were first supplied with another treaty to violate. On the other hand, it was feared that a purely Franco-British agreement would provide Hitler with an excuse to challenge the German-British naval agreement of 1935.[8]

France, in accordance with Britain's wishes, joined in the attempt to negotiate a 'new Locarno'. This was initiated by sending a British questionnaire to Berlin on 6 May. The German government was earnestly requested to declare that it would not change by force the territorial and political *status quo* of Europe, and to complement its non-aggression pledges by pledges of non-interference in the internal affairs of other states; the air agreement which had been an issue for some time was to be completed by an agreement to limit air forces. The British note evaded the problem of Germany's colonial claims, and that of separation of the League of Nations Pact from the Treaty of Versailles which Germany also claimed.[9]

The British questionnaire received no reply. On the eve of a conference which was to bring together in London the British ministers and their new French colleagues (Léon Blum, President of the Council and Yvon Delbos, Minister of Foreign Affairs), the services of the Quai d'Orsay noted that, at the time when the negotiations were to begin, Germany had made no concession, while France had abandoned all her preliminary conditions (notably with regard to the undertaking not to fortify the Rhineland). Their memorandum concluded:[10]

> It is necessary to ask the British government a fundamental question, with particular insistence: what will happen, and what position will Britain take up if, yet again, the attempt at conciliation fails? How then will Franco-British solidarity be asserted in actual fact? What will be the outcome of the pledges undertaken by the British government on 1 April?

[8] Ibid., pp.577–9. [9] Ibid., Vol. II; Documents 35ff.
[10] Ibid., Vol. III, pp.10–17.

At the London Conference on 23 July, Léon Blum insisted on the idea of collective security; peace, he said, cannot be divided. With this he showed not only a doctrinaire attachment to the programme of the Popular Front but, as Briand had done at the time of Locarno, he endeavoured to cover France's allies in Central and Eastern Europe with a general guarantee; this was even more clearly stated by his minister Yvon Delbos.[11]

In the months that followed, France and Britain devoted themselves to the negotiation of this 'new Locarno' to which British opinion seemed attached.[12] The French government went to the trouble of drawing up a detailed proposal, the intentions of which were even more clearly expressed in a memorandum to the British government.[13] Germany, however, as was to be expected, made only evasive replies. Britain willingly consented to these delaying tactics which enabled her to gain time – for her rearmament, the optimists hoped; or, according to the unkindest interpretation, to postpone for as long as possible the moment of adopting a definite attitude.[14] On 20 January 1937 the political directorate of the Quai d'Orsay ascertained that the negotiation was 'bogged down'; it drew up various other proposals, but how could the British be forced to reply?[15]

In order to soothe French impatience, Britain had in fact already replied; in a speech delivered on 20 November 1936, Anthony Eden declared:[16]

> Our arms could be, and if circumstances rendered it necessary, would be, used to defend France and Belgium against unprovoked aggression, in accordance with our present obligations.
> ... Our arms could be, and if a new agreement regarding Western Europe were concluded, would be, used to defend Germany in the event of this power's being the victim of unprovoked aggression on the part of one of the signatories of this agreement.

In other words, Britain still considered herself bound by the Locarno Agreements – with, however, a restrictive shade of meaning with regard to Germany. But this was from then onwards a unilateral agreement which enabled her at the same time to avoid a stricter mutual assistance agreement and to have closer control over French policy. This was precisely what Raymond

---

[11] Ibid., pp.38–41.   [12] Ibid., pp.407–10 (23 September).
[13] Ibid., pp.372–5; see also Document 45.   [14] Ibid., pp.778–81.
[15] Ibid., Vol. IV, pp.555–60.   [16] Ibid., pp.4–5.

Poincaré had wished to avoid. That the French government should now be satisfied with this shows the extent, not of the weakness of character of Poincaré's successors, but of the weakening of the French situation.

The Tripartite Monetary Agreement and its Political Significance

On 25 September 1936, a devaluation of the franc – the second since the 1914–18 war – was announced in the form of a joint declaration by the French, British and American governments.[17] Many people at that time, especially in France, tended to see this declaration merely as a 'cloak', the purpose of which was to make the French public accept a financial manipulation which the government had undertaken to avoid. However, it is not clear why Britain and the United States should in practice be bound by this declaration not to respond to the French devaluation either by further devaluations of their own currencies or by compensating exchange surcharges, merely in order to save the face of a Popular Front government which could not enjoy a preconceived favourable opinion, especially in Britain.

One would have to be able to follow the details of the negotiation which resulted in this agreement. Unfortunately this is impossible, because from the month of June it was conducted in the greatest secrecy – as is natural in financial matters – and the *Documents Diplomatiques Français* are consequently silent on the subject almost to the end. The first text which they provide is a proposal for a French memorandum to the American and British governments, dated 8 September 1936, which proposed a 'pre-stabilization agreement' considered to be 'the only means of putting an end to the development of isolationist tendencies, to reduce restrictions and constraints of all kinds which paralyse exchanges and which create an atmosphere of general insecurity involving the most serious threats to peace'.[18] The connection between economics and politics was thus once more asserted. The reply made two days later by the United States embassy[19] raised, in what was moreover a very moderate form, objections against too general and too definite an undertaking; it maintained in principle the freedom of action of the United States while satisfy-

---

[17] See J. Néré, *La Crise de 1929*, pp.200–2.
[18] DDF, 2nd series, Vol. III, pp.348–9.   [19] Ibid., pp.357–8.

ing France in the immediate future. It was on these foundations that the joint declaration was finally drawn up.[20]

It is natural, however, to see this tripartite monetary agreement as a long-term result of the Franco-Anglo-American discussions which preceded the economic conference in London in 1933.[21] Of course, the situation had altered greatly since then: weakened, France was now the petitioner, and she was obliged to abandon the argument of the gold standard, in theory and in practice. However, in 1936 in certain French circles, an idea which could not be realized in 1933, was seen to reappear: that of regaining political contact with the United States through co-operation in economic matters. A memorandum from the French financial attaché in London, M Monick, who had already played a part in the negotiations of 1933,[22] is very significant in this connection. He described interviews which he had just had with William Bullitt, the United States ambassador in Paris, in accordance with ideas which he, Monick, had previously submitted to his government. The question was to prepare the ground for an initiative by President Roosevelt, the purpose of which was to preserve, or as Monick put it, to 'buy', peace. This meant that the initiative must take place in the economic field. Monick's precise suggestions – to form international companies whose purpose would be to regularize the markets for important raw materials – undoubtedly gave cause for criticism. However, as he himself said: 'The plan which will be adopted by Mr Roosevelt is not the main thing. What we need is to force in some way, by an effort of intelligence, an Anglo-Franco-American initiative, *whatever it may be.*' It was in the same spirit that Delbos considered opening new negotiations with a view to settling the interallied debts.[23] The suggestions achieved nothing, but they were useful as an indication.

The tripartite agreement itself, however, was of a more realistic nature. It was in accordance with the agreement that the British government, who were becoming alarmed about France's persistent gold losses, invited the French government to do whatever was necessary to restore confidence in her currency.[24] The French government replied by denouncing the speculation on the London market, and by appealing for an effective solidarity of the

---

[20] Text published in ibid., pp.422–3.   [21] See Chapter 8.
[22] DDF, 2nd series, Vol. IV, pp.320–8 (22 December 1936).
[23] Ibid., pp.211, 384–5.   [24] Ibid., pp.758–9 (12 February 1937).

financial authorities of the three countries.[25] The British government then refused to go beyond the declaration of intentions of
25 September and to link the three currencies by fixed equivalences
of exchange between them, if not in relation to gold.[26] Experi-
mentation in new financial methods had not yet matured sufficiently to serve as a basis, or at least as a point of departure, for a
close co-operation between the three Western countries.

The Belgian Defection

This problem, which was vital in its practical consequences, over-
lapped closely that of the disappearance of the Locarno Agreement and that of its replacement. For this too it is necessary to go
back to the beginning, which was a considerable time before the
advent of the Popular Front government.

It was on 6 March 1936 – the eve of the remilitarization of the
Rhineland – that the Belgian government denounced the military
agreement which had linked it with France since 1920. It was
therefore not the weakness shown by France on this occasion
which brought about this development in Belgian policy. In any
case, M Vandervelde, one of the heads of the Belgian government,
had not been afraid to declare beforehand to the French ambassador that the clause relating to the demilitarization of the
Rhineland could not be enforced indefinitely.[27]

The result of this was that Belgium was no longer associated
with France except by the obligations of the Locarno Agreement,
which had just collapsed. It was therefore all the more necessary
for France to be a party to the negotiation of a 'new Locarno',
since this attempt seemed to be the only way of keeping Belgium
within the French security system. At this time, the tendency for
Belgian policy to move away from France was attributed basically
to the antagonism between the Walloons and the Flemish; the
Walloons were very Francophile, whereas Flemish opinion seemed
in general inclined at least not to be associated more closely with
France than with Britain, even if it did not feel closer to British
concepts than to French ones.[28] However, the idea of a unilateral

[25] Ibid., pp.788–92 (17 February 1937).
[26] Ibid., pp.821–3 (19 February 1937).
[27] Ibid., Vol. I, p.211 (6 February 1936).
[28] Ibid., Vol. III, pp.28–34 (22 July 1936).

guarantee had just appeared: Belgium would accept a guarantee by France and by Britain, but without guaranteeing them in her turn;[29] she would refuse to become involved in a conflict resulting from France's obligations in Central Europe or from the Franco-Soviet Pact, and she would not consider – assuming that she ever had considered it – that her troops could fight for allies outside Belgian territory.

Faced with this new attitude, the Minister of Foreign Affairs, Delbos, immediately asked the advice of the General Staff concerning the military consequences which would result from it. He received two notes in reply, one giving the point of view of the air force, and the other that of the army; both intended for communication to the British authorities.[30] However, there was a great difference between the two notes. The memorandum from the air force stressed the disadvantages for France and Britain of a new situation in which Belgium would no longer be a guarantor: without the help of the 'Belgian look-out' it would be difficult to secure themselves in time against a German air offensive aimed at Paris and especially London; moreover, the British bomber flights would find it impossible to strike Germany at its sensitive part, in the Ruhr and Westphalia.[31] On the other hand, the memorandum from the army dealt almost exclusively with the drawbacks of this new attitude to Belgium herself. If she settled on a course of neutrality at the beginning of a German offensive she would risk being deprived of French help, which in order to be effective would need to be organized in advance and co-ordinated with Belgian resistance. Belgium would thus be obliged to yield a considerable part of her territory to the invader. The memorandum added simply that 'the French and British forces, deprived of the advance screen made up of the Belgian and French elements fighting on the Meuse, could be hindered in their concentration' and that 'the possibilities of the Allies making their action felt on German territory would be greatly reduced, since the enemy would have conducted hostilities outside its territory from the beginning of the conflict'.

The consequences for France of a break in Franco-Belgian

[29] Ibid., pp.430–2 (29 September 1936).
[30] Ibid., pp.437–41 (30 September 1936).
[31] It is obviously necessary, in order to understand this argument, to take into account the speed and flight range of the aircraft of the period.

military solidarity were different and much more serious. From this time onwards the French army could hardly contemplate 'making their action felt' on German territory. On the contrary its basic plan, since no one doubted that the German offensive must start through Belgium, was to establish itself in a defensive position behind the protection of the Meuse and the Albert Canal, that is, much nearer on the whole to the Belgian-German frontier than to the Franco-Belgian frontier. Since the capacity of Belgium to delay the invader for very long could not really be counted upon, the French manœuvre was feasible only if Belgium appealed to France and gave her the right of passage before the start of the German attack, as soon as a serious threat took shape. The alternative solutions considered – an Antwerp-Namur 'line' which did not exist, or a resistance on the Scheldt which left the main route to Paris through the valley of the Oise open to invasion – did not bear examination.

Under these conditions, the most positive position of the Belgian advocates of neutrality was also the most realistic: France had only to continue the Maginot Line to the sea; Germany would then have no further interest in attacking Belgium, who could even disarm without disadvantage.[32]

No one took this course, however. On 14 October 1936, the King of the Belgians delivered a speech to the Council of Ministers which was immediately published,[33] and which announced both a considerable strengthening of the army and a policy of strict neutrality, following the example of the Netherlands and Switzerland.

The French Minister of Foreign Affairs, Delbos, reacted at first with energy and lucidity. He pointed out to the Belgian ambassador that France had not considered that Belgian soldiers would enter her territory to come to her aid but, on the other hand, that assistance given by France to Belgium could not be improvised at the last minute, since it would naturally require an adjustment in mobilization plans and, consequently, preliminary discussions between the General Staffs. He even added this prophetic warning: 'If Belgium were invaded by Germany after the attack against France, her momentary false security would prevent concerted action. There would be hesitations which would be disastrous for our defence.'[34]

[32] DDF, 2nd series, Vol. III, pp.456–7.   [33] Ibid., pp.520–1.
[34] Ibid., pp.590–4.

On 23 April 1937 the Belgian government indicated that it would give right of entry to foreign troops on her territory only in accordance with clause 16 of the League of Nations Pact, after a decision by the Council of the League – that is, too late, whatever the circumstances. Later it restricted further the functioning of the right of passage in such a way as to exclude the case of assistance to Czechoslovakia.[35] Nevertheless, France and Britain unilaterally maintained the pledge to assist Belgium as stipulated in the Locarno Agreements. How can we explain this decision which contributed perhaps more than any other to the disaster of 1940?

It is necessary at this point to recall in the first place the ambiguity in the attitude of the French General Staff. It allowed a state of mind to prevail which was no doubt fairly widespread and often expressed, notably by the French ambassador in Brussels.[36] This attitude was characterized by a concern to avoid any gesture which could discourage France's friends in Belgium, and to leave the door open for a sudden change in Belgian opinion, which was still hoped for. This was a serious underestimation of the strength of a tendency which considerably strengthened the traditional hostility between the Flemings and the Walloons: the aspiration towards historical neutrality – in fact the very natural but unromantic desire to take shelter – was now such that it resulted in a disregard both of the precedent of 1914 and of geographical facts. We will add that the ambiguity of the attitude of certain Belgian authorities, notably the President of the Council, Van Zeeland, without doubt contributed to keeping French policy in a state of uncertainty.[37]

Franco-German Relations: the Schacht Mission

While the abortive attempt to negotiate another Locarno was taking place, there appeared paradoxically enough a hint of direct discussions between the Germany of the Nazis and the France of the Popular Front. The occasion for this was the visit to Paris of

[35] See P. Renouvin, *Histoire des relations internationales*, Vol. VIII, Part 2, pp.160–1.
[36] See in particular DDF, 2nd series, Vol. III, pp.627, 629; Vol. IV, pp.427–30, 514–18.
[37] In connection with this ambiguity on the part of Van Zeeland, see especially H. de Man, *Après coup*, Brussels, n.d. (1941), pp.262–3.

Dr Hjalmar Schacht, who was still at that time Minister of Economy of the Reich and President of the Reichsbank.

The episode remains shrouded in mystery, and the French sources which refer to it are very incomplete. During the summer of 1936 Dr Schacht travelled all over Europe, ostensibly for formal visits to his colleagues who directed the various issuing banks. After a tour of the Balkans he came to Paris, where a new governor, M Labeyrie, had just been appointed to the Bank of France. However, he also had meetings not only with the Minister of Finance, Vincent Auriol, but with the Minister of Foreign Affairs, Yvon Delbos, and with the President of the Council, Léon Blum. We have a report only of the last interview, which came from Léon Blum himself and in which the impression was given that Dr Schacht let his interlocutor talk without compromising himself.[38]

The dispatches in which the ambassador[39] and, above all, the financial attaché in Berlin[40] announced his visit, let it be understood that, in accordance with his duties, Dr Schacht would seek economic, financial and even currency agreements. In these texts we find the hope, still widespread at the time, that it would be possible by means of economic agreements to achieve a lessening of political tension with Germany.

However, the direct report of the Blum-Schacht interview gives quite a different impression. In it Léon Blum appeared to reply to proposals previously formulated by Dr Schacht, which were fundamentally of a political nature. Had Hitler himself prepared these proposals or had he merely given Dr Schacht a general authority with a view to spying out the land? It is very difficult to answer this question. In his Memoirs Dr Schacht claimed that he took the initiative and gained Hitler's approval for a project aimed fundamentally at German colonial claims.[41] The Schacht Memoirs are, however, very unreliable.

According to the French document, Dr Schacht's proposals were in the form of a bargain: in exchange for satisfactions in colonial matters, Germany would offer 'a general guarantee system' which could pave the way for 'a reduction of armaments'.

[38] DDF, 2nd series, Vol. III, pp.307–11 (28 August 1936).
[39] Ibid., p.275 (24 August).
[40] Ibid., pp.302–5 (27 August).
[41] H. Schacht, *Memoirs of a Magician*, Vol. II, pp.139–40.

However, it was this offer made in exchange by Germany which needed much closer examination. A primary feature seemed to be that the USSR would be excluded from the new diplomatic system, at least at the beginning. To this Léon Blum replied that a disarmament agreement would have no meaning without the signature of the USSR, and that furthermore he did not seek a tête-à-tête agreement but a general ruling, for everything hung together. His attachment to the idea of collective security was obvious. From the brief and evasive replies of Dr Schacht one seems to sense, on the contrary, a wish to negotiate with France in private, isolating her as much as possible from her traditional associates or allies – dislocating, in fact, the diplomatic system which successive French governments had been to so much pains to build up. If this impression is accurate, then the presentation of the German proposals was particularly deceptive: far from the 'guarantee system for general peace' being a concession by Hitler in exchange for colonial satisfactions – with which he never seemed much concerned – it was a manœuvre designed to dislocate the European diplomatic system which had become the basic plan.

Did this attempt achieve anything? In an interview with the ambassador to France which took place immediately afterwards[42] on 2 September 1936, Hitler seemed satisfied with Dr Schacht's journey, but it also seems that what he had most set his heart on at that time was to separate France from the USSR. Later, after the tripartite currency agreement of 25 September, the French ambassador saw Dr Schacht himself.[43] Schacht did not seem discouraged or irritated by the fact that France had devalued without notifying him and without associating him in the operation; moreover, he did not believe at that time that it was possible for Germany to devalue to any useful purpose. On the other hand – and this point should be noted – Schacht showed his resentment of the fact that the currency agreement between France, Britain and the United States suggested a political *entente* between them, an *entente* whose extent he perhaps exaggerated. A little later,[44] the financial attaché in Berlin indicated that Dr Schacht had fallen greatly from favour and that Hitler blamed him for the failure of the Paris talks. It seems doubtful that he attached such importance

[42] DDF, 2nd series, Vol. III, pp.496–9.
[43] Ibid., pp.542–3 (14 October).
[44] Ibid., pp.600–1 (22 October 1936).

to not having been associated with a devaluation which, whatever happened, he was determined to avoid.[45] Did the reluctance of Britain to make extensive colonial sacrifices play a decisive part, as Schacht maintained? It seems to us more likely that to Hitler, who was basically preoccupied with European policy, France's refusal to commit herself in an exclusive private meeting was the determining factor, and that it was this which led him to conclude that Schacht's mission had been a failure.

Franco-Soviet Relations

Franco-Soviet relations, at the time of the Léon Blum government, seemed to be very perplexing. This assertion may seem astonishing when one considers that the conclusion of the Franco-Soviet mutual assistance pact played an important part in the formation of the Popular Front, even if one does not go so far as to claim, like certain Right and Left extremists in France,[46] that the fundamental purpose of the change in tactics by the French communist party, without which the Popular Front could not have been formed, was to make the Franco-Soviet alliance fully effective.

However, the coming to power of the Popular Front did not in any way contribute to the strengthening of friendship between the two countries.

On the Soviet side there was disappointment over the negotiation of the 'new Locarno', in which there was a tendency to see a new manœuvre liable to isolate the USSR.[47] Numerous documents show us that at that time this was indeed Hitler's dominant idea. But adopting this course was precisely what Léon Blum refused to do in his interview with Dr Schacht; the Soviets, however, did not know this.

We are, on the other hand, obviously much better informed about the doubts and alarms which were displayed on the French side. These went so far that the new French ambassador in Moscow, Robert Coulondre, in his first interview with Litvinov,[48]

[45] Cf. J. Néré, op. cit., p.164.

[46] See the book by Daniel Guérin, *Front Populaire, révolution manquée* (Paris, 1963).

[47] DDF, 2nd series, Vol. III, pp.52–5 (24 July), pp.434–6 (29 September).

[48] Ibid., pp.748–51 (12 November). Coulondre was only echoing the fears of Delbos himself. See R. Coulondre, *De Staline à Hitler*, p.13.

was not afraid to devote the whole of his statement to the 'uneasiness' – that was the word he used – of Franco-Soviet relations. According to him there were two, not unconnected, reasons for this uneasiness: one was the interference of the USSR in French internal policy through the French Communist Party, and the other was the fear of French opinion, which saw the agreement with the USSR as a means of safeguarding peace, of finding France involved, on the other hand, in an ideological conflict. On the first point, the Soviet leaders were bound to reply that they were not influencing the French Communist Party – and in so doing they had no hope of convincing their interlocutors.[49]

As for the fear of being involved in a war with ideological motives, it was perhaps firmly rooted in French opinion; and it is known with what care Léon Blum endeavoured to dispel this suspicion.[50] However, competent French diplomats did nothing to encourage it; on the contrary, they stressed that Stalin was practising more and more a Russian national policy rather than an international revolutionary one, and the trials of Trotskyites which were taking place at the time in Moscow served to illustrate this idea.[51] However, Blum's government drove the love of peace and the desire for conciliation to the furthest limit, while the USSR declared herself so convinced that an attitude of firmness towards Germany was necessary that the Soviet leaders began publicly to think: how much better it would be if one were dealing with good French conservative nationalists like Poincaré and Barthou.[52] However, the balance of power had changed too fundamentally for it to be possible to find another Poincaré.

This difference in attitude would not perhaps have been sufficient to breed distrust if it had not been complicated by certain ulterior motives. On the one hand, the sharp variations in Soviet foreign policy, for example, the energetic support given to the Treaty of Versailles and the League of Nations which were formerly so despised, did not fail to arouse a certain scepticism: were we safe from new reversals? On the other hand, if it were accepted that the USSR did not practise an ideological policy,

---

[49] DDF, 2nd series, Vol. III, pp.783–7 (16 November).
[50] See Document 44.
[51] See in particular DDF, 2nd series, Vol. III, pp.557–9; Vol. IV, pp.607–611, 713, 715, 720.
[52] Ibid., Vol. IV, pp.81–2.

what was her intention in supporting the civil war in Spain? Would it be to divert the threatening storm towards the West or, to speak plainly, to induce Germany by a chain of circumstances to attack France first and not the USSR? This suspicion was expressed in the clearest and most brutal form in a report by General Schweisguth on Soviet manœuvres in White Russia.[53] Doubtless one can discern behind these accusations the fear of Franco-Soviet military talks which the French General Staff wanted to have nothing to do with, for reasons we have already described. The same idea, however, was expressed by the French chargé d'affaires in Moscow who was not influenced by such considerations.[54] If conflict broke out in the West, what would be the use to France of an alliance with the USSR, since the USSR did not share any frontiers with Germany? This alarm was so widespread that the French government had to question the USSR officially on the subject, and we have the reply which the Soviet ambassador brought in person to Léon Blum.[55] This reply inevitably raised the question of the Polish attitude. If Poland allowed the passage of Soviet troops, the problem was simple. However, even if Poland 'for incomprehensible reasons' refused passage, the USSR offered to send troops to France by sea. This suggestion, if it was sincere, proved merely that the Russian General Staff, which was essentially that of a landbound army, greatly underestimated the difficulties and dangers of this sea route, which events were to prove so dramatically in 1941–2. It is certain, however, that it could not bring great comfort to the French military experts.

Moreover at this time, the indications received concerning the approaching downfall of Marshal Tukhachevski[56] added further alarms concerning the Germanophile tendencies of the Soviet army and, before long, even its military usefulness.

Thus the Franco-Soviet agreement, in spite of apparently favourable circumstances, did not succeed in finding expression in concerted action. Moreover, it seemed obstructed from then onwards, not only by the incompatibility of the two strategies, but by a psychological obstacle: mutual distrust.

[53] Ibid., Vol. III, pp.510–14 (13 October 1936).
[54] Ibid., p.586 (21 October 1936).
[55] Ibid., Vol. IV, pp.787–8 (17 February 1937).
[56] Ibid., pp.781–2 (10 February 1937).

Break-Up of the Eastern Alliances

This title is surprising for a period in which France was actually endeavouring to strengthen her alliances. But the failure of these efforts in itself had a singularly threatening significance.

However, a *rapprochement* with Poland was being outlined which appeared fruitful, if one judged from appearances. But it happens that in this matter we are acquainted with the underlying facts. The French ambassador in Warsaw, Léon Noël, had suggested to the new government in June 1936 that talks should be held between the French and Polish General Staffs with a view to establishing the terms and conditions of the assistance to be given to the Polish army; but in his opinion French assistance must be subordinated to the removal of Colonel Beck, the Polish Minister of Foreign Affairs, who was reputed to be the champion of Germanophile policy and with whom it seemed impossible to establish relations of trust.[57] In fact, a journey was made to Warsaw in August 1936 by General Gamelin, followed by a visit to Paris by General Smigly-Rydz, Supreme Commander of the Polish army. The report which General Gamelin made about his visit has not been found, but according to Léon Noël,[58] he succeeded in avoiding exhaustive technical discussions which would have obliged him to make inconvenient admissions. General Smigly-Rydz, for his part, obtained by the Rambouillet Agreement[59] considerable credit facilities for Polish rearmament, without any political concessions. The position of Colonel Beck seemed rather to be consolidated as a result of this journey,[60] and General Smigly-Rydz, when asked by Delbos what Poland's attitude would be with respect to Czechoslovakia if the latter were involved in a conflict with Germany, took refuge behind the vaguest possible formulae.[61] Doubtless, the vote for a Polish loan to be placed with France was the occasion for great demonstrations of Franco-Polish friendship.[62] At the same time, however, Beck was suspected of manœuvring to isolate Czechoslovakia,

[57] L. Noël, *L'Agression allemande contre la Pologne*, pp.139–40.
[58] Ibid., pp.141–2, 148.
[59] DDF, 2nd series, Vol. III, pp.377–8 (6 September 1936).
[60] Ibid., pp.668–9 (2 November 1936).
[61] Ibid., pp.441–2 (30 September 1936). See Document 46.
[62] Ibid., Vol. IV, pp.443–4, 480–2.

especially by his approach to Rumania and Yugoslavia with a mutual anti-communist intention, whereas Czechoslovakia was associated with the USSR by a pact of mutual assistance.[63] If this suspicion had a foundation, Poland contributed to the failure of the supreme effort which France was making at that time to find in the Little *Entente* a true support for her policy.

The Little *Entente*, however, had seemed on the point of achieving a cohesion and effectiveness which it had never permanently had until then. At a meeting of the heads of the General Staffs of the three states, held in Bucharest from 15 to 20 June 1936, the principle of the single command was adopted as from the period of political tension or, at the latest, on mobilization. In a general hypothesis of European war involving all the individual cases of localized conflict, it was anticipated that Hungary would be put out of action immediately and *a priori* (even if she declared herself neutral in the first place), simply because her territory was essential to the joining of the forces of the Little *Entente*. This operation would be carried out basically by Rumania, with the help of Yugoslavia, since Czechoslovakia would have to preserve the main part of her forces in order to face Germany. The second phase would have to consist of a combined offensive by France and the Little *Entente* against Germany.[64]

However, after 7 March, Czechoslovakia had been offered a proposal for a pact of non-aggression by Germany, and, if her government undertook direct bilateral negotiations with Hitler, she would run a great risk of being drawn into his orbit. A possibility of avoiding what would be a very severe blow to French foreign policy presented itself: to take up the suggestion of the Rumanian diplomat Titulescu, which visualized a mutual assistance pact between France and the Little *Entente* as a whole (for France was only linked with each of the states of the Little *Entente* individually); this would assume a reinforcement and generalization of the agreements which made up the Little *Entente*, a political ratification, by a written undertaking, of the agreements by the General Staffs which we have just analysed.[65] The effort of French diplomacy in the months that followed would be devoted to the concluding of these two pacts. This induced the French government to accept, contrary to logic, that the negotiations

[63] Ibid., pp.724–5.   [64] Ibid., Vol. II, pp.545–51 (28 June 1936).
[65] Ibid., pp.723–6.

between France and the Little *Entente* would take place at the same time as those which aimed to ensure the cohesion of the Little *Entente* itself. [66]

Nevertheless, this diplomatic undertaking rapidly came up against considerable obstacles. France herself objected to a Czech proposal: [67] in the state of international opinion at that time, it was necessary to avoid drawing up a treaty which would reproduce almost word for word the text of the Franco-Soviet Pact and the Czech-Soviet Pact; the new pact must not appear as a closed agreement but, on the contrary, as the beginning of a much wider *entente*, whose purpose would be simply to guarantee the application of clause 16 of the League of Nations Pact. [68] These objections show how timid French diplomacy was already; nevertheless, they referred only to the form. What was much more serious was that Rumania and Yugoslavia showed an ever-increasing reluctance to associate themselves with Czechoslovakia, who seemed more directly threatened than themselves. Until June 1936 it was understood that the three states would intervene militarily in the case of an attempt at restoration of the Habsburgs, an *Anschluss,* or rearmament of Hungary. In September, however, it was decided that military action would be engaged only if the neutrality of Italy and Germany were guaranteed; [69] in other words, there would be very little opportunity for armed intervention to take place. The seriousness of this retrograde step is measured by recalling that the Little *Entente* had been formed basically against Hungary.

To what could this new direction be attributed? First of all, a ministerial reshuffle had taken place in Rumania. Mr Titulescu, the faithful friend of France and supporter of a *rapprochement* with the USSR, had left the Ministry of Foreign Affairs. [70] His successor, Mr Antonescu, while protesting his fidelity to the French alliance, suggested replacing the single treaty contemplated between France and the Little *Entente* by three treaties which would intervene between France and each of the members of this group. This would add nothing to the pledges which already linked them separately with France; on the contrary, it would remove any

[66] Ibid., Vol. III, pp.715–16 (10 November 1936).
[67] Ibid., pp.733–7.   [68] Ibid., Vol. IV, pp.465–8.
[69] Ibid., Vol. III, pp.718–20.
[70] Ibid., Vol. III, pp.329–31 (2 September)

attempt at effective solidarity between the members of the Little *Entente* themselves.[71]

The attitude of Yugoslavia, however, was an even greater source of anxiety, for there French influence itself seemed to be waning. The President of the Yugoslav Council raised various objections to the proposed treaties, the chief of which was that they risked bringing about a final agreement between Italy and Germany and bringing down reprisals, especially of an economic nature, on Yugoslavia.[72] In fact, the problem was a veritable crisis of confidence: the setback suffered by Britain in the Ethiopian affair and the inaction of France at the time of the remilitarization of the Rhineland, added their effects to those of the German economic ascendancy over Yugoslavia, whose Prince Regent dreaded moreover 'the interference of communism in French policy' and did not wish to be 'involved in a war caused by the Soviets'.[73]

In the face of all these reservations and setbacks, it was soon evident that the attempt to transform the Little *Entente* into an important auxiliary of French policy would not succeed. As Anthony Eden said, another method of saving Czechoslovakia must be found.[74]

Were there any other methods, however? For the French army, which was dedicated to defence of its front, the problem was to send reinforcements to her allies to enable them to resist too. Since Italy could no longer be depended upon, the only theoretical route would be that which joined the Yugoslav coast to Slovakia across the Hungarian plain. This was closed from now on. It appeared from that moment very imprudent on the part of French diplomacy to continue to oppose a direct German-Czechoslovak negotiation.[75]

The War in Spain: Non-Intervention and Attempt at Mediation

The foreign policy of the Popular Front was dominated, almost from its coming to power, by the repercussions of the Spanish Civil War. For nearly two years these blotted out from the eyes of the public any other question of foreign policy, and even resulted in serious internal divisions; but they also held the

[71] Ibid., Vol. IV, pp.571–3.
[72] Ibid., pp.255–6, 292–7.
[73] Ibid., Vol. III, pp.728–30.
[74] Ibid., Vol. IV, pp.705–6.
[75] Ibid., pp.764–70.

attention of a large part of the chancelleries, as is shown by the mass of documents which referred to them. However, it is not possible fully to explain the attitude of the French government in this affair without bearing in mind her diplomatic position as a whole, and this is what has led us to leave the account of the Spanish problem to the end of this chapter.

The military insurrection of General Franco broke out on 17 July 1936. Immediately, the Spanish Republican government requested France to deliver a small quantity of armaments, and at first received a favourable reply. However, on 25 July the French attitude changed, and from this time on tended towards the prohibition of arms deliveries.

Why this change? An account from the envoy of the Spanish government, Fernando de Los Rios, which was published later,[76] attributed it to various causes: a campaign by part of the French press who had been alerted by an indiscretion; the influence of the President of the Republic and of the President of the Chamber of Deputies, Edouard Herriot. This allegation cannot be checked, and we do not have a report from the Council of Ministers. However, on 23 July the Commission of Foreign Affairs of the Senate showed its hostility to arms deliveries,[77] and on 25 July it was the political Directorate of the Quai d'Orsay who were on guard against the possibility of a serious international conflict: what would happen if Germany and Italy recognized Franco and sent him arms?[78]

These anxieties felt by professional diplomats are easily explained. From the beginning it was presumed, and it was soon proved, that Germany and Italy in fact supported Franco. There was indeed the risk of an international conflict taking place and under the worst conditions since France would be isolated. Britain and Belgium, with whom France was attempting at the time to negotiate a 'new Locarno' which would be the basis of French security, seemed to be more in favour of Franco[79] and in any case did not show any sympathy with the republicans. The Little *Entente*, which it was still hoped could be consolidated, would certainly break up completely if Rumania and Yugoslavia feared to be associated with a conflict in the interest of the 'communists'

[76] Ibid., Vol. IV, pp.201–2.   [77] Ibid., Vol. III, p.37.
[78] Ibid., p.58; see also Document 47.
[79] See especially DDF, 2nd series, Vol. III, pp.158–9.

The Sultan of Morocco himself was tempted to recognize General Franco (who was in possession of 'Spanish' Morocco)[80] as a belligerent, which could create an inextricable situation in 'French' Morocco. To this we must add the fear, expressed later by Léon Blum, that the violence of the divisions of French opinion over the Spanish affair would cause a civil war, of which Hitler would take advantage by attacking France. Léon Blum was not the only one to consider this idea: according to the Hossbach memorandum, at the end of 1937 Hitler still thought of attacking, either in the event of a civil war in France or in the event of a Franco-Italian war: either of these would of course have been brought about by the Spanish conflict.

Another element to be considered, however, was of course the opinion which the French government could form of the situation in Spain itself. We know how it was informed, in particular by its military attaché in Madrid, Lieutenant-Colonel Morel, who did not conceal his sympathy for the Spanish republicans, 'people who knew why they were fighting and dying' which, on their opponents' side, 'was true only of the officers'. However, on 31 July he wrote: 'In the long run it seems that even lukewarm discipline, even imposed order, must stamp out spasmodic enthusiasm.'[81] On 14 October, having praised the energetic war effort undertaken by the new government of Largo Caballero, he stressed in spite of everything that 'all the enemy [i.e. Franco's] attacks have succeeded' and announced that the fall of Madrid could not be far away.

Of course, this prophecy proved false; the pro-Franco offensive was finally checked in the suburbs of Madrid. However, this improvement in the Spanish Republic's situation – it would be too much to speak of a reversal – was accompanied by an increased fear of external complications. If Madrid did not fall, this was owing to the intervention of foreign units, 'a microcosm of international communism', whose organization was accurately described by Lieutenant-Colonel Morel.[82]

On 7 December he concluded:

Until now, the Republican military command had failed because it had to contend with the Spanish temperament, the political parties,

---

[80] Ibid., p.199.   [81] Ibid., pp.94–6.
[82] Ibid., Vol. IV, pp.72–3 (27 November 1936) and especially pp.167–73 (7 December 1936).

the regional autonomies, and against an enemy which was materially and technically superior. Could the breathing-space provided by the resistance of Madrid, the Russian help in equipment and political and military advisers allow the organization of a regular republican army? The beginning of a reply could be given in three months.

However, without waiting, the military attaché could perceive other phenomena, for example, a possible reaction of purely Spanish elements against invasion by foreigners, whether they were Russian communists or Italian fascists.[83]

There were, then, many reasons for France not to risk diplomatic isolation, even armed conflict, to uphold a cause which at least until October 1936 seemed doomed in advance. Nevertheless, it was very difficult for the Popular Front French government, whatever its wish to avoid opposition between ideological blocs, to take absolutely no interest in the fate of its Spanish brother. Since it could not or dared not support it directly, the French government endeavoured to make sure that General Franco's insurgents did not benefit from foreign support either. Such was the principle of the policy of non-intervention.

The first move of this policy was to obtain concerted action from Britain which was, moreover, a major concern of French diplomacy in all questions at this time.[84] The task was not easy, for if Britain attached importance to French abstention, even a unilateral one,[85] the prohibition of the export of arms would encounter legal difficulties in her case.[86] To persuade her, it was necessary for the French government to threaten to resume freedom of action if the other countries concerned did not adopt an attitude similar to hers.[87] Britain's co-operation was necessary for several reasons: first because of her ascendancy over Portugal, which was the only country apart from France to have joint land frontiers with Spain and was thus a particularly easy route for supplies for Franco's insurgents:[88] also because Germany and Italy continued to deal tactfully with her, so that she had a certain moral influence over Franco's two great supporters. In fact, during the month of August, a large number of countries, including all those mainly concerned, came round officially to the principle of non-intervention; and on 9 September a non-

[83] Ibid., pp.217–19 (12 December 1936).
[84] Ibid., pp.97–8 (1 August 1936).   [85] Ibid., p.117.
[86] Ibid., p.116.   [87] Ibid., pp.100–1.   [88] Ibid., pp.99–100.

intervention committee held its first purely formal meeting in London.[89] Very quickly, however, the meetings consisted of listening to violent mutual accusations, especially between the USSR on the one hand and Italy and Germany on the other, without any great practical results.[90]

After all, French policy – and this fact has hardly been stressed until now – did not consist solely in preventing the Spanish Civil War from degenerating into an international conflict; France also tried to put an end to the war itself. On 5 August 1936 Admiral Darlan and Rear-Admiral Decoux went to London to draw the attention of their British colleagues to the dangers which collusion between Germany, Italy and General Franco presented to Britain herself; Darlan referred to proposals by Italy for the seizure of the Balearic Islands, and by Germany of the Canary Islands. In order to avoid such dangerous possibilities, Darlan suggested that 'steps should be taken in an attempt to mediate between the Popular Front and the nationalists with the hope of promoting the formation of a democratic government, with the support of the Spanish people as a whole'. The British reply at that time was discouraging.[91]

This initiative was officially resumed on 26 November by the Minister of Foreign Affairs, Delbos.[92] This time the British reply was prompt and favourable.[93] It must not be forgotten that the Spanish situation changed at that time, and that now not only was German or Italian seizure of certain parts of Spain to be feared, but also Russian seizure of other parts, an argument to which the British could not be indifferent. However, the French government was also nursing the hope, or the illusion perhaps, that it would be possible by means of moderate Spanish opinion to assert authority against the intrusions of foreigners, Italians, Germans, or Russians, which were increasing. And, perhaps, this prospect would make Italy and Germany, who were no longer so sure of the success of their protégé Franco, stop and think?

This, however, proved a vain hope. The German reply[94] was a politely disguised refusal: Germany had already recognized Franco's government, thereby indicating that it regarded it as the sole representative of the Spanish people. The German note

---

[89] Ibid., pp.352–3.   [90] See especially ibid., pp.494–5.
[91] Ibid., pp.130–3.   [92] Ibid., Vol. IV, pp.53–4; see also Document 48.
[93] DDF, 2nd series, Vol. IV, pp.84–6 (30 November 1936).
[94] Ibid., pp.209–10 (12 December 1936).

also raised the question of foreign volunteers. The Italian reply was similar to the German reply, but less clear; it stressed the practical difficulties of a consultation of the people in Spain.[95] As for Portugal, she did not see the possibility of mediation in a 'fight between two civilizations'.[96] The French attempt at mediation thus ended in failure. At least it forced each country to declare its position without hypocrisy; this was the only occasion in the whole history of the Spanish conflict in which such a feat was accomplished. Moreover, the fact that none of the totalitarian countries wanted anything to do with a compromise peace in Spain was *a contrario* a justification of the French attitude.

From now on, however, the question of the supply of armaments to Spain was eclipsed by the question of foreign volunteers. The French government asked the other countries this question over the head of the London committee,[97] and it obtained British support without difficulty.[98] The German reply was apparently very positive, but it raised other questions, such as that of 'agitators and political propagandists', and somewhat ingenuously expressed the wish to 're-establish the situation of August last year', which meant the time, before the international brigades had entered the battle line but while Italian and German intervention was already considerable, when the Spanish Republic seemed condemned to a swift downfall.[99] The Italian[100] and Portuguese[101] replies were of a similar nature. As for the USSR, she stressed the necessity for control.[102] However, there was nothing to indicate that this proposal would have crystallized, even in Spain, a desire to unite the Spaniards against the interference of foreigners – and it was on this hope, this illusion, that the French government probably based its action.

At this time it was aware that Italy and Germany were determined to violate all pledges of non-intervention which they had made or would make, and that the USSR, in return, would do the same. Moreover, the French government itself closed its eyes to the help which was, in truth, of very modest proportions, which a large number of its partisans gave to the Spanish republicans. It

[95] Ibid., pp.220–1 (13 December 1936).
[96] Ibid., pp.203–7 (12 December 1936).
[97] Ibid., p.347 (24 December 1936).
[98] Ibid., pp.404–5, 454–5.
[99] Ibid., pp.597–8 (25 January 1937).
[100] Ibid., pp.601–2.
[101] Ibid., pp.399–401.
[102] Ibid., pp.370–1.

would be tedious to give an account of all the violated decisions which made non-intervention a veritable farce. Only once was the declared intention to prevent rival interventions applied effectively: the Nyon Conference (September 1937), which met to put an end to the undeclared naval war which was being established in the Mediterranean, achieved the desired result, owing to the British navy's taking action. This leads one to wonder whether Britain could not in fact have prevented all forms of intervention with this weapon.

Putting aside this regret, however, what balance-sheet can we draw up for the policy of non-intervention? It prevented neither German nor Italian action, nor the final crushing of the Spanish Republic; on the other hand, it reduced the risks of a particularly inopportune international conflict, and perhaps enabled General Franco to adopt an attitude of neutrality during the Second World War, thus saving France from a much dreaded third front. Moreover, the Spanish Civil War and the attitude adopted by the French government enabled France and Britain to co-operate much more closely than they had done previously, but this was a question of an agreement to yield, not to resist. Finally, it is certain that the Spanish conflict contributed a great deal towards the moral estrangement of the USSR with regard to her possible Western allies. It was already possible to pass a judgment which would be passed also on later events: an inglorious, but doubtless inevitable, operation.

The balance-sheet of the foreign policy of the Popular Front appeared heavily negative. In spite of intense diplomatic activity, of which we have been unable to give a complete picture here, in spite of an unprecedented effort of rearmament, the situation of France in Europe did not cease to deteriorate. What part in this decline can we assign to France's internal difficulties? A great deal was said on this subject in the chancelleries but was this not also a means of avoiding unpleasant admissions? Almost everywhere, there was from now on fear of Germany. The League of Nations, France and Britain had demonstrated their impotence in the Ethiopian affair; and since the remilitarization of the Rhineland, questions were asked, without the courage to establish clearly defined conclusions, about the consequences of France's defensive strategy. It was the misfortune of Léon Blum's government to set the seal on the effects of previous events or decisions.

Chapter 14

Munich

The Calm before the Storm

Between March 1936 and March 1938 Europe did not experience any serious alarms, apart of course from the vicissitudes of the Spanish Civil War. It was, however, a deceptive calm, for it was at this time that the mechanisms for the decisive conflicts were being set up. In November 1936 for the first time Mussolini associated himself officially with Hitler by the proclamation of the 'Rome-Berlin Axis', and in November 1937 Italy acceded to the 'Anti-Comintern Pact' which had already been concluded between Germany and Japan exactly a year before. A new Triple Alliance was being built, chiefly against the USSR but also indirectly against France. On 30 January 1937 Germany had unilaterally repudiated clause 231 of the Treaty of Versailles. The event had passed unnoticed at the time, but if we remember the violence of the controversies raised, especially in Germany, by the question of responsibility for the war, we realize that the demolition of the Europe of 1919 was continuing relentlessly. In November 1937 Hitler revealed to his confidants his next objectives: Czechoslovakia and Austria. Soon afterwards, he got rid of the last of those assistants in his army and diplomatic service who seemed inclined to restrain his action. From that time events were to rush headlong forward.

The Annexation of Austria

On 13 March 1938 German troops entered Austria; it was a matter of preventing a plebiscite announced by the Austrian government on the question of national independence. The operation, which was sudden, was of an improvised nature. It succeeded nevertheless because it did not encounter any resistance, either Austrian or international.

The absence of French reaction to an act against which all her leaders, including Briand, had protested in advance with notable energy, obviously did not fail to cause problems. This was one of the cases in which France's political weakness and especially the instability of her cabinet had been most blamed, for once again France was in a crisis: the Chautemps cabinet resigned on 9 March and its successor did not assume office until 13 March. A great deal has been spoken and written on the subject of Chautemps's having resigned from power in order not to take any responsibility in the Austrian crisis. The explanation is perhaps in keeping with the psychology of the man himself, but it is irreconcilable with the facts. It was on 9 March that the acute phase of the Austrian crisis began, with the announcement of the plebiscite: could Chautemps have known what Hitler would do before Hitler himself did? And in any case what could a French government, even one which was sure of its stability, do for Austria in March 1938? Immediate action was possible only with the co-operation of Italy, and Mussolini had also no doubt been taken unawares, like the rest of the world, by the suddenness of the German attack: Hitler had not had time to inform him, and had thus launched into the venture without being sure that Italy would not react. France, however, had not been in close contact with Italy since the Ethiopian affair and the Spanish Civil War had prevented the resumption of more friendly relations. Moreover, an attempt at an Anglo-Italian *rapprochement*, attempted in 1937 without France, had not achieved tangible results. Whether he liked it or not, Mussolini was tied to Hitler both by his ambitions and by his isolation, and by November 1937 he had let his partner know that he was practically resigned to the *Anschluss*.

However, the event which France was completely powerless to prevent had none the less serious consequences for her. It was then clear to everyone that her ally Czechoslovakia was doomed to an impending aggression: her vital centre, Bohemia, was completely surrounded by German territories, and the defences which she had hastily built to confront Germany – and which were pompously baptized the 'Czechoslovak Maginot Line' – were easily circumvented through Austria and the Moravian gap.

The Preliminaries of the Czech Affair

The method chosen to break Czechoslovakia up, which had been suspected for some time, was to stir up agitation in the Germanic minority who had settled on the periphery of Bohemia. On 24 April 1938 the 'German party of the Sudetenlanders', which was to be manipulated by Hitler throughout the crisis, demanded an autonomous government in that area. This claim, however, comprised both the industrial power of Czechoslovakia and her national defence, for the German groups were settled precisely in the mountains of the periphery, which was the only possible line of resistance.

France was associated with Czechoslovakia by a definite treaty of mutual assistance. However, when the Daladier cabinet, which lasted until 1940, was formed in April 1938, the Ministry of Foreign Affairs passed from Joseph Paul-Boncour to Georges Bonnet. Paul-Boncour was an unswerving champion of collective security and French alliances. Daladier abandoned this policy – Paul-Boncour himself recorded – because he considered that such a policy was no longer within France's means. Now Daladier had been responsible for national defence for a long time; he knew the limits and the gaps of the French military force of which many diplomats were still unaware, and his choice showed from that moment that the French government would seek the path of conciliation rather than that of resistance.

British influence could only push him in the same direction. On 28 and 29 April Daladier and Bonnet met those responsible for British policy, Neville Chamberlain and Lord Halifax, in London. The British statesmen had many illusions about the possibilities of reaching an understanding with Hitler, but they had far fewer with regard to the material and moral strength of France. Britain had never made any pledges regarding Czechoslovakia, apart from those resulting from the League of Nations Pact. Part of British opinion, moreover, considered that the claims of the Sudetenlanders were legitimate. Nevertheless, if France went to war to fulfil her obligations to Czechoslovakia, Britain would be more or less inevitably drawn into the conflict: this is what all those responsible for British diplomacy would be led to state in various forms.

The USSR was associated with Czechoslovakia by a mutual assistance agreement, which would come into force only if the Franco-Czechoslovak pact was also put into force. The USSR, however, did not have any joint frontier with either Czecho-slovakia or Germany. In the event of a conflict her forces would therefore have to pass through either Rumania or Poland. Again the possibility of their passing through Rumania was largely theoretical, for on this side there were very few means of communication, and these could easily be cut off by German aviation. As for Poland, she was on bad terms with Czechoslovakia, and full of suspicion regarding Soviet intentions, and since 1934 she had had a non-aggression agreement with Germany. It is true that she was also associated with France by a mutual assistance agreement. It was therefore between France and the USSR that the question of Soviet intervention would be discussed. The USSR declared that she was prepared to keep to her agreements if France would keep to hers, but she asked two questions.

The first concerned French military arrangements. The USSR again asked for Franco-Soviet talks between the General Staffs, and once more encountered an unacknowledged reserve[1] for which we, however, know the reason: the French defensive strategy would make such talks very difficult.

The second question considered the Polish attitude and the possibility that France would be able to influence it; the French evaded this question.[2] However, the debate has remained open among French diplomats themselves: could France, by speaking more loudly and more firmly, have forced Poland into allowing the passage of Soviet troops if necessary? It seems that the answer would be negative. Poland for some time had been bent on showing that she was not a 'satellite' of France; and her fear of seeing the Russians established on her territory, never to leave it, was too fundamental to yield to the influence of a far-off ally. Obviously it remained possible for France to denounce the Polish alliance, in the event of a refusal, and hence to give Russia a free hand in the East. However, confidence in the intentions of the USSR and her actual military force was not sufficient in France for this extreme measure to be envisaged.

A last point which must obviously be considered is Czechoslovakia's wish to resist and the possibility of her resisting. French diplomacy could not fail to have doubts on this subject: we have already seen that she had been alarmed for some time about Czech inclination to a direct *entente* with Germany. What was more serious, however, was that at the end of April 1938 Georges Bonnet entrusted Léon Noël, the former ambassador to Prague,

---

[1] R. Coulondre, *De Staline à Hitler*, pp.142–6.   [2] Ibid., pp.152–3.

with a special information mission to Czechoslovakia. The conclusions reached from this mission were entirely pessimistic: Czechoslovakia was, because of her various national minorities, in the throes of internal disintegration.[3]

Britain Appears on the Scene

On 20 July the British government announced to the French government that it was sending an unofficial intermediary, Lord Runciman, to Czechoslovakia. The problem was to determine what concessions, extracted from Czechoslovakia, would be likely to satisfy Hitler and calm the conflict.

It is easy to explain why Britain should have decided to play an active part: since she would be involved in a war whether she liked it or not, in spite of her refusal to have any commitments in Central Europe, it was necessary for her to try to find a compromise with a view to avoiding the conflict.

France, however, accepted the Runciman mission, which was already a fairly daring interpretation of her undertakings with regard to Czechoslovakia. There are several explanations for this. In the first place it would commit Britain in an area from which she had always remained aloof and, by extending Franco-British co-operation to a new field, would thus reinforce it, which was considered vital. Britain would subsequently be morally obliged to guarantee a ruling, to the establishment of which she herself had largely contributed.

Other reasons could be set forth, however, concerned with French internal policy. One of these, which is somewhat cynical, was presented by Noël as follows: 'In order to avoid any parliamentary difficulty, it was a matter of letting the British government take responsibility for abandoning the Czechs.'[4] A more fundamental reason can be found, however: a large part of French opinion still regarded Czechoslovakia as untouchable and the French commitments regarding her as unconditional. Since the Runciman mission could not fail to take some time, it was a matter of accustoming French public opinion to the idea that a compromise, infringing the integrity of Czechoslovakia, was legitimate and reasonable.

[3] L. Noël, *L'Agression allemande contre la Pologne*, pp.198ff.
[4] Ibid., p.202.

However, the Runciman mission failed: it was not possible to obtain the agreement of the parties in question to a compromise, since the more concessions the Czechoslovak government made, the more inflated the demands of the Sudeten Party became. This should already have enlightened people as to what Hitler's real intentions were.

The September Crisis

With Hitler's speech at the Nuremberg Rally on 12 September, events hurtled forward and the crisis entered its acute phase. When the signal was given, the German Sudeten Party provoked a number of disturbances, and on 15 September asked for Sudetenland to be attached to the Reich. On the same day, at his request, Neville Chamberlain met Hitler at Berchtesgaden and acknowledged the principle of detachment of the Sudetenland territories. On 19 September Czechoslovakia found herself presented with a proposal endorsed not only by Britain but also by France, which stipulated that all territories with at least 50 per cent Germanic population should be attached to Germany. On 21 September, under Franco-British pressure, the Czech government yielded reluctantly.

On 22 September Chamberlain, who brought this capitulation to Hitler at Godesberg, came up against new demands concerning the date of occupation of Sudetenland – fixed for 1 October – and the claims presented meanwhile by the Poles and the Hungarians for portions of Czechoslovakia.

Chamberlain then protested at this procedure which was, nevertheless, quite in keeping with Hitler's tactics: to request in stages whatever one could not obtain all at once, the first concession inevitably bringing about all the rest. Indeed, while mobilization measures and military precautions were adopted on both sides, many people in France and Britain wondered whether, having granted the basic principle, it was really possible to go to war for what seemed to be questions of procedure. President Roosevelt, having clearly indicated that the United States would not intervene in the conflict in any circumstances, proposed an international conference. The same proposal was taken up in a different form by Mussolini: a conference limited to France, Germany, Britain and Italy – a relic of the Four-Power Pact so dear to Mussolini – met in Munich on 29 September. The next day, in the absence of the Czechs, the agreement was made: it was hardly any different from the Godesberg conditions, except for the date limit which was put back from 1 to 10 October, and the fact that an international commission was provided to regulate the terms and conditions for the transfer of the territories.[5]

The only problem we have to deal with here is that of the French attitude during this crisis. On this point, although the *Documents Diplomatiques Français* have not yet been published, we have one of the most valuable accounts, if we consider it to be authentic in spite of the circumstances in which it was published. This is the *Carnets secrets* of Jean Zay, a minister of the Daladier cabinet, which were published during the German occupation, by Philippe Henriot who collaborated with the Germans, with the very ostentatious purpose of discrediting the French 'war-mongers' of whom Jean Zay was one. These *Carnets* give us a report of two Councils of Ministers.

The purpose of the meeting of 19 September was to ratify the Franco-British proposals, for which the President of the Council, Daladier, took personal responsibility. He asserted that Beneš himself, the President of the Czech republic, accepted the principle of territorial transfers; if a conflict broke out, France could not save Czechoslovakia, because of the appalling inferiority of her air force, and because of the length of time and the sacrifices required to cross the Siegfried Line. The ministers unanimously came round to this view. Nevertheless, protests took shape during the days which followed.

It was, however, between Godesberg and Munich that the division which was to split French opinion without regard for party limits became obvious within the government itself, bringing into opposition notably the President of the Council, Daladier, and his Minister of Foreign Affairs, Georges Bonnet.

At the meeting of 27 September, Bonnet recalled that France, in her diplomatically isolated and militarily powerless position, could not go to war; the raising of these arguments, although they were known to all, aroused real indignation in the Council. Daladier in particular, it seems, exclaimed that if it had been decided to abandon Czechoslovakia, this should have been said earlier, and

[5] See the official account by Georges Bonnet of the differences between the Godesberg Plan and that of Munich in the *Livre Jaune Français 1938–9*.

that in the present conditions Hitler could take anything. All of this took place as though the men responsible for French diplomacy, who had long since decided on concessions after lucid assessment of the balance of power, had not been able to manage without some sort of moral justification for their policy, based on the German law of nationalities, which could, provided it was not examined too closely, be confused with the French concept of the right of peoples to self-determination. However, the succession of German demands from Berchtesgaden to Godesberg aimed at stamping the situation with a 'dynamism' which was to result in the breaking up and destruction of the Czech state in a few days, and even the extermination of the Czech people if they resisted. Daladier understood this, as his declarations at the Munich Conference show; and, by the final agreement, he thought that he had preserved the existence of Czechoslovakia. The most curious thing is that according to several accounts, Hitler soon showed his disappointment with the Munich agreement, which nevertheless yielded to him in fact all that he had officially demanded, and this tended to prove that in September 1938 he was less interested in Sudetenland than in the elimination of Czechoslovakia. He had thought that he could reach this objective immediately; as it was, he needed several months of intrigues and threats to achieve it.

The Munich agreement was to bring about a fundamental confusion in French opinion, and violent arguments in all French parties between 'Munichers' and 'Anti-Munichers'. On the moral level, the 'Anti-Munichers' were indisputably right: whatever the diplomatic forms used, France had abandoned an ally and failed in a formal undertaking; once more, might had been right, and this time France had agreed to it without resistance.

The only serious argument in favour of the 'Munichers' was on the level of material possibilities and the balance of power. It was obviously difficult to discuss this openly at the time, but we can do so today. Firstly, as far as the diplomatic situation was concerned, the following comments could be made. It is rather fruitless to wonder – without having access to documents which would enable us to answer the question – whether the USSR did or did not sincerely intend to uphold her undertakings regarding Czechoslovakia: in any case she was unable to do so. As far as Britain was concerned, the exact meaning of this or that declaration and the origin of this or that dispatch have been much discussed, but to what purpose? Those British leaders to whom intervention in Central Europe was most repugnant never denied that once France had gone to war, Britain would be practically obliged to support her. It has not been denied either, however, that British aid at the beginning could only have been insignificant: two divisions and a still embryonic air force.

In fact, then, in order to save Czechoslovakia, France would have had to rely on her own forces only. How long could the Czech troops have resisted? Obviously we are reduced to making hypotheses, based on the example of Poland in 1939. No doubt the Czechs were better armed than the Poles and could rely on natural defences; they were also less numerous and had much less space available; it must not be forgotten either that with the annexation of Austria Czech defences had been circumvented, and that a German onslaught across Moravia would no doubt have very quickly cut off Bohemia from Slovakia.

What opportunities did the French army have in this short space of time? France's inferiority in the air was dramatic. General Vuillemin, the Chief of French Aviation, had declared that if war broke out, after a fortnight there would not be a single French aircraft in the sky; and this declaration, which carried a great deal of weight in the government's decision, was not exaggerated pessimism. An argument used retrospectively by the 'Anti-Munichers' was that at this time the Siegfried Line facing the French frontier was not completed, that it was only weakly defended by troops and that it was still possible to penetrate it. This is no doubt true, but what would have been the outcome of a pitched battle in the Swabian mountains and plateaux between an unprotected French army far from its bases, and German troops who could very easily and very quickly return from Bohemia? In fact there was no reason to suppose that a campaign launched in 1938 would have been less disastrous than that of 1940.

One final criticism has been directed against French policy. If, in April or May, the French government had been aware of the fact that France could not effectively support Czechoslovakia, why did it let her think otherwise until September? Several explanations can be put forward. First of all, French opinion had to be prepared for a backing down which it had as yet hardly considered. Moreover, the Czech crisis had occurred in different conditions from those of the previous crises. Until then Hitler had always used surprise tactics, operating with sudden shows of force invariably followed by peaceful declarations. The gradual mounting of international tension from May 1938 was a new phenomenon. It gave rise to the idea that Hitler had not really decided to risk a war, and that he was relying on intimidation, 'bluffing' in fact; in this case a firm attitude would save everything. This brought about the panic of the last days, in the face of Hitler's increasingly threatening attitude, and the feeling that nothing remained now but final disaster.

The Consequences of Munich

Was the Munich agreement simply a compromise hastily contrived in desperate circumstances, in order to avoid the worst? Was it not at the same time the start of a new policy?

One fact often stressed is that the USSR did not take part in the conference. She had not been invited, perhaps because she had always displayed a deliberate intransigence, laying on France the responsibility for actual decisions. However, it was also, and above all, because France and Britain had simply accommodated themselves to the initiative of Mussolini, who seemed to be the only one at the time who could restrain Hitler. However, did this exclusion of the USSR and this agreement with Germany and Italy not signify, to certain people, that from now on Germany was being given a free hand in the East? In this case, one would simply have made a calculation identical with that of Stalin in 1939 when he concluded his pact with Hitler.

The debate basically revolves round the Franco-German declaration of 6 December 1938.[6] Its official content was singularly thin, consisting of a declaration of good-neighbourliness, mutual respect of established frontiers and an undertaking for consultation between the two governments 'with the exception of their individual relationships with third powers'. What, however, was the meaning and implication of a declaration such as that?

The negotiation can be traced back at least to 17 October, at the time of the farewell visit of the ambassador François-Poncet to Hitler. On that occasion Hitler 'stressed the difficulties which could be caused by a non-aggression formula, if it had to be accompanied by reservations relating to the League of Nations

[6] *Livre Jaune Français 1938–9*, p.38.

Covenant or the existence of pacts concluded with third parties'. However, 'at no time [did he ask] that France should give up her pact with Soviet Russia'. François-Poncet, however, was no fool; he was sure that 'the Führer remained faithful to his preoccupation with disrupting the Franco-British bloc and with stabilizing peace in the West in order to have his hands free in the East'. Nevertheless, he advised that these advances should be followed up, simply because no chance of peace should be ignored.[7] The French government gave a favourable reply, while making 'the necessary contacts with the British government' on this subject.[8] However, when he came to Paris to sign this apparently harmless declaration, the German Minister, von Ribbentrop, in a conversation with Georges Bonnet, launched an attack against the USSR and also against Britain.[9] The German aim was hence quite clear: it was a matter of ensuring the diplomatic isolation of France by this bilateral agreement. In the same discussion, Georges Bonnet tried to induce Germany to moderate Italy's anti-French demonstrations.[10] He subsequently always defended himself vigorously against the German claim, that France dissociated herself from the fate of Czechoslovakia and Poland by this declaration.[11]

This official history is duplicated by another more secret one. After the Munich Agreement, the French ambassador to Warsaw, Léon Noël, took a number of steps with his government to ensure that French pledges with regard to Poland would be revised and would no longer be automatic.[12] Undoubtedly, Poland's attitude towards Czechoslovakia when the latter was in great danger would have been quite sufficient to justify this new policy. The French military chiefs had moreover always considered that French obligations to Poland were too extensive, and criticized in particular the guarantee which was given against a Russian attack. Georges Bonnet gave Noël a reply which the latter interpreted as favourable, but no action followed. Noël explained his final failure as having been caused by the pressure of public opinion, which made another Munich operation impossible.[13]

This is not a digression, for the first condition of a policy whose purpose was to turn the storm towards the East by leaving

[7] Ibid., pp.27–30. [8] Ibid., p.31.
[9] Ibid., pp.42–4. [10] See below p.233.
[11] *Livre Jaune Français 1938–9*, pp.228–31; see also Document 49.
[12] L. Noël, op. cit., pp.248–59. [13] Ibid., pp.303–9.

Germany's hands free there, was obviously for France to extricate herself from her obligations towards Poland which would inevitably involve her in any eastern conflict. If, then, certain people in France were inclined to follow a policy of 'a free hand in the East', the fact is that in the end this policy was not put into effect.

Chapter 15

The Beginning of the War

The Italian Claims

The Munich Agreement, by which France and Britain believed they had compromised successfully and limited the risk of damage, was very widely interpreted in the world as an abdication of the Western powers; the result was a collapse of whatever remained of their friendships in Europe, and a stimulation of covetousness which until then had been more or less restrained. Mussolini, in particular, whose intervention had been requested to avoid a war over Czechoslovakia, thought the time had come to reward himself very handsomely for his co-operation. On 17 December he officially denounced the Rome Agreements of January 1935. He wanted complete control of the port and railway of Djibouti; new management of the Suez Canal Company (use of the Canal being henceforth essential for relations between Italy and Ethiopia); and finally an undefined revision of the status of the Italians in Tunisia.[1] However, he committed the serious error of supporting these demands with a public campaign of intimidation in the German manner: there were demonstrations in the streets, in the press and even in the *Camera dei Fasci* to the shouts of 'Tunisia! Corsica!' and even 'Nice and Savoy!' This was a serious miscalculation of the difference in situations and strength. French opinion greeted these demonstrations with a mixture of scorn and indignation[2] which forced the government to adopt an attitude of categorical refusal. Nevertheless, it tried to find a compromise in this matter which it considered of secondary importance, since an improvement of Franco-Italian relations seemed necessary in view of the constant threat of a massive confrontation with Germany. However, it was necessary to have recourse to an unofficial intermediary, Paul Baudouin, who was instructed to offer purely

[1] J. B. Duroselle, *Histoire diplomatique*, pp.246-7.
[2] Parisian students organized a procession on the theme of 'Venice for France!'

economic concessions, which Mussolini refused.[3] Since Mussolini did not dare to, and could not, go further, the affair did not have any practical consequences.

The psychological consequences, however, must not be ignored, for this incident clearly revealed the indirect repercussions of the Munich Agreement, and hence the impossibility of contemplating another compromise of the same kind. To be more precise, a trend had been discernible in France in favour of a certain dissociation from European affairs; French forces were henceforth to devote themselves to the defence and development of France's overseas empire. This inclination towards an 'imperial withdrawal' was obviously strangled at birth by the Italian claims.

The Prague Coup

There is no doubt that Hitler was never resigned to the limits which the Munich Agreement set, in spite of everything, to his actions regarding Czechoslovakia. His objective was primarily to achieve the complete bondage of this country in order to make it a springboard towards the oil of Rumania and the wheat of the Ukraine.[4] The Czechs, however, with that supple flexibility which had enabled them to survive through the centuries, instinctively tried to preserve a certain degree at least of internal autonomy. Hence Hitler would guarantee the Czech frontiers as he had undertaken at Munich, on condition that a programme to ensure dependence on Germany was carried out, which would consist in particular of a German right to oversee all Czech officials.[5] This was a programme which obviously no government could accept. From that moment Czechoslovakia's fate was sealed. The pretext for the final liquidation was Slovakian autonomist agitation. It is not necessary to describe the details of this distressing affair. On 15 March 1939 Bohemia and Moravia were occupied by German troops and practically annexed to the Reich. Slovakia was occupied likewise, shortly afterwards.

The 'Prague coup' was to result in a sudden and fundamental change in British diplomacy and, at the same time, in that of France, which was closely associated with it. It would be inaccurate, however, to maintain that France had only followed

[3] A. François-Poncet, *Au Palais Farnèse*, pp.81–90.
[4] *Livre Jaune Français 1938–9*, pp.81–9.   [5] Ibid., p.65 (18 February 1939).

Britain more or less willingly. In fact, as had already happened during the Ethiopian affair, the development of the two countries had been for the most part parallel. From 17 March – before Neville Chamberlain had given the signal for a policy of firmness – Daladier, according to the *Carnets secrets* of Jean Zay, declared to the Council of Ministers that 'all we could do was to prepare for war'.

Why this change in the face of a *coup de force*, which was only the continuation of an already long series, and which had been foreseen by many for a long time? It was because French policy, like that of Britain, could not be shaped solely in relation to the balance of power – which did not improve. Until then, out of a love of peace, people had wanted to believe that Hitler would only carry out, in his own brutal way, the programme of the pan-Germanists which had already been defined by Stresemann: to attach to the Reich all regions which could be regarded as populated by Germans. Moreover, since the collapse of collective security, a large part of Western opinion was more or less resigned to this programme. From then on, however, with the annexation of numerous populations which had no Germanic element whatever, it was a different matter: it was a vast campaign of domination which would gradually spread over all Europe, even over the whole world. In the face of this threat, moral indignation was also accompanied by a defensive reflex.

The Policy of Guarantees

Britain and France now acted in great haste, trying to reassure and bolster all countries which might feel threatened by Germany or Italy, or would be ready to yield to their pressure. On 23 March Franco-British armed intervention was promised in the event of German aggression against the Netherlands, Belgium or Switzerland; such aggression would obviously have been only a preliminary to a general offensive towards the West. Britain and France, however, did not confine themselves to these purely defensive precautions. They meant to put a stop to German or Italian expansion all along the line; and this time it really was a policy of blocs, independent of any distinction or shade of opinion, which came into force. On 13 April Britain and France promised help to Greece, who was threatened by the Italian occupation of

Albania, and to Rumania. This last guarantee has been particularly criticized. Rumania, it was said, did not ask for anything; on the contrary, her policy was one of *rapprochement* with Germany, with whom she had signed an important commercial agreement on 10 December 1938. Germany, however, did not discourage Hungarian or Bulgarian territorial claims against Rumania, and from now on people were accustomed to the volte-faces of Hitler's policy. Now if Germany undertook a war, it would be necessary for it first of all to be sure of Rumanian oil.[6] The purpose of the guarantee to Rumania was to strengthen her against any German pressure, direct or indirect. On 12 May Britain signed an agreement with Turkey which, this time, included mutual assistance. In order to enter into this treaty, France did not hesitate to hand over to the Turks on 23 June 1939 the sanjak of Alexandretta which was part of Syria under a mandate.

On 31 March Britain had offered her guarantee to Poland with whom France, on her part, had a treaty of alliance. However, it was not obvious to the Western powers at that time that Poland would be the next victim. No doubt on 24 October 1938 Germany had already informed Poland of its immediate claims: the return of Danzig to the Reich, a German means of communication through the Polish Corridor with privilege of exterritoriality. Poland did not consider any concessions, and it even seems that for a certain time she did not take the German claims very seriously. The Polish leaders who made the German-Polish Agreement of January 1934 did not seem to have understood that in Hitler's mind this agreement could have only one meaning: to make Poland a satellite and an auxiliary in the great expansion towards the East at the expense of the USSR. One proof of their blindness is that they neglected for a long time to inform their French ally of their difficulties with Germany. It was only in the last days of March 1939 that these difficulties were made public.

Negotiations with the USSR

After the 'Prague coup', exchanges of opinion had begun between Britain and the USSR, who until then had not been bound by any particular agreement. When Poland appeared to be decidedly the

---

[6] Jean Zay, *Carnets secrets* (11 April 1939).

most threatened state, the question of the Soviet attitude became of prime importance. However, 'forming a united bloc against the aggressor' was a simple matter only on paper. Poland and Rumania were bound to each other only by an agreement directed against the USSR and not against Germany. Britain herself was reluctant to associate herself with the USSR by an agreement of automatic mutual assistance. Another, completely unexpected, difficulty began to appear, in addition to these difficulties of long standing.

On 7 May 1939 the French ambassador in Berlin announced to his government that Hitler was considering an agreement with the Soviet Union in order to remove the obstacle of Poland.[7] The ambassador raised the question of this contingency several times,[8] conjuring up the possibility of Poland's being divided between the Germans and the Russians. No doubt this information met with a certain disbelief: how would it be possible for Hitler and Stalin, after having founded all their international propaganda on their unshakable ideological antagonism, to reverse their opinion to such an extent without losing face? Nevertheless, the negotiations between the Westerners and the Russians took place, because of this, in an atmosphere of mutual distrust, each side suspecting the ulterior motives of the other. The Soviets saw the Munich Agreement as an attempt to exclude them from European affairs; it was now impossible for the French negotiators to dismiss the idea of a future Soviet volte-face.

Nevertheless, on 27 May, Anglo-French proposals, which met Soviet views, were sent: mutual assistance was considered if war broke out in connection with aggression against Poland, Rumania, Greece, Turkey or Belgium. The Russians, however, presented new demands. They wanted the guarantee to be extended to the Baltic States (whether they liked it or not) and to cover also cases of indirect aggression: these had already appeared, we remember, in the definition of the aggressor proposed by the USSR at the League of Nations. However, they could be interpreted in such a way that the USSR would be able at any time to intervene in the internal policy of the Baltic States, and thus to rebuild the empire

[7] *Livre Jaune Français 1938–9*, pp.153–5. For this episode see especially the account of General Stehlin, *Témoignage pour l'histoire*, pp.147–52.

[8] *Livre Jaune Français 1938–9*, pp.163–5 (9 May), pp.172–3 (22 May), pp.184–5 (13 June), p.210 (4 July).

of the tsars in this region. Finally, the Russians subordinated the conclusion of the political agreement to the negotiation of a military agreement. Perhaps they had been led to make this demand by the memory of the Franco-Soviet treaty which had never been followed by a military agreement. However, they perhaps already knew that a German-Polish war was imminent, and to a certain extent made their political choice – an *entente* with Germany or an agreement with the Western powers – depend on the military arrangements which could be made with the latter.

French and British military missions were therefore sent to Moscow. However, their task proved singularly difficult from the beginning, for France was prepared for only a purely defensive war; Britain was in no way prepared for a war of any kind; and finally, Poland would not permit the entry of Russian troops on her territory. This was why French instructions, drawn up between 13 and 27 July 1939, stipulated the supply and repair of war equipment, the supply of raw materials, air support, perhaps if necessary the intervention of mechanized units (which were considered incapable of permanently occupying the territory), but nothing more.[9] The French concept made sense, in military terms – apart from any diplomatic consideration – only if the Polish front could hold; but British experts did not conceal the belief that, in their opinion, Poland if left on her own could be crushed in two weeks.[10]

Military discussions as such began on 13 August. Immediately, the Russians demanded that the Western countries should reveal their definite plans. This was impossible for both the French and the British experts. In the first place, the modesty of the actions contemplated in the case of France and the means available in the case of the British, could not be disclosed to the Russians without giving the latter a very bad impression; then there could be no question of divulging real military secrets, which ran the risk of being communicated to the Germans. They got over the difficulty by declarations which were so optimistic that they could be called a bluff: the French talked of a Maginot Line extended to the sea and of a 'powerful attack' which they reckoned to organize in a short time; the British alluded to a first convoy of sixteen divisions.[11] In spite of this, the Russians were disagreeably impressed

[9] General Beaufré, *Le Drame de 1940*, pp.120–3.   [10] Ibid., p.152.
[11] M. Baumont, *Les Origines de la Deuxième Guerre Mondiale*, pp.330–1.

by the fact that the Western countries did not contemplate holding back much more than forty German divisions on their front, which implied that the majority of Hitler's forces would weigh upon the Eastern front.[12]

Immediately afterwards, however, the Russians asked the fundamental question: they themselves did not consider concluding a military agreement without active participation of their army in the contemplated battle, which implied the entry of the Russian army into Poland. The French delegation did everything in its power, including sending one of its members in all haste to Warsaw, to obtain Poland's agreement. The Poles remained unyielding: not only did they fear that once the Russians were established in Poland, they would never leave, but they did not believe that the Soviet forces wished to fight or were capable of fighting effectively against the Germans.[13]

In these conditions the discussions could not succeed, and it is rather fruitless to criticize the way in which they were carried out on the French and British side. It was not in anyone's power completely to change, several months or several weeks before hostilities, strategic arrangements, a military organization and an alliance, which had been established for at least ten years. The best that could therefore be expected from the USSR was a benevolent neutrality. However, a German-Russian agreement including a secret clause on the partition of Poland[14] was obviously quite another matter.

The Last Hesitations and the Declaration of War

It must not be thought that from 31 March 1939 until the outbreak of war, the policy of the Western democracies maintained from first to last an attitude of unwavering firmness towards unconditional support of Poland. As it had done before Munich, by intensifying its pressure and its manœuvres of intimidation and by increasing international tension, Germany ended by obtaining some results. France had already shown that she was ill-prepared to maintain a war of nerves. She began to increase her advice to Poland to be careful – as if there was a danger of war

[12] General Beaufré, op. cit., p.139.
[13] Ibid., p.139.
[14] See the text of this clause, ibid., p.186.

breaking out as the result of a chance incident and not of a deliberate decision by Hitler! Also, the apparently limited nature of
the German claims led many to wonder whether it was worth
'dying for Danzig', a 'free city' which was almost purely German,
and already so completely dominated from within by the Nazis
that its official attachment to the Reich would make little difference. As Coulondre, the French ambassador to Berlin, wrote very
lucidly on 22 June:[15]

> The majority of accredited diplomats in Berlin try to see what could
> be a compromise solution and are alarmed that they do not see one.
> Thus they are trapped in a sort of contradiction, for the moment one
> admits, and they admit it, the unlimited nature of the German
> National-Socialist demands, there is then no hope of ending them by
> settling the question of Danzig, and consequently there is no ad-
> vantage in compromising oneself on the subject. On the contrary
> there are major disadvantages.

However Coulondre himself, according to the evidence of his
military attaché,[16] was to be one of those to weaken at the last
moment. This fact, which is not decisive in itself, merely reveals
the atmosphere at the time.

This hesitation, not to say weakening, was naturally aggravated
by the signing of the German-Soviet pact. According to the
Carnets secrets of Jean Zay, Chautemps exclaimed at the Council
of Ministers on 22 August: 'We would certainly die for Danzig,
provided we had a Russian shield'. The first concession was thus
formulated in an official dispatch to the French ambassador in
Warsaw:[17]

> The French government . . . earnestly recommends the Polish
> government to refrain from any military reaction in the event of a
> proclamation of attachment of the Free City to Germany by the
> Danzig Senate. It is important that Poland should reply to a decision
> of this kind only by an action of similar nature, by formulating all
> reservations and all appropriate legal remedies through diplomatic
> channels.

In other words, France virtually sacrificed Polish rights to
Danzig. In the Council of Ministers the 'Anti-Munich' group was

[15] *Livre Jaune Français 1938–9*, p.194.
[16] General Stehlin, op. cit., p.176.
[17] *Livre Jaune Français 1938–9*, p.302 (24 August).

alarmed at the tendency of certain colleagues to understand the nature of French pledges to Poland as conditional.[18] Britain, too, while signing a treaty of alliance with Poland on 25 August, advised the Poles to carry out direct negotiations with Germany. The Austrian and Czech precedents clearly showed the Poles where such an encounter with their dangerous neighbour would lead them. Indeed, Hitler promptly increased his demands: it was no longer a matter of Danzig, nor even of the Corridor and Upper Silesia, but of a complete alignment of Poland with Germany.[19]

Even when German troops entered Poland, this did not put an end to all diplomatic attempts. Italy, who was not anxious to be involved in a general war, proposed an international conference. The Minister of Foreign Affairs, Georges Bonnet, was of the opinion that this should be accepted, provided it had a wider aim 'and that it would propose, as the first British note suggested, a study of all conditions for re-establishing peace in the world'. This was increasing the dangers beyond all limits, as Daladier, the President of the Council, remarked plainly.[20] In any case this conference could not meet until German troops had withdrawn from Poland, according to the British condition; Bonnet would perhaps have been content with a cessation of hostilities. However, Hitler continued his war and intended to see it through to the end. France, therefore, did not evade the issue and on 3 September 1939 she in turn went to war.

Why did France adopt two totally different attitudes within the space of one year? Why did she enter the war on account of Poland, while forcing Czechoslovakia to yield? This was an apparently irrational change.

Was it military considerations which tipped the balance to one side and then to the other? On one point, indeed, these were more favourable in 1939. At the time of Munich, those responsible for French aviation were entirely pessimistic, but now, according to the Air Minister, France had a modern fighter air force and her bomber aircraft were becoming available.[21] As far as the army was concerned, the General Staff had less reason for confidence, but it

---

[18] Jean Zay, *Carnets secrets* (24 August 1939).
[19] *Livre Jaune Français 1938–9*, p.375.
[20] Jean Zay, op. cit. (31 August 1939).
[21] Ibid. (22 August 1939).

did not dare advise against armed intervention.[22] It hoped that the Polish army – helped not only by 'General Winter', but before that, owing to the autumn rains, by 'General Mud' – would be able to hold out until the Spring, which was when British help would become effective.[23]

From the diplomatic point of view, the situation in 1939 was very different from that of 1938. It is true that the German-Soviet agreement was a hard blow, but after Munich one could hardly count on Russian help in practice. Meanwhile, the British attitude had changed radically. It was hardly possible for France, having spent all her efforts over twenty years to convince Britain of the seriousness of the German danger, to take evasive action at the very moment when Britain decided to face up to it.

However, the new French attitude should not be explained only by the change in British policy. It must be seen that a new Munich Agreement was literally impossible. The determination of the Poles not to be a party to any compromise left France with one alternative: either to support them or to lose face by failing, not only morally but officially, to keep her word.

Nevertheless, the debate must be extended: the French government entered the war not to save Poland – it was not sure of being able to do so – but because it was from that time on convinced, at least in its majority, that Hitler's ambitions knew no bounds and that if France abandoned her allies she would soon have to face direct aggression without any outside help.[24]

The 'Phoney War'

However, if this decision was inevitable, it none the less represented the dramatic crushing of the hopes of the generation who had taken part in the war of 1914–18, and who were exhausted by it. The reward of the victory which had cost so much bloodshed was destroyed even before the first shot was fired, and for those who had sacrificed everything in order that the First World War should be 'the war to end all wars', the beginning of another war twenty years later was a political and moral defeat of the first magnitude.

[22] J. Néré, *La Troisième République, 1914–1940*, p.188 and note.
[23] L. Noël, *L'Agression allemande contre la Pologne*, pp.427–8.
[24] *Livre Jaune Français 1938–9*, pp.401–2; see also Document 50.

The Beginning of the War

At first, hostilities occurred in the way in which the balance of power between France and Germany and the opposition of their strategies made it easy to foresee. The Poles were crushed quickly, before the French army had done more than make a show of coming to their assistance, there was no question of France's launching a direct attack on the Siegfried Line. She did not even dare to attack it from the air, for fear of reprisals which she would have been unable to prevent. As planned, she established herself in a waiting position: awaiting the mobilization of the British Empire and awaiting the arrival of American equipment. Hope could now be permitted, since in October 1939 the United States Congress had lifted the embargo on exports destined for the belligerents, to replace it by the 'cash and carry' clause. Nevertheless, France could not make full use of the American industrial capacity, for she had to economize her limited financial resources in anticipation of a long war.

What the General Staff had not foreseen was that this waiting without a definite purpose was to have a profoundly demoralizing effect on the troops and on the nation. It reached such proportions that many people believed it was a deliberate calculation on the part of Hitler, to let the war 'go rotten' in order to sap his enemy's will to resist. We now know that this was not so and that throughout the autumn and winter Hitler discussed with his generals plans for a western offensive.[25] However, immediately after Poland had been crushed, on 6 October, he made a public peace proposal, which the President of the French Council, Daladier, rejected on the 10th, declaring: 'We will only lay down our arms when we have a guarantee of security which will not be challenged every six months'. This was a perfectly logical reply, since it was for vital reasons of general policy and not particularly for Poland, that France had entered the war. Nevertheless, a large part of French opinion and political personnel began to hope that the war would finish before it had begun. The government could not rely on the sacred unity of the 1914–18 war. The weakness of its political foundation could not fail to influence its conducting of the war, as it would influence her reactions to military defeat.

Serious questions remained. First of all, there was Belgium's attitude. In September 1939 Belgium remained out of the war and

[25] See the detailed account of these plans in L. Koeltz, *Comment s'est joué notre destin*, Paris, 1957.

she continued to refuse to make military preparations for with-
standing a German attack; she refused to appeal for French troops
as a preventive measure if the Germans threatened her. The
French army would therefore not have the time to establish itself
in Belgium at the only theoretically conceivable defensive position,
that of the Meuse and the Albert Canal. The French General Staff
none the less, and this was to prove fatal, made preparations to
come to the aid of Belgium if the latter were attacked.

However, this was not the only fault in the ideally imagined
system of strategy.[26] France placed a great deal of her hopes in the
economic attrition of Germany, which would be brought about
by the maritime blockade guaranteed by the British fleet. However, in the circumstances of 1939, this blockade was largely
ineffective, for Germany had practically all the resources of
Central and Eastern Europe at its disposal. Moreover, on the
strength of the agreements of 23 August 1939 and 11 February
1940 it received an abundant supply of raw materials from the
USSR.

The anxiety to reinforce on land a blockade which would be
inadequate if it remained purely maritime, together with the need
to 'do something' and to give France a new 'fighting spirit', were
to lead the French government to take initiatives. Britain participated in some of these, in accordance with her own 'peripheral
strategy' of an essentially maritime power. However, these
initiatives were destined to end quickly or badly.

A first proposal was to start a second front in the Balkans,
inspired by the 'Salonika Front' formed during the First World
War. France and Britain had given their guarantee to Greece and
Rumania. On 19 October they concluded an alliance with Turkey.
An army was sent to Syria under the command of General
Weygand, who was in principle to keep himself in readiness for
rapid intervention. However, it achieved nothing. Not only was
it not resolved to act in the Mediterranean, to deal tactfully with
Italy who remained a 'non-belligerent' but, after the crushing of
Poland, the Balkan states, anxious not to suffer the same fate,
carefully avoided being drawn into the conflict.[27]

The Russo-Finnish war, which claimed attention during the
winter of 1939–40, gave birth to other ideas. The heroic resistance,
which was at first apparently victorious, of the tiny Finland

[26] See Chapter 7.   [27] General Beaufré, op. cit., pp.219–20.

against the gigantic Russia, gave credence to the idea which had been maintained for a long time in certain circles that the USSR was a colossus with feet of clay. And so it seems that certain responsible Frenchmen conceived a grandiose and above all fanciful scheme:[28] that of coming to Finland's rescue and thus of holding the USSR in a vice between Finland in the north and Weygand's army in the south. This was not a matter of adding an ideological crusade to the defensive war against Germany. Germany was still the primary aim. It was hoped that she could be deprived of Russian resources, especially oil from Baku, which was the object of the particular attention of Weygand. The defeat of Finland put an end to these proposals and the Daladier cabinet fell before the combined reservations of those who wanted a more energetic management of the war and those who, without daring to say so, dreamed rather of peace (22 March 1940).

The new President of the Council, Paul Reynaud, appeared to be a man of bold initiatives. The first, which had already been prepared by his predecessor, encroached upon the neutrality of the Scandinavian countries, especially that of Norway. Sweden, like Norway, contrary to the stipulations of the League of Nations Pact, had refused the right of passage of French and British troops who were to go to the aid of Finland. On this occasion, however, attention had been drawn to the Swedish-Norwegian railway from Lulea to Narvik, which was the only outlet for the Swedish iron ore indispensable to German industry. Hitler, for his part, had been contemplating an operation in Norway since December 1939,[29] no doubt to evade the maritime obstacle formed by Britain. On both sides, therefore, concern about the blockade led to an extension of the conflict. Almost simultaneously, on 8 and 9 April, the Franco-British fleet and then a German expeditionary force, came into action in Norway. Norwegian neutrality had not been strictly respected by either side. It must be noted, however, that the German action was much more of the nature of direct aggression, so that the Norwegians came over to the side of the Allies. In spite of this, the Franco-British expedition rapidly ended in failure, owing to inadequate preparation and, above all, to inadequate support from the air.

[28] General Stehlin, op. cit., pp.211–16.
[29] L. Koeltz, op. cit., pp.193–9.

Chapter 16

Woe to the Vanquished

Military Disaster and Political Disaster

On 10 May 1940 the German army launched a great offensive on the western front. Six weeks later France capitulated.

The causes of the military defeat, which stupefied opinion at the time, are now well known. They are of several kinds. First of all, French material inferiority, especially in aviation, in anti-aircraft weapons and in anti-tank weapons, was overwhelming. Next, the French army, unwisely engaged in Belgium outside her fortified lines, was in no way prepared to face a sudden attack and carry out a war of movement. The intellectual inferiority of the French Command was perhaps even more serious than the inadequacy of its means.[1] Nevertheless, we must not lose sight of the fact that the new war of movement required a completely new way of thinking, which had not been fully achieved even in the German High Command which had created its theory. The German victory, or at least the swiftness of this victory, was due to a great extent to the disobedience of several commanders of armoured divisions, deaf to the orders of their superiors who became alarmed at their foolhardiness and directed them to stop their advance.

However, did the military defeat which made all organized resistance impossible in France, necessarily have to lead to the armistice, that is, to political abdication? We will not recall here the ignoble dispute between the civilians and the military who each laid the blame for the disaster on the other: a capitulation in the field would have appeared to put the responsibility solely on the military, while the armistice, which was an act of government, implied a civil responsibility. In fact the real problem was to know whether the French government would transfer to North Africa

[1] See J. Néré, *La Troisiéme Rèpublique, 1914–1940*, pp.193–201, and above all A. Goutard, *La Guerre des occasions perdues*, Paris, 1956, for the details of the operations.

to continue the fight. This idea was discussed for several days, but it must be recognized that Paul Reynaud himself did not appear very decided about adopting this solution, since he made almost no preparations for putting it into practice. When he surrendered the power to Marshal Pétain, whose declared intention was to request an armistice, it is not fitting to make the latter alone responsible for the events which followed.

What chances could this continuation of resistance in North Africa offer? This question also gave rise to heated debates without any possible conclusion, for history cannot be remade. It is certain that France had only very limited military and economic resources available in North Africa, and that she would have had the means to transfer only a few political and administrative leaders, the navy and a few aircraft, in the last days of the collapse. I, however, believe that it would have been possible for the French government, by establishing itself in North Africa, to hold together in the struggle, until the final victory. One argument can be given in support of this idea: Hitler, anxious to have done with the war in the West, would keep his essential resources in reserve for the one opponent who still remained standing: Britain.

However, we must look back to the state of people's minds at that time: the armistice was requested not only on account of the military disaster but in view of a peace which seemed to be very near.[2] French opinion was in fact divided. One section, the supporters of the armistice, were convinced that Britain herself would soon be forced to make peace. The other section, the ones who rebelled against acceptance of disaster, anxiously wondered whether Britain wished to and was able to hold out, and did not begin to feel reassured on this point until the September equinox was past; for from now on, for six months at least, a German embarkation for Britain was impossible, which gave the British world time to arm.[3]

If the concluding of the armistice is explained largely by the circumstances at the time, its consequences were to prove extraordinarily serious. In fact, this book could end here, for from now

[2] See A. D. Hytier, *Two Years of French Foreign Policy: Vichy 1940–1942*, p.139.

[3] For the whole of this chapter, the author cannot help but draw on his personal recollections; he was a soldier in 1939–40 and passed the entire period of 1940–4 in the occupied zone and in the forbidden coastal zone.

on France did not have any foreign policy, properly speaking, since she did not possess the essential means: independence and the freedom to control her own forces.

The Impotence of the Vichy Regime

The Pétain government, which was soon established in Vichy, was reduced to impotence by the very terms of the armistice. Three-fifths of France were from now on occupied by German troops, and all the coasts of the Channel and the Atlantic – the only convenient means of communication with Britain and the United States – were in this occupied zone. The capital, Paris, the only place from which France, which had for a long time been extremely centralized, could be effectively governed, was also in this zone. Finally, all the regions which were vital to the French economy, both agricultural and industrial, were also in the occupied zone. Now the Vichy government was not in a condition to carry out any political action in occupied France where there were only purely administrative bodies which often received their orders directly from the Germans, with the possibility only of moderating or even avoiding them by individual initiative.

In the 'unoccupied zone', however, the Vichy government was far from being able to lead an existence which was independent of the occupier. In the first place the Germans could at any time, without any possible resistance, invade the regions which had remained free, and this is what they did at the end of 1942. However, without even having recourse to this extreme measure which in theory would free the French government from the armistice stipulations, the Germans had methods of exerting pressure which, without display, even without formal violation of the armistice agreement, could succeed in paralysing what remained of life in France: they could more or less completely close the Demarcation Line separating the occupied from the unoccupied zone.[4] They could also, by means of exorbitant occupation payment, 'buy' whatever they had not yet taken in France, without its costing them anything.[5] Owing to these means of exerting

---

[4] A. D. Hytier, op. cit., p.121.

[5] This mechanism, which was too complex to be summarized here, is described in A. D. Hytier, op. cit., p.123; it is a basic work for the whole of this paragraph.

pressure, the Germans continued to make demands which went far beyond the rights conferred on them by the armistice, and these demands were always met sooner or later.

What else could have been done? The Pétain government in the armistice agreement avoided handing over to the Germans the French fleet which was a formidable maritime force – and it did not fear to boast of this. It also retained under its authority its overseas empire which was not within immediate reach of German troops. If the German demands became excessive could it not have departed with the fleet, rallied the empire and renewed the war? This possibility was purely theoretical and was not realized even when the free zone was occupied in its turn in 1942. It is important to understand why. For Pétain and those who had followed him, such an action would lose for them their *raison d'être*. Pétain's great argument in favour of concluding the armistice, against those who advocated with more or less sincerity and energy the retreat to Africa, was that it was not possible to pretend to maintain a French state outside the metropolitan area, nor to govern the French by sheltering oneself from their daily ordeals. However, this general argument was very quickly to become loaded with a whole passionate content which it would no longer be possible to ignore. To abandon an ally who was continuing the fight alone, like Britain in 1940, was only permissible if France could assert deep grievances against this ally. Now there was no lack of grievances.[6] Was it not Britain who had done everything, for more than fifteen years, to annul the Treaty of Versailles and favour the restoration of Germany? Then, when Germany had again become too strong for France, was it not Britain again who drew France into the war in 1939, giving her only ludicrous help, thus causing a too docile French government to conduct a policy 'à la Gribouille'.[7] Once the war had begun, had not Britain been in a hurry to re-embark her troops at Dunkirk, leaving the French at the mercy of the triumphant German army?[8] Once the armistice had been concluded, British aggression against the French ships immobilized in the Oran port

[6] See A. D. Hytier, op. cit., pp.33–4.

[7] Gribouille, a character in French folklore famous for his illogicality: for example, when taken unawares by a shower of rain, he jumped into the water to avoid getting wet.

[8] See J. Néré, *La Troisième République, 1914–1940*, p.200.

of Mers-el-Kebir[9] could not fail to upset the whole of French opinion. This was, moreover, followed by the breaking-off of diplomatic relations between France and Britain; from now on anti-British propaganda could be given a free rein in France.

This was not all, however. The presence on Britain's side of a handful of Frenchmen who continued to fight was a living reproach to all those who had accepted the armistice. It was therefore necessary to represent them in the most unfavourable light. This destruction of the French conscience was indeed one of the most grievous and irreparable consequences of the armistice. With every day that passed, however, in the unfolding of mutual reproaches, a future volte-face of the Vichy regime and its servants became morally more difficult. After the Anglo-American embarkation for North Africa in November 1942, when certain high officials of the Vichy regime who had some authority in Africa asked themselves whether they could return to the war on the side of the Allies, they were prevented from actually doing so by the very absurdity of their position.[10]

If a resumption of the struggle against Germany was never seriously contemplated,[11] those responsible for Vichy policy on the other hand soon adopted the course of collaboration with the Germans to an increasing extent. The most acceptable motive for this was to obtain an alleviation of the severities of the occupation regime, by willingly granting to the Germans what they were in a position to command in any case. This, it seems, was the idea of Marshal Pétain in his moments of lucidity. However, what could have been hoped for in fact by taking this course? Economic collaboration was in any case inescapable. The occupying force could give businesses of any importance the alternative of either closing down or working for it; resistance and sabotage could come only from the lower executive ranks. It seems, however, that the two successive heads of government, Laval and Darlan, had aimed further and had thought of something quite different from a waiting policy. Gambling on a German victory, they tried to negotiate without further delay a package deal which would

[9] See A. D. Hytier, op. cit., pp.51ff.

[10] See, for example, the official document quoted by General Stehlin, *Témoignage pour l'histoire*, pp.318–20.

[11] Apart from certain military men, such as Weygand, who never took part in political decisions.

guarantee France her place in the 'new order'.[12] Hitler, however, did not want to commit himself in advance, for he calculated that when once he had finished the war he could reveal demands concerning France which it was inopportune to disclose too soon. It certainly seems that Darlan, at least, had contemplated a military collaboration with the Germans which would logically result in a war with Britain.[13] Such a policy, however, could not succeed either, for in order for France to re-enter the war on their side, the Germans would have been obliged to relax their grip and, in particular, to allow the French a certain degree of rearmament. This they had no intention whatever of doing. Being well informed of the real feelings of the French, they were not going to allow them arms, knowing perfectly well to what use they would be put in the end.[14]

Thus the Vichy regime was incapable equally of resisting the Germans and of establishing true co-operation with them. It was because of this double impotence rather than a deliberate intention to play a double game that the contradictory guarantees given by Vichy to the Germans and to the British in the autumn of 1940 are explained. At the time of the Montoire interview, the Vichy government had undertaken to reconquer the African colonies that had fallen into the power of the Free French.[15] In December 1940, by the secret Halifax-Chevalier agreements, the same government undertook to respect the *status quo* in the 'Gaullist' colonies.[16] In practice, Vichy could not give the overseas territories any instructions other than to make a gesture of defence in case of attack; it was in no condition to organize offensive operations which would have immediately started a conflict with Britain. Moreover, it was subjected to too strong pressures on the metropolitan territory to refuse the Germans access indefinitely to certain overseas territories, when the Germans imperiously demanded it, as was the case with Syria.[17]

The Impotence of Free France

On 18 June 1940 the appeal made by General de Gaulle was to

[12] A. D. Hytier, op. cit., *passim*, especially pp.176, 227–8, 328.
[13] Ibid., p.267.   [14] Ibid., p.294.   [15] Ibid., pp.171–3.
[16] See, for example, A. D. Hytier, op. cit., pp.106ff.
[17] Ibid., pp.275ff. See p.256.

keep France in the war, or rather, to get her back into it. However, during four years of fighting and even until French territory was liberated, de Gaulle and his colleagues did not succeed in achieving their main objective: to ensure that France and those who continued the fight in her name were accorded the rights and the dignity of an ally in the war against Hitler. This is one of the most painful chapters of this tragic history which remains for us to discuss.

It must first be recognized that, materially, in numbers of men, ships and territories, de Gaulle and the Free French represented very little. It could not be otherwise, however. Those who had the strongest motives to join the Free French in England or elsewhere were the French people in the occupied zone who were in direct contact with the Germans and for whom the Vichy regime did not form a screen to hide reality from them. However, these were the very people who found escape most difficult and most dangerous, owing to the efficiency of German surveillance. Conversely, it was easier to join de Gaulle from the free zone, and even more so from the overseas territories. However, especially for the latter, the mortal peril which the German occupation represented seemed far away and rather insubstantial. This contradiction between the will and the means of accomplishment, which was so obvious in space, also proved to be so in time: it was during the first days of the capitulation, when faced with a still incomplete German occupation and a Vichy government which was just beginning to become organized and take over the administration, that circumstances were most favourable for people to respond to the appeal of General de Gaulle. At that time, however, the French people were scattered along the exodus routes, isolated and without means, dazed by the blow of a disaster which they could not understand, not knowing, moreover, whether Britain would or could continue the fight. It was only when the September equinox was past that the evidence asserted itself: Britain, spared from the threat of a surprise invasion, was to take advantage of the winter months to build up her defences, and could hold out. However, to join Britain was from then onwards a difficult and hazardous venture which needed long preparations.[18]

Qualitatively, too, the Free French were not able immediately to inspire their fellow-countrymen with confidence; at first they

[18] Here again the author draws upon his personal recollections.

did not include a single important politician, and very few administrators, diplomats or officials of high rank. To join the Free French was to sacrifice everything: position, career, livelihood; to expose one's family to the worst reprisals; and to lead an outlaw existence. This was easier for the young and obscure than for those whom a well-developed career had already tired physically and morally and who, moreover, being more in the public eye, were more vulnerable. The allies, besides, had faulty vision in this connection: it was not the prestige and influence of one or other pre-war personality which could rally the French to resistance, but simply the presence of the enemy. On the other hand, those who used all their strength to resist the enemy became by the same token the natural leaders of the French people.

One of the first tasks of the Free French was obviously to guarantee a base in the overseas territories, out of reach of the enemy. French Equatorial Africa appeared most promising in this respect: it was far away, very far from the influence of Vichy, but on the other hand it was near the British colonies and the Belgian Congo which were still in the war. Above all, its sparsely populated territories, where only a few men were needed to tip the balance one way or the other, were the territories for action dreamed of for bold individual initiative; and this was more or less the only asset of Free France. At the beginning of August 1940 de Gaulle sent there some of his first followers, Pleven, General de Larminat and the future General Leclerc. Between the end of August and the first days of September, Chad, Cameroon, Central Congo, Oubangi Chari and then Gabon joined Free France. The daring and the faith of a few men had achieved a miracle without shedding any French blood.

However, the results were not unrelated to the scantiness of the means used: Equatorial Africa was too weak and too far away to serve as a real base for Free France. Its contribution to the war effort was limited in practice to the airfield at Fort Lamy, a turntable in the centre of Africa, and to what seemed a very remote means of threatening Italian Libya from the south.

French West Africa was much more inviting because of its extent, its population, its resources and the strategic situation of Dakar which commanded the South Atlantic and sea and air links with South America. However, Dakar was a large town, a place of great importance, abundantly provided with troops and a central administration which was naturally inclined to obey the government in office; the appearance of a few determined men and a flag could not be sufficient to guarantee this base. This was why de Gaulle had developed a plan consisting of a landing on the Ivory Coast or at Conakry which would establish a number of rallying points round about, spreading to come closer together.[19] Churchill, however, haunted by the needs and the dangers of naval warfare, did not wish to wait for the results of these long-term tactics. He ordered a frontal attack on Dakar, with the participation of large British naval forces.[20] This was a very dangerous operation which was compromised by ill-fortune. The most serious mishap was the passage of a French flotilla from the Mediterranean to the Atlantic, as a result of the inexplicable negligence of the British authorities at Gibraltar; this brought to Dakar, besides a considerable reinforcement to its defence, a contingent of sailors who were enraged at the British aggression against Mers-el-Kebir. On 23 September the Dakar operation failed. The consequences of this failure were particularly serious: not only did all hope of winning over West Africa to Free France have to be abandoned but, most unjustly, de Gaulle was held responsible for the failure. He partly lost the confidence of the British and, also, it seems, of the Americans.[21]

Although the winning-over of overseas territories to Free France thus rapidly found its limits, it would appear that the recruiting of individual Frenchmen abroad would be easy. This, however, was not the case. When diplomatic and consular representatives, maintained by the administrative machine, continued to obey the Vichy government – with which, moreover, the non-belligerent countries were obliged to keep up diplomatic relations – Frenchmen who did not wish to submit were in a very difficult situation. They had no passport, which was particularly serious in a neutral country in time of war, their action was paralysed and they were exposed to all denunciations. Their life would soon have become impossible if there had not been some success in making certain countries acknowledge unofficial Free

[19] J. Soustelle, *Envers et contre tout*, Vol. I, p.139.
[20] D. S. White, *Seeds of Discord*, pp.212–13. De Gaulle, *Mémoires de Guerre*, Vol. II, pp.96–9.
[21] D. S. White, op. cit., p.235.

French delegations who were at least invested with consular powers.[22]

The real strength of Free France lay in fact in the moral adherence of an ever-increasing part of metropolitan France, especially the occupied zone. How could this adherence be shown, however? Public demonstration could hardly be considered, and the security requirements of the secret struggle demanded tight segregation of the organizations, which could not be more unfavourable to the expression of a common will.[23]

During the summer of 1940 when Britain, faced with immediate and deadly peril, had to make an arrow out of any piece of wood, anything seemed possible: the worst and the best. The worst was obviously the aggression against Mers-el-Kebir. The best was the agreement of 7 August 1940[24] by which Churchill recognized to some extent that Free France did exist and granted it material and financial help. The main British support to the French cause was the availability of the BBC – subject, however, to control and certain reservations. Without the daily encouragement of Radio London, the mass of French people who instinctively rejected German domination would have been reduced to a hopeless wait-and-see policy.

However, in spite of comradeship in arms, relations between Britain and the Free French soon deteriorated. First of all, from October 1940, the British government adopted the course of a *modus vivendi* with the Vichy regime, and even tried to make secret agreements which would have enabled the French navy and French North Africa to re-enter the war.[25] Must it be thought that after the failure of Dakar, the British tried to find other means of reaching their strategic objectives on the sea and in Africa, and that from now on de Gaulle and the Free French were only a secondary trump-card?[26] There is hardly any doubt that the persistent illusions concerning the actual intentions and the possibilities of the Vichy regime weighed heavily on the relationship between Free France and her allies.

[22] J. Soustelle, op. cit., Vol. I, pp.204–5, 223–4.
[23] Ibid., pp.307, 317–18.
[24] See the text of the agreement and explanatory letters: General de Gaulle, op. cit., Vol. I, pp.278–83.
[25] A. D. Hytier, op. cit., pp.268–9.
[26] J. Soustelle, op. cit., Vol. I, p.368.

Another, quite different, factor which aggravated this relationship was Syria, a traditional object of Franco-British rivalry. Syria, which remained under the authority of Vichy, afforded a useful field of manœuvres for the intrigues of the Germans, who calculated that they could make use of her, especially for stirring up a revolt against the British in Iraq. Admiral Darlan granted the right of passage to Germany for its war materials and aircraft. In June 1941, British and Free French forces penetrated into Syria. The Vichy forces resisted vigorously, and the campaign cost several thousand lives. When the Vichy representative capitulated, the British endeavoured to eliminate the Free French from Syria, and the frictions and grievances resulting from this continued until 1945. The origin of the affair, which poisoned Franco-British relations, was perhaps not even a strategic consideration associated with the fight against Germany, but the preoccupation of the British and Free French with outdistancing each other in the Middle East.[27]

However, the attitude of Britain towards Free France, as well as towards other countries, was to be more and more influenced by the position of the United States. The latter, while they were not officially belligerents, had maintained diplomatic relations with the Vichy government, as was customary. In addition to this they tried by this method to influence Vichy and keep it from going too far on the path of collaboration with Germany. This naturally resulted in a reserved and even distant attitude as far as Free France was concerned. On the other hand, the United States by tradition closely watched all European possessions which formed part of the Americas, particularly the French Antilles which remained under the sovereignty of Vichy. By the Havana Agreements of July–August 1940, the various American republics undertook jointly to oppose any transfer of sovereignty of these European possessions.[28]

In June 1941, de Gaulle sent René Pleven to Washington, where he had great difficulty in obtaining a meeting with some of the American ministers. Nevertheless, in September, the American State Department agreed to the presence in Washington of an official Free French Delegation, and on 11 November President Roosevelt extended the benefit of Lend-Lease 'to the territories'

[27] This is the theory of A. D. Hytier, op. cit., pp.276–8.
[28] D. S. White, op. cit., pp.162–7.

within the jurisdiction of Free France; however, it pretended to deal with the actual authorities in the locality, without recognizing the central authority to which they belonged.[29] The entry of the United States into the war as a result of the attack on Pearl Harbour did not put an end to these difficulties. On the contrary, in December 1941, the rallying to Free France of the little islands of Saint Pierre and Miquelon along the Newfoundland coast, resulted in a very violent incident between the American State Department and General de Gaulle.[30] In the United States this rallying, which in the eyes of the French was a purely French affair, was regarded as a challenge to the policy expressed by the Havana Agreements. This reaction, and the whole attitude of the United States government regarding Free France, while they were engaged in the same war against the same enemies, are still difficult for a Frenchman to understand today. However, the obliteration of France and the material weakness of Free France were part of the explanation: France was no longer an ally, an agent of history, but a mere pawn which could be used at will.

The lack of understanding and perhaps the ignorance[31] of the Americans regarding the real French situation led them to take a serious step, which was to weigh heavily on the last two years of the war. Being unable to attempt an embarkation for Europe in 1942, and urged by the Russians to act without further delay to relieve the eastern front, the British and Americans decided on an intervention in French North Africa in the autumn of 1942. However, in order to obtain co-operation in this territory, which was a necessary base for their future operations, at the least cost, the Americans did not wish to appeal to the Gaullist groups established there. On the contrary, they 'fabricated' a new leader to bring France into the fight, General Giraud, who had recently escaped from a German prisoner-of-war camp. Giraud was largely unknown to the French public and he had displayed unfortunate affinities with the Vichy regime in their internal policy. In any case, given the circumstances which had brought him out of obscurity, he ran a great risk of appearing simply as an agent of a foreign country, even if it was an ally. This calculation

[29] D. S. White, op. cit., pp.322–6.
[30] D. S. White thought that he could make this incident the basis of his book.
[31] See D. S. White, op. cit., p.348.

did not even achieve the immediate results which had been proposed. When the Americans landed they were greeted by gunfire, in spite of the name of Giraud, and many fell who need not have done so. When, as a result of complex and obscure vicissitudes which we cannot even summarize here, Giraud was put into power in Algiers, he carefully retained the men, the institutions and the shibboleths of Vichy, and this could only put an obstacle in the way of resuming the fight against the Germans.[32] However, a new division was introduced within France herself, and this was at the wish of an ally. Far from being able to have a foreign policy, France saw external pressures overthrowing her internal policy.

This position of Giraud was, moreover, singularly weak, for his authority could neither rely on the legitimacy of Vichy – which had disowned him – nor on that of the Republic. Meanwhile, a year was needed – from November 1942 to November 1943 – for a normal situation in accordance with reality to be restored in North Africa. Nevertheless, General de Gaulle showed conciliating tendencies throughout this episode which he did not always adopt in other circumstances. De Gaulle had tried to contact Giraud directly, even before meeting him at the Anfa interview imposed by President Roosevelt and which, moreover, did not achieve any tangible result.[33] Now they had to wait until May 1943 for Giraud, chiefly under the pressure of representative institutions in Algeria who were meeting again, to give his consent to de Gaulle and the National Committee to establish themselves in Algiers. It was in November 1943, with the meeting of a consultative assembly in Algiers, that the provisional government of the French Republic was provided with all the administrative agencies permitted by circumstances. For all that, it was not recognized by its allies without reservations. On the eve of the landings of June 1944, the American authorities, it seems, again considered administering the liberated French territories directly.[34] However, these inclinations, if they existed, were soon swept aside by the facts. At the end of 1944, the authority of General de Gaulle was established almost everywhere: Free France had become simply France.

[32] J. Soustelle, op. cit., Vol. II, especially pp.212–13.
[33] See de Gaulle, op. cit., Vol. II, pp.429–33: texts of telegrams exchanged between de Gaulle and Giraud before the Anfa interview.
[34] J. Soustelle, op. cit., Vol. II, p.389.

Nevertheless, France was still a long way from resuming her international status and her means of external action. It is sufficient to point out that she was not present at the Yalta Conference (February 1945) and the Potsdam Conference (July 1945) at which the destiny of Europe was fixed without Europe herself being consulted. This simple statement enables us to measure the enormity of the disaster into which Hitler had swept the whole of Europe, a disaster from which France, in spite of a very large number of unprecedented individual acts of heroism, has been unable to escape.

Conclusion

The history of French foreign policy from 1914 to 1945 is one of a vast retreat, slow at first, then gathering speed, and finally culminating in an unprecedented collapse. Frenchmen who came suddenly face to face with the result did not fail, as is natural in such circumstances, to try to find those who were to blame among the men who wielded power during that period, and even more in the institutions within whose framework this authority had been exerted. We certainly do not claim that errors were not committed. There were some on the diplomatic level such as, no doubt, the weakness shown during the Disarmament Conference, and most certainly the almost unbelievable miscalculation made in the Ethiopian affair. There were again more errors implicating those responsible for military matters and general policy, such as inaction when Hitler reoccupied the Rhineland; or the unpardonable rashness of launching unprotected into Belgium to meet the German invasion, troops which had been trained to defend themselves only in organized positions. However, these errors are not on the whole greater than those which, since men are not infallible, are committed in even the healthiest and soundest political systems. The study of the *Documents Diplomatiques Français* too, as they are published, shows us all the efforts made by French policy during these years to remedy a situation whose deterioration was clearly recognized. If these efforts as often as not proved in vain, this is because French policy was faced with a task which was both necessary and unattainable. The Europe defined by the Treaty of Versailles was the only means conceivable at the time of avoiding German hegemony, and it was in order not to suffer this hegemony that France had sacrificed everything. On the other hand, the peace of Versailles was impossible to maintain without the active co-operation of the three allies who had won the war. Once this co-operation had disappeared, everything was to crumble as if by an inescapable fate, and French statesmen, beginning with Briand, were well aware of this. These men later found themselves reproached with having given their allegiance to Britain or

Conclusion

America; the futility of their efforts, with respect to allies who were too slow to understand, is one of the most tragic chapters of this story. And yet these great allies believed themselves protected from the German threat. But what of the persistent blindness of Poland and Czechoslovakia who were in direct contact with the danger and who continued, in the case of Poland, to keep up conflicts with all her neighbours and, in the case of Czechoslovakia, to despise Italy, the only road through which help could come?

The world of 1939 has very little in common with the world of today. Franco-German antagonism, which was a basic reality of the period we have discussed, has no purpose today; and the Europe which was still Utopian at the time of Briand can now perhaps be achieved. The Marshall Plan, which removed all problems of debts and reparations, has shown to what extent it was possible for men of action to learn practical lessons from history. As far as France is concerned, she seems now to have recovered her material and her vital forces. Let us not deceive ourselves, however. This fall has injured even those who do not know the details of this past or who do not wish to remember them. Assurance, confidence in herself and in her free institutions, and even a certain *joie de vivre*, have vanished from France. Politically and morally, she has received a wound from which she has not recovered.

Appendix

Documents

Introduction

The present series of documents may appear not only very incomplete – that is self-evident – but also very unevenly distributed. It is in fact based essentially on the publication of the *Documents Diplomatiques Français* which still only covers extremely limited chronological periods. For this era we have hardly any private documents, especially correspondence between statesmen, which could not only fill in the gaps of the official publications but in certain cases could also reveal the ulterior motives of the principal figures in diplomacy. We have had no alternative but to have recourse in certain cases to declarations in Parliament, even to newspaper articles. Nevertheless we feel that in spite of all its inadequacies this collection can throw light on certain basic and often unknown aspects of French foreign policy.

List of Documents

1 Memorandum sent by Aristide Briand, President of the Council, to the American Ambassador (10 January 1917). (Question of war aims.)
2 Letter from Aristide Briand to Paul Cambon (12 January 1917). (Question of war aims.)
3 Memorandum from Maurice Paléologue, Director of Political Affairs, to Pokrovsky, Russian Minister of Foreign Affairs (14 February 1917). (Question of war aims.)
4 Clemenceau's reply to Lloyd George's memorandum of 16 March 1919.
5 Article by André Tardieu: 'M Clemenceau and the American risk' (*L'Illustration*, 20–7 March 1920).
6 Extract from the inaugural speech by Aristide Briand (20 January 1921).
7 Speech by Aristide Briand to the Chamber of Deputies (extract: 12 April 1921).

8 Aristide Briand and the Washington Conference (extracts: Briand's speech to the Chamber of Deputies, 21 and 25 October 1921; Briand's speech at the Washington Conference, 21 November 1921).

9 Discussion between Lloyd George and Aristide Briand (21 December 1921). (Question of the British guarantee.)

10 Aristide Briand's reply to the British memorandum on the Guarantee Pact (8 January 1922).

11 Speech by Clemenceau at the Metropolitan Opera in New York (22 November 1922). (Question of guarantees.)

12 Ministerial declaration of the Herriot government (extract: 17 June 1924).

13 'The right to security and international reciprocity' (article by Aristide Briand in *L'Europe Nouvelle*, 18 December 1924).

14 Sanctions and guarantee pact (memorandum from Philippe Berthelot to Aristide Briand, April or May 1925).

15 Origin and justification of Locarno (extracts: Aristide Briand's speech to the Chamber of Deputies, 25 February 1926).

16 Memorandum by Aristide Briand on European Union (17 May 1930).

17 'Cutting our losses' (article on reparations from the *Dépêche de Toulouse*, 3 January 1932).

18 The 'Confidence Pact' (July 1932).

19 Note from Germain-Martin to Edouard Herriot (15 October 1932).

20 Memorandum from the American government (23 November 1932). (Question of war debts.)

21 Memorandum to the American government (1 December 1932).

22 French aide-mémoire of 9 November 1933 on measures taken regarding American trade.

23 Dispatch from the French Ambassador in Brussels (3 November 1932). (Belgian attitude.)

24 Unofficial memorandum to Arthur Henderson (12 July 1933). (French disarmament plans.)

25 Dispatch from André François-Poncet to Pierre Etienne Flandin (25 March 1936). (History of the Franco-Soviet pact.)

26 Memorandum from General Weygand (16 January 1933). (French strategic problems.)

27 The Four-Power Pact: French counter-proposal (24 March 1933).
28 The Four-Power Pact: final text (30 May 1933).
29 Paul-Boncour circular (25 July 1933). (Question of national minorities.)
30 Dispatch from Henri de Jouvenel to Joseph Paul-Boncour (28 June 1933).
31 Memorandum intended for Mussolini (10 September 1933). (Consolidation of Central Europe.)
32 Note from the Political Directorate (19 July 1933). (Franco-Soviet *rapprochement*.)
33 The Franco-Soviet mutual assistance agreement of May 1935, accompanied by the signature formalities.
34 'Free hand' (Laval-Mussolini correspondence on Ethiopia, December 1935–January 1936).
35 Clause 16 of the League of Nations Pact (Legal basis for sanctions).
36 Memorandum from the Army General Staff (18 January 1936).
37 Meeting of the Military High Committee (18 January 1936).
38 Memorandum (probably from General Gamelin) (27 January 1936).
39 Report of a military meeting with General Gamelin (8 March 1936).
40 Flandin administrative memorandum (11 March 1936). (Discussions between the Locarno signatories.)
41 Massigli memorandum (12 March 1936). (Consequences of remilitarization of the Rhineland.)
42 Memorandum from the Director of Political Affairs (30 June 1936). (Fragility of the French system of alliances.)
43 Programme of the Rassemblement Populaire (Section devoted to foreign policy).
44 'The problem of peaceful co-existence' (article by Léon Blum in *Le Populaire*, 28 August 1937).
45 Memorandum to the British government (16 September 1936). (Proposal for a 'new Locarno'.)
46 Delbos–Smigly-Rydz talks (30 September 1936). (Guarantees to Czechoslovakia.)
47 Memorandum from the Political Directorate (25 July 1936). (Arms deliveries to Spain.)

48 From Yvon Delbos to Charles Corbin, French Ambassador in London (26 November 1936). (Proposal for mediation in Spain.)

49 Letter from Georges Bonnet to Joachim von Ribbentrop (21 July 1939).

50 Declaration of the Government to the Chambers (2 September 1939). (Entry into the war.)

1. *Memorandum sent on behalf of the* Entente *by Aristide Briand, President of the Council, to the American Ambassador (10 January 1917).*

(War aims of the Allies.)

(1) Restoration of Belgium, Serbia and Montenegro, with the compensations which are due to them;

(2) Withdrawal from invaded territories in France, Russia and Rumania with just reparations;

(3) Reorganization of Europe, guaranteed by a stable regime and based as much on respect of nationalities and on the right to full security and freedom of economic development possessed by all nations, large and small, as on territorial agreements and international rulings calculated to guarantee land and sea frontiers against unjustified attacks;

(4) Restitution of provinces or territories formerly seized from the Allies by force or against the wish of the population;

(5) Liberation of the Italians, Slavs, Rumanians and Czechoslovaks from foreign domination;

(6) Liberation of populations subjected to the bloody tyranny of the Turks; expulsion from Europe of the Ottoman Empire, which is decidedly alien to Western civilization;

(7) The intentions of His Majesty the Emperor of Russia with respect to Poland were clearly indicated by the proclamation which he addressed to his armies;

(8) The Allies have never had the intention of exterminating German peoples or causing them to disappear politically.

2. *Letter from Aristide Briand to Paul Cambon (12 January 1917)* (in G. Suarez, *Briand, le pilote dans la tempête*, Vol. II, pp.128–30).

By your letter of 10 September last [which does not appear in the correspondence of Paul Cambon], you informed me of your private conversation with Lord Grey about the conditions for the future peace and you pointed out to me that the Principal Secretary of State for Foreign Affairs considered that an exchange of views among the Allies on this subject would be useful, so that they would be able to reply to any armistice proposals which a neutral power, notably the United States, could make.

The government of the Republic considers that when the present conflict is finally settled, it would be desirable as far as possible to put aside the intervention of powers which did not take part, but it nevertheless believes it advisable to determine now the general conditions according to which the Allied powers could consider peace, in order to avoid any future misunderstanding between them.

Every power has its own aspirations, and it is important to know them in order to balance in some way the satisfactions which can be granted or the sacrifices which can be requested of each of them. Thus the negotiation which will open in London with Italy on the subject of Asia Minor will not be considered in isolation and without taking into account the considerable advantages which the Rome government has in mind both in the Adriatic region and in the Alps. The very opening of this negotiation indicates how urgent it is for France and Britain to exchange their views on general conditions for future agreements.

We have the same interest as far as Russia is concerned, about which country Lord Grey also appears to be concerned. We can have the greatest confidence in the loyalty of the Emperor Nicholas, but everyone in Europe knows to what intrigues about nothing the world of the Court and the lowest strata of the revolutionary parties in Petrograd are exposed.

I would therefore see advantages in resuming and carrying on the discussions, for which Lord Grey took the initiative, so that we could show in Petrograd and Rome that our views are closely united with those of the British government. It would be premature to go into too precise details, but I would like to give you general instructions from which you must draw your inspiration.

You have clearly indicated to Lord Grey that not only must there be no question about the recovery of Alsace-Lorraine, but it must not be considered as an advantage, or a new acquisition. Alsace-Lorraine must not, as it were, enter into the calculations. We recover our property which was torn from us against the will of the population. It must be understood that Alsace and Lorraine must be restored to us, not mutilated as they were after the treaties of 1815, but demarcated as they were before 1790. We would thus have the geographical and mining basin of the Saar, the possession of which is essential to our industry, and the memory of the successive mutilations of our ancient frontier must be effaced. There is, however, one question which will inevitably be asked on this occasion, and it is that of the left bank of the Rhine. Some well-meaning people in France who are attached to the oldest traditions of our national policy, claim it as the lost heritage of the French Revolution which is necessary to form what Richelieu called our 'pré carré' [neatly rounded-off territory].

It is to be feared, however, that the recovery of the Rhineland provinces which were taken from us a century ago might be considered as a conquest and would be of a nature to create great difficulties for us.

What is more important than a glorious but precarious advantage is to create a state of affairs which would be a guarantee for Europe as well as for us and which would be a cover for our territory.

In our eyes, Germany must no longer have a foot beyond the Rhine; the organization of these territories, their neutrality and their temporary occupation must be considered in exchanges of opinion between the Allies. It is, however, important that France, being the most directly concerned with the territorial status of this region, should have the casting vote in examining the solution of this serious question.

3. *Memorandum from Maurice Paléologue, Director of Political Affairs at the French Ministry of Foreign Affairs, to Pokrovsky, Russian Minister of Foreign Affairs (14 February 1917).*
I have the honour of declaring to the Imperial government that the government of the Republic proposes to have among the peace conditions which will be imposed on Germany the following claims and guarantees of a territorial nature:

(1) Alsace-Lorraine will be returned to France;

(2) Its frontiers will extend at least as far as the boundaries of the former duchy of Lorraine; they will be mapped out in such a way as to provide for strategic needs and to re-integrate into French territory all the coal-mining basin of the Saar valley;

(3) The other territories situated on the left bank of the Rhine,

at present incorporated in the German Empire will be completely detached from Germany and freed from any political and economic dependence on it;

(4) The territories of the left bank of the Rhine which are not incorporated in French territory will form an autonomous and neutralized state; they will be occupied by French troops as long as the enemy states have not completely fulfilled all the conditions and guarantees stipulated in the peace treaty.

Consequently, the government of the Republic will be happy to be able to count on the support of the Imperial government in achieving her plans.

4. *Clemenceau's reply to Lloyd George's memorandum of 16 March 1919* (from A. Tardieu, *La Paix*, pp.130–2).

II . . . Before the war Germany was a great world power whose future was on the water. It is of this world power that it became proud. It is the loss of this world power for which it cannot console itself.

Now we have taken from it, or will take from it, without being stopped by fear of its resentment, all its colonies, all its navy, a large part of its commercial fleet (by way of reparations), and the foreign markets over which it reigned.

We thus deal it the blow to which it will be most sensitive, and we believe that we can appease it by a few improvements in territorial conditions. This is a pure illusion and the remedy is not on the same scale as the evil.

If, for reasons of a general order, we wish to give Germany satisfaction, we must not look for this in Europe. . . . In order to appease it (if we are determined to do so) we must offer it colonial satisfactions, naval satisfactions and satisfactions of commercial expansion. The memorandum of 26 March considers only European territorial satisfactions.

III The memorandum of Mr Lloyd George expresses the fear that too severe territorial conditions imposed on Germany will play into the hands of the Bolsheviks. Is it not to be feared that the method which he suggested might have precisely this result?

The conference has decided to create a certain number of new states. Without being unjust, can it sacrifice them by forcing unacceptable frontiers on them out of consideration to Germany? If these peoples – especially Poland and Bohemia – have resisted

Bolshevism up to now, this is because of national feeling. If violence is done to these feelings, they will fall a prey to Bolshevism and the only barrier which separates Russian Bolshevism and German Bolshevism will be broken down.

The result will be either an Eastern and Central European Confederation under the direction of Bolshevik Germany, or the enslaving of these same countries by a Germany which will have again become reactionary, owing to general anarchy. In either of these two cases the Allies will have lost the war.

The policy of the French government, on the contrary, is resolutely to help these young nations, with the support of all that is liberal in Europe, and not to look for mitigations – which would in any case be invalid – for naval and commercial disaster inflicted on Germany by the peace, at the expense of these peoples.

If, by giving these young nations the frontiers which are necessary for them to live, we are obliged to transfer Germans, the sons of those who dominated them, to their sovereignty, this is to be regretted and it must be done in moderation, but it cannot be avoided. . . .

IV . . . If we follow the method suggested in the memorandum of 16 March what would be the result? A certain number of total and final guarantees would be acquired for maritime peoples who have not known invasion. The surrender of the German colonies is total and final. The surrender of the German navy is total and final. The surrender of a large part of the German merchant fleet is total and final. The exclusion of Germany from foreign markets, if not final, is total and lasting.

Partial or temporary solutions, on the other hand, would be reserved for the continental countries, that is, for those who suffered most from the war: the reduced frontiers suggested for Poland and Bohemia are a partial solution. The defensive undertaking offered to France for the protection of her territory is a temporary solution. The system proposed for the coal of the Saar is a temporary solution. Here there is an inequality which may run the risk of having a bad influence on relations between the Allies themselves after the war, which is even more important than their relations with Germany after the war.

5. *André Tardieu, 'M Clemenceau and the American risk'*
(L'Illustration, *20–7 March 1920*).

[The non-ratification of the Treaty of Versailles by the Senate of the USA destroys at the same time the Anglo-American guarantee treaty to France. Had Clemenceau provided nothing to face this eventuality?]

On 22 April 1919 the text of article 429 [of the Treaty of Versailles] was worded and approved as follows:

'If the conditions of the present treaty are faithfully observed by Germany, the occupation (of fifteen years) stipulated in article 428 will be successively reduced, as follows:

(1) After five years . . .;

(2) After ten years . . .;

(3) After fifteen years the rest of the occupied German territories will be evacuated.'

If we refer to the treaty signed on 28 June, we ascertain that clause 429 contains an additional paragraph. This paragraph is drafted as follows:

'If at this time (at the end of fifteen years) the guarantees against unprovoked aggression by Germany are not considered adequate by the Allied and associated governments, the withdrawal of occupation troops could be delayed to the extent considered necessary for obtaining the aforesaid guarantees.'

This final paragraph had been adopted on 22 and 29 April at the request of M Clemenceau. What was its origin? What were its meaning and implication?

On 23 April, in a private meeting, M Clemenceau asked Mr Wilson the following question:

'The treaty, as it stands, satisfies me from the point of view of guarantees. The future, however, is not yours or mine. You have a Senate, just as I have a Parliament. Neither you nor I can be sure what they will do in ten years, or what they will do tomorrow. If, for example, the treaties with the USA and Britain are not ratified, what will be France's situation? What replacement guarantee will be available to her?'

President Wilson replied:

'Your comment is perfectly fair. However, it presents a difficult problem. Let us try to find a solution.'

This attempt lasted for more than a week. On five occasions the two presidents exchanged suggestions and texts. The sequence of these texts (which exist), fully illuminates their effort.

On the evening of 29 April, President Wilson and M Clemenceau in agreement with Lloyd George decreed the final edition, which became the final paragraph of article 429, and which I quoted above. Let us re-read this text and then we will understand.

'At the end of fifteen years, on 10 January 1935, the Allied and associated governments, according to the terms of the final paragraph, would have to decide whether the guarantees against unprovoked aggression by Germany were or were not adequate. Which guarantees were meant? Those stipulated by the treaty with Germany and the two British and American treaties at Versailles, on 28 June 1919 – that is, for a far-off and unspecified future, the League of Nations; for a nearer future, the occupation, completed by the two treaties. In what circumstance could these guarantees be considered insufficient in 1935? Obviously, when the two treaties fail; that is, precisely, in the present case. In this case, what would happen? The withdrawal could be delayed to the extent considered necessary in order to obtain the aforesaid guarantees.'

In other words, if, failing the ratification of the British and American treaties, France has no other security guarantee than the occupation of the left bank of the Rhine and the bridgeheads after fifteen years, *this occupation could be prolonged until there were other guarantees*, that is, until either the two treaties signed on 18 June or equivalent agreements came into force. Thus the final paragraph of clause 429, the culmination of M Clemenceau's efforts, supplied an answer to the question asked of the President of the USA by the head of the French government on 23 April 1919, and to the question presented on 19 March 1920 by the American Senate; an answer which, in all hypotheses, safeguards the interests of France.

6. *Inaugural speech by Aristide Briand, 20 January 1921* (quoted by G. Suarez in *Briand, sa vie, son œuvre*, Vol. V, p.109).
This agreement [between France and her allies] is the basic condition for settling all questions which keep effective settlement of peace in suspense. We will do everything to uphold it and develop it. We are highly confident that our great friend and ally, Britain, will help us with all her forces. Nothing, in fact, can sever the relations between these two great countries who have learned to know each other better and to esteem each other more in the arduous combats in which they shed their blood together. . . .

The century-long friendship between France and the USA, the unforgettable memories of our common history, which have in the past and will, if necessary, in the future mingle the blood of our soldiers on the battlefields of liberty, guarantee our union both in peace and in war. We are sure that our American friends will give us as compensation for our damages the same invaluable support which decided the victory in the Great War in which we jointly defended the cause of civilization.

7. *Speech by Aristide Briand to the Senate, with no date given, and to the Chamber, on 12 April 1921* (quoted by G. Suarez in *Briand, sa vie, son œuvre*, Vol. V, pp.175–6).

Tomorrow, if, when the occasion arises, Germany tries to withdraw from its pledges and its undertakings by new machinations, a strong hand will fall on its shoulder. . . .

This is not the time for discussions on how much or how little patience has been shown in the service of our right nor the time for measuring Germany's capacity for payment. It is no longer words, but acts and results which must be offered to a country which has waited for two years. Our resolution has definitely been made: on 1 May Germany will be faced with the consequences of all the successive violations of the treaty which it signed.

This treaty includes its recognition of its responsibility and obligation to pay for the damage it caused, to the utmost of its ability; it includes the undertaking to disarm in conditions which were clearly pointed out to it, and the punishment of those responsible for the crimes committed.

On 1 May Germany was faced with the balance-sheet of its obligations on the one hand, and the balance-sheet of what it has fulfilled on the other hand. We have in our hands an enforceable warrant. When the bailiff has been sent, if the debtor persists in being recalcitrant, then he must be accompanied by the police.

It is not a matter of war; it is not a matter of disturbing the peace, or of resuming the military operations which Germany imposed on us. It is a matter of going with an executed, signed and valid document, and after jurisdiction has been accepted and the Reparations Commission has supported it with its sentence; it is a matter, I repeat, of going to find the debtor if he does not want to pay, and of forcing him by all the means of coercion within our power.

8. *Aristide Briand and the Washington Conference.*

(1) [speech by Briand to the Chamber of Deputies, 21 October 1921] It is necessary that we show them there[1] that we are not the troublemakers we are made out to be, that we have peaceful ideas, and that it is not for pleasure that we keep thousands of men under the colours, and that, if we make enormous budgetary efforts to maintain an army, this is because of a perfectly natural concern for our security. . . .

Then arises the question, I shall not say of disarmament, but of limitation of armaments, from the naval and land points of view. We will talk. We will say exactly what we think. . . . We will say: what would have become of France, if, exhausted by the war of 1871, she had given way, if she had given up guaranteeing her own safety; if, exhausted by the enormous sums the conqueror had exacted from her, she had taken refuge solely in considerations of economic progress? At the hour when the freedom of the world was in peril . . . there would not have been one French soldier on guard at the frontier of world liberty. . . .

Let everything be done so that she will not be threatened in the future. . . . Let all guarantees be given so that France has nothing to fear, so that liberty has nothing to fear, and France will not be the last to limit her armaments. However, we must have these guarantees; they are essential. France must demand them for herself and for the world.

(2) [speech by Briand to the Chamber of Deputies, 25 October 1921] France shows at present, by the moderate use she makes of her force, always at the service of her rights, that she has none of the ulterior motives which others have attempted to attribute to her. It is very costly to maintain this force; she keeps it only for security reasons. On the day that an international situation is created which would give France, not a verbal security, not a vague declaration subject to interpretation, but a certain security for the integrity of her territory, France would listen to any proposals of this nature which may be made to her.

(3) [speech by Briand at the Washington Conference, 21 November 1921] [Briand has just pointed out the efforts which France is

[1]At the Washington Conference.

already making in the way of disarmament, especially the reduction of the length of military service by half.]

In this way the home army will be reduced to half of its effectives. To go beyond this, and I say this very clearly and frankly, is impossible. France could not do this without exposing herself to the greatest danger. If someone said to us, today or tomorrow: 'We, as well as you, can see this danger; we understand it and we will share it with you; we will offer you all the means of security you could wish': immediately France would adopt a different course.

... We understand the anxieties of other nations, and their difficulties in a world which is still troubled, and we are not so egotistic as to require other nations to use their national sovereignty to our advantage. But then ... if France must remain alone in the face of a situation such as I have described without exaggeration, such as it is in reality,[2] then she must be left the possibility of guaranteeing her security to the extent compatible with the needs of the present hour.

I would like to be able to say that all the questions must be asked, examined, discussed and solved, but I would like to call your attention to this point: the moral isolation of France would be a poor condition for hastening the hour when peace is finally established in Europe and in the world. It is important that everyone should know that France has still the goodwill, the heart of all civilized peoples and of all those who fought at her side, to guarantee the triumph of freedom in the world.

The true condition of disarmament of all the malevolent elements which I indicated at the beginning of my talk is that it should be known in Germany that France is not alone, that it is certain that all the poisonous propaganda designed to disfigure the face of France will come up against impenetrable barriers, and that those who were with us yesterday are morally still with us today.

If this is known in Germany, the reasonable men who are trying to consolidate the Republic will gain the upper hand. The words

[2] Briand had spoken previously about the industrial power of Germany, its capacity to make use of considerable armed forces disguised as police forces, in addition to the *Reichswehr*, and also the formidable unknown quantity, Russia.

which incited the former Germany[3] will resound hollowly. It will be impossible for those who dream of revenge to carry out their intentions, democracy will be established in the country, and from this time on one may seriously hope to see peace reign finally in the world.

9. *Memorandum (dictated by Aristide Briand) on the subject of a discussion between Lloyd George and Briand at Downing Street, on 21 December 1921* (quoted by G. Suarez, *Briand, sa vie, son œuvre*, Vol. V, pp.350–1).

[Lloyd George has just said that Britain can give complete guarantee concerning the French frontier but is reluctant to undertake any commitments regarding the eastern frontiers of Germany.]

M Briand said that he had in mind an alliance of much wider scope than that outlined by Mr Lloyd George. He understood very well that the British public was not concerned with giving unconditional support to the countries of Eastern Europe. However, from the French point of view, the first result of a firm agreement would be to reduce France's military burdens and to bring them to proportions more in keeping with her resources. This was the strong desire of at least three-quarters of the population of France, and its conviction was that this result could only be achieved by close ties between France and Britain. It was not impossible to imagine that other nations would adhere to this agreement, even Germany itself. M Briand thought that there was much to be said in favour of such an arrangement, of the same type as the treaty between the four powers on the subject of the Pacific, which had just been concluded in Washington. Such an agreement would not impose very strict military obligations on the powers but would make it possible for them to consult with each other in the event of a crisis which could threaten their interests or the *status quo*. This arrangement could include three or four powers, but its nucleus would be a complete alliance between Britain and France round whom other nations could be grouped. He repeated earnestly that Germany could be a party to this agreement.

---

[3] Briand had read extracts from a book by General Ludendorff which extolled in particular the moral value of war.

Mr Lloyd George said that British public opinion was at that time hardly prepared to contemplate such an extensive alliance, but that there would be a majority in Parliament and in the country for granting France a simple guarantee against invasion, although this guarantee would in fact encounter today more opposition by the minority than it would have done two years ago. M Briand, however, contemplated something which would extend beyond the two countries. If it were possible to involve Germany, all the better. He would like to consult his colleagues about M Briand's suggestion and continue the discussion at their coming meeting in Cannes.

M Briand said that he would prefer to put his ideas on paper and submit them for Mr Lloyd George's examination. His main object was to build around a Franco-British agreement a general organization whose aim would be to uphold peace in Europe. If other nations had the impression of a firm agreement between France and Britain for maintaining peace and order, peace would not be threatened for long and Germany would find it an advantage to join them. This act alone would obstruct the path of reactionary forces in Germany, by making the order of things, which they wished to destroy, unshakable. Such an agreement between France and Britain would prevent the Germans from making plans against the peoples on their frontier. Such a guarantee would probably force the Germans to give up their military intentions against Poland and Russia, for example. This would also help German democracy to promote Germany's return to the community of nations and this would tend, in a general way, to stabilize Europe for a long period.

10. *Aristide Briand's reply to the British memorandum on the Guarantee Pact (8 January 1922)* (quoted in G. Suarez, *Briand, sa vie, son œuvre*, Vol. V, pp.373–5).

For France, one question dominates all the others: that of her security. This country, which has suffered so much . . . cannot forget that Germany has 20 million more inhabitants than has France, that for the majority of Germans democracy is still a word devoid of meaning and that this disciplined, industrious people, gifted with a fertile genius for organization, but among whom active political and intellectual propaganda, especially in universities and schools, fosters an aggressive spirit and a passionate desire for revenge, could one day make the disarmament measures laid down by the Treaty of Versailles ineffective.

The best guarantee against such an eventuality is that Germany would be certain that France would not be isolated if Germany attacked her. The negotiators of the Treaty of Versailles had understood this, since they considered it necessary in 1919 to complement the provisions of this treaty with treaties between France and the United States and between France and Britain, which were not ratified.

The situation is not quite the same today. The USA seem to want to remain aloof from European political affairs. Moreover, for two years, the peace settlement and the difficulties raised by the solution of the different problems which the general situation presented have caused differences of opinion to arise between France and Britain, which did not appear in 1919. It would therefore be necessary for the agreement, which would be concluded between France and Britain against a German attack, to show in addition the desire of the two countries to act in complete agreement with regard to upholding peace. A treaty which included only a military guarantee would carry insufficient weight with regard to Germany, if the latter could, on the other hand, see the possibility of provoking and making use of Franco-British dissent to destroy the agreement.

In the eyes of the French government the purely defensive treaty which would intervene must contain bilateral undertakings. A unilateral guarantee like that of the Franco-British Treaty of 1919, which had the similar Franco-American Treaty as a corollary, would not suit the present circumstances. It is necessary to make a public display of the solidarity of the two countries in the event of possible aggression by Germany. Moreover, if Britain can believe she is safe from German attacks, no one can assert, although she is infinitely safer than France in this respect, that changes in war methods and equipment will not make her lose all or part of the advantages she enjoys from her natural defences.

The French government therefore considers that the *entente* which is to be concluded must contain terms so that in the case of direct aggression on the part of Germany against one of the two countries, the other country should immediately come to her aid with military, naval and air forces. It would be specified, moreover, that the British government would undertake to consider the upholding of the German disarmament conditions stipulated in the Treaty of Versailles, and notably the special references to the Rhineland regions which appear in clauses 42, 43 and 44 of this treaty, as indispensable to the safeguarding of French territory; and that any violation of these latter provisions would constitute a case of direct aggression against the security of France in the eyes of the British government, just as much as aggression against French territory as such. Moreover, any violation by Germany of military, naval or air clauses of the Peace Treaty would be considered on both sides, as being of a nature to motivate the concerted action of both powers.

In order to give this undertaking its full weight, the two governments would engage to regulate the size of their respective armaments by mutual agreement . . . and an *entente* between the General Staffs would be provided for. These clauses, while organizing . . . future military collaboration between the two countries would enable the question of armaments to be regulated to their mutual satisfaction.

On the other hand, since constant collaboration between the two countries would constitute the best guarantee against any action which could disturb the security of Europe, the two governments would agree to act together with regard to any question of such a nature as to endanger general peace.

11. *Georges Clemenceau*: '*What I told the Americans*' (L'Illustration, *9 December 1922, speech delivered on 22 November 1922 at the New York Metropolitan Opera*).

I am not sure that the Rhine is an absolutely effective defence, especially with the new weapons of war which, unless there were an absolutely rigorous surveillance, could cause horrifying surprise attacks on the part of a state on its neighbour.

However, this should at least give us safety from the first blow, and this is why at the Peace Conference, I claimed, by a document which is in all the chancelleries, not the annexation of German territory, but the military frontier of the Rhine.

The next day Mr Lloyd George took me on one side and said:

'If you give up your military frontier of the Rhine I will offer you the naval and military guarantee of Britain. I undertake, moreover, to do my best to obtain a similar guarantee from President Wilson.'

After careful consideration, rather than choose the Rhine and the breach of the Franco-Anglo-American *entente*, I accepted the proposal. However, in order to be able to test the good faith of Germany, I obtained an occupation of fifteen years. I obtained permission for this occupation to extend beyond this period if Germany did not carry out all the commitments of the treaty or if the military guarantees were considered inadequate.

I am not dwelling on these discussions. However, it is quite clear that Mr Lloyd George has not given what he promised. In my opinion France must resume her right in its entirety, if she is not guaranteed satisfaction.

The authorization of the Parliaments was necessary. Britain voted for the treaty; we were offered protection. It would be better to rely on oneself for one's own defence than on a contract, however loyal it might be on either side, whose clauses are easy to evade. Mr Lloyd George has not given us his guarantee and the USA is not interested in the implementation of the Treaty.

I do not ask for anything, but I nevertheless draw your attention to the consequences of an agreement which would prevent German militarism from having access to the Rhine. Nothing would be more in accordance with your views and those of Britain, for, if you give your guarantee to the Rhine frontier, everyone will understand that a no less decisive guarantee works in Germany's favour, since we could not attack it ourselves without losing the support of our best friends.

Hence there would be security for all. This would be a beginning of co-operation with a view to preserving peace which, by its certain success, could not fail to produce an effect of appeasement in numerous parts of Europe.

12. *Ministerial declaration of the Herriot government (extract:*
17 June 1924).

France expressly renounces all thought of annexation or conquest. What she desires is security with dignity and independence. What she wants is peace, primarily for herself, but for other nations too.

We must speak without misunderstanding. Our democratic government will steadfastly defend the rights of our country as set forth in the Treaties. We have a right to reparations. We want them in the name of justice. The new international order which we hope for must not be founded on an iniquity. However, when

Germany has put itself in order with the Treaty from the point of view of these reparations and security, it will depend only on Germany whether it enters the League of Nations.

We are hostile to the policy of isolation and force which leads to occupations and the taking of territories as a guarantee. Faced with the present state of Germany, and in view of the necessity to secure not only France, but all peoples, against an offensive return of nationalist pan-Germanism, we do not believe that it is possible to withdraw from the Ruhr before the pledges stipulated by the experts, whose report we accept without reservation, have been settled and submitted to the international organizations qualified to control them, with just and effective guarantees of execution.

We also believe that in the interests of peace we must control disarmament of Germany by the joint effort of the Allies and, as soon as possible, by the action of the League of Nations. We must solve security problems by guarantee agreements, which in turn are placed under the control of this League. . . .

. . . France does not know hatred; for her it is sufficient to be supported by justice. Our government will not show any weakness with regard to those in Germany, who have not given up violating the Treaties, in order to foster ideas of restoration of the monarchy, with a spirit of revenge. Our government hopes to see the strengthening of German democracy.

13. 'The right to security and international reciprocity' (article submitted by Aristide Briand to L'Europe Nouvelle, 18 December 1924).
Geneva? This is where, little by little, the administration is organized which alone can guarantee peace to nations by covering one continent then another with a network of obligations and sanctions. Nearly all the Ministers of Foreign Affairs of the world, or their delegates, are present. They work to create an atmosphere of international solidarity, a method for management of the external interests of the countries which have elected them with a view to guaranteeing the security of one and all.

The right to security – this is indeed the first principle of the declaration of the rights of nations which the fifth assembly of the League of Nations is working on at this moment. It is vital, like the right to bread, the right to work, the right to education. It can be guaranteed only by the co-operation of the powers in a vast reciprocal action, which was attempted many times during the nineteenth century, but whose covenant in the Treaty of Versailles is so far the most perfect charter. Even during the war – at the very beginning of the war – there were many of us in France who thought that this task could be entrusted only to a joint stock company of peace, like the League of today. I had occasion to refer to it in the ministerial declaration of the first cabinet I formed after 1914. I spoke of it again in 1916 to the delegates from the Duma when they were received in Paris by the President of the Chamber.

Since then I have never forsaken the League of Nations. I have always tried to serve it. At Cannes, when I tried to find formulae which would guarantee Europe against any aggression, I thought of the possibility of bringing the secular arm, by roundabout ways, to the League of Nations where it was lacking. A double system of alliances was already rising from the discussions which had been undertaken, an Anglo-Franco-Belgian agreement was to guarantee security of the Rhineland, and a second pact between interested nations was to uphold order in Eastern and Southern Europe. These two systems of agreements, combined and united under the aegis of the League of Nations, should have contributed to the latter effective forces which would have speeded the solution of problems with which it is now still faced, especially since these agreements did not tilt their lances towards anyone. Their negotiators even indicated in private conversations that Germany could be called upon to take part in these new combinations once it had subscribed to the non-aggression agreement which was to be defined at Genoa. However, the right to security has never seemed to me to be a claim for European nations alone. It equally concerns the Pacific states. I went to Washington, and I gave France's approval to the Pacific agreements, still carrying out this same task on the other side of the Atlantic: seeking for each continental group peace systems which, united and organized jointly would give the League of Nations an ever richer and stronger life. The absence of the USA at Geneva is a weakness for the League. Let us hope that the obstacles which stand in the way of her membership at this moment will gradually fall. I therefore was pleased to accept the opportunity of being part of the French delegation and of resuming in a more extensive, more direct and so much more attractive form, the quest for international guarantees. Soon, I hope, a definition will be found for the concept of aggression, and the concept of compulsory arbitration will be accepted. The voices of all the peoples who are inscribed in the martyrology of the war, the voices of all those whose only crime is the misfortune of having been born in a dangerous area, are raised to ask for assistance. May security be guaranteed for them in order to enable them to devote themselves entirely to working for peace.

14. *Sanctions and guarantee pact (memorandum from Philippe Berthelot to Aristide Briand, April or May 1925)* (quoted by G. Suarez, *Briand, sa vie, son œuvre*, Vol. IV, pp.83–4).

The starting point of the debate is bad; we seek British co-operation in possible coercive measures against Germany. This, however, is impossible. Britain will be able to give effective co-operation only if she herself considers that Germany is to blame. If failure must be asserted by a committee which will automatically put sanctions into operation, Britain would wish to have an effective right to veto in order to maintain her freedom of judgement and action.

Conversely, it is also inconceivable that France could finally give up her own freedom of action and submit in advance to the future advice of Britain.

These comments apply to Franco-British co-operation as a whole and show how illusory was the guarantee pact devised in 1919 so that Clemenceau, who made a parliamentary argument of it which was taken too seriously, would yield.

A guarantee agreement is of positive value only when it is in the form of a military alliance, which is incompatible with Britain's traditional policy.

Moreover, the guarantor state would become either a protector state or an auxiliary state: a guarantee pact is a pact of bondage.

At present it is wise to define the dispute and not to enlarge it.

Britain cannot and does not wish to put herself under the lead of the Franco-Belgian pair. If the latter considered that an action, in which Britain did not wish to co-operate, was necessary, the most we would have to do would be to ask her to allow us to act alone (which was what she did with regard to the Ruhr, while expressing reservations). If it were possible to regularize the procedure followed at that time *a posteriori*, this would be a

success. It cannot be accepted that the refusal of one of the contracting parties is sufficient to paralyse all the others completely.

Failing an agreement of this kind, an assertion of mutual goodwill will be sufficient, and each party will in fact retain its freedom.

15. *Origin and justification of Locarno (speech by Aristide Briand
before the Chamber of Deputies, 25 February 1926).*

What struck me at the time of the discussion of the Treaty of
Versailles, which I mentioned at the Commission of Foreign
Affairs and must repeat to you now, was the tragic dialogue which
was carried on between different members of the Chamber at that
time, over the pressing concern to guarantee the security of
France.

This was indeed the thought which dominated the whole
assembly. The material conditions of the Treaty, although they
were important, were a secondary consideration. We were emerging from a hideous war, and we had only one idea: to avoid
another war, and the whole discussion centred on this point. This
was the dialogue that I heard:

Are we certain that the clause of the Treaty in which we
renounce the guarantee of a natural frontier, the clause which
promises us the combined guarantee of the USA and Britain, will
work? Certain indications from the USA, certain disturbing
political facts which could give rise to the thought that the Treaty
would not be ratified, were set forth as a justification for these
doubts.

The honourable president of the Council at that time, whom you
could not reproach with not being concerned with his country's
security, said, 'I hope that the USA will ratify the Treaty.'

When one speaker added, 'But if the Treaty is not ratified by the
USA, what will become of the British guarantee?', M Clemenceau
replied, 'I hope that the British guarantee will work.'

When someone insisted again, saying, 'This British guarantee
is bound up with the American guarantee; it is an integral part of
it, and if the latter country fails, and Britain consequently considers herself free, what will happen then?', I can still see M
Clemenceau raising his hands and murmuring, 'Well, then, there
will be no longer a Treaty; there will be nothing.'

Well! gentlemen, when chance circumstances brought me to
power in 1921, I considered that my first duty was to use all my

strength, all my mind and all my heart, to try to fill in this gap. . . .

At the Cannes Conference, and even before that conference, discussions were undertaken and continued on this subject with representatives of the British government. Their outcome was favourable. . . . It was agreed that the British guarantee would be given. The text of the proposal for the agreement was published.

At the same time, gentlemen, the notion of the Geneva protocol was born in Cannes. There the organization of the Genoa Conference for the whole of Europe was being prepared, in which no nation could participate without previously signing a non-aggression pact. Hence we thought that we could bring to the nations of Europe a whole vast system of peace, a whole vast plan of international organization.

Was it a matter of an ordinary alliance, similar to all the others between Britain and France? No, gentlemen! And you will find in the Blue Book, which the British government published at the time, a record of discussions during which it had been perfectly understood that, when a guarantee agreement had been made between Britain and France, Germany could, and even must, enter.

Gentlemen, this is the very essence of the Locarno Treaty. When the worthy M Herriot had the reparations plan with which you are acquainted accepted in London, the question of an understanding between the peoples of Europe was naturally again put forward to carry out this plan.

It was then that the suggestion of Mr Stresemann, that is, the suggestion of the German government, originated. I seized upon this suggestion. In it I found again the thought that I had had at Cannes. I considered that the events which had taken place since 1921 were such as to strengthen in my mind the wish to form a new agreement whose necessity had become apparent to me, and I gave this my greatest attention.

16. *Memorandum by Aristide Briand of 17 May 1930 on European Union* (from G. Suarez, *Briand, sa vie, son œuvre*, Vol. VI, pp.331–4. This text is not literal throughout. Certain points have been summarized by Suarez).

Introduction
The proposal examined by twenty-seven European governments

will find its justification in the very definite feeling of collective responsibility in the face of the danger which threatens European peace, from the political as well as the economic and social points of view, from the fact that the general economy of Europe is still in an unco-ordinated state. The need to establish a permanent system of agreed solidarity for the rational organization of Europe results in fact from the very conditions of security and well-being of the peoples which their geographical situation calls them to share, in this part of the world, a solidarity of fact. No one today doubts that lack of cohesion in the grouping of Europe's material and moral forces is in practice the most serious impediment to the development and effectiveness of all political or juridical institutions on which the first ventures of a universal peace organization tend to be founded. . . .

Proposals
(1) To establish a basic agreement whose purpose is to assert the principle of European moral union, reserving all the prerogatives of the League of Nations and presented as a regional agreement, in accordance with the provisions of clause 21 of the Treaty [of Versailles];

(2) To form a representative and responsible organization in the form of a regular institution, the 'European conference', and an executive organization in the form of a 'permanent political committee', a study organization and an instrument for action of European Union sitting in Geneva; these two organizations will be presided over by the nations in rotation.

[This committee, which was of necessity restricted, had to make it possible for representatives of other European governments who were or were not part of the League of Nations, who might be interested in studying a question, to be invited at any time. Moreover, it would have the right to invite a representative of an extra-European power, who might or might not form part of the League of Nations, to be present at or even take part in discussions of a problem in which she was interested (either with a consultative or deliberative voice). . . .]

(3) The memorandum recognized the need to decide in advance the basic directives which would determine the general concepts of the European Committee and guide it in its preparatory work of developing the programme of European organization. In these

general concepts it would subordinate the economic problem to the political problem.

Since any possibility of progress on the way to economic union is determined strictly by the question of security, and since this question is closely linked with that of progress which can be achieved on the path of political union, the constructive effort which would tend to give Europe its organic structure would have to be carried out first of all on the political level.

Again, the economic policy of Europe in its general outlines must subsequently be developed on this level, as well as the customs policy of each European state in particular.

A reverse order would not only be ineffectual, but would appear to the weakest nations as liable to expose them, without guarantees or compensation, to the risks of a political domination which could result from the industrial domination of the most highly organized states.

It is therefore logical and normal that the economic sacrifices to be made to collectivity could be justified only by the development of a political situation which would inspire confidence between peoples, and true peace of mind.

European political co-operation must lead to the establishing of a federation founded on the idea of union and not unity. This concept . . . could consequently imply for Europe a general system of arbitration and security and progressive extension of the policy of international guarantees which was inaugurated at Locarno, to the whole European collectivity, until agreements on series of particular agreements are integrated into a more general system.

Economic organization of Europe must lead to a *rapprochement* of European economies, achieved under the political responsibility of interdependent governments by establishing a common market whose aim is to raise human well-being to the highest possible level for the territories of the European community as a whole, 'in which circulation of goods, capital and pensions would be facilitated'.

17. *'Cutting our losses'*
[*Dépêche de Toulouse*, 3 January 1932] Since all is indeed lost, we will no longer risk much by cancelling Germany's total and final debt. Not only would we lose nothing by this final cutting of our losses,

but we would doubtless gain by disarming the prejudices of the great German public and by somehow overturning Hitler's electoral springboard. . . . Hitler's party . . . have managed to convince the mass of the electorate that the Reparations – which were represented in the Reich's budget as 12 per cent of their expenses – are the sole and abominable cause of the German downfall. Deprive Hitler of this argument and you will take away three-quarters of his followers. Hence, perhaps we could prevent a German revolution whose future or entire repercussions cannot be foreseen. . . . It is true that this generosity would make a hole in our national budget, but the hole is there already. Moreover, there would be occasion for talks with the USA. The USA has taken a hand in this affair to urge us to help Germany. When we have helped it even beyond American wishes, when we have hence shown the example of a nation which sacrifices its credits in the interest of universal peace, we will no doubt have the right to point out to the men of Washington that our generosity has furthermore put us in Germany's place and that it is we who are insolvent. What would they say to that? What we ourselves would reply to the arguments from beyond the Rhine. The USA would perhaps grumble, but they would have nothing to say in reply. They would accept what we cannot prevent. . . . Up to now, and from the first day, Germany has tirelessly applied itself to nibbling at the reparations. It has not ceased to be successful in this, and our legitimate resistance to agreeing to these unwarranted curtailments has made us appear to be an arrogant and greedy conqueror. Consequently we have not had the benefit of our successive concessions. The sponge which would clean up everything would not fail to impress the German population on this occasion.

[*Dépêche de Toulouse*, 17 January 1932] What does it [Europe] think of us? We should not perhaps count on German gratitude. However, we must reckon with European misunderstanding. For goodness' sake, let us not deceive ourselves! Europe misunderstands us at this moment. Our prestige is intact, our power undisputed, but the sympathy which we formerly enjoyed has ended by cooling off. . . . Yes, indeed, we are right to assert the legitimacy of our claims. We must only remember that it is one thing to establish one's right, and another to flog it to death. . . .

Europe is breaking away from us, not because Europe disputes the origins and the legitimacy of our claim against Germany but because in the long run our demands, however just, prolong the mentality of war during a state of peace.

18. *The 'Confidence Pact' (July 1932)* (DDF, 1st series, Vol. I, p.31).

In the declaration which forms part of the Final Act of the Lausanne Conference, the signatory powers expressed the hope that the work achieved would be followed by new achievements. They asserted that these achievements would be all the easier to accomplish if the peoples upheld this new accomplishment of peace which, in order to be complete, must be applied simultaneously to the economic order and to the political order. In the same declaration the signatory powers asserted their intention to endeavour to solve the problems already presented and those which would be presented in the future, in the same spirit which dictated the Lausanne Treaty.

Taking inspiration from these ideas the British government and the French government have decided to make an immediate mutual effort to this effect, as set forth below:

(1) Should the need arise, they intend to carry out in complete frankness and in accordance with the spirit of the League of Nations agreement, a mutual exchange of views concerning any question coming to their knowledge, which has the same origin as that which was so happily settled at Lausanne and which relates to the European system. They will mutually keep themselves informed of the development of these questions. They hope that other governments will wish to join them and adopt the same procedure.

(2) They intend to work together and with other delegations in Geneva to find a solution for the disarmament problem which will be advantageous and just to all the powers concerned.

(3) They will consult together, among themselves and with other interested governments, to make careful and practical preparations for the world economic conference.

(4) While awaiting the outcome of a new trade agreement between the two countries at a future date, they will avoid any act of a discriminatory nature on the part of one of the two countries against the interest of the other.

Appendix

19. *The question of war debts (memorandum from Germain-Martin,*
   Minister of Finance to Edouard Herriot, Minister of Foreign
   Affairs, 15 October 1932) (DDF, 1st series, Vol. I, pp.426–7).

It is not fruitless to remember, moreover, that there is no connection by law between reparations and war debts, since such a
connection has always been refused by the USA.

On the other hand, close connections exist in practice between
the two, on the initiative of the USA themselves, since the
American intervention of June 1931:

(a) The proposition for a moratorium by President Hoover,
which was formulated at the request of Germany with the basic
object of appeasing the latter, referred to all intergovernmental
debts without distinction;

(b) The resolution of Congress which ratified it, explicitly
applied it to the powers who were in debt to the USA on the strict
condition that these powers themselves would allow their own
debtors to benefit from it;

(c) Meanwhile the communiqué drawn up at the time of M
Laval's visit to Washington referred also to new temporary
arrangements for all intergovernmental debts.

In this connection it is useless to insist on the fact that the
American initiative of 1931 finally broke the mechanism built up
by the Young Plan, a mechanism which in other circumstances
could have been reorganized to take into account the exceptional
seriousness of the crisis in conditions which would protect the
rights of the creditor to a greater extent. . . .

It would be fruitless, however, to hide the fact that
American opinion still seems a long way from giving the
above considerations their true importance; these considerations, in the eyes of the debtors, and especially since the
Lausanne Conference, tell in favour of a radical revision of
the debt agreements. . . .

(a) The USA still hold to the principle of individual negotiations with each of their debtors, and it does not seem as if they
will modify their attitude on this point;

(b) If they seem to insist less on an exhaustive study of the
capabilities of their debtors, they will certainly tend to attach
great importance to the respective extents of the concessions
agreed to in the original agreements, and the changes which came
about in the situation of the debtors since the agreements were

concluded. This attitude is obviously more favourable to Britain than to France;

(c) They seem prepared to take into account the special political or commercial advantages which their various debtors are likely to offer them;

(d) Finally, those in favour of total cancellation or a really substantial reduction seem to insist on an immediate payment on the capital and on establishing a certain connection between the revision of existing agreements and a minimum European disarmament.

The situation becomes complicated, as far as France is concerned, on account of the withdrawals of gold which were made at the Federal Reserve Bank. The USA Issuing Institute has never opposed these withdrawals. Its leaders even declared that they preferred an immediate withdrawal according to a plan determined in advance rather than withdrawals in successive batches at indefinite dates. Parliamentary and financial circles finally congratulated themselves that they had seen the mortgage which rested on their country lifted. Recent declarations by President Hoover, indicating that the USA had nearly abandoned the gold standard, gave them a certain justification in retrospect. However, public opinion would remain impressed by this.

. . . Mindful of all these difficulties, well-disposed Americans who are friends of France, who are anxious to spare her credit without, however, committing her future, now advise her to face the payment date of 15 December 1932, a payment date which is, moreover, not likely to benefit from the postponement clauses represented in the Mellon-Bérenger agreement, while making all sorts of reservations as far as the fate of subsequent payments is concerned.

There is no question of appreciating here the difficulties of internal policy which would be the result for the French government of such a payment. Moreover, it would be necessary to be able to put forward considered reasons of foreign policy which the government could find for carrying it out when the time came.

. . . It is no less certain that a resumption of the integral service of debt agreements, on 15 December 1932, would constitute a dangerous precedent for the future. Britain, who is no doubt assured here and now of seeing the annual instalments of the Baldwin-Mellon agreement reduced proportionally at least to the level of the annual instalments of the Mellon-Bérenger agreement, if she requests it, can perhaps expose herself to this without too great a risk. This risk would be considerable for France.

On the other hand, in the absence of a collective action with which Britain would be associated and which is difficult to foresee on this account – meaning a unilateral repudiation of the debt agreements – France would not be able to denounce the debt agreements purely and simply; that is understood. . . .

Moreover, as far as Germany is concerned, we cannot uphold the idea of inviolability of contracts and treaties and repudiate undertakings which have been validly signed. This consideration alone appears to be decisive.

In order to avoid the payment which falls due on 15 December without denouncing the Mellon-Bérenger agreement, there remains therefore one possibility: to negotiate with the USA before that date either a new arrangement, or a temporary moratorium, while awaiting something better.

In the first part of this memorandum we have set forth at great length the difficulties which the settlement of a new satisfactory arrangement would encounter. It seems, however, that France could use very forceful arguments in her favour.

In the first place there was the fact that at Lausanne France followed the suggestions of the USA, that she only agreed to enormous sacrifices after the agreement come to on the necessity of no longer carrying on transfers which did not correspond to actual movement of goods or services, in the relationship between one people and another. The abnormal transfers, following upon the settlements of credits resulting from the war, appeared to be the deep-rooted cause of the persistence of international disturbances.

Moreover, France is justified in invoking the effort of European reconstruction, which has been carried out so far in the collective interest by the French government and which was particularly in evidence at the Stresa Conference. The broad outlines of this effort can be summarized as follows:

(1) Offer of a guaranteed loan to Germany in 1931; this loan was doubtless matched with certain conditions, but, if its principle had been accepted, it could not have failed to mitigate German difficulties considerably;

(2) Advances of 350 million francs to Hungary in 1931. Loan of

300 million francs to Yugoslavia in 1931, to mitigate the effects of the Hoover moratorium. Extension of the dates of Yugoslav payments to France in 1932;

(3) Guarantee of a loan of 600 million francs to Czechoslovakia in 1932;

(4) France's renunciation, in practice, of the German Reparations at Lausanne in 1932, since the net balance which France could expect for future payments from Germany had to be at the very least re-lent to Central and Eastern Europe;

(5) Guarantee to Austria for issue of a new loan granted by France;

(6) Substantial loans to the Reichsbank and to various central banks of Central and Eastern Europe granted by the Bank of France;

(7) French effort to form a body of exchange in Central and Eastern Europe and for raising the price of cereals in the same area.

Now it is clear that this reconstruction effort was rendered necessary to a great extent by withdrawals of American capital from Europe since 1931, and by the present total absence of the American market with regard to the financial affairs of Europe.

Subject to France's bringing to the world conference views which continue to be positive, she must therefore be justified in invoking her policy of European reconstruction in order to obtain from the USA, who were directly concerned with this reconstruction, favourable treatment in the matter of debts. . . .

It is quite obvious, moreover, that the preparation and signing of a final agreement about debts cannot occur between 8 November and 15 December; once the negotiations are undertaken, a request for a moratorium for the next payment date could be based on both the opening of the negotiation and the awaiting of the results of the world conference. If this request were rejected, the question would be asked – and then only – as to whether it would be advisable or not to guarantee the payment of 15 December. However, it can hardly be imagined how, having imposed the moratorium on Europe in 1931, the USA could refuse to give her the benefit of its temporary extension in 1932, while talks about a final settlement were in progress.

Since the aim seems clear (a contractual payment in capital similar to that of Lausanne) . . . how can it be achieved, taking into account the especially difficult position of France?

This can only be done, it seems, if Britain takes the initiative of undertaking a discussion with the USA to achieve this herself and hence creates a precedent for France, Italy and the other debtors of the USA.

Will Britain agree to do this? She is bound by the declarations of her representatives at Lausanne and by the gentlemen's agreement signed at the conference: before any negotiation, France, Britain, Italy and Belgium must have a consultation. If one of the four powers is not satisfied with the agreements she has made with her creditors, she can refuse to ratify the results of Lausanne. As it stands, the gentlemen's agreement obliges Britain, if she wishes final ratification of the Lausanne acts, which is obviously in her interests, to obtain a satisfactory enough agreement from the USA, for her to have nothing or very little to demand from her own debtors. So long as they do not incautiously hasten the talks, France and Italy will almost inevitably benefit from the Anglo-American precedent. . . .

It therefore appears essential to get Britain to take the initiative as soon as possible and to make a demand, under conditions which would have received the consent of her own debtors, either for a moratorium, or for revision of the agreements in force; it would be specified that, should the principle of a moratorium not be accepted, the debtor powers would maintain a common attitude. France would undertake her own negotiations soon afterwards and would base her own attitude on that of Britain. No doubt Italy would be prepared to do the same. A French initiative, on the other hand, would seem to run the risk of being insufficiently supported by Britain and of being probably opposed by Italy, a double risk to which we cannot expose ourselves.

20. *Memorandum from the American government (reply to the French memorandum of 10 November) 23 November 1932*
    (DDF, 1st series, Vol. II).

Your present proposal greatly exceeds what has been considered or proposed up to now either by President Hoover or by this government. Hence you will allow me to recall very briefly some of the basic conditions and reservations which would define any new study of the question of debts on the part of this government, and would influence the results of this study. Not only is the final decision regarding consolidation, payment or modifications of the intergovernmental obligations in question reserved for the Congress of the USA, but the Congress itself has created in the past, in the form of the Commission of World-War Debts, the organization whose task it is to study facts and make recommendations, according to which such an action could be undertaken. The executive power could make recommendations, but the facts and proofs were submitted to Congress, and decisions were made by Congress who acted through this organization.

Moreover, since the time when these obligations were created, under President Wilson, this government has constantly maintained in the way in which it negotiated them, so far as it was concerned, that they must be negotiated as completely distinct from reparations resulting from the war. Its insistence on this difference is quite natural since, after the war, it refused to accept reparations on its own account, and also since its position as a creditor was different from that of all the other nations: not only had this government not received any compensation in the form of territory, economic privileges or governmental indemnities at the end of the war, but since it had no obligation of any sort towards the others, it could only be of disadvantage to the USA to treat debts and reparations as if there were a connection between them. No concession regarding a credit of this government has in whole or in part any counterpart in the claims of any one of its creditors. On the contrary, any concession of this nature would inevitably result in transfer of the burden of taxes from the taxpayers of some other country to the taxpayers of our own country, without the possibility of finding compensation elsewhere.

The debts due to the USA thus fell quite naturally into the category of ordinary debts between individual nations and have been treated as such. The American Congress made arrangements with each of its debtors, which it intended and believed were generous and entirely within the limit of the debtor's capacity for payment, without the latter's running the risk of compromising its finances or its currency, or being prevented from maintaining, or if possible improving, the standard of living of its citizens. I recognize the importance of the decision, quoted in your memorandum, which has been made by the governments at Lausanne, with regard to the reparations owed to them by Germany, as well as the possible effect of the loss of this source of revenue to these creditor countries. Moreover, I do not forget either, that the world depression and the parallel drop in prices have increased the weight of debts in numerous parts of the world, nor that the decrease in international commerce has increased the difficulties of obtaining foreign currencies. I also recognize the influence these events can have on the process of improvement (of world conditions). On the other hand, it is important to take into consideration the fact that the consequences of the depression also made themselves felt with all their weight on the American people.

I assume that this government adopted the system I have described in order to give, with great caution and care, full weight to the contradictory elements in the world situation which obviously differ from one country to another. I acknowledge that I can find no decisive reason which would be of a nature to induce the American Congress to act in any way differently on this point from the manner and the principles which guided it in the past.

I also believe that it would not be opportune to try to undertake discussions on this subject, except in this manner and according to these principles.

The attitude of the President is therefore that, for any possible future study of intergovernmental financial obligations as they exist at present, a certain organization of the type I have mentioned, should be formed to study the question with each government individually as has been done up to now. As he has declared several times in public, he also considers that some basis could be found to give the American people adequate compensation in a form other than cash payment. The President is prepared to recommend to Congress the formation of an organization of this kind to study the question as a whole.

As far as the suspension of payment of the French debt of 15 December, requested in your memorandum, is concerned, the executive has no power to grant an extension and no fact has been put in our possession which could be presented to Congress for favourable examination on the strength of the above-mentioned principles. The memorandum from the French government refers to the work of the Lausanne Conference. It seems to me that the situation with which the Lausanne Conference was faced in its examination of the question of German reparations was quite different from that which we are dealing with here, owing to the fact that the Conference had before it the report of the Basle experts.

The American government and people attach importance to the upholding of the agreements in force and the payment of 15 December, an importance such that it by far exceeds all the reasons now set forth in favour of its suspension, and if the payment were made, the future prospects of a favourable examination of the question as a whole would, in my opinion, be thereby greatly enhanced.

21. *Memorandum from the French government to the American government (1 December 1932)* (DDF, 1st series, Vol. II).

When he made his proposal for a moratorium in 1931, the President of the USA asserted that the attitude of the federal authorities showed their wish to contribute to the future restoration of world prosperity, with which the American nation is so deeply concerned. 'The duty of statesmen', indicated the Washington communiqué of October 1931, 'is not to neglect any practical means of co-operation for the well-being of all. This principle is especially important at a time when the world awaits guidance which will help it to overcome the present deadly depression in so many homes.'

The economic depression, which prompted both the American President's proposal and his call for co-operation among nations, has worsened since the spring of 1931. Misery and unemployment are increasing everywhere. This depression can only increase if the payment of intergovernmental debts must be resumed before the foreseen general arrangement can be reached.

The French government is acquainted with the formal reservations which were made by the American Congress at the time of the Hoover moratorium, and it does not in any way intend to question its prerogatives. However, it must recall that the French Parliament, in its turn, subordinated its approbation to its interpretation of the moratorium proposed by President Hoover.

It must also recall that the committee of experts which met in Basle in December 1931 as a result of the Washington meeting, and in which an eminent American personality took part, did not confine itself to recognizing the temporary impossibility for Germany of facing its reparations obligations. It unanimously and officially condemned the transfers of capital without a return, which were necessitated by payments of war debts, as being particularly harmful to the restoration of the world economy. The report ended as follows: 'In the first place, any transfer from one country to another, made on such a large scale that it upsets the balance of payments, can only exacerbate the present chaos. In the second place, it is advisable not to lose sight of the fact that any alleviation in favour of a debtor country, which is unable to bear the burden of certain payments, runs the risk of transferring this burden to a creditor country which, being itself a debtor, would in its turn be unable to support it. An adjustment of intergovernmental debts as a whole to the present troubled world situation – an adjustment which would have to be made without delay to avoid further disasters – is the only durable measure which would be capable of restoring the confidence which is the very basis of economic stability and true peace.'

The government of the Republic was actuated by these considerations of a general nature when it accepted the Lausanne Agreements, subject to the approval of the French Parliament. In spite of a budget with a deficit of nearly 500 million dollars, the restoration of whose balance has already demanded and will again demand the severest measures, France will have thus voluntarily renounced an annual net balance, after payment of her war debts, of nearly 85 million dollars, in the interests of world economic recovery.

She has agreed to this heavy sacrifice in the conviction that the payments stipulated by the existing agreements could not be made without involving deep-rooted financial and economic disturbances.

In this respect, and as far as she is concerned, the situation has often been misunderstood and needs to be defined. The rush of gold to France which took place over the last years was basically caused, or made inevitable, by existing world conditions. This gold does not belong by any right to the French Treasury. It is not a permanent source of riches for France. It is the guarantee of all French or foreign deposits made in France. Its normal and desirable redistribution can result only from a general regaining of confidence and the needs which would follow from this.

The slight improvement which took place after the Lausanne Agreements, expressed the hope of the nations in this respect for the intervention of a worldwide settlement. The recovery which was then taking shape could not be continued if future payments of intergovernmental debts were demanded. It is advisable to note in particular that failing a radical reversal of the trade balance of the USA with Europe, a balance which is at present largely in their favour, these payments, in view of the progressive reduction of foreign revenues of the debtors, will require increasing interventions, which will soon be ruinous for the whole world, on the credit and exchange markets.

The French government cannot believe that, all things considered, the American people would find it in their interest to carry out an undertaking which, when strictly applied, would have the effect of creating more chaos and misery in the world, since the transfer of sums which do not correspond to exchange can only upset the balance of international relations even more fundamentally.

It was the influence of these serious anxieties, and the awareness of the responsibilities weighing on the great powers with regard to safeguarding social and economic order, which prompted the French government to request of the Federal Government, on 11 November last, a postponement of the payment which fell due on 15 December.

In entreating the Federal Government to re-examine the request in the light of the above considerations, the French government considers that it is fulfilling a duty which is not only national but international.

It is fully aware of the part which France is called upon by circumstances to play in Europe. It does not intend to take advantage of the efforts it has already achieved towards restoration of economic stability and the recovery of affairs, nor of the inclination which it still has for co-operation to this purpose in the future, but it wonders with apprehension how France can continue on this course if, contrary to all expectation, the co-operation of the USA, on which she believed she could rely for support in her efforts, failed her.

These are the considerations which now lead the French government to renew, through me, its urgent and carefully considered request to your Excellency, to reconsider the request to suspend the payments which fall due on 15 December.

The reception of this request is awaited with confidence by my government, which measures all the consequences which the decision of the President of the USA could have on the improvement or deterioration of the tragic situation resulting from the war.

22. *French memorandum sent on 9 November 1933 to Mr Feis, the economic adviser to the American State Department, concerning measures taken regarding American trade* (DDF, 1st series, Vol. IV, pp.749–50).

At the time when the American government will be called upon to make modifications to its customs tariff which are of great importance to French exports, it seems appropriate to recall that the French government over the past years has continued to prove as favourably disposed with respect to American trade as circumstances have permitted.

In 1927, when the French customs tariff was raised, the government of the Republic agreed to grant American goods the concession of the minimum tariff, or a continuation of the rights previously levied. It was understood that trade negotiations would soon begin and that certain administrative impediments from which French products suffered in the USA would be removed. In spite of this agreement, none of the modifications requested in the administrative order has been granted by the Federal Government.

At the time of the customs revision in 1927–8, the French government benevolently and unilaterally applied the arrangements of the *modus vivendi* of 1927 to American goods. The USA has been the only country which has benefited from these advantages without giving anything in return.

Since 1928 the French government has continued to take into account the arrangements of the *modus vivendi* of 1927, although no steps have been taken by the USA in favour of French products, the majority of which have on the contrary been heavily hit by the application of the new American tariff of June 1930. At the time when the tariffs were raised, various decrees were passed to spare certain American goods or at least to put them in a more favourable position than that which existed previously in relation to other similar foreign products (decrees of 19 November 1931 for asparagus; 25 December 1931 for stockings and cotton socks; 5 August 1932 for ham; 6 August 1933 for oil-yielding products; and 19 September 1933 for frozen pigs' livers).

However, in addition to the advantages which have been granted to American trade strictly in the field of customs, it is also necessary to point out the particularly favourable treatment which American goods have enjoyed so far as the application of the system of quotas is concerned.

By the agreement of 31 May 1932, the French government had accepted that the quota established for an American product was not reduced to a figure lower than 10 per cent of the total imports of this product during 1931, when American importation would have been, during the same year 1931, equal to or greater than this percentage by 10 per cent. If it had been less than 10 per cent of the total imports, the quota would be fixed at the 1931 level of American imports. The French government informed the American Chargé d'Affaires in Paris on 8 September 1933 that it had decided not to apply to the USA the system of distribution of quotas which would come into force on 1 January of the following year, and which would include an automatic allocation of 25 per cent only of these quotas to foreign countries, the rest to be subject to negotiation. The arrangement of 31 May 1932 therefore remains in force, and the fixed-quota American goods continue to benefit from the rule of distribution proportional to previous imports. The effect of this decision, as the French Minister of Foreign Affairs pointed out to the American Chargé d'Affaires, was to place American trade in a privileged position on the French market in relation to trade from other countries.

Finally, it is not superfluous to recall that the French government continues to exonerate American goods from the exchange surcharge, although the dollar has depreciated for more than ten months, and that all the other countries whose exchange has depreciated have had this surcharge imposed, and that many of these countries have protested against the favourable treatment reserved for the USA. The concern of the French government regarding currency has been not to interfere with the experiment which is being carried out in the USA in the industrial field, and which is followed with great sympathy in France.

While thus accommodating American interests, the French government has endeavoured to co-operate closely with the American government on the international level. It has most eagerly welcomed the suggestions of President Roosevelt as far as the customs truce is concerned, and its goodwill has also been demonstrated in the discussions which ended with the corn agreement to which the USA attached great importance.

In spite of the increasingly alarming lack of balance in its trade figures, the French government has been bent on maintaining the flow of exchanges between the USA and France, by granting favourable conditions. Statistics show that this liberal policy has not been without effect on American exports. Purchases of American goods by France have increased to 1,494 million francs during the first six months of 1933, while French sales to the USA have not exceeded 377 million francs.

23. *Dispatch from the French Ambassador in Brussels (3 November 1932) (DDF, 1st series, Vol. I, pp.650–1).*
I have already had occasion to draw the attention of the Department to the articles published in the *Revue Générale* by M Jaspar . . . (former Prime Minister, at present Minister of Finance in Belgium). In the 15 October issue of the periodical in question, under the title 'A policy of realities', M Jaspar, on the pretext of 'the agony of the Disarmament Conference', examines the various guarantees of an international order which at present surround the security of Belgium. . . . In the first place he recalls the system established by the London Conference of 1831 and hardly disguises his nostalgia for the happy period of 'guaranteed' neutrality under the vigilant protection of Britain. This British protection . . . in his eyes has as much value as the Locarno Treaty, in which he is pleased to see 'the restoration of the system of 1831 in a new form, and, in a different spirit, the return to Belgium of the diplomatic security which she lacked' and 'the establishment on firm foundations of the status of Belgium'. However, the Rhineland pact . . . does not yet seem to him to be adequate. . . . What does M Jaspar want, in order for the security of Belgium to be finally and wholly guaranteed? The conclusion of a defensive military agreement with Britain on the model of the Franco-Belgian agreement. . . .

. . . No doubt the considerations which he sets forth in the above-mentioned article are in response to a feeling which tends to become more and more evident. . . . With every day that passes, a tendency in favour of a narrower concept of Belgian interests is increasingly asserted. Belgium prefers to let the great powers sort out the tangled skein of international affairs by themselves while she confines herself to playing the part of a power with limited interest, a part less glorious perhaps, but a calmer one. Without yet declaring it openly, she hopes for a return to the state of neutrality. M Jaspar is not the first to give a public indication in this direction. M Poullet, following, moreover, M Vandervelde, took this into account in his report on the budget of the Minister of Foreign Affairs. . . . Since 1918 opinions have changed, and so also have events. Today there are Belgian politicians – and not the least important ones – who seem most of all to be afraid of seeing their country enfeoffed to a France which is too isolated.

24. *Unofficial memorandum sent to Arthur Henderson following his talks of 11 July with M Daladier and M Paul-Boncour (Paris, 12 July 1933)* (DDF, 1st series, Vol. III, pp.897–9).
The question of disarmament is at present dominated by a definite problem: what is the aim of the German government?

The chancellor Hitler, in his speech of 17 May, and the German representatives at Geneva maintained that the Reich had no wish to increase its armaments. However, at the same time, we see that Germany is developing a programme which is, in practice, equivalent to a programme of rearmament, both in the field of effectives and in that of equipment, especially aviation equipment. Whatever reason one looks for in order to explain these facts, it remains that, in many countries, the government and public opinion view the events developing beyond the Rhine with a legitimate alarm. At a time when it is a matter of making it possible to conclude an agreement which, for certain powers, would involve an important reduction of their military force and a considerable modification of the balance of power to their disadvantage, it is natural that these powers feel the necessity for certain precautions more urgently than ever.

I   When, with a view to facilitating the solution of the problem of equality of rights, the French government proposed a standard-ization of the type of continental European army on the basis of short-term service and limited manpower, by an initiative which the British proposal had taken up on her account, it was aware that its proposal would involve sacrifices for France.

(a) France gave up the future advantages which strict observance of the peace-treaty system was calculated to guarantee to her as far as the possession of trained reserves was concerned, and she did this at the very moment when the application of this system of the treaties could have begun to have its full effect in Germany, as a result of the ageing of those recruits who took part in the war;

(b) As far as forces intended for immediate defence of the home territory were concerned, France accepted equality of manpower, duration of service and number of officers, with Germany and Italy;

(c) The application of this proposal included, moreover, an important reduction of current average manpower, both for the French forces as a whole and for the forces of metropolitan France and of the duration of service of those called under the colours in metropolitan France.

II   In the present state of Europe and in view of the anxieties referred to above, one must take the necessary precautions for the modification, in a direction favourable to Germany, of the present ratio of armaments of the European continent not to put the security of France and that of other countries in danger.

The experience of the Geneva discussions seems to prove that it is not possible at present, in the field of mutual assistance, to obtain the collective guarantees which would have made a reduction of their military power easier for the different governments. This, however, in no way constitutes a reason for giving up the achievement of progress in the political field which the work at Geneva enables us to anticipate (non-recourse to force, definition of the aggressor, etc.) and which could, moreover, be expressed at an international level by less strict formulae than those which it is desirable and possible to apply to continental Europe.

In any case, however, it will be essential to be certain that the new system which is to be inaugurated as far as armaments are concerned, will be more faithfully observed than that created by the peace treaties.

The technical work, especially that of the manpower committee, has brought to light the real difficulties of the problem and the scope which a dishonest state could have for evading the limitation undertakings which would result from the future convention. For example, as far as manpower is concerned, it is important to prevent the limitations being evaded by development of pre-military instruction, instruction of a military nature outside the army or police forces; moreover, Germany must not be able to add a conscripted army to its regular army, when it should be substituting one for the other. It is no less important that the increase of German manpower should not be accompanied by increase of armaments.

In a politically critical hour, France, who from now on agrees to a reduction of her manpower cannot, even in the interests of peace, also agree to an immediate reduction of her equipment, before the exercise of strict control of armaments limitations has enabled it to be established with certainty that the transformation of the armies to a defensive type has been faithfully carried out.

III   From the above remarks it follows that, when measures for limiting and reducing armaments are carried out, it is advisable to establish chronological order and progression.

(a) During an initial period of four years, known as the trial period, the mechanism of the convention will be prepared in detail; at the same time the arms race will be stopped and the first operations for reducing armaments will be carried out. Among the measures to be taken during this period, and whose application will be the object of a regular and permanent control, we will quote the following in particular:

(1) Transfer, according to a progression defined year by year, from the present situation with regard to manpower and length of service, to the situation which will be laid down by the agreement (it will be necessary to discuss with the British delegation certain modifications of figures which she put forward); parallel to this, all paramilitary instruction will be eliminated in accordance with the conclusions of the manpower committee. With regard to pre-military instruction, this will be the subject of very strict ruling in conditions which will guarantee equivalent advantages to all states. It is pointed out for the record that the French delegation has already defined its position time and again, with regard to the question of trained reserves, with regard to the duration of periods of reserve which must be limited, and with regard to a separate system for overseas forces.

(2) As far as equipment is concerned, and subject to possible special arrangements for fixed artillery for shore or fortress use;

(i)   For states whose land armaments are not at present the object of any limitation: (*a*) cessation of all manufacture of artillery above 155mm calibre and any tank construction above a tonnage limit to be fixed; (*b*) storage of the most powerful equipment on national territory, but under League of Nations control;

(ii) As far as states bound by military clauses of peace treaties are concerned, they will continue to observe the qualitative limitations of equipment to which they are subject at present;

(3) Annual manufacture of equipment authorized by the agreement will be carried out only in certain specific factories (private or state-owned), which will be subject to international control and within the limit of the quotas which will be fixed for each state.

(4) Controlled publicity of armaments expenditure, with a view to providing the technical conditions necessary to enforce a limitation of these expenditures in the second phase of application of the agreement.

(5) Establishment of an efficient system of inspection which must in particular enable regular and periodic inspections to be made on site (at least once a year).

(b) For the second period of four years, if it is agreed that the control organizations should continue with improvements which experience may suggest, the convention must stipulate the following measures:

(1) Completion, if necessary, and continuation of implementation of the measures stipulated for the first period;

(2) Enforcing the limitation of expenditure;

(3) In this second period, if the permanent disarmament commission has ascertained that the progressive execution and control of limitations and reductions stipulated for the first period have been carried out satisfactorily, by a majority vote qualified under conditions which will be defined, the equipment listed below will be handed over to the League of Nations which can either keep it to make it available to an attacked state [this solution was preferred by the French delegation] or to prescribe its total or partial destruction, for which it would be responsible in any case:

(i) All artillery above 220mm calibre which has not been converted to fixed coast or fortress artillery;

(ii) All tanks exceeding the authorized tonnage.

IV The convention must contain clauses the aim of which is to point out consequences of any violation of the commitments undertaken.

In view of the realization of a new stage in the reduction of armaments, the agreement must stipulate the future conclusion of a second agreement which will be duly reached in conditions which will prevent (in accordance with clause 8 of the pact) the signatories of the first agreement from resuming their freedom on its expiry.

25. *Dispatch from André François-Poncet to Pierre Etienne Flandin (25 March 1936)* (DDF, 2nd series, Vol. I, p.657).

(Historical account of the Franco-Soviet pact)

Nobody recalls . . . that the agreement of 2 May is only the residue of a more far-reaching operation, of which Germany had been informed and which it had repeatedly been invited to join. Even before the project for an Eastern pact had been made public, M Louis Barthou had taken care to communicate its terms to the government of the Reich.

On his instructions, I had paid a visit to Herr von Bülow on 7 June 1934. I had urged the Secretary of State not to adopt a negative attitude prematurely, with respect to the proposals which had been made to his country. I entreated him to examine favourably a combination which was in no way directed against the Reich but on the contrary offered Germany pledges of security and provided it with the means of emerging from its isolation. I had set out before my interlocutor the advantage of a multilateral agreement which was inspired solely by the concern to organize the peace of Europe rationally and methodically.

I had not omitted to add that if Germany met our suggestions with a categorical refusal, it would perhaps succeed in destroying the work to which we had applied ourselves; but that it must expect that we would then achieve a bilateral *entente* with Moscow, after a private meeting about which the government of the Reich would not be in a position to complain, since it would have caused it and made it inevitable.

On 12 July 1934 the British Ambassador had approached Baron von Neurath in a similar manner.

During the months that followed we did not let slip any opportunity of reminding Germany that the Eastern pact was still accessible to it and that we hoped to see it departing from its dilatory attitude. We insisted to this effect shortly after the London Conference in February 1935. We renewed our entreaties and Germany even seemed for a moment ready to yield, at the time of the Stresa Conference. Later, while our meetings with the Russians were developing, we again endeavoured to point out to Hitler's government that the contemplated pact was, in a way, of a provisional nature and would change its character when the Reich agreed to join, and that in this case a much wider and more effective system of security could emerge from a limited arrangement.

26. *Memorandum from General Weygand, Vice-President of the Conseil Supérieur de la Guerre (16 January 1933)* (DDF, 1st series, Vol. II, pp.457–9).

(French strategic problems)

At a time when reorganization of the military forces of France is on the agenda, as a result of estimates to be made because of the reduction in contingents during the years 1935 to 1940, and negotiations in Geneva regarding limitation of armaments, as well as budgetary difficulties of 1933, it is important to define what France requires of her national forces as a whole. If we do not settle what purpose they must serve, we run the risk of treating these serious problems, whose solution determines the future and independence of the country, from a purely subjective point of view, losing sight of the very purpose of these forces. We thus become involved in arrangements of detail, partial concessions and reductions decided without a thorough inquiry. Pared down in this manner by retrenchments, none of which seems vital to those who agree to them but whose total and incidence multiply the destructive effects, the military forces will eventually suffer very grave impairment. If such procedures continue, these forces, in spite of the admirable devotion of the cadres, will gradually become incapable of fulfilling their basic function.

... The old formula, 'We must have an army which corresponds to the needs of our policy', has lost none of its value. It means that an army can be organized according to just principles only if the policy, which she must see carried out, is clearly defined.

France is profoundly pacifist. This is true, this is simple, but it is just too simple to be sufficient to define her policy. The policy of a great country like ours, which through her possessions has spread over the whole surface of the globe, has to reckon with various and complex elements which are the results of her geographic and demographic situation, the nature of her frontiers and the inclinations of her neighbours, the treaties in force and the agreements made with other powers.

(1) France has land frontiers of more than 1,000km, of which she shares about 300km with Italy, and which are reinforced by the barrier of the Alps; she shares 300km of frontier with Germany without natural protection to the west of the Rhine. She is the only European country to have maritime frontiers opening on the north, west and south, on three seas which are free of ice all the year round. Her eastern and south-eastern neighbours openly assert a policy of destruction of the state of things established by the treaties, and of aggressive intentions towards her. They do not even leave her ignorant of the terms and conditions of the future conflict, summed up in the newly fashionable term, 'sudden war', by land, sea and air.

The result is that the first duty of the military, air and naval forces of the national defence is to defend the territory while defending themselves against these attacks. However, the new conditions of sudden attack and barbarism which one is obliged to consider, force France, who refuses to be the aggressor, to withstand the attack and consequently to have on her frontiers a defence system which is always in good order and easily alerted. This necessity creates obligations as far as the present manpower, equipment service and calling up of reserves are concerned.

On the other hand, it must be made clear that the often-used term, 'defensive army', has no meaning. Even in the defensive, especially in the defensive, an army which has neither the will nor the means to manœuvre is doomed to defeat. Consequently, the defence system must include large manœuvring units, in addition to the fortress units.

(2) The German frontier, however, is common to France and Belgium. They are linked by an agreement for their joint defence. Belgium does not have the means of protecting the 120km which stretch from the south of Luxembourg to the Dutch Limburg against invasion. France must go to her rescue without delay in order to stop the enemy on this line. . . . There she will have the advantages of having to block 120km with the support of the Belgian army instead of 350km with her own forces alone, and of keeping the enemy at a distance from the rich country of the north. The extent of territory to be covered by French strategic

deployment is therefore increased by a substantial part of Belgian territory. Consequently, new large manœuvring units, certain of which must be capable of special speed, are seen to be indispensable on this account.

(3) We have another ally, Poland. The invasion of Polish Pomerania by the Germans is a common topic of conversation. What will be the attitude of France if this manifestation of 'sudden war' surprises her in the midst of peace? Will she immediately enter Germany to make the Germans respect the treaties and to take securities there? What will her present military condition allow her to do without having recourse to any mobilization measures? If what she can do is not sufficient, what preparations should she make?

(4) Other agreements link us with the nations which form the Little *Entente*. In what obligations will they involve us, and involve themselves? What instructions will the governments give to their General Staffs, in case of conflict, as to how to conduct the war? Against which enemy will the initial effort be made? What co-operation in the way of equipment would be useful to these countries?

(5) Since a cluster of alliances or agreements combines our action with that of powers in Eastern or Central Europe, this action cannot be pursued without a material link between them and France. By what route? The Baltic which, moreover, is not free of ice at all times, will obviously be closed at the Straits. Only the Salonika route remains. Hence the necessity for our naval action in the Eastern Mediterranean, which must have a base there for this purpose. Hence also the importance of our presence in the Levant and a firm presence in Tripoli made necessary, moreover, by the outlet of the Mosul pipe-line and the sea-plane port, the first stage of the air route to Indo-China.

(6) Corsica, because of its situation, is a base indispensable for the protection of our transmediterranean transport, an exceptional 'aircraft carrier' at no great distance from the vital points of Italy, and a gateway into the closed lake of the Tyrrhenian Sea. Defence work is in progress there at present. Will this be sufficient to make it the base which it must become for essential operations?

(7) Spanish Morocco seems to be threatened with relapsing into anarchy very soon. What forecasts are to be made and what precautions must be taken to confirm the sovereign authority of the

Maghzen there and to prevent the establishment of another European power?

(8) The study of these questions, all of which are important to the organization of our national defence forces, will necessarily lead to combinations of manpower from the home territory, North Africa or the colonies. Bearing in mind the moral and material disadvantages of an unplanned augmentation, what is the maximum manpower of these overseas contingents which could be stationed in France? Also, taking into account the security of our colonies and protectorate countries, what is the minimum manpower of the forces of each nationality which must be maintained there?

If we leave questions of this magnitude without examining or solving them, we shall be led inexorably day by day, under the pressure of budgetary necessities, political influences or international blackmail, to take measures which will gradually drain our national forces of their substance. They will become merely a façade and will not be in a condition to fulfil their mission at the hour of danger.

It therefore appears absolutely essential to begin this methodical and exhaustive study without delay. Its results will be the obligatory basis for all organization or reorganization of the national defence forces. It can only be done by responsible chiefs: ministers and military chiefs, that is, by a reduced and rationally formed council of national defence.

27. *The Four-Power Pact: French Counter-proposal* (*24 March 1933*)
     (DDF, 1st series, Vol. III, pp.70–1).
Germany, France, Britain and Italy:
Aware of the special responsibilities imposed upon them by their capacity as permanent members of the League of Nations Council with respect to the League itself and its members;

Convinced that the state of unease which prevails in Europe can be dispelled only by an affirmation of peace which will restore confidence;

Aware of the solemn nature of the undertakings contained with respect to this in the League of Nations Pact, the Locarno Treaty and the Briand-Kellogg Pact of which they are signatories, as well as in the declaration of non-recourse to force whose principle has already been adopted by the political commission of the conference for limitation and reduction of armaments on 2 March last;

Declare, in the same spirit, that they wish to achieve among themselves within the framework of League of Nations procedures, an effective policy of continuous co-operation with a view to preserving peace.

For this purpose the four powers, in order to adopt the same lines of conduct with respect to them whenever possible, decide to examine jointly all questions of application in Europe of clauses 11, 12, 15 and 19 of the Pact, which could be referred to the League of Nations, in order to give the methods and procedures stipulated by these clauses their full effect, and from which they agree that they will in no way depart.

The four powers assert, in general, their wish to act together on all questions of common interest to Europe, especially on all questions concerning restoration of its economy, whose settlement, without being the subject of a procedure before the League of Nations could, it would seem, be usefully investigated within the framework of the study commission for European Union.

28. *The Four-Power Pact: final text (30 May 1933)* (DDF, 1st series, Vol. III, pp.592-4).

Aware of the responsibilities imposed upon them by their capacity as permanent members of the League of Nations Council, with respect to the League itself and its members, and those which result from their joint signatures of the Locarno Agreements;

Convinced that the state of unease which prevails in the world can be dispelled only by strengthening their solidarity which will be likely to affirm confidence in peace in Europe;

Faithful to the commitments they have undertaken through the League of Nations Pact, the Locarno Treaty and the Briand-Kellogg Pact, and referring to the declaration of non-recourse to force, the principle of which was proclaimed in the resolution signed in Geneva on 11 December 1932 by their delegates at the aforesaid conference and adopted on 2 March last by the political commission of the Disarmament Conference;

Mindful of giving all the clauses of the League of Nations pact their full effectiveness, and conforming to the methods and procedures stipulated there and from which they agree not to depart;

Respectful of the rights of each state which must be established only by the party concerned.

. . . (formal provisions) . . .

Clause 1

The contracting High Parties will act together on all questions which concern them. They undertake to make every effort to practise a policy of effective co-operation between all powers, within the framework of the League of Nations, with a view to maintaining peace.

Clause 2

With regard to the League of Nations Pact, and notably its clauses 10, 16 and 19, the contracting High Parties decide to examine among themselves any proposal relating to methods and procedures which would be suitable for guaranteeing the application of these clauses, subject to decisions which can only be made by the regular agencies of the League of Nations.

Clause 3

The contracting High Parties recognize that the preservation of peace necessitates reduction of national armaments to the minimum compatible with national security, the geographical situation and the special conditions of each state, and that the success of the Disarmament Conference is the best means of achieving this end. They renew their desire to co-operate with the other powers represented at the conference, in order to develop as quickly as possible an agreement which will guarantee a substantial reduction and limitation of armaments with subsequent provisions with a view to further reductions.

France, Britain and Italy declare that the principle of equal rights, as recognized in the declaration of 11 December 1932, must have a practical value for Germany and the other states which were disarmed by treaty.

France, Britain, Italy and Germany will consult together regarding the terms and conditions to be applied in order to achieve this principle in stages.

Clause 4

The contracting High Parties assert their wish to act together on any question of an economic nature which is of common interest to Europe, especially for her economic recovery, with a view to establishing an arrangement within the framework of the League of Nations.

Clause 5

The present agreement is concluded for a period of ten years, reckoning from the exchange of ratifications. If, before the end of the eighth year, any of the contracting High Parties has not notified the others of its intention to end it, it will be regarded as renewed and will remain in force without any time limit, each of the contracting High Parties retaining the ability to terminate it, subject to a declaration to this effect two years in advance.

The present agreement will be registered at the League of Nations in accordance with the pact of the League.

Clause 6

(League of Nations deposition procedure.)

29. *Circular from Joseph Paul-Boncour, Minister of Foreign Affairs, to the French ministers in Prague, Bucharest and Belgrade (25 July 1933)* (DDF, 1st series, Vol. IV, pp.68–71).
(Question of national minorities)

If one can understand from the emotional point of view, the impatience felt with regard to the minorities clauses by the states which are subjected to them, when they see that others are free from them, one must also inquire from the political point of view to what practical conclusion an action of the kind they are contemplating would lead. Indeed I cannot imagine that they are under the illusion that they can persuade all the member states of the League of Nations, or even all the European states, to accept a system of minorities similar to that laid down by the special treaties which they have signed: they know very well that neither Italy, nor Britain, nor even France nor, doubtless, Germany would be so disposed. The final objective of these tactics can therefore only be to embarrass the great powers, and to ascertain their refusal in order to draw certain inferences from it and thus to prepare the way for their own liberation. This is an implied warning, one veiled by the request for generalization, and this is what gives this request a tactical meaning and value. However, I doubt whether the Assembly will wish to pay attention to this warning, and that it will in fact serve the interests of the states who dream of having recourse to it.

One can no doubt allege that Germany made use of a method of this kind over the question of the limitation of armaments and that on the whole it has gained and hopes further to gain substantial advantages from it. I would offer two replies to this allegation.

The first is that at the head of the section of the Treaty of Versailles dealing with disarmament of Germany, there is a formal reference, with which the representatives of the Reich have been able to support their argument, for 'general limitation of armaments' which the disarmament of the vanquished states must prepare and make possible. On the contrary, nowhere in the individual treaties or in the Pact is there a similar clause, regarding the protection of minorities which the states with minorities could use, and which insists upon general application of this system as a kind of moral undertaking with respect to states with minorities.

The second is that while seeking to free itself from the Treaty of Versailles, even beyond and outside the texts, Germany has been acting within the boundaries of its general policy. One may wonder, on the other hand, whether it is in the interest of our friends in Central and Eastern Europe to follow them in this path and to lend a hand in what would amount to a revision of the treaties.

Revision is indeed the subject we must discuss and we must even go further than this. If it can be admitted that the treaties contain clauses of different value and that the territorial clauses are clauses of the first importance, which are more immutable than the others, then it is among these that the provisions relating to the protection of minorities are drawn up. Clauses 86 and 93, which state that minorities agreements will be concluded for Czechoslovakia and Poland respectively, appear in Part 3 of the Treaty of Versailles (European political clauses). This is also the case in the Saint-Germain and Trianon treaties for minority agreements signed by the successor states. . . . The provisions for minorities certainly seem in the first place like bondage, a kind of mortgaging of certain territories at the time when they were assigned to new or enlarged states of Central or Eastern Europe. They are bound to this situation by a legal and moral bond, from which these states cannot free themselves without giving Germany a plausible pretext for questioning this aspect.

I know that in time these memories will fade and that Germany, since the advent of the Hitlerite regime, has done all it could to undermine the moral foundations of the protection of minorities, from which it, nevertheless, benefits the most. However, even when faced with these violations, it is important to keep an exact tally of the possibilities, all the more so since this matter touches the problem of the upholding or the revision of the territorial *status quo* by close associations.

I would like to point out in this connection that our friends of Central and Eastern Europe do not seem sufficiently aware of the services which the protection of minorities gives them, and could give them, if instead of their regarding it primarily as an inconvenience from which it would be advisable to free themselves, they exerted themselves in a constructive spirit to making good use of it. Indeed nothing could better serve German revisionist propaganda than the cleverly fostered fable of bad treatment suffered by minorities in the new states. Now, every conscientious examination which has been made of the true situation of minorities – I am not referring here to Czechoslovakia which is irrelevant, but to other states, notably Poland – has enabled it to be established that this fable was, if not completely unfounded, at least greatly exaggerated. For my part I cannot see a better contradiction with which these states could counter German propaganda, than these reports and letters proceeding from League of Nations organizations. . . .

I understand that in the frequency of these procedures, in their initiation associated with complaints which were often trivial, there was no doubt something which could offend their *amour-propre*. If every teacher who is refused the right to teach, if every owner of a field to whom a law of agrarian reform is applied, if every wine merchant whose licence has been taken away can, from the moment he belongs to a minority, put his case before the League of Nations, while if he belonged to the majority he often could not even legally contend the matter, this is obviously an abuse. The present circumstances, and the mistakes – now found out – made by Germany after having for so long made itself the champion of the cause of the minorities, no doubt provide a favourable opportunity for carrying out the necessary rectification.

In this task of reform, our friends of Central and Eastern Europe can be assured that we will be on their side. . . . However, with regard to the considerations recalled above, we could not pursue matters any further.

If they wished to take this course, using the German attitude to the Jewish question as a justification, I am very much afraid, as I said at the end of my circular letter about the Bernheim petition, that they will not have a very favourable reception from the League of Nations, and that, according to the old wise saying, they will lose all while wanting to gain all.

30. *Dispatch from Henri de Jouvenel to Joseph Paul-Boncour (28 June 1933) (DDF, 1st series, Vol. III, pp.778–81).*
The false tidings of the last days, the actions they seem to have caused, the resurrection of the defunct Tardieu plan[4] have not exactly advanced the solution of the complicated problems of Central Europe. It has made the *rapprochement* between Italy and the Little *Entente* more difficult for the time being. It is necessary to let the fire die down and when all is calm to resume a negotiation in which our strength lies in the fact that we are right.

Since exports from Austria to Hungary represent only 6 per cent of the total Austrian exports, and her imports from Hungary do not exceed 10 per cent of her total imports, it appears futile to look for a remedy for the deficiency in the Austrian economy in some Austro-Hungarian agreement. The result of such an agreement could only be to establish German supremacy over Austria and Hungary; Germany buys 17 per cent of Austrian exports and 10 per cent of Hungarian exports, and supplies 21 per cent of Austrian imports and 21·70 per cent of Hungarian imports.

An Austro-Hungarian agreement would in no way serve the economic interest of Italy; with purchases which do not exceed 9·5 per cent of Austrian sales, 12·8 per cent of Hungarian sales, and sales reaching exactly 4 per cent of Austrian purchases and 4·9 per cent of Hungarian purchases, she would be incapable of balancing the power of German export and production in this area. On the other hand, it would directly threaten the political interest of Italy by contributing to drawing Austria and Hungary into Germany's orbit and by widening the prospect of the *Anschluss*.

On the other hand, it is to be feared that an economic agreement limited to Austria, Hungary and the three countries of the Little *Entente* would be doomed to fall under German influence. We realize that Czechoslovak industry, when called upon to exercise

[4] This must refer to the Beneš plan for Franco-Italian negotiations.

an industrial quasi-monopoly in this grouping with agricultural countries, expects to benefit from this. However, one might as well note that Mr Beneš has not yet even been able to achieve the 'economic Little *Entente*', for the formation of a Council and a secretariat was not sufficient, and that in 1932, in the middle of bargaining on the Danubian plan, he had to resign himself to seeing a German-Rumanian treaty put into force. On the other hand, his talks with the Yugoslav minister, as reported in a telegram from our minister in Prague of 11 May 1932, 'showed him that in Belgrade they cannot imagine that an economic system of the five Danubian states does not reserve special conditions for Italy'. The fact is that economics has its reasons which politics sometimes forgets, and Yugoslavia is not carrying hostility with her neighbour so far as to refuse her trade and to fail to recognize that 28 per cent of her production goes to Italy, whereas 8 per cent goes to Czechoslovakia and 3 per cent to Rumania.

With regard to the Italian position, this has not changed since M de Beaumarchais described it to the Department on 23 May 1932 as that of a state which is heir to the former Austria-Hungary, believing that it has the right to be regarded as in a special situation, and opposed to any project which would refuse her this.

[Note to the Document: 'In telegram no. 543, the French Ambassador in Rome underlined that as far as reorganization of Central Europe was concerned, Italy considered that she had a certain priority from her victory over the Habsburgs, hence her opposition to the Tardieu Plan. Messieurs Beneš and Marinko-vitch were prepared to recognize that Rome was in a special situation. Hence, before any joint negotiation with the other European countries, France should talk with Italy.]

To undertake a Danubian negotiation repeating 'neither Italy nor Germany' is to return to checkmate. What must be said is 'either Italy or Germany'. In fact, if the year 1930 is taken as a basis for calculation, which seems reasonable, and we add up the figures for the exchanges of Austria, Hungary, the three countries of the Little *Entente* and Italy, it is seen that the total exceeds that of the trade of the five Danubian countries with Germany.

Austria sells to the five other countries 51·3 per cent of her exports as against 17 per cent to Germany. She buys from them 49·4 per cent of her imports as against 21 per cent from Germany.

Hungary buys from the above-mentioned countries as a whole

55·6 per cent of her imports as against 21 per cent coming from Germany, and sends 66·1 per cent of her exports there as against 10·2 per cent to Germany.

If they are allowed to follow their natural bent, economic trends can only induce Austria and Hungary to develop their exchanges with Italy and the countries of the Little *Entente* and promote the formation of a vast market of Central and Southern Europe.

Of the three countries of the Little *Entente*, the one whose economy seems most orientated towards Germany – Rumania – still sells 39·8 per cent of her exports on the market we have just considered as against 18·8 per cent on the German market, and she derives from it 41 per cent of her imports as against 25 per cent from Germany.

Czechoslovakia obtains 28·1 per cent of her imports from there as against 17 per cent from Germany, and she sends them 43·6 per cent of her exports as against 17 per cent to Germany.

As for Yugoslavia, she buys from them 54·6 per cent of her imports as against 17·6 per cent from Germany, and sells them 61·3 per cent of her exports as against 17·7 per cent to Germany.

By increasing her exchanges with the Danubian countries, Italy alone would not be able to balance what she would lose by isolating herself from her main client, Germany, because the percentages from Austria, Hungary and the three countries of the Little *Entente* in her imports and exports do not reach the 12·6 per cent and 12·8 per cent represented by the purchases and sales of Germany in Italy, even on considering the overall quantities.

Hence it would not be in her interest to enter the association on the same level as the others, but she could merely enjoy a special situation in it which could bring her economic advantages of three kinds:

(1) The more and more pronounced tendencies of the Reich towards national self-sufficiency should at present provide her with the opportunity of taking Germany's place in the Danubian and Balkan markets by turning the cheapness of her products to advantage, provided that Italian industry could achieve agreements with what is no doubt her most direct rival, Czechoslovak industry;

(2) Economic reorganization of Central Europe should afford her the possibility of saving the ports of Trieste and Fiume, by endowing them with the hinterland for lack of which they are

dying, on condition that transport tariffs in favour of the Adriatic ports can be established in these regions;

(3) A new field will be open to the Italian work force, on condition that the great international works contemplated in London by M Daladier are provided in this part of Europe.

31. *Memorandum intended for Mussolini* (*10 September 1933*)
(DDF, 1st series, Vol. IV, pp.328–9).
(*Consolidation of Central Europe*)

The French government has not ceased to recommend to the Danubian countries that they should form agreements among themselves of such a nature as to facilitate their economic recovery. However, since it is convinced, as it has already shown on two occasions, that this recovery requires support from other countries, it considers that study and preparation of appropriate measures should include in particular a close co-operation with the Italian government and that an overall plan should be recommended to the countries concerned at the joint initiative of the two countries.

It seems to the French government that the first condition for success must be to put aside any special preoccupations of a political nature and not to let several rival economic groups form in the Danubian countries. It is therefore on a footing of complete moral and material equality that the states directly concerned – by which we must understand Austria, Hungary, Czechoslovakia, Yugoslavia, Rumania and possibly Bulgaria – must endeavour to organize economic co-operation among themselves and by bilateral agreements.

This co-operation could be established by any arrangements of an economic nature, which the studies would show to be useful, notably by establishing preferential tariffs and by better organization of means of transport. It must not exclude the development of economic relations with third-party states, especially with neighbouring states, by means of trade agreements which could include advantages which would tend to the exclusive benefit of Danubian agricultural products.

The organization must be completed by industrial agreements whose purpose would be to interest non-Danubian states in the hoped-for improvement of the markets of Central Europe, while reserving for the latter the possibility of developing her own internal market and co-ordinating her economic forces more satisfactorily.

The function of these private agreements which must, moreover, be limited to certain important products, would enable a suitable part to be reserved for Germany, and would also satisfy Poland who has always shown very great interest in the Danubian market. It would call for co-operation on the part of Italy, and it would obviously be part of its function to define this co-operation; it appears, however, that she can already see the main elements of this.

In another field, that of transport, whose development is of such great interest not only because of its repercussions on general activities but for its own sake, the geographical situation of the ports of Trieste and Fiume and the intensity of the flow of goods likely to converge there, assign to Italy a particularly useful part in supporting the Danubian group.

The advantage of this formula is not to take inspiration from any political consideration which could be an obstacle to its achievement. It takes the situation of Germany into account, and does not raise any obstacles to its normal economic activity in the region under consideration. The formula's chances of success lie also in the fact that, since the initiative for its presentation must rest jointly with France and Italy, it does not run the risk of arousing prejudices on the part of any of the countries concerned.

The French government would be happy to be assured that the views recalled here are in general in accordance with those of the royal government, as it has been led to believe by the meetings which this mission has already held on this subject.

32. *Note from the Political Directorate (19 July 1933)* (DDF, 1st series, Vol. IV, pp.32–3).

(*Franco-Soviet* rapprochement)

A proposal has been made to us by the Soviet government to conclude a verbal and secret agreement under which the two governments would communicate their views concerning questions of a general nature which could be of interest to either country, and agreements which they would contemplate making with third-party powers. On this occasion it was pointed out to us that it is an agreement similar to that which is in force between the USSR and Germany, which was a complement to the Rapallo

Treaty and to which secret clauses have been attributed until now, although it is impossible to be certain about this. The proposal gives rise to the following comments:

(1) In principle we must congratulate ourselves on the feelings of confidence which are thus displayed towards us. One cannot, however, refrain from remarking that if such an undertaking has been made by the USSR with regard to Germany, the communication which has been made to us is a contradiction to this undertaking. We would like to hope, however, that the commitments undertaken with respect to us will be better observed;

(2) We have already made undertakings of this nature: the European confidence agreement of Lausanne in 1932, the Four-Power Pact in Rome. It is true that these are collective agreements, and of too vast a scope not to allow a certain latitude as far as the obligation to communicate our views or to disclose our negotiations on questions of a general nature are concerned. However, we do have stricter bilateral undertakings incorporated in clearly defined agreements which compel us to keep one another informed and to act together jointly with other countries on the same questions on which Franco-Soviet exchanges of views have a bearing. These other countries are precisely those with which we have particularly close links: Poland, Czechoslovakia, Yugoslavia and Rumania.

If a relationship of trust with the USSR must be governed by the agreement which has been proposed to us, we would from this time on be *obliged* to inform these governments of all communications which come to us from Moscow, as well as to inform Moscow of all communications proceeding from these governments. What is more, the Soviet government would be equally *obliged* to communicate the same information to the German government. An agreement must be kept, or if it cannot be kept, it should not be made. Otherwise, this creates suspicion and doubt from the beginning between those very nations who undertook to observe such conditions;

(3) The confidence agreement, the Four-Power Pact, our agreements with Poland and the Little *Entente* are written down, published, registered, or are about to be registered, at the League of Nations. In other words, 'We know what is in them', and what their aim is.

What could the proposed agreement lead to? Either confidence exists, in which case there is no need for it, or confidence is lost, in which case the agreement is no longer valid, especially if, since the agreement consists only of the one undertaking to consult together as in the present case, the parties do not need to fear the loss of the benefit of other stipulations by making it null and void;

(4) With regard to third parties, however, an agreement, even devoid of substance, can have an effect from the very fact that it would be secret. It would alarm them because one day, willingly or otherwise, they would come to suspect its existence without knowing whether and to what extent it could threaten them.

If this is to be the result, if not the purpose, of the agreement which has been proposed to us, this consideration should decide us to refuse it outright. Such a method would be an absolute contradiction of all our policy, which is to develop confidence or, if necessary, to cause certain countries to reflect, to do this openly and as far as possible by having recourse to the procedures of the League of Nations;

(5) Finally, it is advisable to note that if the *rapprochement* which has been taking place for two years between the governments of Paris and Moscow is beneficial in that it could restrain Germany's ideas of having recourse to force, if this purpose is not clearly defined, it could seriously alarm Britain who has her own interests to defend in Asia.

For reasons of principle, as well as from obvious political motives, the proposal which has been made to us can only be followed up if the idea of a *secret* agreement is first of all clearly put aside; and if in addition every precaution is taken, so that when made public, it cannot be considered as being directed against Britain, since the understanding with Britain remains the basis of all French policy.

33. *The Franco-Soviet mutual assistance agreement* (*May 1935*).
The President of the French Republic and the Central Executive Committee of the Union of Soviet Socialist Republics,

Prompted by the desire to assert peace in Europe and to guarantee its benefits to their respective countries by more completely guaranteeing the exact application of the clauses of the League of Nations Pact which aim to maintain national security, territorial integrity and political independence of states,

Resolved to devote their efforts to the preparation and conclusion of a European agreement to this purpose, and expecting to contribute, as far as it is within their power, to effective application of the clauses of the League of Nations Pact,

Have resolved to conclude a treaty to this effect. . . .

Clause 1

In the event of France or the USSR being the object of a threat, or in danger of aggression, on the part of a European state, the USSR and France undertake mutually to hold an immediate consultation as to what measures to take to see that the provisions of clause 10 of the League of Nations Pact are observed.

Clause 2

In a case in which, in the conditions stipulated by clause 15, paragraph 7 of the League of Nations Pact, France or the USSR would be the victim of unprovoked aggression on the part of a European state, in spite of the peaceful intentions of both countries, the USSR and reciprocally France would immediately agree to give aid and assistance.

Clause 3

Taking into consideration the fact that, according to clause 16 of the League of Nations Pact, any member of the League who has recourse to war in contradiction to the undertakings made in clauses 12, 13 and 15 of the Pact is *ipso facto* considered as having committed an act of war against all the other members of the League, France and reciprocally the USSR undertake in the event of one of them being the object of an unprovoked aggression by a European state in these conditions and in spite of the sincerely peaceful intentions of the two countries, immediately to offer aid and assistance, acting according to the application of clause 16 of the Pact.

The same obligation is assumed for the case in which France or the USSR is the object of an aggressive action on the part of a European state in the conditions stipulated in clause 17, paragraphs 1 and 3 of the League of Nations Pact.

Clause 4

Since the undertakings stipulated above are in accordance with the obligations of the contracting High Parties, as members of the

League of Nations, nothing in the present Treaty will be interpreted as restricting the mission of the latter to take appropriate measures for safeguarding effectively the peace of the world or as restricting the obligations of the contracting High Parties, resulting from the League of Nations Pact.

Clause 5
The present Treaty . . . will be registered at the Secretariat of the League of Nations. It will take effect as from the exchange of ratified documents and will remain in force for five years. If it is not denounced by one of the contracting High Parties, with an advance notice of at least one year before the expiry of this period, it will remain in force without a time limit, each of the contracting High Parties being able to end it by a declaration to this effect with advance notice of one year. . . .

Formalities of Signature
At the time of signing the Franco-Soviet Mutual Assistance Treaty of today's date, the Plenipotentiaries signed the following Protocol which will be included in the exchange of ratifications of the Treaty.

I. It is understood that the effect of clause 3 is to oblige each Contracting Party to offer immediate assistance to the other, while conforming immediately with the recommendations of the League of Nations Council, as soon as they have been stated with respect to clause 16 of the Pact. It is likewise understood that the two Contracting Parties will act jointly so that the Council can state its recommendations with all the speed which the circumstances will require and that if nevertheless for some reason the Council does not state any recommendation or if it does not achieve a unanimous vote, the obligation to assist will be no less applicable. It is also understood that the undertakings to assist stipulated in the present Treaty relate only to the case of an aggressive action carried out against the actual territory of one or the other Contracting Party.

II. Since the joint intention of the two governments is not to contradict in any respect, by the present Treaty, the previous undertakings with respect to third-party states by France and by the USSR in virtue of the published treaties, it is agreed that the provisions of the aforesaid Treaty cannot be given an application which, being incompatible with the treaty obligations assumed by a Contracting Party, would expose the latter to sanctions of an international character.

III. The two governments, considering it desirable to conclude a regional agreement which would aim to organize security between contracting States and which could include, or be accompanied by, mutual assistance undertakings, recognize that they have the right to participate by mutual consent, and if the need arose, in similar agreements in such a form, direct or indirect, as would seem appropriate, the undertakings of these various agreements taking the place of those resulting from the present Treaty.

IV. The two governments declare that the negotiations which have just resulted in the signing of the present Treaty were undertaken in the first place with a view to complementing a security agreement encompassing the countries of North-Eastern Europe, that is, the Union of Soviet Socialist Republics, Germany, Czechoslovakia, Poland and the Baltic States adjoining the USSR; alongside this agreement a Treaty of Assistance was to be concluded between the Union of Soviet Socialist Republics, France and Germany, each of these three states having to undertake to offer assistance to whichever of them was the object of aggression on the part of one of these three states. Although circumstances have not yet enabled these agreements which the two parties continue to consider desirable, to be concluded, it still remains that the undertakings stated in the Franco-Soviet Treaty of mutual assistance must be understood as coming into force only within the limits contemplated in the previously proposed tripartite agreement. Independently of the obligations arising from the present Treaty, it is at the same time recalled that, in accordance with the Franco-Soviet Pact of non-aggression signed on 19 November 1932 and without interfering in other respects with the universality of the undertakings of this Pact, in the event of one of the Parties becoming the object of an aggression on the part of one or several third-party European powers not alluded to in the above-mentioned tripartite agreement, the other Party must refrain, for the duration of the conflict, from any direct or indirect aid or assistance to the aggressor or aggressors, each Party declaring moreover that it is not bound by any assistance agreement which would be in contradiction with this undertaking.

34. *'Free hand.'*

(1) *Letter from Pierre Laval to Mussolini* (*Paris, 22 December 1935*)
  (published in H. Lagardelle, *Mission à Rome*, pp.275–6).

My dear President,

The present situation obliges me to send you this letter. You will excuse its terms, but I would be failing for the first time in the duties of friendship towards you if I did not express myself with complete frankness. As you have recalled, I was fortunate in being able to complete an often interrupted negotiation which had lasted for several years, in Rome on 7 January last, and it seems to me to be useful to point out in what spirit we made our agreements. In a general declaration we affirmed our wish to develop the traditional friendship which unites our two nations and to co-operate in upholding peace in a spirit of mutual confidence.

I have not hesitated to sacrifice important economic advantages which long and costly efforts had produced for my country in East Africa. I agreed to limit these interests in Ethiopia to the zone necessary to supply the railway traffic from Djibouti to Addis Ababa. . . .

There is no need to add that the rich future prospects laid open by this agreement did not extend beyond the economic field. They could not have gone beyond this limit without coming up against the guarantees set up around the sovereign independence and territorial integrity of Ethiopia by international acts in which Italy and France had participated. . . .

During our talks, I did not omit to stress all the advantages which you could obtain from our agreements for the development of your peaceful action in Ethiopia. You have shown me your wish to make use of our agreements only for peaceful purposes. Last February, at the time when large Italian military forces were sent to Eritrea and Somaliland, I did not omit to point out to you in a friendly manner the danger of measures which appeared to exceed the requirements of the immediate defence of your two colonies.

(2) *Letter from Mussolini to Pierre Laval* (*Rome, 25 December 1935*)
  (ibid., p.279).

My dear President,

I appreciate the frankness with which you spoke to me, and in my reply I would not wish to have recourse to any other method or style. . . .

You told me that your concessions relating to Abyssinia were concerned only with the recognition of an economic superiority of Italy in this country and that I had undertaken to develop a peace policy. I cannot agree with your argument; I venture to remind you, if only to affirm the spirit of these agreements, that the interview we had in Rome was also determined by the necessity for a verbal understanding, since it was understood that as far as the question of 'desisting' was concerned, it would not have been possible to say everything in written records. So it was that in our conversations there was occasion to mention several times the 'free hand' which had been allowed to me in Abyssinia, except for the reservations for your rights which were expressly specified in the document. . . . Moreover, even an examination of the specific clauses of the document is sufficient to show that something which went beyond mere economic achievements in favour of Italy was under consideration.

It is furthermore obvious that none of Italy's requirements would have found satisfaction in Ethiopia if it had not been based on the guarantee of a political control.

Naturally, I do not hereby mean to say that you have given your approval to this war which ensuing circumstances made inevitable.

(3) *Letter from Pierre Laval to Mussolini (Paris, 23 January 1936)*
   (ibid., p.285).

My dear President,

I do not wish to leave the ministry without replying to your letter of 25 December last.

. . . You remind me that the expression 'free hand' came up again during our talks. You interpret these words as an extending of the scope of the agreements of 7 January.

I was able to use this colloquialism, with the freedom of tone justified by the friendly nature of a conversation at the Farnese Palace on the evening of 6 January.

I believe that it is even more useless to cavil at the meaning of these words since your letter of 25 December gave what was to me the essential evidence, that is, that I had never given my approval to the war which you subsequently believed yourself obliged to undertake.

35. *Clause 16 of the League of Nations Pact.*
(*The legal basis for sanctions*)
(1) If a member of the League has recourse to war contrary to the pledges undertaken in clauses 12, 13 and 15, he is *ipso facto* considered as having committed an act of war against all the other members of the League. The latter undertake to break all commercial or financial relations with that country immediately, and to forbid any relations between their nationals and those of the state which has broken the Pact, and to cease any financial, commercial and personal communications between their nationals and those of this state whether it is or is not a member of the League;

(2) In this case it is the duty of the Council to recommend to the various governments concerned, the military, naval or air effectives which the members of the League will contribute respectively to the armed forces which are to see that the undertakings of the League are enforced;

(3) The members of the League agree, moreover, to afford each other mutual support in applying the economic and financial measures to be taken on the strength of the preceding clause and to reduce to a minimum the losses and disadvantages which could result from this. They afford each other mutual support to resist any special measure directed against one of them by the state which has broken the Pact. They take the necessary steps to facilitate the passage across their territory of forces of any member of the League who is participating in a joint action to see that the pledges of the League are observed;

(4) Any member who has made himself guilty of violation of one of the undertakings resulting from the Pact can be excluded from the League; the exclusion is declared by the vote of all the other members of the League who are represented at the Council.

36. *Memorandum from the Army General Staff for the Military High Committee* (*18 January 1936*) (DDF, 2nd series, Vol. I, pp.116–20).
The development of the international situation and the increase of German military power clearly stress the lack of balance between our military forces and those of our chief adversary, in spite of the efforts we have already made. . . .

I. [Since the Anglo-Italian conflict] our total force dedicated to

the defence of the North-East is therefore much reduced: definitely
by ten divisions and two brigades of cavalry and possibly by four
brigades (from North Africa) whose arrival in France can be
delayed for a more or less long period of time.

II. Germany has permanently at its disposal at the present time
the strength of its land forces (not including the anti-aircraft
defence) totalling 790,000 men, distributed as follows:

Army	520,000
Militarized police	30,000
Auxiliary troops quarters in barracks (SS)	40,000
Labour service	200,000

In 1936 or, at the latest, during 1937, this strength will approach
a total of 1 million men, when the current programme is achieved.

At present the German regular army is composed of: 10 army
corps (24 infantry divisions and a mountain brigade, 2 cavalry
divisions and 1 independent brigade, and 3 armoured divisions).

It is approaching the figure of 12 army corps and 36 divisions,
which was established by the law of 16 March 1935, and which
will probably be achieved at the end of 1936 or during 1937.

Independently of this increase of manpower, the increase of
German military power is expressed by the development of the
artillery strength of the units and by mechanization. . . .

III. In a situation of this kind, which does not allow us to unite
all our forces at the most vulnerable frontier, we must make up for
the deficiency in manpower in the field by increasing the artillery
strength and material obstacles. Hence the pursuit of the programme of national defence (at present in the course of development) beyond the figure of 2,629 millions approved by the Council
of Ministers on 21 June 1935, is presented as of primary importance.

. . . In short, the intensive rearmament of Germany, an artillery
which is powerful in quality as well as in quantity, a mass of tanks
which, for the armoured divisions alone, approaches 2,000 units,
can only be opposed by the present French programme, with an
artillery system based on the equipment in service during the
First World War, limited armament and anti-tank defences,
especially with regard to the fortified regions, and modern tanks
which barely cover a third of our needs.

Appendix

37. *Report of the meeting of the Military High Committee (18 January 1936)* (DDF, 2nd series, Vol. I, pp.121–4).

[those present: the Ministers of War, Navy, Air and the Chiefs of General Staff].

(reading of the above memorandum)

The War Minister pointed out that the reversal of our policy with regard to Italy compels us to maintain on the Alps and in the Mediterranean basin nearly a fifth of the total of our forces, whereas after the Rome Agreements it was possible for us to have them intervene in the north-east almost in their entirety. He then drew attention to the importance of the results already obtained in Germany in completing the military programme decreed by the Hitler government. The French programme of April 1935 is thus notoriously inadequate, particularly as far as armaments are concerned: an effort is imperative especially for artillery and armoured equipment. . . .

[General Gamelin] then pointed out the aims which our enemies seemed to be pursuing by creating powerful armoured units. It is to be feared that certain of our allies cannot ward off the attacks of such divisions which are intended, it would seem, for action on free or slightly built up terrain. The delay shown by the Belgians in improving the measures already taken for the defence of their territory creates in this respect a situation which is particularly favourable to an enemy attempting to outflank our fortified regions through the plains of the North (Belgium and the Netherlands). This constitutes a problem for France which deserves our attention from three angles: manpower, equipment and fortifications.

In conclusion General Gamelin again pointed out the considerable advantage which France has at present in her system of fortifications which, by making our north-eastern frontier particularly strong, compels our possible enemy to seek yet again the decision of invading Belgium, and probably even the Netherlands, using costly equipment which takes a relatively long time to prepare.

The War Minister concluded by indicating that the plan of April 1935 which covered a relatively favourable situation no longer enabled us to face a singularly aggravated state of affairs. The million men which Germany could have in arms in peacetime from 1936 was matched in France by effectives which were indeed considerable, but which, unless some new measure were introduced in this connection, ran the risk of again finding themselves even more clearly inferior in numbers. As regards equipment, Germany is on the point of overtaking us outright. Our superiority therefore remains in our fortifications alone, and to this day, in the ability of our High Command, the number and training of our officers, and finally in the undeniable advance which we owe to a military organization whose function and development nothing has so far impeded. . . .

General Gamelin estimates that, if it is impossible for us to equal Germany in the fight for manpower, this does not apply to equipment. . . .

. . . General Gamelin then showed how the military action of the Reich seemed to be able to develop against the powers of the Little *Entente*. First of all, it would no doubt be a matter of neutralizing the French army by establishing a fortified barrier similar to ours on the western frontiers (the demilitarized zone would be reoccupied as soon as possible for this purpose). Thus freed from any fear of an offensive on our part, Germany would be completely at liberty to settle the fate of the powers of the Little *Entente*, in whose favour only Russia and Poland would be able to intervene directly. The intervention of Russian forces against Germany can be achieved only by crossing Polish or Rumanian territories; it is doubtful whether either of these two powers would accept this possibility. . . .

The Air Minister pointed out the narrow rear zone which the Russian aviation called upon to operate in Czechoslovakia would have available; the slightest German advance would risk compromising the security of the airfields. The question of providing spares or repair of equipment based in this manner outside the national territory, moreover presents problems which are often difficult to solve.

The War Minister considers that Britain and Poland[5] remain with France the only powers around which resistance to an aggression from the Reich could be organized.

38. *Memorandum (probably from General Gamelin) taken from the War Archives, dated 27 January 1936* (DDF, 2nd series, Vol. I, pp.152–4).

At the time when the question of the ratification of the Franco-

[5] The omission of Czechoslovakia appears significant.

Soviet treaty of mutual assistance arises, it appears useful to calculate its possible repercussions. These repercussions can be by the action of Germany, or Poland, or Belgium. . . .

(1) Germany has violently taken up a position against the letter and the spirit of the treaty. . . .

It is of hardly any importance whether the German objections are more or less well founded. We know with what total absence of good faith our neighbours from beyond the Rhine can affirm the most questionable arguments when necessary. What is important, what is serious, is the systematic attitude adopted by the Reich in this affair. One cannot help having the impression that it is looking for an excuse to rid itself of the pledges undertaken at Locarno which inconvenience it considerably in its present military reorganization.

A large volume of information from very different sources confirms that the German command wishes to achieve in a very short time this military reoccupation of the line of the Rhine which will enable it to cover itself better from the West, in particular by putting into effect a programme of fortifications which would already be complete.

The chancellor Hitler declared that Germany would respect Locarno if the other signatories respected it likewise. Hence German propaganda, orientated by the Wilhelmstrasse, is on the lookout for violations, real or imagined. It has been seen how Franco-British military talks were exploited against Locarno, talks which nevertheless were held on the occasion of the threat of a conflict in the Mediterranean. The ratification of the Franco-Soviet treaty would be a better battleground.

It is possible that this ratification may provide the Germans with the awaited opportunity to reoccupy the Rhineland. Should this danger be eliminated at the time of ratification, it could appear in a more threatening form if the treaty were followed by a military agreement;

(2) Poland protests her fidelity to the French alliance and, in spite of the German-Polish pact of non-aggression which represents a simple *modus vivendi*, she declares that she still considers Germany as the main enemy; however, she does not want Russian support against Germany at any price, for she holds the USSR in such distrust that she would not under any circumstances allow passage of the Red Army over her territory.

The Franco-Soviet Treaty has given rise to numerous criticisms in Poland. Its ratification will probably be an obstacle to renewal of the Franco-Polish alliance which is looming ahead, and will be of a nature to bring Warsaw closer to Berlin.

The affair would take a more serious turn if it were a question of extending the political treaty concluded with the USSR by a military agreement. The Polish military alliance seems incompatible with the Russian military alliance. A choice will have to be made;

(3) Belgium, although geographically far removed from the USSR, pays an attention to the treaty, on account of its possible effects on Locarno, which must be emphasized.

A large part of the public fears in fact that Belgium, as a signatory of Locarno, may be involved because of France in a conflict which may break out initially between Germany and the USSR, but which may subsequently have repercussions on the Rhine through the working of the Franco-Soviet Treaty.

Ratification of the treaty, and with greater reason, a Franco-Soviet military agreement would run the risk of having troublesome consequences for us in Belgium, at a time when propaganda for a policy of neutrality is becoming more pronounced in that country and when the Franco-Belgian military agreement of 1920 is violently breached.

39. *Report of a military meeting with General Gamelin (8 March 1936)* (DDF, 2nd series, Vol. I, pp.444–6).
Those present: General Gamelin, Admiral Durand-Viel, General Pujo, General Georges, General Picard, Vice-Admiral Abrial, Colonel de Saint-Vincent (DAT), Colonel Jeannel.
[General Gamelin] The government has asked me, 'Are you able to hold out?' I replied that if a conflict between Germany and France were confined to the land front on the Franco-German frontier, there would be effectives on both sides which would be broadly sufficient for saturation to be achieved rapidly. The fronts will become stabilized. Aviation alone will be able to carry out offensives into enemy country. If the theatre of operations begins with Belgium, what will Britain do?
[Admiral Durand-Viel] According to the exchanges of views which took place yesterday evening at the Ministry of Foreign Affairs (MM Sarraut, Flandin, Piétri, General Maurin, Déat,

General Gamelin, Admiral Durand-Viel, General Pujo . . .)[6] the French government, after having brought the question before the League of Nations Council (article 4 of the Locarno Treaty) will request that a commission of inquiry should be sent to the Rhineland by the League of Nations, Germany being declared as the aggressor. It is in order to examine what our attitude would then be, that the government asks the military, 'Are you in a position to drive the Germans back out of the zone?'

[General Gamelin] War would be started from the moment we entered the zone. Such an action would therefore necessitate general mobilization.

Before the ratification of the Franco-Soviet pact, General Gamelin had given in writing his opinion of the probable consequences of this ratification (occupation of the demilitarized zone by the Germans).

He had had a conversation on this subject with M Léger and with M Sarraut and had said to them, 'If we oppose this occupation with force, this is war.' M Léger replied that everything had been done to eliminate from this agreement anything which could be dangerous, and that the discussion of ratification had been delayed as long as possible, but that now it was no longer possible to delay it any further.

General Gamelin considered that we could enter the Rhineland zone only if we went there . . . at the same time as the other guarantor powers . . . of the Locarno treaties (Britain, Italy. . . . It is necessary for British and Italian contingents to be with us and the Belgians . . .).

[Admiral Durand-Viel] At present Britain could hardly give us anything but moral support. Above all it would be necessary for the Ethiopian affair to be settled. It is difficult to see how a joint action can be contemplated by two powers who are themselves in a state of mutual hostility (Britain-Italy). When this hostility has ceased, at least fifteen days will be needed for the British naval forces to be ready to act in the North Sea and the Channel. At present the British Isles are devoid of any naval protection.

[General Pujo] At the moment Britain has 150 fighter aircraft and 150 modern bomber aircraft. The 150 fighter aircraft will very probably be assigned to the defence of London. However, Britain

---

[6] No report of this exchange of views has been found in the archives of the Ministry of Foreign Affairs.

could meanwhile send us a few as well as part of the 150 bombers.
The Belgians have 18 squadrons. . . .

The Italians have completely reconstructed their home aviation
formations. At present they have in Italy about 900 aircraft, the
majority of which are of recent construction. They could send us
about 100 bombers.

Utilization of USSR aviation would require munitions and
spares to be sent to Czechoslovakia. It is reported that airfields
with underground shelters have been prepared in Czechoslovakia
for Russian aviation.

General Gamelin wonders whether the Germans would not
compromise if faced with a very firm attitude. He requested that a
general should go to Geneva, where important technical questions
would be dealt with. In particular it will be very important to
arrange for British and Italian troops to come immediately to
France and for us to go to Belgium.

Measures already taken. Measures to be taken
General Gamelin enumerates the arrangements made by the War
Ministry to counter a possible sudden attack.

Placing of troops in the shelters of the fortified regions and in
the gaps between the shelters.

Leave of absence for twenty-four hours has been cancelled
in the East. Nothing has been done about the rest of the
country.

It is decided that the Air will work in harmony with the
Interior and will then specify the special surveillance system in the
frontier sub-sectors from Belfort to the sea and in the Boulogne
sub-sector.

General Gamelin requests Admiral Durand-Viel to point out to
M Piétri the fundamental importance of settling the question of
petrol stores.

It was agreed that the three departments would communicate
with each other by a bulletin at least once a day about the measures
taken.

40. *Administrative memorandum from Flandin to the diplomatic
representatives in London, Berlin, Rome, Warsaw, Moscow,
Brussels, Ankara, Berne, Madrid, Washington, Prague, Bucharest,
Belgrade, Vienna, Athens, Lisbon, Copenhagen, Stockholm,*

Appendix

Oslo, Kaunas, The Hague (11 March 1936) (DDF, 2nd series, Vol. I, pp.493–4).

After the declarations by Mr Eden to the House of Commons, we could not venture to hope that a complete agreement between the French and British points of view could result from the first exchange of views between the Locarno powers.

Yesterday's meeting was none the less important because it enabled the British representatives to see the extent of the mistake they had made in their appraisal of the attitude which the French and Belgian governments had been led to adopt due to necessity, when faced with the initiative taken by Germany in the Rhineland.[7] Mr Eden who, in yesterday's declaration, seemed to retain only those Locarno obligations which relate to the case of a clearly defined aggression, has been obliged to understand that British responsibility was also equally committed in the case of a simple contravention of clause 43.

Mr Van Zeeland, having stressed that the Locarno Treaty was the basic element of the international status of Belgium, and that the fallacious pretext used by the Reich to justify its gesture was in any case not valid with respect to his country, very clearly indicated that he was in no doubt that the guarantor governments were prepared to stand by all their obligations of assistance and that he awaited their declarations to this effect.

As far as I am concerned, I have defined the French position both in relation to the problem of our own security and in relation to the more general problem of respect of international order and observation of the pledges which were freely made.

From the second point of view, the League of Nations is committed especially after the resolution voted by its Council on 17 April 1935 shortly after Stresa, and a failure on its part would irrevocably compromise all organization of collective security. Besides, the powers which signed the Locarno Treaty have individual obligations which they must honour.

In practice I have not excluded any possibility of negotiation for the future, but on the express condition that the situation which existed before the German gesture be re-established and that, consequently, the reign of international law be restored. The

[7] The first meeting of the four Locarno powers (other than Germany) took place on 10 March at the Quai d'Orsay; no report of this meeting has been found in the French Archives.

guarantor powers must now exert themselves with us to restoring the former situation, having recourse to all kinds of pressure which may be necessary.

Those various comments convinced the British ministers that a further exchange of views between them and their colleagues was essential; it was under these conditions that the modifications to the programme of future meetings which were announced by the press occurred.

I add that the Italian delegate still adopts an attitude of great caution, having noted from the beginning that, since he represented a 'sanctioned' state, he must refrain from any declaration and confine himself to playing the part of an 'observer'.

41. *Memorandum for the Minister from René Massigli, Assistant Director of Political Affairs (12 March 1936)* (DDF, 2nd series, Vol. I, p.525).

(Consequences of remilitarization of the Rhineland)

In the Paris meeting (of 10 March), the French argument was set forth from the double point of view of our security and of respect to League of Nation principles, or generally speaking, of international law. It could be useful today to show the British ministers the practical consequences of a failure of the Western Powers.

The communication from the Japanese ambassador in Paris[8] already defines these consequences for a part of the world which interests Britain in particular. In Europe the danger would be no less and it is not possible that the Foreign Office has not already received cries of alarm from its representatives abroad.

Poland is showing great enthusiasm, but if matters end with a German triumph, Colonel Beck would quickly draw inferences from this, and so would the Baltic States.

A German success would likewise not fail to encourage elements which, in Yugoslavia, look towards Berlin. It will encourage them more especially since at present the Yugoslav government has decided to support us without reservations, and has informed us of this. In Rumania this will be a victory of the elements of the Right which have been stirred by Hitlerite propaganda. All that will remain for Czechoslovakia is to come to terms with Germany. Austria does not conceal her anxiety. 'Next time it will be our turn', the French Minister in Vienna was told.

[8] No reference in the DDF.

Turkey, who has increasingly close economic relations with
Germany but who, politically, remains in the Franco-British axis,
can be induced to modify her line. The Scandinavian countries,
Denmark in particular, are alarmed.

The question at the moment is that of knowing whether Europe
will or will not be German.

42. *Memorandum from the Director of Political Affairs* (*M Bargeton*)
(*30 June 1936*) (DDF, 2nd series, Vol. II, pp.563–4).
(*French security*)
Putting aside the Rhineland pact denounced by Germany, the
treaties concluded by France in view of the consolidation of peace
and the safeguard of her own security, are as follows:

A number of treaties concluded with Poland in 1921, with
Czechoslovakia in 1924, with Rumania in 1926 and with Yugoslavia in 1927, described in current language as treaties of alliance,
but in fact consisting only of an undertaking to act together within
the framework of the League of Nations with a view to safeguarding common interests. They are consequently of limited
scope with regard to the assistance to be given, but on the other
hand, of unlimited scope with regard to the countries which could
threaten the aforesaid interests. However, although they have
these two features in common, these four treaties are not identical
in form, and the intention with which some of them were concluded could make their operation very difficult. Hence, from the
beginning, the Polish treaty has been considered as applying to a
Russian threat at least as much as to a German threat.

Two other treaties were concluded by France with Poland and
with Czechoslovakia in Locarno, which were unlimited as far as
the assistance to be given was concerned, but limited on the other
hand as to the countries against which assistance would be due.
These commitments were undertaken without appearing to be
directed against a third-party country, for it was a matter not of an
alliance but of a guarantee given for carrying out the commitment,
which occurred the same day, and by the consent of all, between
France and Germany, Germany and Poland and Germany and
Czechoslovakia not to have recourse to arms and to settle by
peaceful means all differences which could arise between two
countries.

Finally, France has concluded a treaty of assistance with the

USSR whose functions have been even more precisely stipulated than the preceding ones, with the exception, it is true, of the functions of the Rhineland pact and Locarno. This is a treaty which in principle was not a bilateral treaty, nor is it a treaty guaranteeing undertakings made by a third party. It is a treaty which remains open to Germany in particular, without the latter having entered into it.

There is a disparity among these various treaties – one has only to read the texts to be convinced of this – which makes their application very difficult and which, from now onwards, would be enough to put us in an embarrassing situation if one of our 'allies' took it into its head to benefit from an agreement which was as strict as any other made by friendly countries.

Politically, our system of alliances is even less coherent. Among the five countries of which each has a treaty known as an 'alliance' with France, there are few who regard themselves as allies of one another. There is no need to dwell on the relations between the USSR and Poland, between Poland and Czechoslovakia, on the mutual distrust of Poland and Rumania, born of Polish-Russian hostility, and which makes the Polish-Rumanian alliance a figment of the imagination, the absence of an undertaking of assistance between the three states of the Little *Entente*, except against Hungary, the situation of Yugoslavia, who is hypnotized by fear of Italy and continues to ignore the Soviet Union, without mentioning less apparent but persistent rivalries and differences.

These facts lead one to think that – if there were no other motive for ruling out a 'policy of alliances' – such a policy is not practicable, for it assumes first of all that the participants are, in fact, all allied among themselves. The result of the present situation is not only weakness. It also results in the concentration on France of any attempt made against peace, France being – and how inadequately – the only link between countries which would be inclined to oppose such an attempt.

How otherwise can indivisible peace be established on a system of agreements which allows such divisions between its supporters?

The effort which will be made to render clause 16 of the League of Nations Pact effective, must enable us to give the assistance pledges a form which will enable our different agreements to operate, and allow them to blend in an undertaking resulting from the Pact which would be imposed, in their mutual relations, on all countries who had already made such undertakings with France.

This solidarity which already results from paragraph 3 of clause 16 for countries applying economic sanctions, must be established likewise between countries who would offer military assistance.

43. *Programme of the Rassemblement Populaire (Section devoted to foreign policy).*

II Defence of peace:

(1) Appeal for co-operation of the people, and especially of the working masses, for the preservation and organization of peace;

(2) International co-operation within the framework of the League of Nations for collective security, by the definition of the aggressor and the automatic and joint application of sanctions in the case of aggression;

(3) Incessant effort to progress from armed peace to unarmed peace, firstly by a limitation agreement, and then by simultaneous and controlled general reduction of armaments;

(4) Nationalization of war industries and elimination of private arms trade;

(5) Repudiation of secret diplomacy, international action and public negotiations to bring back to Geneva those countries who have set themselves apart from it, without infringing the constitutive principles of the League of Nations: collective security and individual peace;

(6) Achievement of flexibility in the procedure stipulated by the League of Nations Pact for adjustment of treaties which are dangerous to world peace;

(7) Extension of the system of pacts open to all, especially to Eastern and Central Europe, according to the principles of the Franco-Soviet Pact.

44. *'The problem of peaceful co-existence' (article by Léon Blum in* Le Populaire, *28 August 1937).*

. . . The real question is not to guarantee peaceful co-existence of democracies and dictatorships in Europe. The real question is to guarantee co-existence 'without risk of explosions' between the nations who resolutely desire peace and the states who do not want it, or who want it less.

Democracies will peacefully tolerate the existence of dictatorial states alongside them. Whether one blames them for this or praises them, the fact remains. Britain and France have gone so far as to sign the Four-Power Pact with the Führer's Germany and the Duce's Italy. One has the right to assume that the reverse is true. At least M Hitler and M Mussolini have not so far declared the intention of having peaceful relations only with states founded on the same principles which they have caused to prevail in their own country. This does not therefore constitute the real division. The real blocs are not demarcated by this formula.

There are, however, nations who work with complete sincerity to preserve, stabilize and organize the general peace, nations to which it would be ridiculous to attribute the slightest ulterior motive of aggression or conquest. We can vouch with pride that republican France is one of these. On the other hand, there are those who do not exclude war as a means of achieving their political ambitions, who so far have been reluctant to take part in any united effort towards settlement and organization, and from whom plans of aggression or conquest can reasonably be expected. Italy has conquered Ethiopia, Japan is methodically carving up China, Italy is celebrating the seizure of Santander as a victory of her own arms, and no one could protest that it is absurd and impossible to speak of designs on Austria or Czechoslovakia.

All things considered, it is not a matter of democracy and anti-democracy. Nor is it a matter of communism and anti-communism, although this distinction is the one which pleases the dictators. Germany and Italy may find it useful to explain their intervention in Spanish affairs by the wish to obstruct the road to communism, and Japan is in the course of following their example with regard to China. However, what settled the question is that the Duce and even the Führer have for a long time maintained more friendly relations with Soviet Russia than have Britain or France. The theory of communist and anti-communist blocs is only a clever diversion, a tactical procedure, a propaganda method by which no responsible statesman can be justified in remaining deceived.

The sole criterion which allows nations to be classed and distinguished from one another is their position with respect to peace, their more or less frank, more or less active, more or less constant desire to preserve it by regulating the present, and to consolidate it by arranging the future. This is how the two blocs are really separated. This is how the problem of 'peaceful co-existence' must be correctly formulated. This comes back to saying that it does not present itself to the group of peaceful powers, for to them it was determined in advance; they are prepared in advance for all forms of *entente* and co-operation with a view to peace. It is to the others that it presents itself: it is on them that the solution depends.

45. *Memorandum to the British government* (*16 September 1936*)
   (DDF, 2nd series, Vol. III, pp.372–5).
(*Proposal for a 'new Locarno'*)
(1) With a view to preparing negotiations, the principle of which was agreed upon in London and whose purpose was to be to strengthen the preservation of peace between the powers of Western Europe by a revision of the Locarno Treaty, the government of the French Republic has considered it useful to set forth before His Britannic Majesty's government . . . the bases on which in its opinion a new agreement could be founded;

(2) The French government considers that the clauses of the Locarno Treaty must be maintained as far as possible, with the exception of modifications and additions which the present circumstances render necessary and which acquired experience seems to render desirable;

(3) Since it has been suggested that the Netherlands should be included in the new agreement . . . the French government is prepared, as far as it is concerned, to accept this extension. It is likewise prepared to examine the opportunity of making a place for the Free State of Ireland in the new agreement;

(4) It will certainly not have escaped the attention of the British government that the disappearance of the demilitarized zone creates a new situation as far as Luxembourg is concerned, independently of the consequences it will have for the security of French and Belgian territories . . .;

(5) The basis of the Locarno Treaty is a guarantee of the territorial *status quo* resulting from the frontiers between Germany and Belgium and between Germany and France, and a guarantee of the inviolability of these frontiers. The new agreement could likewise ascertain that there is no territorial dispute between the contracting parties and that consequently they will guarantee each other individually and collectively, in their mutual relations, the territorial *status quo* as well as the inviolability of the frontiers of their possessions and dependencies;

(6) Each signatory would undertake to each of the other signatories not to surrender to any attack or invasion and not to have recourse to force in any circumstances;

(7) It is self-evident that the obligation thus contracted would not prevent a signatory power from exercising the right to legitimate defence, that is, the right to resist the violation of the above-stated undertaking;

(8) In the case of failure to observe the undertaking of non-aggression, assistance must be supplied by the other signatory powers to the attacked power. The undertaking of assistance must not be less extensive than that which was undertaken in the Locarno Treaty. The French government upholds the acceptance it gave, in the provisions decreed on 19 March, to mutual assistance to the advantage of Britain and Italy. With regard to the point of knowing whether assistance to those two powers would be owed by all the signatories or only by some, whether it would be due in every case or only in some cases, the French government will readily hold talks with the parties concerned; it will likewise readily exchange views on the arrangements to be made in the Netherlands as far as assistance is concerned, should the Netherlands be party to the agreement;

(9) Since the effectiveness of assistance depends to a great extent on the rapidity with which it will be supplied, the government of the Republic considers that if a solution which would ensure that this assistance would follow automatically in satisfactory conditions cannot be found, the mechanism stipulated by the Locarno Treaty (clause 4) must nevertheless be maintained (except for the addition which will be indicated in the future for warding off sudden aerial attack). In this case, the distinction between the case in which the League of Nations Council ascertains the violation of the non-aggression agreement – which sets in motion the obligation of immediate assistance – and the case of so-called flagrant violation in which the obligation to give mutual assistance comes into immediate operation without previous verification from the Council, the latter only intervening later, would be preserved;

(10) The undertaking made by France in the Locarno Treaty, never to surrender to any attack or invasion by Germany, includes certain limits set forth in clause 1 of this Treaty; the same applies to Germany and Belgium. The same idea would be taken up again

in more simple terms, if it were specified that the benefit of the new treaty (and especially the assistance which results from it) cannot be invoked by a signatory state which has failed in the undertakings set forth in the Treaty or who in Europe has taken action against the territorial integrity or political independence of another power, especially by directing an attack against the latter;

(11) The government of the Republic insists on this occasion on underlining that it would not for its part accept a solution which would limit the freedom of action which was to be guaranteed to it by the Locarno Treaty, as well as to the other signatories, in the case of an act of aggression committed by one of the contracting countries against a non-contracting country; it does not doubt that the British government shares its attitude on this point, in accordance with the principles of the League of Nations Pact. Moreover, the German government has been acquainted with the treaties concluded at Locarno, either between the French government and the Polish government, or between the French and Czech governments: the government of the Republic expressly agrees to uphold these treaties whose execution it must be possible to guarantee at any time, without there being any failure to fulfil the commitments inscribed in the new agreement.

As for the Franco-Soviet Pact, whose compatibility with the Locarno Treaty has been recognized by the British government as well as by the Belgian and Italian governments, and on the subject of which the governments represented in London proposed in vain to Germany on 19 March last to obtain a decision at the International Permanent Court of Justice, the French government is bent on recalling that its signatories declared themselves ready to replace it with a new treaty to which Germany would be a party.

Moreover, in order to justify the violation of the demilitarized zone of the Rhineland, the government of the Reich put forward precisely the necessity of restoring a balance which, according to her, the conclusion of the Franco-Soviet Pact had destroyed. The German government does not seem disposed to consider withdrawal from the Rhineland zone; the other powers concerned seem to have given up asking her; the very argument which it put forward on 7 March now forbids the Reich from insisting on this point.

Being a faithful member of the League of Nations, resolved to respect the obligations which devolve on it by virtue of this, but also resolved to exercise the rights which the Pact confers on it, the government of the Republic cannot accept moreover that the legitimacy of its diplomatic action could be disputed from the moment that it conforms with the principles of the Pact;

(12) If it is considered, in accordance with the Franco-British proposals of 1935 and with the suggestions contained in the German memoranda of 7 and 31 March 1936, that it is advisable to provide for the danger of sudden aggression from the air by means of an automatic and effective reaction on the part of each of the signatory powers, the French government declares itself ready to participate in an agreement of this nature which would also include undertakings to limit air armaments. This agreement could take the form of a special protocol. It would be stipulated that in the case of an aggression accompanied or unaccompanied by a land or sea attack, which the air forces of one of the contracting powers would carry out against another contracting power, the other signatories would immediately bring their air forces into action to help the victim of the aggression and carry out the most suitable military reaction for its benefit. It would, moreover, be specified that an air action carried out in reply to hostilities effectively opened or undertaken to carry out commitments resulting from the new agreement would not give rise to this assistance;

[13, 14, 15, 16, 17: detailed measures]

(18) The programme thus outlined does not, however, exhaust the subject of the contemplated negotiation as far as settlement of the situation created on 7 March 1936 is concerned. In particular, and in accordance with the arrangements decreed on 19 March 1936, the adoption of suitable provisions to forbid or limit further establishment of fortifications in a given zone could be successfully achieved;

(19) The French government in no way intended in this memorandum to consider all the questions which would arise during the coming conference; it limited itself deliberately to the main problems connected with the negotiation of the treaty which must replace the Locarno Treaty. It is, however, evident that without even calling to mind the questions relating to European security for the solution of which the co-operation of other

countries bordering on or near to Germany would be indispensable, the delegates of the powers which will be represented at the conference will have to discuss more general problems on the subject of which the French government reserves the right to make its view known subsequently. The government of the Republic places the stopping of the arms race among the foremost of these problems. Without prejudice to the discussions which may take place on this subject at Geneva during the coming assembly, it is bent on recording here its conviction that if Europe is to be saved from a catastrophe, it is important to consider without delay a limitation and then a general controlled reduction of armaments. The government of the Republic reserves the right to formulate any proposals which appear appropriate in this connection in due course.

46. *Report of the Delbos–Smigly-Rydz talks (30 September 1936)*
    (DDF, 2nd series, Vol. III, pp.441–2).
(Guarantees to Czechoslovakia)
    I.   Questions which M Delbos asked General Smigly-Rydz at the request of the Czechoslovak minister (on the occasion of the signing of the Rambouillet Agreement):
    A. *In the event of France's being attacked by Germany*, to what extent could *Poland* be counted on:
    (a) to help Czechoslovakia carry out her obligations to France?
    (b) to facilitate the execution of these obligations?
    (c) not to hinder this execution?
    (Reciprocity being guaranteed, *mutatis mutandis*, on the part of Czechoslovakia with respect to Poland.)
    B. *In the event of Czechoslovakia's being attacked by Germany*, to what extent could *Poland* be relied upon:
    (a) to assist,
    (b) to facilitate,
    (c) not to hinder the execution of the obligations of France with respect to Czechoslovakia?
    II.   Assurances given by General Smigly-Rydz:
(1) In the first case (A), Poland, not being bound by any undertaking of any kind with respect to Czechoslovakia, would do nothing which could hinder the execution of her obligations of assistance to France;
(2) In the second case (B), Czechoslovakia could count on the

fidelity of Poland to her obligations as a member of the League of Nations, just as France could count on the fidelity of Poland to her obligations as an ally;

(3) In a case in which Czechoslovakia is exposed only to a threat from Germany, since the carrying out of this threat must involve France in the same state of war, it would obviously be in France's interests to hold talks with Czechoslovakia, but also with Poland on the strength of the clauses of the Franco-Polish Treaty. The connection would thus in fact be guaranteed indirectly by the intervention of France between Czechoslovakia and Poland;

(4) If Czechoslovakia believed she must go to the expense of fortifications on the Polish frontier, 'this would really be money wasted'.

47. *Memorandum from the Political Directorate of the Ministry of Foreign Affairs (Paris, 25 July 1936)* (DDF, 2nd series, Vol. III, p.58).

(Political and legal implications of arms deliveries to Spain; possible consequences of governmental support)

The implications of arms deliveries to a foreign country are quite different depending on whether it is a question of:

(1) supply made directly by private arrangement by manufacturers to foreign authorities;

(2) private supplies made with the authorization of the government of the country of manufacture;

(3) supplies made by the government of the country of manufacture itself or at its instigation.

In the last case, the operation has the characteristics of intervention in the internal affairs of another state. A part of the armed forces of the delivering state is in effect placed at the disposal of a foreign authority.

All the seriousness of this act would become apparent if the insurgents came to be recognized by foreign states as the *de facto* government. The latter could in their turn give official support by similar assistance to insurrectionist authorities.

In the present case, should recognition of the insurgents as the actual government follow by the Reich or the Italian government, the situation would immediately become apparent in all its seriousness.

48. *From Yvon Delbos, Minister of Foreign Affairs, to Charles Corbin,*
    French Ambassador in London (26 November 1936) (DDF, 2nd
    series, Vol. IV, pp.53–4).

(Proposal for mediation in Spain)

The protraction of the drama which drowns Spain in blood makes
more and more imperative the duty to do everything possible to
end it. On the other hand the risks to the international situation
which can result from the fact that foreign assistances and counter-
assistances to the two combating parties increase from day to day.
The French government consequently considers that it is no
longer possible for the great powers, who are concerned with the
higher interest of peace and European civilization, to oppose this
chain of events with a simple attitude of expectation and non-
intervention, on pain of one day themselves having to suffer the
consequence of a moral abdication of this kind.

Before this chain of events brings about a sort of automatic
inevitability against which any attempt at diplomatic action would
be in vain, it is the duty of the Cabinets of London and Paris
urgently to examine how far their active co-operation in the
present crisis could go.

The French government, for its part, considers that diplomatic
intervention by the two governments, provided it was undertaken fairly quickly and firmly, could be usefully carried out in the
following way:

The pressure of Great Britain and France exerted simultaneously
in Berlin, Rome and Lisbon on the one hand, and in Moscow on
the other hand, would in a general manner tend to represent the
moral obligation which is jointly the duty of all the main powers
concerned to make an exceptional effort, and all necessary sacrifices, should they be needed, to protect the European community
from the agony and danger of prolonging the Spanish drama. To
this end:

(1) The German, Italian and Portuguese governments on the
one hand, and the Soviet government on the other hand, would
be put into the position of reaffirming the great concern for peace
which they have never ceased to profess. Consequently they
would be urged to recognize as a pressing requirement of this
peace policy, the immediate necessity of making an effective
contribution to the easing of the situation in Europe by absolutely
renouncing any direct or indirect activity likely to foster inter-

national competition around the Spanish conflict. A resolution of this nature, required in fact only on a political and higher level which would directly involve the responsibility of the governments, that is, over and above the procedure of the London committee, must intervene in a completely neutral spirit, apart from any argument about the initial responsibilities and justifications set forth on the subject of assistance or counter-assistance. The application of this resolution would be automatically guaranteed by the immediate implementation of the control, whose main terms and conditions the London committee has already decreed;

(2) The aforesaid governments, while themselves renouncing any consideration which could involve them in the giving of assistance would, on the other hand, be invited to associate their action with that of the British and French governments to stop the armed struggle between the government forces and the rebels, by a joint attempt at mediation;

(3) It could be agreed that if this collective mediation succeeded, the armistice obtained would be turned to account to establish a free national consultation in Spain, by means of general elections guaranteed under a provisional regime of international assistance.

This would be the general idea of the double undertaking of conciliation and mediation which would be set in motion by Franco-British initiative.

The French government would be grateful to the British government for any comments or suggestions, regarding the best conditions for achieving such a venture, of which it would like to inform us. However, in view of the urgency, it would set a high value on being informed now, of the agreement in principle of the Cabinet in London.

49. *Personal letter addressed by Georges Bonnet, French Minister of Foreign Affairs, to Joachim von Ribbentrop, German Minister of Foreign Affairs (Paris, 21 August 1939) (Livre Jaune Français 1938–9, pp.228–31).*

Most esteemed M von Ribbentrop,

I have received the letter you sent me marked 'Personal', in reply to the communication I myself sent to Count de Welczeck on 1 July.

There is one point which I would like to have clearly defined. At no time, either before or after the declaration of 6 December, has it been possible for the German government to think that France had decided not to be interested in affairs in Eastern Europe.

At the time of the December meetings I reminded you that we have had a treaty of alliance with Poland since 1921, and a pact with the USSR since 1935, which we intend to abide by. At that time I gave precise assurances to this effect to the Ambassadors of Poland and of the USSR in communications to which the press gave very wide publicity. I even remember that at the time when I reminded you of the treaties which united us with Poland, you willingly replied that these treaties could not interfere with Franco-German relations because your relations with Poland at that time were excellent.

I am all the less astonished at the assurance you gave me that, three months earlier, Chancellor Hitler in his speech of 26 September last at the Sports Palace in Berlin, had quoted the German-Polish agreement as a model of this kind:

'We have succeeded', he said, 'in achieving in less than a year an agreement with him [Marshal Piłsudski] which in its essence removed the danger of conflict for ten years in the first place. We are all convinced that this agreement will bring about a lasting peace. We realize that there are here two peoples who must live side by side with one another. A state of 33 million inhabitants will always tend to seek an access to the sea; it was therefore necessary to find a means for agreement. This agreement has been found and is developing more and more. The decisive element is that the two governments and all reasonable and far-sighted men of the two peoples and the two countries have the firm wish continually to improve their relations.'

Moreover, during our talk of 6 December, one of the most urgent demands I addressed to your Excellency was in connection with the joint guarantee to be given to Czechoslovakia, in carrying out the Munich Agreements. I would not have been able to make such a request if France had not attached importance to what must happen in Eastern Europe.

Since I could not obtain a satisfactory reply on this subject, I sent you a note on 8 February 1939 which invoked the agreement signed in Munich on 29 September to insist again on the need to achieve a rapid agreement on the joint guarantee to Czechoslovakia; to this note you replied on 2 March with a request to wait for clarification of internal developments in Czechoslovakia, and improvement of the relations between this country and neighbouring states, before contemplating a general agreement between the powers which signed the Munich Agreement.

Furthermore, the very declarations which I made when I addressed the French Chamber on 26 January 1939 confirmed this point of view in a way which could not lead to any misunderstanding. These declarations, which you will find in our *Journal Officiel* (p.234) were reproduced in the press of the entire world:

France has also maintained her traditional friendly relationship with Poland. At the time of the Franco-German declaration of 6 December I informed the Polish Ambassador of our intentions, in accordance with the spirit of our agreements. On thanking me for keeping it informed, the Polish government let me know that it expressed satisfaction about an act whose purpose, meaning and scope it appreciated. Therefore, gentlemen, it is necessary to put an end to the fable that our policy would have destroyed the obligations which we undertook in Eastern Europe with the USSR or with Poland. These obligations still hold and they must be applied in the same spirit in which they were created.

There is therefore no ambiguity. You are acquainted with the treaty which unites France and Poland. On the occasion of the Franco-German declaration of 6 December, you never dreamt of asking me to denounce it. At the time when we signed this declaration your relations with Poland were excellent and there was nothing in Franco-Polish relations of a nature to touch a sensitive point on your part.

On 30 January 1939, in his speech at the Reichstag, Chancellor Hitler moreover again expressed satisfaction over the relations between Germany and Poland. 'At the present time', he declared, 'one would hardly find a division of opinion among the true friends of peace, as to the value of this agreement' (the German-Polish Pact of non-aggression). These words had all the more meaning for us in that they were spoken several weeks after an important discussion in Berchtesgaden between Chancellor Hitler and M Beck, the Polish Minister of Foreign Affairs.

In March, relations between Germany and Poland became strained and this created a new situation. France takes no responsibility in the development of these relations between Berlin and Warsaw. In fact she has always refrained – and will continue to refrain – from taking part in any way in questions which, since they are concerned with the special relations between the two neighbouring countries, do not risk affecting the general international situation and the general maintenance of peace.

In accordance with the declarations which I had the honour of making to Count de Welczeck, we sincerely hope that a contractual arrangement can be concluded between Germany and Poland. However, there is one point about which it is my duty to remind you, for the very reason that I had dealings with you on 6 and 7 December in Paris, and that is that France has a treaty of alliance with Poland and that, faithful to her word, she will scrupulously carry out all the obligations undertaken in this treaty.

You wish to point out, by reminding me of all the efforts you yourself have made towards a *rapprochement* between France and Germany, that Chancellor Hitler has always wished for a Franco-German *entente* and described a new war between our two countries as 'folly'.

This assurance corresponds with our sincere wish. Like you, I wish to guarantee the continuation of good relations between France and Germany. This is why in my communication of 1 July which keeps all its justification and all its meaning, I was bent on reminding you, with all the frankness that the circumstances require, of the position of the French government with regard to Poland, especially with regard to the situation in Danzig.

France eagerly desires peace; no one can doubt this. Nor can anyone doubt the resolution of the French government to keep her obligations. However, I could not let it be said that our country would be responsible for the war because it had honoured its signature.

Yours, etc. . . .

50. *Declaration read on 2 September 1939 to the Chamber of Deputies by M Edouard Daladier, President of the Council, and to the Senate by M Camille Chautemps, Vice-President of the Council.*
(*Entry into the war*)
Poland has been the victim of the most unjust and most brutal aggression. The nations who guaranteed her independence are bound to intervene in her defence. Britain and France are not powers who could renounce or think of renouncing their signature. . . .

. . . Moreover, gentlemen, it is not only a question of the honour of our country. It is also a matter of protecting her vital interest. For a France who allowed this aggression to be accomplished would soon be a despised France, an isolated France, a discredited France, without allies and without support and, there can be no doubt of this, she would herself soon be subjected to a terrible attack.

I ask this question of the French nation and of all nations: what would be the value of the guarantee, which was again renewed at the very moment of aggression against Poland; the guarantee given for our Eastern frontier, our Alsace, our Lorraine, after the denouncing of the guarantees successively given to Austria, Czechoslovakia and Poland? Made more powerful by their conquests, gorged with the spoils of Europe, masters of inexhaustible natural riches, the aggressors would soon turn all their forces against France.

Our honour is then only the pledge of our own security. It is not that abstract honour, that archaic honour of which conquerors speak to justify their outrages. It is the dignity of a peaceful nation, which has no hatred for any other nation in the world, and who only ever pledges herself for the well-being of her liberty and her life.

At the price of our honour we would be buying only a precarious and revocable peace, and then tomorrow when we would have to fight, after having lost the esteem of our allies and of the other nations, we would be only a wretched nation doomed to the prospect of defeat and servitude.

Select Bibliography

Until recently it has not been possible to study French foreign policy from 1914 to 1945, owing to lack of first-hand documentation. Even today, the publication of the *Documents Diplomatiques Français* (DDF) is very fragmentary. We have used the volumes which have appeared so far:

First series (1932–5)
    Vol. I   July–November 1932
    Vol. II   November 1932–March 1933
    Vol. III   March–July 1933
    Vol. IV   July–November 1933
Second series (1936–9)
    Vol. I   January–March 1936
    Vol. II   April–July 1936
    Vol. III   July–November 1936
    Vol. IV   November 1936–February 1937

The *Livres Jaunes* (Yellow Books) previously published by the government to defend its position on certain important questions are much less useful, because of their selective nature. We know, for example, that in the *Livre Jaune Français 1938–9* published soon after the war began, all documents liable to incriminate either the USSR (whose alliance it was hoped to retrieve), or the previous attitude of Poland (since France had entered the war to defend her), have been removed.

Our study is naturally written within the general framework of the history of international relations. We have therefore made constant use of three works:

P. RENOUVIN, *Histoire des relations internationales* Vol. VIII: *Les Crises du XXe siècle*, part 1, 1914–1929, Paris, 1957; part 2, 1929–1945, Paris, 1958.

J. B. DUROSELLE, *Histoire diplomatique de 1919 à nos jours*, Paris, 1962.

M. BAUMONT, *Les Origines de la Deuxième Guerre Mondiale*, Paris, 1969.

Another indispensable framework is the general history of France during this period. On this subject consult:

Select Bibliography

J. NÉRÉ, *La Troisième République, 1914–1940*, 3rd ed., Paris, 1969.

We are still very ill-equipped as far as the history of French foreign policy as such is concerned.

R. ALBRECHT-CARRIE, *France, Europe and Two World Wars*, Geneva, 1960, is a remarkable effort in objectivity, but it is already outdated from the documentary point of view.

Interesting ideas can be found in:

A. WOLFERS, *Britain and France between Two Wars; Conflicting Strategies of Peace since Versailles*, New York, 1940.

H. W. JORDAN, *Great Britain, France and the German Problem, 1913–1939*, London, 1943.

On the other hand there is little to be found in:

J. E. HOWARD, *Parliament and Foreign Policy in France, 1919–1939*, New York, 1948.

Of course the Memoirs published by a large number of the principal figures of this period to justify themselves must not be neglected. Among those which cover all or a large part of this period, we particularly mention those of:

G. BONNET, *Défense de la paix*, Vols. I, II, Geneva, 1946–8.

G. BONNET, *Le Quai d'Orsay sous trois Républiques*, Paris, 1962.

P. E. FLANDIN, *Politique française, 1919–1940*, Paris, 1947.

GENERAL M. GAMELIN, *Servir*, Vols. I, II, III, Paris, 1946–7.

E. HERRIOT, *Jadis*, Vol. II, Paris, 1952.

J. PAUL-BONCOUR, *Entre deux guerres*, Vols. II, III.

P. REYNAUD, *Mémoires*, Vols. I, II, Paris, 1963.

For want of something better, we may add to this category:

G. SUAREZ, *Briand, sa vie, son œuvre*, Vols. III, IV, V, VI, Paris, 1939–41, using the personal papers of Briand.

We now come to works limited to certain questions or to certain chronological subdivisions.

For the First World War:

A. PINGAUD, *Histoire diplomatique de la France pendant la Grande Guerre*, Vols. I, II, III, Paris, 1935–45.

F. CHARLES-ROUX, *La Paix des Empires centraux*, Paris, 1947.

G. PEDRONCINI, *Les Négociations secrètes pendant la Grande Guerre*, Paris, 1969.

Special mention should be made of the very accurate and very exhaustive study:

P. RENOUVIN, *L'Armistice de Rethondes*, Paris, 1968.

Select Bibliography

For the Treaty of Versailles alone the bibliography is immense. However, the best description of the French government's approach is:

A. TARDIEU, *La Paix*, Paris, 1921.

To be more specific, for one of the phases of the negotiation:

P. MANTOUX, *Les Délibérations du Conseil des Quatre*, Vols. I, II, Paris, 1955.

G. HANOTAUX, *Le Traité de Versailles du 28 Juin, 1919*, Paris, 1919.

P. BIRDSALL, *Versailles Twenty Years After*, London, 1942.

E. MANTOUX, *La Paix calomniée ou les conséquences économiques de Mr Keynes*, Paris, 1946.

For the implementation of the Treaty:

GENERAL NOLLET, *Une Expérience de désarmement*, Paris, 1932.

E. WEILL-RAYNAL, *Les Réparations allemandes et la France*, Vols. I, II, III, Paris, 1949 (a very exhaustive study).

J. SEYDOUX, *De Versailles au Plan Young*, Paris, 1932. (Collection of articles and studies, contemporary with the events themselves and written by one of Poincaré's closest colleagues.)

A. ANTONUCCI, *Le Bilan des réparations et la crise mondiale*, Paris, 1935.

And, on the level of general policy:

A. FABRE-LUCE, *La Crise des alliances*, Paris, 1922.

A. FABRE-LUCE, *La Victoire*, Paris, 1924.

And in a very different direction, the collections of articles by:

R. PINON, *Chroniques du Ministère Poincaré*, Vol. I, *Le Redressement de la politique française*, Paris, 1922; Vol. II, *La Bataille de la Ruhr*, Paris, 1923.

DORTEN, *La Tragédie rhénane*, 1945.

There is a lack of studies taking an overall view of the eastern alliances of France. Special mention should, however, be made of:

A. MOUSSET, *La Petite Entente*, Paris, 1923.

PIOTR S. WANDYCZ, *France and her Eastern Allies, 1919–1925*, Minneapolis, 1962 (a very exhaustive study but very much influenced by the Polish point of view).

There is no study of the whole problem of national defence and French strategy after the withdrawal from the Rhineland. However, attention should be drawn to:

R. W. CHALLENER, *The French Theory of the Nation in Arms, 1866–1939*, New York, 1955.

For the world economic crisis, a general outline is provided by:

J. NÉRÉ, *La Crise de 1929*, 2nd ed., Paris, 1969.

In connection with the Disarmament Conference:

G. CASTELLAN, *Le Réarmement clandestin de l'Allemagne, 1930–1935*, Paris, 1954.

And also, with regard to the advent of Hitler and its consequences:

Select Bibliography

A. FRANÇOIS-PONCET, *Souvenirs d'une ambassade à Berlin, 1931–1938*, Paris, 1946.

For the fluctuations of Polish policy:

J. LAROCHE, *La Pologne de Piłsudski. Souvenirs d'une Ambassade, 1926–1935*, Paris, 1953.

For the attempt at a Franco-Italian *rapprochement*, especially the de Jouvenel mission:

R. BINION, *Defeated Leaders*, New York, 1960.

For the Franco-Soviet Alliance:

W. E. SCOTT, *Alliance against Hitler: The origins of the Franco-Soviet Pact*, Durham, N.C., 1962.

For the Ethiopian affair:

M. GALLO, *L'Affaire d'Ethiopie. Aux origines de la guerre mondiale*, Paris, 1967. To be complemented by:

P. BARTHOLIN, *Les Conséquences économiques des sanctions*, Paris, 1938.

There are only a few works on the final crisis. We will quote:

H. NOGUERES, *Munich, ou la drôle de paix*, Paris, 1963.

The following memoirs should be consulted:

R. COULONDRE, *De Staline à Hitler*, Paris, 1950 (essential).

L. NOËL, *L'Agression allemande contre la Pologne, une ambassade à Varsovie, 1935–1939*, Paris, 1946.

A. FRANÇOIS-PONCET, *Au Palais Farnèse. Souvenirs d'une ambassade à Rome, 1938–1940*, Paris, 1961.

GENERAL PAUL STEHLIN, *Témoignage pour l'histoire*, Paris, 1965.

GENERAL A. BEAUFRÉ, *Le Drame de 1940*, Paris, 1965.

JEAN ZAY, *Carnets secrets*, Paris, 1942.

The works of the Parliamentary Commission of Enquiry into 'The events which took place in France from 1933 to 1945' naturally must not be forgotten.

As far as the period of German occupation is concerned, the most recent works are:

A. D. HYTIER, *Two Years of French Foreign Policy: Vichy 1940–1942*, Geneva, 1958 (especially notable).

D. S. WHITE, *Les Origines de la discorde; de Gaulle, la France libre et les Alliés (1940–1942)*, Paris, 1967 (translation of *Seeds of Discord*, Syracuse, 1964) (very penetrating study). Also essential is:

GENERAL DE GAULLE, *Mémoires de Guerre*, Vols. I, II, III (published with numerous documents), Paris, 1954–9.

J. SOUSTELLE, *Envers et contre tout*, Vols. I, II, Paris, 1947, 1950.

Everything must be put in its context especially within the framework of the general history of the Second World War, as recollected in the works of A. LATREILLE and HENRI MICHEL (the latter in the collection: *Peuples et Civilisations*).

Index

Abernon, Edgar V., Viscount d', 49, 72

Abyssinia (Ethiopia), 133–4, 193, 233, 260, 326–7; Addis Ababa, 133, 183; non-intervention policy, 152; War with Italy, 173–83; zones of influence, 133–4

Africa: French Equatorial, 253; French North, 247, 257, 310

Aggression, definition of, 119, 127, 161–2, 237, 281, 303

Air forces, allied (1936), 334–5

Albania, 145, 175, 236

Alexander I, King of Yugoslavia, assassination, 151

Alexandretta, 236

Algiers, 258

Aloisi, Pompeo, 176, 181

Alphand, Charles (ambassador), 163, 171

Alsace-Lorraine, 1; restoration to France, 7, 9, 16, 74, 266–7

Alto Adige, 138

Antonescu, Ion, 213

Armaments and disarmament: Allied, 98; Disarmament Conference (1932), 117–31, 137, 144, 301, Germany leaves, 120, 144, 260, control and inspection, 13, 32, 125, 126, 305; Germany, 12–13, 31–3, 75, 93, 124–31 passim, 139, 197–8, 274, 277, 278, 302–6; naval disarmament, 29; Roosevelt and armaments, 114

Auriol, Vincent, 206

Austria, 22, 41, 149–51, 175, 221–222, 292, 319, 337; Anschluss with Germany, 136, 141, 142, 143, 151, 221; customs union with Germany, 90–1, 136, 156; economic conditions, 134, 146, 316, 317–18; independence of, 23, 138, 153, 194; Kredit Anstalt bankruptcy, 102; Nazi party in, 136, 144–5, 146, 149, 150; Vienna rising, 149

Austria-Hungary, 4, 5, 6, 7, 9; break-up of, 21

Bainville, Jacques, 42

Baku, 245

Balearic Islands, 218

Bargeton (Director of Political Affairs), 338–9

Bartholin, M., 178

Barthou, Louis, 57, 129, 166–9, 306; assassination, 151, 168

Baudouin, Paul, 233–4

Baumont, M., 238

Beaufré, A. (general), 238, 244

Beck, Josef (colonel), 211, 337, 351

Belgium, 9, 96, 97, 98, 124, 166, 185, 188, 197, 215, 235, 308–309; frontier guarantee, 73, 74; independence, 7; military agreement with France, 202–5, 243–4, 246; neutrality, 96, 204, 301–2, 333

Beneš, Eduard, 60, 135, 142, 143, 144, 151, 227, 316, 317

Bennet, J. Wheeler, 104

Berchtesgaden meeting, 226
Berthelot, Philippe, 9, 42, 72, 282
Bessarabia, 157
Binion, R., 119, 137
Birdsall, P., 21, 24
Blum, Léon, 195–6, 198, 199, 206, 207, 209, 210, 216; on 'peaceful co-existence', 340–2
Bohemia, 268, 269
Bolsheviks, 268, 269
Bonnet, Georges, 223, 224, 227, 231, 241, 349–52
Bradbury, Sir John, 35
Brazil, 75
Briand, Aristide, 9, 14, 17, 26, 28, 29, 30, 36, 40, 47–8, 65, 69–76 *passim*, 85–92 *passim*, 221, 260, 261, 265, 271–6 *passim*, 280, 282–5 *passim*; character and career, 69–71
Briand-Kellogg Pact, 85–7, 122, 156, 310, 311
Britain, 1, 6, 10, 27, 49, 74, 167–9, 176, 233, 249, 293, 331, 342; air force, 334–5; and France (*Entente*), 60–2, 152, 163, 265–71, 275, 276, 277, 282, confidence agreement, 107, 139, 288, economic disagreements, 108–109, joint policy and guarantees, 169–70, 234, 235, 236, 238, mutual assistance, 196–200; and Free French, 251–6 *passim*; and Italy (MacDonald-Mussolini proposal), 139; Labour Government, 64, 67, 68; Navy, 179–80; 'Peace Ballot', 176–8; Polish guarantee, 236, Alliance, 241; resistance after 1940 armistice, 247; and Rhineland, 15, 188, 190; and sanctions, 153, 176, 177; and Spanish Civil War, 215, 217, 218, 219, 348, 349; and

Turkey, 236; and Vichy government, 255; and world economic crisis, 101
British Commonwealth, 89; Ottawa agreements, 108
Bulgaria, 5, 108, 319
Bullitt, William (ambassador), 201
Bülow, Bernard von (German chancellor), 2
Bülow, Bernhard Wilhelm (German chancellor), 306
Butler, Nicholas Murray, 85

Caballero, Largo, 216
Cambon, Paul, 25
Castellan, G., 13, 118–19
Chamberlain, Neville, 223, 226, 235
Charles-Roux, F., 6
Chautemps, Camille, 166, 222, 240, 352
China, 6, 158, 175, 221
Cieszyn Affair, 44, 60
Clemenceau, Georges, 7, 14, 15, 16, 23, 25, 26, 28, 29, 51, 70, 268, 270, 278–9
Collective security, 24, 66–7, 119, 124, 161, 176, 183, 195, 199, 285, 325, 340
Constantine I, King of Greece, 5
Corbin, Charles (ambassador), 348
Corfu incident, 60
Corsica, 309
Cot, Pierre (air minister), 163, 164
Coulondre, Robert, 208–9, 224, 240
Cru, Jean Norton, 95
Cuno, Wilhelm (German chancellor), 52, 55
Customs Truce (1933), 112–15, 299–301
Czechoslovakia, 9, 21, 22, 42, 43, 99, 135, 142, 144, 161, 192, 193, 205, 213, 214, 221–31, 241, 261,

292, 314, 316–17, 318, 319, 321, 331, 338, 350; and Hungary, 226; and Poland, 44, 60, 73, 166–7, 211, 212, 226, 346–7; Prague Coup, 234–5; Runciman mission, 225–6; unemployment in, 134

Dakar, 253–4
Daladier, Edouard, 126, 130, 191, 223, 227, 228, 235, 241, 243, 302, 319, 352
Danube: commercial association, 146–8, 319–20; Pact, 152; region, 41–2
Danzig, 22, 236, 240, 241
Dardanelles, 45–6; Chanak affair, 46
Darlan, Jean (admiral), 218, 250, 251, 256
Dawes, Charles G., plan, *see* Reparations
Decoux, Jean (rear-admiral), 218
De Gaulle, Charles, 190, 251–5 *passim*, 257, 258; authority established, 258
Delbos, Yvon, 198, 199, 201, 203, 204, 206, 218, 346, 348–9
Delcassé, Théophile, 2, 5
De Man, H., 205
Denis, Ernest, 9
Denmark, 338
Desticker (general), 65
Disarmament, *see* Armaments
Djibouti, 133, 233
Dollfuss, Engelbert, 149; assassination, 150
Dulles, John Foster, 19
Dunkirk, 249
Durand-Viel (admiral), 187, 333–4
Duroselle, J. B., 85, 129, 151, 233

Eden, Anthony, 174, 190, 199, 214, 336

Eisenmann, Louis, 9
Entente, Little, 42–3, 44, 60, 135, 141, 142, 143, 144, 148, 151, 167, 212, 213, 215, 309, 316, 321, 331, 339; economic organization, 147, 317–18
Entente, Triple, 3–7 *passim*; war aims, 8–9
Ethiopia, *see* Abyssinia
European Union, 87–9, 285–6
Eyck, Erich, 57

Fabre-Luce, A., 37
Fernando de los Rios (envoy), 215
First World War, 3, 242; Allied agreement, 3–4; armistice, 9–10, 11; French losses in, 11, 18–20, 93; peace conditions, 265–9
Fiume, 147
Flandin, Pierre Etienne, 169, 170, 186, 187, 188, 190, 306, 335–337
Foch, Ferdinand (marshal), 10, 13, 16, 40, 51, 65, 93, 94
Four-Power Pact, 140, 142, 148, 162, 310–13, 321, 341
France: and Abyssinia, 133–4; air force, 229, 241, 246; alliance with Britain, 27–8, 30, 60–2, 107, 271, 275, 276, 277, 282, joint policies, 169–70, 196–7, 233, 234–6, 238, Anglo-American guarantee, 15–16, 26–31 *passim*, 270, 283; armistice with Germany (Second World War), 246–7; army strength (1933), 191; Cartel des Gauches, 63–8 *passim*; colonial empire, 61, 158; Communist Party and USSR, 209; as continental power, 1; Czech alliance, 60, 222, 223; depreciation of currency, 50, 57, 77–8, 200, stabilization of franc, 79, 82, 101;

fleet, 132–3, 249–50, 309; Franco-Soviet Treaty, 155–72, 184–5, 224, 238, 306–7, 320–5, 332–3, 338, 344, 350; Free French, 251–9 *passim*, and Dakar, 253–5, and French Equatorial Africa, 253; General Staff and Supreme Command, 242–4, 328–31, and Belgium, 203–5, intellectual inferiority of, 246, and Rhineland, 185–9, 190–1; internal divisions in France, 183–4; invasion by Germany (1940), 246; Italian *rapprochement*, 132–54, 184; losses in First World War, 11, 18–20, 93; 'Manifestos' of intellectuals, 177–8; military doctrines, 94–9, 307–10; national debt (1922), 34; occupation by Germany (1940), 248; pacifism in, 94, 192; Polish Alliance, 40, 134, 211–212, 232, 350; Popular Front, 185, 189, 193, policy of, 195–220, 340; provisional government (1943), 258; rearmament, (1936), 196; Franco-Russian Alliance (First World War), 2, 3; security (1936), 338–40; and Spanish Civil War, 215–21 *passim*, 347–9; Vichy government, 248–59 *passim*, collaboration with Germany, 250; war aims (1917), 8, 21, 265; war with Germany (1939), 241, 352–353; and world economic crisis, 100–16 *passim*, 296

Franco, Francisco (general), 215, 216, 218, 220

François-Poncet, André, 129, 230, 231, 234, 306–7

Funk, Walther (German minister), 128

Gallo, M., 180

Gamelin, Maurice (general), 94, 185, 191, 211, 330, 331–5

Geneva Protocol, 67–8, 119, 284

Genoa Conference, 29–30, 284

Germain-Martin (Minister of Finance), 148, 289

Germany, 1, 8, 101, 175, 183, 194, 218, 245, 291, 306–7, 316, 320; Anti-Comintern Pact, 221; army, 13, 31–3, compulsory service, 152, 170, strength (1933), 191; blockade strategy (1939), 244; currency crisis, 48–9; and Czechoslovakia, 212, 221, 234–5; disarmament, 12–13, 31–3, 75, 302–6, 314, Control Commission, 32; economic agreements, 108–9; Franco-German frontier, 72–4; German-Polish pact, 141, 236; German-Soviet pact, 240, 242, 244; Imperialism of, 2; industrial party, 52; international loan to, 103–4; invasion of France, 246; invasion of Poland, 241, 352–3; paramilitary organizations, 71, 90, 104, 125; population, 1, 11, 276; rearmament, 118–31, 139, 328–9, 330–1; *Reichswehr*, 119, 127; reparations payments, 20, 47–8, 50, 52–3; Rome-Berlin Axis, 221; and Rumania, 234, 236; security guarantees to, 124; Silesian problem, 36, 40–1; and Spanish Civil War, 215, 216, 218, 219; Weimar Republic, 33, 59, 91; withdrawal from League of Nations, 128; world policy (*Weltpolitik*), 2; *see also* Rhineland; Saar; Sudetenland

Gibraltar, 179, 254

Gilbert, Parker (agent for reparations), 58, 81, 82, 83
Giraud, Henri (general), 257-8
Godesberg meeting, 226, 227
Goemboes, Gyula (Hungarian minister), 143
Goering, Hermann, 191
Gold and gold standard, 101-2, 201, 202, 290; Britain and, 110
Goutard, A., 246
Greece, 5; Franco-British aid, 235-6; and Italy, 60
Grey, Edward, Viscount, 7, 265, 266

Habsburgs, 41, 42, 135-6
Halifax, E. F. L. Wood, Viscount, 223
Hanotaux, Gabriel, 24
Hauser, Henri, 2-3
Havana agreements, 256, 257
Henderson, Arthur, 302
Henriot, Philippe, 227
Herriot, Edouard, 63, 64, 65, 106, 112, 113, 123, 159, 163, 170, 215, 279, 284, 289; and collective security, 66-7; and war debts, 110
Hesnard (assistant to Briand), 76, 77
Hindenburg, Paul von, German President, 90
Hitler, Adolf, 33, 90, 118, 127, 128, 132, 139, 140, 141, 152, 169, 184, 185, 187, 189, 198, 206, 207, 208, 212, 216, 221, 222, 226, 227, 229, 230, 234, 235, 237, 241, 243, 247, 251, 259, 287, 302, 332, 341, 350, 351; comes to power, 160-1
Hoare, Sir Samuel: Laval-Hoare plan, 180-2; resignation, 182
Hoover, Herbert, 293, 295; Moratorium, 102-7, 289, 296; on

gold standard, 290; on reduction of armaments, 120
House, Edward M., 7, 10
Hungary, 5, 41, 42, 44, 108, 143, 144, 175, 212, 291, 316, 317, 319, 339; territorial claims, 135, 226
Hytier, A. D., 247-51 *passim*, 256

Iraq, 256
Italy, 7, 9, 73, 74, 108, 123, 124, 127, 137, 183, 241, 316, 317, 320, 339; air force, 335; and Alto Adige region, 138; Anti-Comintern Pact, 221; defeat at Adowa, 133; Italo-Soviet Pact, 162; naval equality, 132-3; 'non-belligerence' (1939), 244; *rapprochement* with France, 132-154; Rome agreements, 150, 152, 174, 184, 233, 330; Rome-Berlin Axis, 221; and Somaliland, 133, 174; and Spanish Civil War, 215, 219; territorial claims, 4, 233, in Albania, 145; war with Abyssinia, 173-83, 341

Japan, 6, 175, 221; relations with China, 158, 341
Jaspar, Henri (Belgian minister), 301, 302
Jouvenel, Henri de, mission of, 137-8, 140, 142, 146, 316-19
Justice, International Court of, 91, 189

Karl, Emperor of Austria-Hungary, 7, 41, 42
Kellogg, Frank Billings, 86
Kemal (Mustapha) Ataturk, 45
Keynes, J. M., 24, 28, 34
Koeltz, L., 243, 244
Kun, Béla, 41

Larminat, Edgard de (general), 253
Laroche, Jules (ambassador), 135
Lattre de Tassigny, Jean de (colonel), 171
Lausanne Conference, *see* Reparations
Laval, Pierre, 104, 105, 151, 158, 169, 170, 190, 250, 289, 326; Laval-Hoare plan, 180–2; resignation, 182
Law, Andrew Bonar, plan on reparations, 53, 65–6, 109
League of Nations, 8, 17, 23–4, 26, 41, 60, 67, 123, 140, 153, 209, 220, 280, 281, 285, 336, 340; and Abyssinia, 174–83 *passim*; entry of Germany, 74, 75; German withdrawal, 128; International Force of, 119, 121; Manchuria Commission, 158; Pact of, 75, 85, 86, 139, 167, 198, 205, 213, 245, 310, 311, 328, 339; and Rhineland, 187–9; USSR and, 160, 165, 168
Lebanon, 137
Leclerc, Jean (general), 253
Léger, Alexis (secretary to Laval), 171
Leopold III, King of Belgium, 204
Levinson, Salmon O., 85
Litvinov, Maxim, 161, 162, 167, 193
Lloyd George, David, 15, 22, 23, 28, 29, 30, 35, 46, 47, 88, 268, 271, 275, 276, 278, 279
Locarno Agreements and Treaty, 29, 71, 73, 85, 86, 98, 134, 137, 184, 189, 196, 199, 283, 284, 301, 310, 311, 336, 338; denounced by Hitler, 187, 332; revision of, 342–6
London Conference, 32, 306
London Economic Conference (1933), 111–15 *passim*, 201

Lowe, C. J., 174
Ludendorff, Erich (general), 275

MacDonald, J. Ramsay, 66, 123, 125, 139; Armies Plan, 125
Machray, R., 60
Madrid, 216
Maginot Line, 93, 95–7, 122, 192, 204, 238; gaps in, 95–6; Czech, 99
Manchukuo, 158
Mangin, Charles M. E. (general), 16
Mantoux, E., 24
Marshall Plan, 181, 261
Masaryk, Thomas, 9
Massigli, René, 193, 337–8
Maurin (general), 186
Mers-el-Kebir, 250, 254, 255
Monick (financial attaché), 201
Morel (lieutenant-colonel), 216, 217
Morocco, 216, 309–10
Mosul oilfield, 45
Munich agreement, 227–32 *passim*, 233, 350; repercussions of, 234
Mussolini, Benito, 138, 139, 140, 143, 145, 146, 150, 151, 174, 181, 184, 193, 221, 222, 226–7, 233, 234, 319, 326, 327, 341

Nationalities, principle of, 21–2; national minorities, 38–9, 138, 313–16
Naumann, Friedrich, 45
Néré, J., 39, 48, 130, 246
Netherlands, 235, 342
Neurath, Konstantin von (German minister), 306
Nicholas II, Tsar, 8–9, 266
Noël, Léon (ambassador), 142, 211, 224–5, 231
Nollet (general), 13, 31, 126

Norway, invasion by Germany, 245

Nyon Conference, 220

Paléologue, Maurice, 41, 42, 267

Papen, Franz von (German chancellor), 106

Pas de Calais, 11, 17

Paul-Boncour, Joseph, 123, 125, 130, 137, 138, 142–3, 147, 149, 163, 165, 223, 302, 313–16

Peace Conference (1919), 23; Treaties, 25

Pearl Harbour, 257

Pedroncini, G., 6

Pétain, Philippe (Marshal), 10, 94, 247, 248, 249, 250

Pierrefeu, Jean de, 94

Piłsudski, Jósef (Polish premier), 39, 40, 134, 350

Pingaud, A., 4

Pinon, René (assistant to Poincaré), 24, 51, 59, 171

Pleven, René, 253, 256

Poincaré, Raymond, 7, 16, 28, 30, 47, 48, 50–1, 55, 56, 63, 64, 66, 77–8, 81–2, 83, 200; plan on reparations, 53, 58–9

Poland, 8, 21, 43, 75, 98, 124, 134, 140–1, 166–7, 168, 231, 237–42 *passim*, 261, 268, 269, 309, 314, 315, 321, 331, 337, 338, 346, 350, 352; and Czechoslovakia, 44, 60, 339; British guarantee and alliance, 236, 241; frontiers, 22, 38–9, 40, 73; German-Polish pact, 141, 166, 332, 350, 351, 352; Poles in France, 135; Polish Corridor, 22, 138, 140, 236; and USSR, 156–7, 159, 210–11, 224, 333; war with Russia (1920), 40, 42

Portugal, 217, 219

Potsdam Conference, 259

Prussia, 13, 14

Pujo (general), 334–5

Rapallo Agreement (1922), 75, 156, 320

Rathenau, Walther (German minister), 32, 37

Renouvin, Pierre, ix, 10, 14, 152, 185, 205

Reparations (First World War), 10, 15, 33–8, 294; assessment, 18–21, 36–7; Commission, 20, 35; Dawes Plan, 57–9, 77–83 *passim*, 272, implementation of, 64–6, 76; distribution of, 36; final payment, 106, 286–7; Lausanne Conference on, 106, 107, 109, 110, 111, 288; moratorium on, 47–8, 50, 52–3, 57, 102–7, 292, 293, 295, 297, 321; Wiesbaden Agreements, 37–8; Young Plan, 82, 83–5, 102, 104, 105–6, 110, 289,–93

Reynaud, Paul, 190, 245, 247

Rhineland, 26, 267, 268, 278, 338; evacuation of, 90, 93; evacuation of Cologne area, 65, 71; guarantee of frontier, 29; left bank, detachment, 9, 10, 14; military occupation, 15, 27, 185, 271, 279; remilitarization by Germany, 184–7, 220, 260, 332, 334, 336, 337–8, 344; separatist movements, 27, 55, 56

Ribbentrop, Joachim von, 231, 349

Roosevelt, Franklin D., 111, 112, 114, 115, 125–6, 226, 256; and de Gaulle (Anfa interview), 258; and peace, 201

Rousseau, C., 174

Ruhr, occupation of, 36, 51, 64, 93, 280; Interallied Mission,

Ruhr, occupation of, *cont.*
53–4; 'passive resistance' movement, 54–5, 65; withdrawal from, 65
Rumania, 5–6, 9, 42, 43, 157, 159, 161, 167, 212, 213, 215, 224, 237, 319, 321, 337, 338, 339; and Germany, 234, 236
Runciman, Walter, Viscount, 225–6
Russia, 2, 4, 38; Franco-Russian alliance, 2, 3; revolution in, 12; *see also* USSR

Saar, 16, 96; detached from Germany, 17, 267, 269; returned to Germany, 169
Saint Pierre and Miquelon, 257
Salonika, 5
Sanctions, 75, 153, 328; against Italy, 175–83 *passim*
Sarraut, Albert (Minister of Foreign Affairs), 187
Sauvy, A., 50
Schacht, Hjalmar, 57–83; mission to France, 206–8
Schleicher, Kurt von (German minister), 119
Schuschnigg, Kurt von, 150
Scott, W. E., 107, 119, 152, 155, 157–8, 161, 163
Second World War, 18, 24, 241, 352–3; capitulation of France, 246; 'Phoney War', 242–5
Seeckt, Hans von (general), 71
Serbia, 3, 5
Sèvres, Treaty of, 45
Seydoux, Jacques, 51, 84
Shotwell, James T., 85
Siegfried Line, 227, 229, 243
Silesia, Upper, 36, 40; partition, 41
Sixtus, Prince of Bourbon-Parma, 7

Smigly-Rydz, Edward (general), 211, 346
Snowden, Philip, 83
Somaliland, 133, 174
Soustelle, Jacques, 254, 255, 258
Spa Conference, 31, 35–6, 39
Spain, 75; Civil War in, 214–21 *passim*, arms deliveries, 347, international brigades, 219; non-intervention policy, 217, 219–20, 348–9; Republican government, 215
Stalin, Josef, 209, 230
Stehlin, Paul (general), 237, 240, 245, 250
Stresa Conference (1934), 153, 291, 306
Stresa Economic Conference (1932), 107–9, 134
Stresemann, Gustav, 52, 55, 56, 57, 69, 71–90 *passim*, 91, 284
Suarez, Georges, 69, 73, 271, 272, 275, 276, 282, 284
Sudetenland, 22, 223, 228; attached to Germany, 226
Suez Canal, 174, 179, 233
Sweden, 245
Switzerland, 175, 235
Syria, 45, 137, 236, 251; invasion (1941), 256

Tangier, 133
Tardieu, André, 18, 26, 27, 96, 146, 159, 268, 269–71, 317; Tardieu Plan, 119, 121, 316
Taylor, A. J. P., 30
Thoiry interview (Briand-Stresemann), 76–8, 82
Titulescu, Nicolae, 212, 213
Trieste, 147
Tripolitania, 133
Tukhachevski, Mikhail N. (marshal), 210
Tunisia, 133, 137, 152, 233

Turkey, 5, 9, 45–6, 236, 244, 338

Ukraine, 39
USA, 6, 27, 28, 175, 200, 201, 277, 287, 290; and arms, 98, 'cash and carry' policy, 243; financial crisis, 11–13; and Free French, 257; intervention in First World War, 8; and League of Nations, 26, 281; 'lend-lease', 256–7; and Rhineland, 15; opposes Tardieu Plan, 119; and Treaty of Versailles, 26, 270; and Vichy government, 256; and Young Plan, 84
USSR, 43, 75, 76, 218; and Britain, 236–9; and Czechoslovakia, 223–4, 228, 230; Finnish war, 244–5; Franco-Soviet Treaty, 155–72, 184–5, 208–10, 224, 238, 306–7, 320–5, 332–3, 338, 344; German-Soviet Pact, 240, 242, 244; non-aggression pacts, 156; opposes Tardieu Plan, 119; relations with Poland, 38–40, 42, 76, 239, 339, Pact, 157, 159; and Spanish Civil War, 219; *see also* Russia

Vandervelde, Emile (Belgian minister), 202, 302
Vansittart, Sir Robert, 181, 182
Van Zeeland (Belgian minister), 205, 336
Venizelos, Eleutherios, 5
Versailles, Treaty of, 14, 24, 26, 31–8 *passim*, 51, 59, 61, 77, 79, 93, 117, 125, 127, 130, 189, 198, 209, 221, 249, 260, 270, 277, 278, 281, 283, 314; revisions, 36, 72–3, 83, 103, 138, 139,

143–4; and the Ruhr, 53–4
Vuillemin (general), 229

Walwal incident, 174
Wandycz, Piotr S., 22, 60
War, outlawry of, 85–6
War debts, 49–50, 78–80, 109–16, 291, 293–5, 297; Balfour declaration on, 49, 53; Hoover Moratorium, 102–7, 289, 296
Warsaw, 40
Washington Conference (1921), 29, 132, 173
Weill-Raynal, E., 35, 65, 76, 80, 102, 107
Weygand, Maxime (general), 39, 40, 94, 97, 99, 121–2, 244, 245, 250, 307–10
White, D. S., 254, 256, 257
Wiggin, Albert, 104
Wilhelm II, Emperor, 2
Wilson, Woodrow, 7, 8, 10, 15, 17, 18, 26, 132, 270, 278; Fourteen Points of, 8, 9, 10, 19, 22
Wirth, Joseph (German minister), 32, 37
Wolfers, Arnold, 28
World economic crisis, 100–16, 296–8
World War, *see* First World War; Second World War
Wrangel, Peter N. (general), 39

Yalta Conference, 259
Yugoslavia, 42, 43, 136, 137, 145, 151, 161, 167, 213, 214, 215, 292, 317, 318, 319, 321, 337, 338, 339; Serbo-Croat antagonism, 135, 151

Zay, Jean, 227, 235, 236, 240, 241